After the Disciplines

Critical Studies in Education and Culture Series

After the Disciplines

The Emergence of Cultural Studies

EDITED BY

Michael Peters

CRITICAL STUDIES IN EDUCATION AND CULTURE
Edited by Henry A. Giroux

BERGIN & GARVEY
Westport, Connecticut • London

Library of Congress Cataloging-in-Publication Data

After the disciplines : the emergence of cultural studies /
   edited by Michael Peters.
       p.   cm.—(Critical studies in education and culture series,
   ISSN 1064–8615)
     Includes bibliographical references and index.
     ISBN 0–89789–626–2 (alk. paper).—ISBN 0–89789–627–0 (pbk. :
   alk. paper)
       1. Universities and colleges—New Zealand—Curricula.
   2. Universities and colleges—United States—Curricula.   3. Culture—
   Study and teaching (Higher)—New Zealand.   4. Culture—Study and
   teaching (Higher)—United States.   5. Education, Humanistic.
   6. Postmodernism and education.   I. Peters, Michael (Michael A.),
   1948– .   II. Series.
   LB2362.N45A48   1999
   378.1'99—dc21   98–51218

British Library Cataloguing in Publication Data is available.

Library of Congress Catalog Card Number: 98–51218
ISBN: 0–89789–626–2
      0–89789–627–0 (pbk.)
ISSN: 1064–8615

First published in 1999

Bergin & Garvey, 88 Post Road West, Westport, CT 06881
An imprint of Greenwood Publishing Group, Inc.
www.greenwood.com

Printed in the United States of America

The paper used in this book complies with the
Permanent Paper Standard issued by the National
Information Standards Organization (Z39.48–1984).

10 9 8 7 6 5 4 3 2 1

Copyright Acknowledgment

Chapter 4, "Fragmented Visions: Excavating the Future of Area Studies in a Post-American
World," appeared in *Review: A Journal of the Fernand Braudel Center*, XIX, 3, Summer
1996, pp. 269–315. Reprinted with permission.

Chapter 11, Henry A. Giroux, "Doing Cultural Studies: Youth and the Challenge of
Pedagogy," *Harvard Educational Review* 64:3 (Fall 1994), pp. 278–308. Copyright © 1994
by the President and Fellows of Harvard College. All rights reserved.

Contents

Series Foreword

Educational reform has fallen upon hard times. The traditional assumption that schooling is fundamentally tied to the imperatives of citizenship designed to educate students to exercise civic leadership and public service has been eroded. The schools are now the key institution for producing professional, technically trained, credentialized workers for whom the demands of citizenship are subordinated to the vicissitudes of the marketplace and the commercial public sphere. Given the current corporate and right wing assault on public and higher education, coupled with the emergence of a moral and political climate that has shifted to a new Social Darwinism, the issues which framed the democratic meaning, purpose, and use to which education might aspire have been displaced by more vocational and narrowly ideological considerations.

The war waged against the possibilities of an education wedded to the precepts of a real democracy is not merely ideological. Against the backdrop of reduced funding for public schooling, the call for privatization, vouchers, cultural uniformity, and choice, there are the often ignored larger social realities of material power and oppression. On the national level, there has been a vast resurgence of racism. This is evident in the passing of anti-immigration laws such as Proposition 187 in California, the dismantling of the welfare state, the demonization of black youth that is taking place in the popular media, and the remarkable attention provided by the media to forms of race talk that argue for the intellectual inferiority of blacks or dismiss calls for racial justice as simply a holdover from the "morally bankrupt" legacy of the 1960s.

Poverty is on the rise among children in the United States, with 20 percent of all children under the age of eighteen living below the poverty line.

Unemployment is growing at an alarming rate for poor youth of color, especially in the urban centers. While black youth are policed and disciplined in and out of the nation's schools, conservative and liberal educators define education through the ethically limp discourses of privatization, national standards, and global competitiveness.

Many writers in the critical education tradition have attempted to challenge the right wing fundamentalism behind educational and social reform in both the United States and abroad while simultaneously providing ethical signposts for a public discourse about education and democracy that is both prophetic and transformative. Eschewing traditional categories, a diverse number of critical theorists and educators have successfully exposed the political and ethical implications of the cynicism and despair that has become endemic to the discourse of schooling and civic life. In its place, such educators strive to provide a language of hope that inextricably links the struggle over schooling to understanding and transforming our present social and cultural dangers.

At the risk of overgeneralizing, both cultural studies theorists and critical educators have emphasized the importance of understanding theory as the grounded basis for "intervening into contexts and power . . . in order to enable people to act more strategically in ways that may change their context for the better."[1] Moreover, theorists in both fields have argued for the primacy of the political by calling for and struggling to produce critical public spaces, regardless of how fleeting they may be, in which "popular cultural resistance is explored as a form of political resistance."[2] Such writers have analyzed the challenges that teachers will have to face in redefining a new mission for education, one that is linked to honoring the experiences, concerns, and diverse histories and languages that give expression to the multiple narratives that engage and challenge the legacy of democracy.

Equally significant is the insight of recent critical educational work that connects the politics of difference with concrete strategies for addressing the crucial relationships between schooling and the economy, and citizenship and the politics of meaning in communities of multicultural, multiracial, and multilingual schools.

Critical Studies in Education and Culture attempts to address and demonstrate how scholars working in the fields of cultural studies and the critical pedagogy might join together in a radical project and practice informed by theoretically rigorous discourses that affirm the critical but refuse the cynical, and establish hope as central to a critical pedagogical and political practice but eschew a romantic utopianism. Central to such a project is the issue of how pedagogy might provide cultural studies theorists and educators with an opportunity to engage pedagogical practices that are not only transdisciplinary, transgressive, and oppositional, but also connected to a wider project designed to further racial, economic, and political democracy.[3] By taking seriously the relations between culture and power, we further the possibilities of resistance, struggle, and change.

Critical Studies in Education and Culture is committed to publishing work that opens a narrative space that affirms the contextual and the specific while simultaneously recognizing the ways in which such spaces are shot through with issues of power. The series attempts to continue an important legacy of theoretical work in cultural studies in which related debates on pedagogy are understood and addressed within the larger context of social responsibility, civic courage, and the reconstruction of democratic public life. We must keep in mind Raymond Williams's insight that the "deepest impulse (informing cultural politics) is the desire to make learning part of the process of social change itself."[4] Education as a cultural pedagogical practice takes place across multiple sites, which include not only schools and universities but also the mass media, popular culture, and other public spheres, and signals how within diverse contexts, education makes us both subjects of and subject to relations of power.

This series challenges the current return to the primacy of market values and simultaneous retreat from politics so evident in the recent work of educational theorists, legislators, and policy analysts. Professional relegitimation in a troubled time seems to be the order of the day as an increasing number of academics both refuse to recognize public and higher education as critical public spheres and offer little or no resistance to the ongoing vocationalization of schooling, the continuing evisceration of the intellectual labor force, and the current assaults on the working poor, the elderly, and women and children.[5]

Emphasizing the centrality of politics, culture, and power, *Critical Studies in Education and Culture* will deal with pedagogical issues that contribute in imaginative and transformative ways to our understanding of how critical knowledge, democratic values, and social practices can provide a basis for teachers, students, and other cultural workers to redefine their role as engaged and public intellectuals. Each volume will attempt to rethink the relationship between language and experience, pedagogy and human agency, and ethics and social responsibility as part of a larger project for engaging and deepening the prospects of democratic schooling in a multiracial and multicultural society. *Critical Studies in Education and Culture* takes on the responsibility of witnessing and addressing the most pressing problems of public schooling and civic life, and engages culture as a crucial site and strategic force for productive social change.

Henry A. Giroux

NOTES

1. Lawrence Grossberg, "Toward a Genealogy of the State of Cultural Studies," in Cary Nelson and Dilip Parameshwar Gaonkar, eds., *Disciplinary and Dissent in Cultural Studies* (New York: Routledge, 1996), 143.

2. David Bailey and Stuart Hall, "The Vertigo of Displacement,"*Ten 8* (2:3) (1992), 19.

3. My notion of transdisciplinary comes from Mas'ud Zavarzadeh and Donald Morton, "Theory, Pedagogy, Politics: The Crisis of the 'Subject' in the Humanities," in Mas'ud Zavarzadeh and Donald Morton, eds., *Theory Pedagogy Politics: Texts for Change* (Urbana: University of Illinois Press, 1992), 10. At issue here is neither ignoring the boundaries of discipline-based knowledge nor simply fusing different disciplines, but creating theoretical paradigms, questions, and knowledge that cannot be taken up within the policed boundaries of the existing disciplines.

4. Raymond Williams, "Adult Education and Social Change," in *What I Came to Say* (London: Hutchinson-Radus, 1989), 158.

5. The term "professional legitimation" comes from a personal correspondence with Professor Jeff Williams of East Carolina University.

Preface

This collection, in the main, is comprised of chapters contributed by academics from New Zealand (and overwhelmingly, the University of Auckland) and the United States. In these terms it might be said to be an exemplification of a set of relations between the local and the global, the large and the small, the "metropolis" and the satellite. The collection is an attempt to take seriously the notion of the "disciplines" in the humanities and social sciences and to examine its multiple histories, its specific national locations, the emerging economy of studies, and the politics that accompany new developments of interdisciplinarity and transdisciplinarity.

It is my understanding that in New Zealand there is no such thing as cultural studies, at least in any disciplinary or institutional sense where it is possible, for example, to refer to a separate department or school within a university or tertiary education institution. In discussing this proposition with colleagues I have been informed that New Zealand does have its own form of cultural studies; it is one mediated through, perhaps, a Boasian (and American structural functionalist), anthropological notion of culture, a strong revisionist sense of the history of both British colonialism and Maori resistance, with an inflection toward first or early contact studies—and, most importantly, pursued *within* the established disciplines of anthropology, English and history. Not only is such a view put forward as an explanatory hypothesis but it is also positively favored: that is, cultural studies within the existing disciplines, it is held, is better than some independent hybrid. I am less convinced of this reading and more inclined to accept the view at the explanatory level that New Zealand universities on the whole have not been receptive to new disciplinary developments, and that new areas of study have struggled to gain academic recognition and to be able to present courses as part of the university curriculum. Certainly, it seems the examples of Maori studies, film studies and women's studies in New Zealand would tend to support this interpretation. I am inclined also to accept the view that cultural studies as a new area of study, separate from (although related to) existing disciplines, is preferable to cultural studies remaining within the disciplines. How else might we take account of Asian cultural studies, for instance, or new areas of study that develop independent of or completely outside the cultural prism of the European traditional university curriculum?

More recently, the effects of so-called French theory and contemporary discourses of "postmodernism" and "poststructuralism" have been felt and taken up in the humanities and social sciences in New Zealand universities, although these newer discourses and movements of thought have also been actively resisted as "imported rhetoric" through a variety of exclusory strategies. (This collection, for instance, despite an international co-publishing agreement and handsome independent sponsorship, was dismissed by one university press as "too trendy.") Where they have been taken up (and increasingly more so in recent years), they have contributed to refocusing questions of the relations between issues of culture and power: the politics of identity in relation to Maori, feminism, community and the nation. These developments are, perhaps, clearest in media and communication studies, film studies, art history, art criticism and the visual arts, but they also have a strong presence in sociology, education and the other social sciences.

Disciplinarity, a notion that refers to the study of the disciplines—the history of their formation—is now a firmly entrenched feature of cultural studies. It is an excellent example of an area of study where questions of culture and power intersect, and as an emerging area of study, it seems both to stand outside the scope of traditional disciplines (but is close to history and epistemology) and yet deserve serious attention. It is to be hoped that this collection will inspire further reflection upon the formation of the disciplines in the humanities and social sciences.

As always, there are a large number of people to thank: the members of the original seminar and the present contributors. I should like to acknowledge the willingness and support for putting this collection together from especially Timothy Luke and Bob Markley. I would like to thank Henry Giroux, who has been tremendously supportive of my work over the years, and specifically for his support for publishing this collection in his series. Henry is an exemplary public intellectual who works across the areas of critical pedagogy, cultural and youth studies. I would like also to specifically acknowledge the support of my friend and colleague Colin Lankshear. Brian Opie, president of the Humanities Society of New Zealand (HUMANZ), has been inspiring in his intellectual leadership, reinventing the humanities for New Zealand in the twenty-first century and contributing to the definition and formation of appropriate knowledge and culture policies.

I would like to acknowledge the editorial direction from Jane Garry at Bergin and Garvey and editorial help from Jan Duncan in the School of Education, the University of Auckland, in preparing the manuscript for publication.

Finally, I would like to acknowledge the financial assistance of the Auckland Medical Aid Trust, whose research objectives supported a generous grant that helped to bring this project to fruition.

Michael Peters
The University of Auckland

After the Disciplines

Introduction: Disciplinarity and the Emergence of Cultural Studies

MICHAEL PETERS

Can one accept, as such, the distinction between the major types of discourse, or that between such forms or genres as science, literature, philosophy, religion, history, fiction, etc., and which tend to create great historical individualities? . . . "Literature" and "politics" are recent categories, which can be applied to medieval culture, or even classical culture, only by a retrospective hypothesis, and by an interplay of formal analogies or semantic resemblances; but neither literature, nor politics, nor philosophy and the sciences articulated the field of discourse, in the seventeenth or eighteenth century, as they did in the nineteenth century. In any case, these divisions—whether our own, or those contemporary with the discourse under examination—are always themselves reflexive categories, principles of classification, normative rules, institutionalized types; they, in turn, are facts of discourse that deserve to be analyzed beside others; of course, they also have complex relations with each other, but they are not intrinsic, autochthonous, and universally recognizable characteristics.

—Michel Foucault, *The Archaeology of Knowledge* (1992: 23)

For only two centuries, knowledge has assumed a disciplinary form; for less than one, it has been produced in academic institutions by professionally trained knowers. Yet we have come to see these circumstances as so natural that we tend to forget their historical novelty and fail to imagine how else we might produce and organize knowledge.

—Ellen Messer-Davidow, David R. Shumway and
David J. Sylvan (eds.), *Knowledges* (1993: viii)

DISCIPLINARITY: AFTER FOUCAULT?

If I begin with Michel Foucault, it is because it is difficult to go past or beyond him. Standing on the shoulders of Gaston Bachelard, Georges Canguilhem, Michel Serres, Martial Guéroult, and Louis Althusser, he was among the first, now almost thirty years ago, to raise questions concerning the unities of discourse and of disciplines; to interrogate the notion of "disciplinarity." "Archaeology" as the "epistemological mutation of history" *is* a form of structuralism but one that is decentered through the operation of Nietzschean genealogy which askews the search for origins and foundations. Foucault was forever questioning and progressively refining his own project as one that concerned the *problematique* of the subject, and his archaeology of knowledge is also defined in these terms. As he says, "Making historical analysis the discourse of the continuous and making human consciousness the original subject of all historical development and action are two sides of the same system of thought" (Foucault 1992: 12). It is no wonder then that when he assumed his chair at the prestigious Collège de France in 1970 at the age of forty-four, he called it "The History of Systems of Thought." "Systems of thought," he suggested, "are the forms in which, during a given time, knowledges individualize, achieve an equilibrium, and enter into communication." As Paul Rabinow (1997: xi) explains: Foucault divided his work on the history of systems of thought into three interrelated parts, the "reexamination of knowledge, the conditions of knowledge, and the knowing subject." The discursive formation and transformation of knowledge (and its disciplinary forms) is comprised by rules which characterize "its existence, its operation, and its history" (Foucault 1997: 7).

Foucault first takes the disciplinary unities that are already given and he inquires what formally unites them as fields specified in space and individualized in time. By suspending the naturalness of accepted unities, it is possible to describe or define other unities. *The Archaeology of Knowledge* is Foucault's attempt to describe the relations between statements that constitute a field of discourse in terms of the objects to which they refer, the style in which they manifest, the system of concepts they establish and the themes they identify. In Chapter 6, "Science and Knowledge," Foucault (1992: 178) inquires:

If one calls "disciplines" groups of statements that borrow their organization from scientific models, which tend to coherence and demonstrativity, which are accepted, institutionalized, transmitted, and sometimes taught as sciences, could one not say that archaeology describes disciplines that are not really sciences, while epistemology describes sciences that have been formed on the basis of (or in spite of) existing disciplines?

Archaeology defines the rules of formation of a group of statements; it does *not* describe disciplines. Disciplines may serve as starting points for the description of "positivities" but "they do not fix its limits" or "impose definitive divisions upon it" (Foucault 1992: 179). By "positivities" Foucault means that which characterizes the unity of a discourse through time— a *historical a priori* that as a form of positivity defines "a field in which formal identities, thematic continuities, translations of concepts and polemical interchanges may be deployed" (127). In short, positivities do not characterize forms of knowledge.

Yet "archaeology" was still too static and while different from structuralism per se, it bore all its traces. The conception of disciplines as "structures" carried with it the criticisms of structuralism itself. The notion of disciplines as knowledge "structures" or forms assumed a fixed origin, or center, which freezes the play of difference and meaning in a totalizing gesture around a transcendental subject, which, itself, is construed as the fount of all meaning, knowledge and moral action. As is now well known, Foucault went to great pains to dissociate himself from structuralism and his own methods underwent a trajectory that carried him away from "archaeology" towards a genealogical approach strongly indebted to Nietzsche's *Genealogy of Morals* (1956 [1887]) and to Nietzsche's associated concept of the will to power (see Mahon 1992; Peters, 1998). The latter, for instance, Foucault (1997: 11) discusses in one of the Collège course summaries entitled "The Will to Knowledge" where he suggests it is possible to analyze systems of thought at the level of discursive practices.

Discursive practices are characterized by the demarcation of a field of objects, by the definition of a legitimate perspective for a subject of knowledge, by the setting of norms for elaborating concepts and theories. Hence, each of them presupposes a play of prescriptions that governs exclusions and selections.

Principles of exclusion and selection do not refer to a historical or transcendental subject, Foucault argues, but rather "to an anonymous and polymorphous will to knowledge," referencing his remark to Nietzsche's *The Gay Science*, which he describes as presenting "a model of a fundamentally interested knowledge, produced as an event of the will and determining the effect of truth through falsification" (1997: 14).

It is against this kind of Foucauldian understanding that I organized a seminar series called "Disciplinarity: The Emergence of Cultural Studies" at the University of Auckland, New Zealand, in 1996. It was a series that attempted to take the notion of *disciplinarity* seriously, especially in relation to the formation of "cultural studies." I was using the term "cultural studies" in a wider sense than normal, in part in a sense akin to what other have called the "new humanities." The motivation to hold the seminar was part of my own trajectory that brought together interests in contemporary French philosophy, educational theory and the transformation of the modern university. In terms of my own research agenda I had been greatly interested in the work of the French philosopher Jean-François Lyotard, and had recently published a selection of authored, coauthored and edited works concerning the philosophy of Lyotard, especially in relation to the question of the university (Peters 1995); "poststructuralism" and education, more generally, (Peters 1996, 1998); cultural politics and the university (Peters 1997); virtual technologies in higher education and the politics of university restructuring (Peters and Roberts 1998, 1999). It seemed necessary to me not only to analyze the external pressures facing the university—in particular, the neo-liberal paradigm of globalization, the impact of the new communications and information technologies, the incremental privatization of higher education and the commodification of knowledge and teacher–student relations—but also to raise some questions concerning the changing knowledge economy of disciplines—their internal relations, the transmutation, displacement, disappearance and the emergence of different fields of inquiry called "studies." (This is not to conclude that there is an "inside" and an "outside" story, for it is not possible to talk of the development of "cultural studies" within the university without reference to larger movements and events outside the university and, if anything, the relations of the university to society have become more porous, "media saturated," and open to interference.)

In thematizing the seminar and the collection, I had been strongly influenced by Bill Readings' work and the seminar he had mounted from the Department of Comparative Literature at the University of Montreal. Readings[1], a translator of Jean-François Lyotard's work, had examined what he called the "crisis of identity" being faced by the modern university. He had returned to the work of the founders of the modern university—Newman, Kant, the Humboldt brothers—and worked through a number of strategic texts that established a thread to contemporary discourse.

DWELLING IN THE RUINS

In a recent book, the posthumous culmination of the seminar he initiated, Bill Readings (1996) argues that three ideas of the university dominate the modern era: the Kantian idea of reason, the Humboldtian idea of culture and the technological idea of excellence. With the advent of globalization and the alleged decline of the nation state as the principle of economic and cultural organization both the Kantian and Humboldtian conceptions have become problematic. Universities now function as one more bureaucratic subsystem among others harnessed in the service of the goal of national competitiveness in the global economy. In the age of global capitalism, Readings suggests universities have been reduced to a technical ideal of performance within a discourse of "excellence."

For anyone working in an American, Australian, Canadian, British or New Zealand university at any time over the past decade, Readings' observations must constitute an easily recognizable description. The language of managerialism, with a focus on strategic planning, mission statements and performance indicators, seems to have little to do with the traditional governance of the university, and the further the university moves away from the old structures, the more it loses its institutional uniqueness and looks like just another corporation. The neo-liberal policy paradigm now dispenses with any pretence to anything other than the underlying market logic: contestable funding, "providers" and "consumers," student loans and so on, have real consequences and now form the parameters of our daily working lives. In short, the establishment of a new discourse of the university has been accomplished and while we might distance ourselves from the ideology of managerialism or even attempt to subvert it in various ways, we cannot help but be effectively reshaped by it.

In an earlier paper which is the lead article in a special issue of *Oxford Literary Review* commemorating his work, Readings (1995: 16) argues that we must recognize that the university is a *ruined* institution, and he asks us to ponder the question of what it means to dwell in the ruins without falling back on romance or nostalgia. For his part Readings restricts himself to the notion of the culturally oriented humanities, noting that under the impact of the market and the adoption of consumerism as a way of life the (Humboldtian) idea of culture has dropped out of the discourse purporting to give the university a foundation or, at least, no longer appears serviceable. As the editors remark, the university no longer functions as a "privileged site of national cultural self-definition" (Clark and Royle 1995: 16). Readings (1995: 21) himself suggests that the animating idea of culture in cultural studies "is not really an idea in the strong sense proposed by the Modern University."

In the face of such an overriding economic imperative, Readings asks "how thought may be addressed within the University" (1995: 22) or rather "how to think in an institution whose development tends to make thought more and more difficult" (23). His answer is partly construed as a historical response, although clearly it also contains faint traces of a German idealism with its concern to protect, if not an idea, then a *space*. He implicitly defines thought in terms of its disciplinary structures while acknowledging the dissipation of such structures and the opening up of a certain interdisciplinary space. To dwell in the ruins of the university without nostalgia Readings suggests we ought to abandon disciplinary grounding but retain as structurally essential "the *question of the disciplinary form that can be given to knowledges*" (25). In this new context disciplinarity has become a *permanent question*: "we must keep open the question of what it means to group knowledges in certain ways" (25), to ask not only in what it consists but also what it excludes.

I am sympathetic to Readings' interpretation. His project and his thinking acted as a source of inspiration for me. In the spirit of critical thinking I want to respond to aspects of Readings' analysis. Let me briefly summarize my criticisms. First, I think Readings conflates the Kantian and the Humboldtian ideas. He talks of disciplinarity in the humanities, acknowledging the decline of the Humboldtian idea of culture as a central organizing idea for the university, yet the idea he wants to defend, in some limited sense, is a variant of the (Kantian) idea of reason—the idea of thought or thinking and its institutional space. Some clarification is required here: I think there is a suppressed argument in Readings' work that does a lot of work concerning the definition of thought or thinking in humanities in terms of its disciplinary structures. For my part I would want to talk of the *multiplicity* of thought, of the difference between disciplinary and interdisciplinary thinking, of thinking without the disciplines, perhaps even of thinking despite the disciplines.

This new multiplicity of thought in the humanities and social studies is not just a kind of postmodern *bricolage*, assemblage or blind eclecticism driven by fashionable trends in the academic market; it is also a kind of unraveling of the disciplinary purposes of the modern university. It is not without considerable care that Foucault chose the notion of discipline as part of the title of his famous work, *Discipline and Punish*. Michel Foucault was not protesting against the notion of the disciplines as they have developed since the Enlightenment, nor was he anti-Enlightenment. Foucault's development changed over his lifetime. He progressively redefined his object of study as shifting from discourse, to power, to the subject—from the orders of discourse, to the analytics of power, to the different modes by which human beings are made subjects. "Discipline"—a systematically ambiguous term—as a form of moral training establishes the liberal rationality of governance required for our autonomy as subjects and, therefore, also the self-regulating autonomy of the university as a whole. Barry Hindess (1995: 44), for example, argues that "the most influential Western models of a university should be seen, at least in part, as belonging to a liberal rationality of government" in the Foucaultian sense of individual self-regulation. Indeed, the neo-Foucaultian trope of disciplinarity has proved remarkably productive for understanding not only the university and the rise of cultural studies but also modern institutions per se.[2]

Second, I disagree with Readings when it comes to giving up entirely on the idea of culture and on the university as a privileged site for cultural self-definition at the national level. Readings is still too wedded to the idea of the modern university, an idea largely born out of German idealism and one certainly bearing all the traces of a Eurocentric conception. While Readings does entertain a certain resistance to the history of the idea—we now live amongst its *ruins* and we must learn to do so without nostalgia—he does not seek to displace it or dislodge it entirely. More importantly, he does not want to interrogate its cultural expression, its native tradition or the way it expresses a certain typical Euro-universalism and ethnocentrism. The time of the idea is a European time which must be questioned. In non-European cultural traditions the task of the postcolonial university, *in a different cultural time*, may be precisely to focus upon the question of national cultural self-definition and to do so as a means of coming to terms with, confronting, engaging with, or resisting forces of cultural homogeneity that threaten to erode indigenous traditions in the wake of a globalization, which commodifies both word and image.[3] We cannot presume that the university will take place or perform the same functions in non-European cultures as it does/did in European cultures. Some indication of this might be gained from the prescribed purposes of national universities (for example, the National Islamic University of Malaysia) which have a statuary function of protecting and enhancing national religious and cultural traditions.

Third, by concentrating upon the disciplinary shifts in the humanities and social studies alone Readings is not able to provide an analysis of the way in which these shifts respond to or interact with other shifts—for example, between the sciences and the humanities—or the way the whole disciplinary regime is modulated together. His allusion to the shift of philosophy and the presence of certain strands of European philosophy in departments of literature and cultural studies, which are almost totally ignored by philosophy departments, is a good example. Such a question almost certainly requires reference to disciplinary developments in science and an investigation of the adoption of a "scientific" philosophy. Let me briefly elaborate. A genealogy of American philosophy reveals the fracturing of a public intellectual tradition under such figures as Emerson and Dewey when Jewish emigre philosophers, strongly influenced by the Vienna Circle (for example, Hans Reichenbach, Herbert Feigl and Rudolf Carnap), migrated to the United States. In general, analytic philosophy became very narrowly professional and technical, turning in upon itself and, accordingly, less interested in communicating with other disciplines. Under the influence of twentieth-century formalism and logicism, it ditched its "humanity" and "literariness" to become a highly professionalized and a purely technical discipline (see Barradori 1994; Dyke 1993; Rorty 1982).[4]

Fourth, I do not think that Readings sufficiently distinguishes between two kinds of market liberalism: that construed in national economic terms and a neo-liberal economic globalization. They have both impinged upon the university in distinctive ways and in different eras. Neo-liberal economic globalization, at least, presents *new* problems—legal, ethical, epistemological—to the university and operates, partly, outside the strategic imperatives that define national policies. In terms of the convergence of media business interests with both edutainment and infotainment sectors, with the computer industry and with publishing, the full impact of a neo-liberal globalization on the disciplinary economy of universities has yet to be felt. Its "disciplinary effects," or the way such convergence is reconfiguring the disciplines, is only recently being hypothesized. Above all, it is necessary to distinguish the effects of the open economy and the new form of international competition in higher education as part of the neo-liberal project of globalization (as world economic integration) from the new information and communications technologies that support and make possible globalization. The relationship between changes due to globalization (as world economic integration), the internal demands and pressures such changes make nationally, and the challenges to the traditional disciplinary economy require investigation. In particular, it is necessary to explore the ways in which reconfiguration of the state under globalization articulates and informs a reorganization of the university. This aspect requires some further elaboration.

The emergence of electronic digital technology alongside new social (and theoretical) trends such as the "democratization" of higher education, an increasing social and linguistic diversity of the student population, and pressures for more systematic public accountability suggests a new kind of "core" for the liberal arts (Lanham 1993). Are we concerned here with questions about the "efficiency of information" or rather the "reconfiguration of communications exchange" (Poster 1990)? In the hypertextual virtual reality of the World Wide Web, in the space of a complete textual environment based upon text-based computing, what sense can we make of the notions of the "virtual text" and "virtual author"? What does the shift from the "tactile" to the "digital" mean for new new kinds of reading and writing practices? Or even more fundamentally, with the shift to a virtual text based on transient and temporary representations of digital codes stored in a computer's memory, where does the text reside (Bolter 1991)? To claim that electronic text processing "marks the next major shift in text-based information technology after the printed book" (Delany and Landow 1993: 6) is only to acknowledge a shift based on the common denominator of the digital code which has already led one author to speak of "the impending demise of traditional scholarly journals" (Odlyzko 1994). New features of text-based computing have begun to shape the emergent world of digitized and networked information. Such features as the dematerialization, manipulability, open admission, and so-called dispersal of the text help establish new parameters for the emergence of new forms of discourse and study, and the development of hypertext and hypermedia concordances produce new forms of interlinked, multimedia textuality (Delany and Landow 1993: 12–15). In addition, networked text distribution has the potential to upset the gatekeeping hierarchies of written texts surrounding the printing and publishing industries in ways that disturb the market and traditional modes of regulation of the text. The digital code short-circuits the exchange of ideas, fast-tracking academic publishing and changing the temporal scale of communication in the process. The ease of replication, transmission, modification and manipulability raise new legal and "political" problems concerning intellectual property, copyright and plagiarism.

These developments have led some critics (e.g., Landow 1992; Lanham

1993; Poster 1990) to talk of a convergence of French poststructuralism and the new communications technologies, drawing connections between intertextuality, multivocality and decenteredness, particularly with reference to hypertext and hypermedia developments. They draw attention to the concept of "intertextuality" (Kristeva) and the questioning not only of the "author-function," to use Foucault's term—or authorial forms and all forms of authority—but also the universal and the learning subject of the university, in general. If the concept of the author is under threat of redefinition, if the notions of authority based upon it are also open to question, what does it imply for the university, for the relationship between professor and student, and for the *discipline* of the university?

There are clear implications of the shift to digital publishing and cyberspatial learning environments for conceptions of knowledge and modes of investigations: What influence does the Internet as a largely anarchic medium have on the organization of knowledge? What are the ramifications of the shift from "knowledge" to "information" for traditional disciplinary structures? What do the "simulation" and "speed" effects of the Net and forms of electronic communication have upon traditional academic practices, such as reading and writing, which, themselves, form part of the larger network of practices that run across all disciplines?

DISCIPLINARITY: THE CONCEPT

> To some, no doubt, the word *disciplinarity* is a problematic neologism. Why use the term at all? Why not refer simply to the general or comparative study of disciplines? . . . Our answer to these questions is that what we are proposing to study is neither the knowledge produced by individual disciplines nor a discipline itself. Rather, we are interested in what makes for disciplinary knowledge as such: discipline-ness, or, as we shall call it, disciplinarity. . . . Put differently, our concern is with the *possibility conditions* of disciplines.
>
> —Ellen Messer-Davidow, David R. Shumway, and David J. Sylvan (eds.), *Knowledges* (1993: 1–2)

Messer-Davidow and her colleagues, Shumway and Slyvan, draw upon Foucault as a source of inspiration but also for a definition when they neologize the word "disciplinarity." In what has quickly become the standard-bearer in this field, they suggest that the disciplines "discipline" us in four ways (Messer-Davidow et al. 1993: vii–viii):

1. disciplines "specify the objects we can study (genes, deviant persons, classic texts) and the relations that obtain among them (mutation, criminality, canonicity). They provide criteria for our knowledge (truth, significance, impact) and methods (quantification, interpretation, analysis) that regulate our access to it";

2. "disciplines produce practitioners, orthodox and heterodox, specialist and generalist, theoretical and experimental";

3. "disciplines produce economies of value. They manufacture discourse. . . . They provide jobs. . . . They secure funding. . . . They generate prestige . . .";

4. "disciplines produce the idea of progress. They proliferate objects to study and improve explanations. They devise notions that command ever-growing assent. . . ."

I am not entirely clear that the description of the way in which disciplines "discipline" us is exhaustive or is even consistent, methodologically speaking. There is nothing to distinguish the categories that Messer-Davidow et al. (1993) suggest and, in particular, the last category seems somewhat epistemologically naïve. The editors, perhaps, are attempting to remain theoretically and methodologically neutral or agnostic (insofar as it is possible) so as to remain as inclusive as possible and not to rule out different approaches to the study of "disciplinarity." The collection of essays constitutes an important theoretical step forward. The preface establishes the basis for the series and indicates the several different kinds of books to be written that serve as distinguishable theoretical trajectories: *disciplinary histories, institutional topographies*, and *extradisciplinary reports*. The first would investigate the intellectual, political and social milieus in which disciplines arose and the way that a mode of inquiry assumed a particular disciplinary form. The second "would examine the rhetorics and rituals of disciplinary activities as well as the characteristic spaces in which institutional practices occur" (viii). The third, "would look at knowledges that lie beyond disciplines": "the new cross-disciplinary and counter-disciplinary inquiries (feminism, neo-Marxism, cultural studies); non-academic institutions that produce knowledge (museums, missionary schools, public-interest organisations); and forms that non-disciplinary knowledge does and could take" (viii) (for instance, direct-mail surveys, comic books, union organizing, videos).

I am scrutinizing the basis for this series because there are implicit hierarchies and values associated with any categorization of the disciplines, as Messer-Davidow et al. are all too aware. Yet the envisaging of several kinds of book for the series is tantamount to an implicit division. We must ask the question: What does it leave out? First, if the three different kinds of books represent in some way an emergent typology for the study of disciplinarity, I would argue there is not enough recognition of the notion of "disciplines" and of the history of "disciplinarity" itself—the *economy* or system of disciplines and the checkered history of attempts to deliberately overcome the increasing segmentalization of knowledges into fields and subfields. Second, such categorization does not take account of the developments referred to under the concepts of "multidisciplinarity" and "transdisciplinarity." I shall deal with each of these points in turn.

Julie Klein (1998), who has contributed a book to the series on the concept of *interdisciplinarity* (Klein 1993), maintains that there were 8,530 definable knowledge fields by 1987. There is little recognition, perhaps, of the complex transformations *within* disciplines that result from events, pressures, forces and trends—demographic, institutional, social, psychological— external to the disicplines. In particular, I am thinking of the discourse of multiculturalism and the degree that it has (or has not) transformed traditional disciplines in the humanities like history or philosophy. A good example of this kind of reflection and study is the special issue of *Daedalus* (Winter, 1997) devoted to *American Academic Culture in Transformation: Fifty Years, Four Disciplines.* M. H. Abrams (1997: 114) reflecting on the transformation of English studies over the period 1930–1995, for instance, remarks:

Among the theoretical modes that succeeded the New Criticism and its near contemporary, archetypal theory, are phenomenological theory, structuralist theory, reader-response theory, reception theory, semiotic theory, speech-act theory, and Bakhtinian dialogic theory. However, most deeply influential in fostering the radical character of literary studies in America have been the works (often grouped as "postmodern" or "poststructural" of four French writers—the deconstructionist theory of Jacques Derrida, the "power/knowledge" theory of Michel Foucault, the revised Freudian theory of Jacques-Marie Lacan, and the neo-Marxist ideological theory of Louis Althusser.

Abrams suggests that what makes poststructuralism "genuinely revolutionary" is the way it calls radically into question the humanistic paradigm underlying literature, a paradigm that locates the site of literature in the human world and interprets a work of literature as the product of a purposive human author. Poststructural theories, he argues, by contrast, "abstract literary texts from the human world" relocating them in the "play of language-as-such," within the forces of a "discourse already-in-being." This radical shift from the humanistic frame of reference translates the human agent (as writer and reader) as well as the work itself into the "products, effects, or constructs of language and discourse." In other words, as he asserts, "the functions of human agency are transferred to the immanent dynamics of the signifying system" (Abrams 1997: 115). The study of disciplinarity must be able to take account of those epistemic grand movements that involve shifts within an entire set of disciplines (the humanities) but whose effects are highly localized and differential within disciplines.

These grand disciplinary shifts might comprise larger historical reconfigurations: the advent of European formalism per se and its various manifestations and cultural expressions in avant gardes, in structuralisms and poststructuralisms; the development of anticolonialisms, the emergence of philosophies of decolonization and postcoloniality; and in association with this, the revitalisation of indigenous traditions and the recognition of traditional non-Western cultural forms of knowledge, their hybridization and the emergence the new forms of cultural knowledge that spring from these developments.

It must, in addition be recognized that there are specific meanings that govern the use of the terms "disciplinarity" and its cognates—"multidisciplinarity," "interdisciplinarity" and "transdisciplinarity." Basarab Nicolescu (1998a: 1) provides a useful set of definitions. He asserts that "interdisciplinarity" concerns the "transfer of methods from one discipline to another" and suggests that one can distinguish three degrees of interdisciplinarity: a degree of application (when, say, the methods of nuclear physics are transferred to medicine leading to new treatments); an epistemic degree (when, say, the methods of formal logic are transferred to the law); a degree of the generation of new disciplines (when, for example, the transfer of mathematics to physics or meterological phenonmena and stock market processes led to the development of mathematical physics and to chaos theory). Multidisciplinarity or pluridisciplinarity "concerns studying a research topic not in only one discipline but in several at the same time" (Nicolescu 1998a: 2). A painting by Giotto, for example, can be studied within art history, but also within the history of religions, European history and geometry. Marxist philosophy might be studied in philosophy, physics, economics, psychoanalysis and literature. Transdisciplinarity, Nicolescu (1998a: 1) argues, concerns "that which is at once between the disciplines, across the disciplines, and beyond all discipline." The three pillars—levels of reality, the logic of the included middle, and complexity—determine the methodology of transdisciplinary research. Disciplinarity, for instance, concerns at most one level of reality whereas transdisciplinarity concerns the dynamics engendered by the action of several levels of reality at once. Transdisciplinarity, Nicolescu (1998a: 2) argues, is "globally open," entailing a "new vision and a new lived experience." It emerges from the most advanced contemporary sciences (quantum physics and cosmology, molecular biology) and is aimed at a self-transformation, the unity of knowledge and the "creation of a new art of living" (see also Nicolescu 1998b).[5]

Klein (1998) concurs. She first charts the notion of transdisciplinarity as it was defined at the first international seminar on interdisciplinarity, attended by such luminaries as Jean Piaget, Andre Lichnerowicz and Erich Jantsch (1972), who proposed an education-innovation system as a multileveled and multigoaled hierarchy. Since that early beginning, Klein (1998: 2) comments, a new definition has appeared:

Gibbons, et al. (1994) identify a fundamental change in the ways that scientific, social, and cultural knowledge are being produced. The elemental traits are complexity, hybridity, non-linearity, reflexivity, heterogeneity, and transdisciplinarity. The new mode of production is "transdisciplinary" in that it contributes theoretical structures, research methods, and modes of practice that are not located on current disciplinary or interdisciplinary maps. One of its effects is to replace or reform established institutions, practices, and policies. Problem contexts are transient and problem solvers mobile. Emerging out of wider societal and cognitive pressures, knowledge is dynamic. It is stimulated by continuous linking and relinking of influences across a dense communication network with feedback loops. As a result new configurations are continuously generated.

While Klein (1998: 2) concentrates upon the sciences, she acknowledges that the humanities and social sciences "also exhibit complexity and hybridity, heterogeneous practices of the same discipline, overlapping problem domains, and crossfertilization of tools and methods." This academic boundary crossing sometimes termed "postmodernism" or the "new constellation" (Bernstein 1990) reflects the contemporary reality: the erosion of older nation states, the globalization of economic activities, the development of new communication and information technologies and the emergence of new cultural "particularisms" (Klein 1998: 2).

These understandings motivate Nicolescu (1998a) and Klein (1998) to call for the transdisciplinary development of education. Nicolescu (1998a: 2) remarks: "In spite of the enormous diversity of the systems of education from one country to another, the globalization of the challenges of our era involves the globalization of the problems of education," and he invokes a new kind of education based on Jacques Delors' four pillars: learning to know, learning to do, learning to live together, and learning to be. Klein (1998: 3) suggests that the transdisciplinary project will involve a critique of institutional structures and pedagogical strategies, and she draws on the work of Basil Bernstein (1990) to suggest the need for integrated codes in education as society becomes more fragmented and specialized:

Integrated codes are characterized by new forms of interdependence and cooperation. They heighten awareness of the difference between insularity and hybridity. Insulation stresses the interdictory, impermeable quality of cultural boundaries, textual classification, and disciplinary autonomy. Hybridity stresses essential identity and continuity, permeability of classificatory boundaries, cultural meanings, and domains. Hybridity is not dominant, but the framework in education has shifted, putting hybridizers on the offensive, and insulators on the defensive.

It is, perhaps, with cultural studies and the so-called new humanities[6] that this complexity and hybridity is best exemplified.

DISCIPLINARITY AND CULTURAL STUDIES

In an excellent collection of essays *Disciplinarity and Dissent in Cultural Studies*, the editors, Cary Nelson and Dilip Parameshwar Gaonkar (1996: 5) suggests that cultural studies in the 1990s "finds itself being textually inscribed and politically positioned in a time of financial crisis." The "explosion of subdisciplinary programs and interdisciplinary institutes" that many imagine to be the future of cultural studies in the United States has not materialized and "for the most part institutionalization is on hold." While there has been some disciplinary resistance to cultural studies and a conservative backlash, the editors also acknowledge that within existing disciplines conceptual struggles are taking place and cultural studies is in the process of redefining itself.

Lawrence Grossberg (1996: 131) echoes these sentiments when he proclaims that cultural studies "has never been in a more precarious and ambivalent position than it is now in the U.S. academy." In particular, he argues two conditions threaten its viability as a political project. First, in its easy application to a variety of projects, cultural studies has lost sense of its own distinctiveness. Second, media representations have constructed cultural studies in a very narrow sense. Grossberg himself argues against these contradictory forces of expansion and contraction, that cultural studies must remain more modest in its goals and self-understandings. He suggests that in order to question more thoroughly the sites of its institutionalization and commodification cultural studies in the United States must begin to narrate its own history. As he argues:

One could write any number of different "cultural studies" of cultural studies itself, constructing them from a number of different narratives: the empowerment of the margins; the emergence of a hegemonic conservatism; the media-tization of culture and the globalization of capital; the theoretical excesses of "critical theory" (as the term was used in the U.S.); the failures of the traditional "left" political institutions and movements; the crisis of the humanities (and the social sciences) . . . None of these narratives offers a singular vision of a homogeneous, progressively developing field. (Grossberg 1996: 134)

His own preferred normative description of cultural studies as an academic practice is one way of "politicizing theory and theorizing politics" (142) in order to help "reconstitute political strategies" based upon a new authority. While it shares a number of "operational procedures" with other critical practices it is distinctive in terms of its "radical contextuality" (143). The question of cultural studies' own interdisciplinarity is not to be construed as an "aggressive anti-disciplinarity" (144) for its own sake but rather as a consequence of the pursuit of knowledge that happens to transgress disciplinary boundaries, perhaps in unpredictable ways, in the effort to map as rigorously as possible a particular context and "to answer a strategic question" (145). Disciplinarity, as a field within cultural studies, has been established within the last few years: it encourages a philosophical self-reflection for cultural studies and the attempt to provide some parameters in defining its distinctiveness.[7]

Herman Gray (1996) would seem to agree with Grossberg, at least insofar as asking the question whether cultural studies is inflated in the United States and in emphasizing the importance of historical specificity in understanding the formation of cultural studies and its ongoing development. He suggests:

What eventually emerged in quasi-institutional form under the initial impetus and influence of Richard Hoggart, Raymond Williams, E. P. Thompson, and Stuart Hall was first and foremost a political and intellectual project that developed, Hall puts it, as "an adaptation to its terrain" (Hall 1990, 11). That is, cultural studies emerged in conjunction with a particular set of political problems, theoretical crises, and social and cultural transformations in postwar England. (Gray 1996: 206; Hall 1990, 1992)

Gray's point is that cultural studies developed out of a specific set of social and political conditions in England and it did not "spring full-blown as a fully realized intellectual discourse and institutional formation" (Gray 1996: 207). Indeed, as he suggests, it is more accurate to talk of several periods and types of cultural studies: "the period of subcultural and ethnographic studies of popular culture and media; the period of engagement with structural Marxism; the culturalist period; and the period of the new ethnicities and gender studies" (Gray 1996: 208) (see also Palmeri 1997; Rodman 1997; Storey 1997). John Frow (1992: 25) suggests that cultural studies originates, above all, in *the crisis of the universality of value*: it "takes as its theoretical object the culture of everyday life, where the concept of culture is understood in a broadly anthropological sense, as the full range of practices and representations in which meanings and personal and group identities are formed" and it "is concerned as much with the social relations of representation as it is with self-contained texts; it thinks of the cultural, in William's phrase, as 'a way of life' rather than a set of privileged objects."

Stuart Hall (1996), like Grossberg, emphasizes in very general terms the context of social relations in which meanings and the symbolic occur. In addition, he wishes to define cultural studies in relation to questions of power. As he argues,

cultural studies has always looked at this in the context of the social relations in which it occurs, and asked questions about the organization of power. So it's cultural power, I think, that is the crux of what distinguishes cultural studies from, say, classical studies, which is after all the study of the culture of Roman times. There are all

kinds of cultural studies going on, but this interest in combining the study of symbolic forms and meanings with the study of power has always been at the centre.
(24)

Although Hall (1997), in a slightly different or more nuanced way to
Gray, acknowledges the regulative force of William's anthropological notion
of culture as "a whole way of life" (as opposed to "the best that has been
thought or said") in British cultural studies, he denies that there is, or ever
was, *one* regulative notion. In this regard his comments are worth quoting
at some length:

He'd [Williams] hardly written the sentence before a critique of the organicist character of that definition emerged. It was an important move, the sociological, anthropological move, but it was cast in terms of a humanist notion of social and symbolic
practices. The really big shift was the coming of semiotics and structuralism: not
because the definition of culture stopped there, but that remains the defining paradigm shift, nonetheless—signifying practices, rather than a whole way of life. . . . For
Williams, everything is dissolved into practice. Of course, the new model was very
linguistic, very Saussurean, but nevertheless, that was the definitive break. Everything
after that goes back to that moment. Post-structuralism goes back to the structuralist
break. Psychoanalytic models are very influenced by the Levi-Straussian moment, or
the Althusserian moment. If I were writing for students, those are still the two definitions I'd pick out, and I wouldn't say there is a third one. I suppose you might
say that there was a postmodern one, a Deleuzian one, which says that signification
is not meaning, it's a question of affect, but I don't see a break in the regulative idea
of culture there as fundamental as the earlier one. (25)

In the same interview, he remarks upon the global diffusion of cultural
studies and its local differences and distinctiveness comparing the founding
moment of British cultural studies with what cultural studies is today. Hall
acknowledges the varied practices that go under the heading of cultural
studies and suggests that the most distinctive aspect of its rapid global dispersion is its situational or geographical appropriation.

Meaghan Morris (1992) has argued that the emergence of cultural studies
can be closely identified with the reconstruction of *national* schools: the
Birmington Centre for Contemporary Cultural Studies, founded in 1964
under the influence of Stuart Hall and with clear links to Raymond Williams
and Richard Hoggart; an American tradition based on the work of Clifford
Geertz or James Carey, now strongly represented (in a different way) by
James Clifford; a Canadian school based upon the work of Harold Innis
and Marshall McLuhan; and a European strand based upon studies of "everyday life" (for example, Henri Lefebvre, Michel de Certeau). One might
add here, perhaps, the development of "poststructuralist" modes of analysis
which challenge the structualist analyses of culture proposed first in formal
linguistics and later applied and developed most notably by Claude Lévi-

Strauss. Significantly, Morris mentions *transnational* strains of postcolonial/ multicultural criticism (Frantz Fanon, Aimé Cesaire, Ranajit Guha, Edward Said) and feminist criticism.

The reception of cultural studies has been different geographically and uneven on a national basis. Where it is possible to talk of national emergent traditions and reconstructions in the case of the Britain, the United States, Britain and Australia, in Aotearoa/New Zealand the reception and development of cultural studies has been both more recent and piecemeal, and it is difficult yet to talk of a national construction or reception.[8] Maori studies, for instance, only became a separate department at the University of Auckland in 1991 (see Ranginui Walker's chapter in this collection, Chapter 9) and women's studies in New Zealand universities is also a very recent development in the sense of institutionalization (i.e., its own program, courses and department). Aspects of cultural studies approaches had been adopted within the departments of English, sociology and education in New Zealand universities during the 1980s and the more recent development of film and television studies or communications studies has either grown out of existing English departments (see Roger Horrocks chapter in this collection, Chapter 8) or they have been set up with the larger urban polytechnics. The fact is that local differences provide subtle and distinctive hues to the meaning and development of cultural studies. In Aotearoa/New Zealand, *biculturalism*, as both rhetoric and practice, has given cultural studies a clear and distinctive regional meaning, and there have been clear attempts to develop a cultural studies in Aotearoa/New Zealand that bears the imprint of its Pacific location.[9]

DISCIPLINARITY: THE SEMINAR

To the original contributors to the seminar I issued the following series of "orientations" that were to help shape their thinking and provide an overall thematic coherence.

Orientations

> **dis'cipline**, n. Branch of instruction (arch.); mental & moral training, adversity as effecting this; military training, drill, (arch.); trained condition; order maintained among schoolboys, soldiers, prisoners, etc.; system of rules for conduct; control exercised over members of church; chastisement; (Eccl.) mortification by penance. So **dis'ciplinal** (*or*-lin'-) a. [ME, f. OF f. L *disciplina* (*discipulus* DISCIPLE,-INE)]
> —*The Concise Oxford Dictionary*

It was not a bad idea, whoever first conceived and proposed a public means for treating the sum of knowledge (and properly the heads who devote themselves to it), in a quasi *industrial* manner, with a division of labour where, for so many fields as there may be of knowledge, so many public teachers would be allotted, professors being trustees, forming together a kind of common scientific entity, called a university (or high school) and having autonomy (for only scholars can pass judgement on scholars as such); and, thanks to its faculties (various small societies where university teachers are ranged, in keeping with the variety of the main branches of knowledge), the university would be authorised to admit, on the one hand, student-apprentices from the lower schools aspiring to its level, and to grant, on the other hand—after prior examination, and on its own authority—to teachers who are "free" (not drawn from the members themselves) and called "Doctors," a universally recognised rank (conferring upon them a degree)—in short, *creating* them.

> —Immanuel Kant, *The Conflict of the Faculties*,
> (1979 [orig. 1798]: 23)

The history of the modern University can be crudely summarised by saying that the modern University has had three Ideas, the Kantian idea of reason, the Humboldtian notion of culture, and now the technological idea of excellence. The distinguishing feature of the last . . . is that it lacks all referentiality—it is the *simulacrum* of the Idea of a University . . . in the Kantian University [the president's] function is the purely disciplinary one of making decisive judgements in inter-faculty conflicts on the grounds of reason alone. In the University founded on culture, the president incarnates a pandisciplinary ideal of a general cultural orientation. . . . In the contemporary University, however, a president is a bureaucratic administrator . . . From judge to synthesiser to executive.

> —Bill Readings, "For a Heteronomous
> Cultural Politics" (1993: 164)

The first of these "orientations," as is clear, was influenced by Foucault's *Discipline and Punish* (1977) and, less obviously, *The Order of Things* (1974). The OED definition of "discipline" was meant to draw attention to the multiple meanings of the term and, in particular, following Foucault, to draw attention to the way it functions as both a form of knowledge and as a form of power.

The original seminars and the collection of essays were designed to examine the emergence and formation of "cultural studies" (a generic term used to cover newly emergent fields of study) within the university and implications for a new disciplinary economy. Authors of individual chapters were asked to consider two broad questions:

- What are the underlying historical, epistemological and political reasons for the emergence of cultural studies?
- What do these developments imply for the traditional liberal arts curriculum and the traditional discipline-based university?

The concept of "discipline" is a recent one in the history of ideas, but it has governed the organization and production of knowledge (Klein 1993). The traditional disciplines were institutionalized in the eighteenth century with the emergence of the concept of the modern university. They were transported and developed in the New World in a context of political and cultural colonialism, designed for an elite cultural class. They were based upon traditional liberal claims for autonomy, ethics and a disinterested neutrality. While under a Kantian model, based upon a purely rationalist conception of knowledge and division of academic labor, disciplines were said to be critical, yet their critique "has often been blind to the ways in which the high culture it disseminates has worked as an instrument of class legitimation" (Frow 1990). Disciplines have ignored their own critical self-reflection and tended to neglect the institutional framework within which particular knowledges are organized, produced and disseminated. Within "scientific" culture, and especially in the postwar era where developed nations have actively pursued the massification of tertiary education, disciplines have tended to become increasingly "technical," ruled epistemologically by what members of the Frankfurt school have described as "instrumental" or "technocratic" rationality.

Principles underlying a global neo-liberalism and managerialism have been responsible for restructuring universities during the 1980s. Some thought that such developments imperiled the humanities, while others believed that the context of globalization and the development of new communications technologies offered new hope for both interdisciplinary work and the emergence of a critical approach. In this environment the study of culture has become fragmented, curtailing possibilities for cultural critique. Attempts to develop interdisciplinary programs have failed. This has led scholars to advocate "both the development of a critique and the production of cultural forms consonant with emancipatory interests," based upon a counterdisciplinary praxis (Giroux et al. 1994). It has also resulted in calls for educators generally to critically address the politics of their own location and to better understand the ways in which we as educators support, challenge or subvert institutional practices that are at odds with democratic processes.

The concept of "disciplinarity" is a term meant to focus attention on these issues, problematizing the concept of the disciplinary structure of knowledge and the university based upon it. Related terms: "interdisciplinarity," "transdisciplinarity," "multidisciplinarity." In addition, authors were provided with the following questions to help them achieve a coherence with the overall aims of the collection.

- What is "cultural studies"? (i.e., In what ways might the notion of cultural studies be contestable?)

- To what extent does the emergence of cultural studies displace or dislocate traditional disciplines?

- What forms of resistance has cultural studies encountered, and why?
- What does cultural studies mean for the idea of the university, especially in New Zealand/Aotearoa?
- To what extent does the emergence of cultural studies reflect a changing mission of the university and changing relations between the university and the wider society?
- What is the future of cultural studies?

According to these questions and the guiding rubrics, I called the seminar "Disciplinarity: The Emergence of Cultural Studies." At that point in 1996, I was not aware of the recent work on the notion of disciplinarity or, indeed, the new developments in thinking that had recently occurred under associated cognate terms "interdisciplinarity" and "transdisciplinarity." *After the Disciplines* emphasizes that the emergence of extradisciplinary forms of knowledge, came *after* the disciplines, chronologically speaking; that a new economy of knowledges had begun to appear, an economy which was no longer limited by parameters of the traditional disciplines. Yet there is still a question about the longevity of such developments. It may have been equally appropriate or more judicious to have called the collection *Besides the Disciplines*.

The collection incorporates the work of most of the original participants who gave seminars at the University of Auckland, including two visiting American academics, Robert Markley and Timothy Luke. Only at a later stage did I encounter the work of Ravi Palat and Warren Moran at my own university. Both Palat and Morran have strong research interests in area studies. I actively sought contributions from Henry Giroux and Colin Lankshear. The result is a collection which is wider in scope than the original seminar program and, perhaps, more representative of competing views. It is a collection that elaborates both the local and the global—perspectives from both a small country that has not yet overcome its own colonial past or cut its constitutional umbilical cord to the "mother country" and a country that is the dominant world superpower: Aotearoa/New Zealand and the United States. The collection begins with Ruth Butterworth's chapter on the political economy of "studies." For Butterworth, an understanding of the shift from "disciplines" to "studies" requires an analysis of relations within the academy and those between the academy and its sociopolitical context. Such an understanding, for Butterworth, is premised upon the conceptualization of education (and the university) as a system of production. According to this classic approach and conception, the economy of cultural studies is comprised of "three pieces on the chessboard": "the gurus, mainly Franco-German, but including the converted Marxists of the Birmingham School; forty years of mass market academia; and the market in baby boomers." Butterworth's essay, placed as the opening chapter, serves to "keep us honest"; it serves to rail against the culturist "turn"; it serves as an unashamedly old-fashioned Marxist critique and invective against postmodernist tendencies in cultural studies. Butterworth's essay is both a challenge and a purgative to those currently practicing in cultural studies. She suggests that:

At a critical time key academics fled into "discourse," "deconstruction" and "representation" retreating into culturalism and ethnicism. Cultural studies, which is not expensive, was the ideal loss-leader in the window of the academic supermarket. Its representations too accurately "represent" the helpless discontents of the postmodern.

Butterworth sides with Sivanandan (1996) who views "postmodernists" and those who practice cultural studies as intellectuals who have actively helped to embed global capitalism, and while her comments "pull no punches," they are, as always, not without considerable humor.

Robert Markley's chapter (Chapter 2), by contrast, is not a critique from outside the field but rather one deeply embroiled in its most recent skirmishes concerning the cultural study of science and the notorious *Social Text* affair involving Alan Sokal.[10] If anything Markley is shaping up to Sokal—who like Butterworth professes to be an old leftist (and "realist")— and addressing Sokal's "misreading" of his work (especially Markley's "The Irrelevance of Reality: Science, Ideology and the Postmodern Universe"). The purpose of Markley's chapter is "to signal an end to the so-called science wars" and to go beyond a debate simplistically and artificially polarized between "realists" and "constructivists" by considering "contributions that the cultural study of science has made to the development of postdisciplinary programs of study." Markley begins by demonstrating the "shoddiness" of the intellectual attacks of the likes of Paul Gross, Norman Levitt, Martin Lewis and Jean Bricmont—whom he calls "scientific exceptionalists"—on the cultural study of science. Markley defines exceptionalism as "the belief that science remains distinct in theory and practice from other cultural and cognitive practices." He proceeds to show what exactly these scientific exceptionalists would have to maintain in order to "cordon off" science from culture, politics and religion, and finally, he makes the case for what scientists have to gain from the cultural study of science. For Markley, cultural studies challenges disciplinary claims to "transhistorical knowledge and cultural authority" and as such it is not to be defined in terms of an antithesis to science nor should it lead to the abandonment of science for anthropology or literary criticism. Rather it provides an opportunity for scientists to expand the practice of science in order to think through the way in which socioeconomic values "underlie our lived experience of science and technology in the 1990s."

In Chapter 3, Timothy Luke notes that higher education developments in cyberspace have tended to be *extradisciplinary*: "In cyberspace, the world no longer needs to be 'naturally divided' into the conventional units of university-defined disciplinarity." Luke first focuses on postmodernity and the new world order, and he draws upon Jean-François Lyotard's notion of performativity and Fredric Jameson's suggestion of the emerging world space of multinational capital to explain a new regime of flexible accumulation, technical specialization and state deregulation. Postmodernity, for Luke, can be thought of in terms of a historical-geographical condition, a political-economic mode of production and a cultural-ethical regime of representation. In this complex environment the university institution becomes driven by its technical ideal of excellence (Bill Readings) and "cyberschooling" exercises an attraction for the new technocrats and digiterati operating under neo-liberal policy constraints. Cyberschooling "recenters control in the educational experience" and "presumes new disciplinary discursive canons," generating a "new aesthetics of educational performance." The political economy of cyberschooling poses a number of questions: Who owns and controls cyberschool sites? What happens to disciplinarity? That is, who certifies teachers, accepts students, operates infostructures? Who will set prices, fees and costs at cyberschool? Luke's sobering conclusion is that cyberschooling will not save money, though it will lead to new post/trans/antidisciplinary learning environments.

In an ambitious, complex and strongly argued chapter (Chapter 4), Ravi Arvind Palat investigates "how the geopolitical imperatives of U.S. hegemony conditioned the institutional underpinnings and substantive content of area studies." Palat demonstrates how area studies emerged in the context of bipolar rivalry between the United States and the USSR, originating in training programs for soldiers and civilians who were assigned the task of administering occupied territories in Europe and the "Far East." Yet while area studies was envisaged as multidisciplinary, the programs tended toward microlevel analyses; while they generated masses of empircal data on the peoples of Africa, Asia, Latin America, the Middle East and the Pacific, the programs never permitted the diversity of cultural and historical experience of these "areas" to challenge or question the narrowness of Euro–North American theoretical categories. Palat focuses upon the institutionalization of area studies in U.S. universities that reflected a U.S.-led partioning of the globe following the reconstitution of the world market under the Bretton Woods system—what Palat calls "imaginative geographies of U.S. hegemony."

With world economic integration it is no longer clear that the nation-state can serve as the unit of analysis and there have been attempts to redraw boundaries and reconstitute geopolitical units in the aftermath of the Cold War and in the period of economic globalization. Palat comments, for instance, how the term "Asia-Pacific" has gained wide currency (at least up until the recent financial crisis in South Asia) and how such popularity "masks a profound redefinition of both 'Asia' and the 'Pacific' " by excluding most of "peasant" Asia, Australia, New Zealand, the Pacific islands and Central and Latin America. It has become apparent that new programs of study based upon "Asia-Pacific" or "Central Asia" are unable to explain emerging political and economic trends. In the final section of his chapter, Palat examines the continued segmentation of area studies programs under the impetus of studies of "postindustrial" and postmodern economies, arguing that "despite the explicit repudiation of post-European Enlightenment rationality by several new academic specializations, they continue to perpetuate and reinforce the series of binary oppositions between an essentialized and totalized West and its equally essentialized and totalized other(s)."

The crisis of area studies reflects deeper questions concerning the untenability of the nineteenth century institutionalization of knowledge. In this context Palat speaks of an "antidisciplinarity as praxis"—of "richly textured historical narratives within wider relational networks," of "constructing genuine world-scale sets of data," of "the construction of new theoretical and conceptual tools," of facing the "imperialism of departments"—in the attempt to conceptualize a post-American world.

In Chapter 5, Warren Moran picks up on related themes to argue a case for a particular set of relations between geography and areas studies. He argues (in agreement with Maureen Molloy) that disciplinary knowledge makes a special contribution to interdisciplinary knowledge, and he suggests that "geography shapes what the discipline geography is and what geography does." In his chapter, Moran demonstrates this proposition by reference to the development of the academic discipline in New Zealand dating from the late 1930s. Moran then suggests that the practice of area studies "is one prism from which to view globalization." He describes in broad terms the neo-liberal paradigm of globalization and the way in which Maori, as the indigenous people of Aotearoa/New Zealand, have become directly implicated in the globalization process. Moran engages directly with Palat, observing that there is something of a paradox with area studies in that, while the original motive may well have been "strategic," many involved in area studies became deeply committed to the culture and countries they were studying. He adds: "It is tempting to argue that in small countries, or those not central to the major global alliances, there was no strategic need for a specific focus on area studies." Finally, Moran suggests six ways that geography can contribute to area studies, including "a strategic approach to the disciplinary imperative in education."

Maureen Molloy begins Chapter 6 by disputing my use of "cultural studies" to capture the growth of "studies" per se. Her starting argument is that women's studies is not a subset of cultural studies; it "is, in part, interdisciplinary, but also has strong disciplinary bases" and not "all interdisciplinary research and teaching done in the name of women's studies [is] cultural studies." (My difficulty in naming the seminar was not one of ignorance or confusion over the identification of various national schools of cultural studies about which I have written extensively elsewhere [see Peters 1996] but rather of coming up with a single term that embraced extradisciplinary developments or the emerging economy of studies. Molloy suggests Gayatri Spivak's term "marginality studies.") Molloy focuses upon the shift in women's studies to cultural studies approaches and she comments upon implications of this shift for effective teaching at university level, hence her title: "Women's Studies/Cultural Studies: Pedagogy, Seduction and the Real World." Molloy first suggests that the rise of cultural studies in New Zealand is attributable to three factors: the political economy of tertiary training, a social justice agenda, and New Zealand's status as a self-consciously decolonizing nation. She suggests that feminist cultural studies "grew initially out of that attempt to insert women into the Marxist version of culture" and she identifies two matriarchal lines of descent: one via film studies (Laura Mulvey, Teresa de Lauretis and Meaghan Morris) and the other via political philosophy (Carole Pateman). Molloy makes an argument for the "real world": poststructuralism has undercut the notion of "experience" (that was the principle on which Anglo-American feminism stood) and those practicing feminist studies must retrieve the social and social scientific heritage of cultural studies so that "our students are not limited to deconstructive readings." In answering the question what does feminism offer to cultural studies, Molloy writes that "it offers everything—that without the systematic consideration of the gendered-ness of culture, in all its manifest forms, cultural studies can only repeat the existing masculinist hegemonies; that is, it can only be symptomatic of that which it is trying to analyze."

Feminist contributions to theorizing subjectivity and the role of historicized analyses of emotion as a central feature of subjectivity are two *absences* that Megan Boler investigates in Chapter 7. Boler argues that these absences cannot be simply added on to cultural studies: discourses of emotion are central to studies of culture because "emotion appears to be one of the least understood sites of power relations." This chapter is part of a larger book project entitled *Feeling Power: Emotions and Education* (1999). Boler provides an example of the way in which educators and social scientists, part of the "mental hygiene movement" during the 1930s, targeted so-called "emotional" or "labile" students. She then examines two contemporary examples of the "labile" student to show that their explanation requires a cultural studies that is guided by a systematic theory of emotions and power. Boler suggests that feminist philosophies of emotion challenge the traditional separation of emotion and cognition and reject accounts of emotions as "private" and gender-specific: rather, emotions are "collaboratively constructed" and gender-related. In the final section, Boler outlines recent contributions to a politicized theory of emotions.

In "The Late Show: The Production of Film and Television Studies" (Chapter 8), Roger Horrocks presents a case study tracing the introduction of film, television and media studies in schools and universities in New Zealand. He sees the curriculum as a site of struggle in both the institutional and intellectual senses and yet his story is not a "sentimental history" of the struggle of new heroic subjects against the *ancient regime*. Horrocks's story suggests that it was forces from the Right—in particular, a neo-liberal program of market liberalization—rather than challenges to the existing disciplinary order made in the name of cultural theory that finally admitted film studies into the curriculum, at least at the University of Auckland. As he argues, Horrocks does not seek to discredit the idea of discipline, rather he aims "to document a sample local history, highlighting political pressures, the complex chains of cause and effect, and the idiosyncracies of individuals and institutions that often seem more closely related to chaos theory than to the broad generalizations of philosophers of culture."

Horrocks provides an analysis of film and television studies in terms of the school and university curricula in New Zealand from the point of view of one who has been actively involved in its struggles. He documents the introduction of film and television studies at the University of Auckland where it struggled unsuccessfully for fourteen years to be admitted to the B.A. program. He shows that the rational process of curriculum development and evaluation of new subjects is subject to a high level of historical accident and usually to external political forces. He comments that, ironically, film and television studies has benefited more than most from the new political environment, concluding "it is difficult for me to speak of the university and its values being under threat when for years I have heard academics using that same rhetoric to block the development of my own subject."

Ranginui Walker pursues a similar tack in his chapter to explain the development of Maori studies in tertiary education in Aotearoa/New Zealand (Chapter 9). Walker describes the two disparate traditions of Maori and Pakeha (a Maori word for European, the exact meaning of which is still unclear) as the founding cultures of the nation-state in New Zealand and records the cultural subversion, especially through schooling, which took place through the colonialization of the former by the later. Missions and a system of Native Schools assimilated Maori, isolating young Maori from their culture and language. Maori pupils were punished for speaking Maori and, as a consequence, the number who spoke Maori as their first language rapidly declined. Walker documents the efforts and moves made by Sir Apirana Ngata from the early 1920s to include Maori language as a subject of study for the bachelor of arts degree on the same basis as foreign languages. The senate of the University of New Zealand, Walker claims, "stonewalled the request on the grounds there was no literature to support a teaching program." It was through adult education and the establishment of the new

Centre for Continuing Education that the first group of Maori tutors were appointed and, at about the same time in 1951, the appointment of the first lecturer in Maori language located in the anthropology department at Auckland University. Walker highlights the struggles to establish Maori language and culture as legitimate fields of study in the academy, against the arguments and gatekeeping strategies of professors and administrators. Maori studies only emerged from under the mantle of anthropology, at the University of Auckland in 1991, a fact which reminds us of the still active historical legacy of the university as a institutional site of British colonialism and the lack of (a liberal) recognition and toleration for knowledge traditions, skills, understandings, cultural and discursive forms, that differ from Western (or European) ones.

In Chapter 10, Colin Lankshear addresses himself to the question of literacy studies in education. First, he describes the focus on literacy from the early 1950s which, from the contributions of a range of disciplines—anthropology, history, linguistics, sociology, psychology—there emerged a "sociocultural" conception of literacy in opposition to the then dominant functionalist paradigm. In the second leg of the argument Lankshear examines the theoretical and conceptual struggles in education around what has become known variously as "socioliteracy studies," "sociocultural literacy" or "the new literacy studies." Thirdly, Lankshear maps out the current state of literacy studies in education, outlining the elements of a sociocultural approach to literacy which, in conceiving of literacy as social practices, is not only deemed to have the necessary theoretical scope and explanatory power but also is broad enough to support a moral and political basis for pedagogy and social reform. In the final leg of the argument, Lankshear examines the tradition of "critical literacy" in relation to socioliteracy studies as a whole. The critical dimension of literacy involves "developing a critical perspective on literacy per se"; "engaging in critique of particular *texts* or specific instances of *literacy in use*"; and "making 'critical readings' of Discourses and enacting forms of resistance or transformative practice on the basis of preferred ethical, political and educational values/ideals." Both the field socioliteracy studies per se and critical literacy, in particular, are examples of strong multidisciplinary and crossdisciplinary endeavours.

In "Doing Cultural Studies: Youth and the Challenge of Pedagogy" (Chapter 11), Henry A. Giroux begins by explaining the indifference by educational theorists to cultural studies, and the resistance by cultural studies theorists to the importance of critical pedagogy as a form of cultural practice. He suggests that since cultural studies is concerned with the critical relationship among culture, power and knowledge, it ought not to surprise us that mainstream educationalists often dismiss cultural studies as too ideological, ignoring its theoretical interest in deconstructing power relations and privilege within educational institutions and practices. Cultural studies provides the means, for instance, to unravel the disciplinary structures and hierarchies of curricula to reveal the way in which they are socially constructed and bear the traces of the cultural dynamics of sexuality, race, national identity, colonialism, gender and youth. By the same token, Giroux argues for a view which takes seriously the notion of cultural work as involving pedagogical practices. First, he comments upon the absence of pedagogy in cultural studies and makes the case for pedagogy as a central aspect of cultural studies. Indeed, as Giroux points out, cultural studies—according to Raymond Williams—grew out of pedagogical work going on in adult education in the 1930s and 1940s. Second, Giroux focuses upon the centrality of the "problem of youth" (Dick Hebdige's term) and the relation of representation of youth to mass culture. Next, Giroux examines the intersection among cultural studies and pedagogy by focusing upon four films (*River's Edge*, *My Own Private Idaho*, *Slacker*, and *Juice*) as devices that frame youth in diverse ways. Giroux argues that the pedagogical issue is paramount if educators and cultural workers are to address the effects of changing economic conditions on young people, whose identities are constructed at the intersection of electronic media and popular culture, and he lays out the theoretical elements that link cultural studies and critical pedagogy.

In Chapter 12, Brian Opie talks of "Humanities in the Postmodern." Opie suggests, following Geoff Eley and James Sosnoski, that in the postmodern the humanities disciplines have been radically destabilized and that this "breaking down" of disciplines, which is transformative of the modern university, exemplifies key features of postmodernity: a dissolution of boundaries of all kinds, a new decenteredness in social formations, a dispersal of knowledges of all forms of central and bureaucratic control, and of the forces of sociocultural reproduction in general. Opie substitutes the Humanities Society of New Zealand (HUMANZ) for cultural studies in his question concerning the changing mission of the university and the changing relations between the university and the wider society. He takes as his starting point the year of 1984—the year, he suggests, when New Zealand "irrevocably entered postmodernity." The year 1984 was an historical turning point: it represented the end of the protectionist policies of the Muldoon government, on the one hand, which were designed to establish "fortress New Zealand," and the adoption of a neo-liberal paradigm of globalization, on the other, with the election of the fourth Labour government, under the stewardship of Roger Douglas as minister of finance. With the substitution of "the market" for enriched concepts of society and culture, the traditional humanities disciplines could resist only through rejection or withdrawal. Opie traces the effects of this marketization of society and culture on the founding of HUMANZ, providing an account of the fate of the humanities in contemporary New Zealand. Starting from the formulation "the postmodern is our interregnum," Opie suggests, "The departmentization of the humanities in the university is an abberration, a consequence of the industrial mode of the Western university; the interregnum of the postmodern is a transitional period in which profoundly different institutional formations for the conservation and production of knowledge will take shape." In the remainder of his chapter Opie focuses upon four constituent elements that originally comprised the conditions or background against which the humanities developed in the West as disciplinary forms of knowledge: text, technology, the city and the state. In term of the last of these—and, in particular, the New Zealand state—Opie argues the case for cultural policy and cultural policy studies.

The chapters that comprise this collection cover a great deal of territory, and the themes and issues they deal with crisscross one another and overlap. They constitute, one might argue in Wittgensteinian terms, a series of "family resemblances." A number have a local inflection commenting upon, in particular, developments within New Zealand or the United States. What they have in common is a concern for "disciplinarity" and "culture" either explicitly, at the theoretical level, or more indirectly in terms of an exemplification of a crossdisciplinary, multidisciplinary or antidisciplinary approach. Often the terms "postmodern," "postmodernism" and "postmodernity" are used to signal epochal changes, both in the nature of the university as an essentially *modern* institution and its curricula and discourses. By no means are these terms used in the *same* way or with the same *valuations*. We should, I think, as Lyotard has argued, learn to respect intellectual differences: without trying to resolve them into a synthesis or monologue. Without such differences there would be no conversation or debate.

NOTES

Acknowledgement: I would like to acknowledge the helpful and constructive criticisms on an earlier version of this chapter by Peter Roberts, Colin Lankshear and Henry A. Giroux.

1. Bill Readings died in a plane crash in late 1994, only a couple of months before I was to work with him on his research seminar called "The Crisis of Identity of an Institution." The seminar I gave at the University of Montreal was "Cybernetics, Cyberspace and the University: Hermann Hesse's *Glass Bead Game* and the Dream of a Universal Language" (in Peters 1996). Readings earlier had contributed an essay ("Towards a Heteronomous Politics of Education") to a collection I edited on the educational significance of Jean-François Lyotard's (1984) *The Postmodern Condition* (Peters 1995). He had edited (with Paul Griemas) the political writings of Lyotard (1994). For "Lyotardian" readings of the university see also Readings (1993) and Peters (1989, 1996). The crisis of the university is a theme I have addressed most recently in Peters (1997).

2. See, for instance, Caputo and Yount (1993); Elam (1994); Hunter (1994, 1995), Lee and Green (1997); Messer-Davidow et al. (1993); Nelson & Goankar (1996); Roberts and Good (1993); Sosnoski (1995).

3. The question of the postcolonial university and cultural self-definition is addressed, in part, by so-called "subaltern studies" (Guha 1982; Guha and Spivak 1988) but also suggestively by Edward Said (1994a, 1994b), especially in terms of imperialism in literature and representations of the intellectual, and also by Ashis Nandy (1988) in his study of the impact of British science in India.

4. In this respect I find fascinating the comment Foucault makes on Anglo-American philosophy in "La Philosophie analytique de la politique" (orig. 1978, 1994) cited in Davidson (1997: 3):

For Anglo-Saxon analytic philosophy, it is a question of making a critical analysis of thought on the basis of the way in which one says things. I think one could imagine, in the same way, a philosophy that would have as its task to analyze what happens every day in relations of power—a philosophy that would try to show what they are about, what are the forms, the stakes, the objectives of these relations of power. A philosophy, accordingly, that would bear rather on relations of power than on language games, a philosophy that would bear on all these relations that traverse the social body rather than the effects of language that traverse and underlie thought. One could imagine, one should imagine something like an analytico-political philosophy.

5. Nicolescu was instrumental in setting up the International Center for Transciplinary Research (CIRET) as a nonprofit organization in Paris in 1987. CIRET (located at http://perso.club-internet.fr/nicol/ciret/) has the aim of developing research in a new scientific and cultural approach in order to lay bare the nature and characteristics of the flow of information circulating between the different branches of knowledge. CIRET in conjunction with UNESCO convened the International Congress "Which University for Tomorrow? Towards a Transdisciplinary Evolution of the University" (Monte Verit, Lacarno, Switzerland, April 30–May 2, 1997), which led to the *Declaration of Locarno*, issuing a series of recommendations, including the creation of an itinerant UNESCO chair; the development of transdisciplinary courses in universities and the diffusion of innovative transdisciplinary experiences; the transdisciplinary training of university teachers and the development of transdisciplinary pedagogies; the creation of transdisciplinary research centers and spaces; and the development of the project of transdisciplinarity in relation to ethics, the mass media, multimedia, cyberspace, and world peace.

6. I mean by "new" humanities what Abrams calls "postmodernism" or a humanities which renounces the notion that meaning is the product of a human agent (speaking, writing, listening) and emphasizes, by contrast, the language system.

7. See the recent essays by Palmeri, Rodman and Storey contributed to a 1997 issue of the *Journal of Communication Inquiry*, 21(2). Palmeri discusses Robert McChesney's left critique of the "postmodern" tendencies of contemporary cultural studies, which suggests that it requires the development of principled critiques of the market and capitalism, as well attention to social movements. Rodman, in the wake of the impact of the Sokal affair, discusses the claim that cultural studies has no means to distinguish genuine critical scholarship from jargon-filled hoaxes. He concludes that cultural studies suffers from a lack of articulation: it needs to link up with other political projects and to communicate better to a wider audience. Storey concludes with Tony Bennett that cultural studies needs to be more "disciplined to withstand the increasing hostility of others, if we are to build on the foundations of what has already been achieved."

8. *Sites* as the major New Zealand cultural studies journal is advertised as having

a South Pacific perspective (see: http://www.massey.ac.nz/~NZSRDA/nzssreps/journals/sites/sites.htm). The journal's editorial policy statement is as follows: "*Sites* is a multi-disciplinary journal established in 1981 to promote the study of cultural questions within the broad tradition of left scholarship. We publish articles with a predominantly Aotearoa/New Zealand and South Pacific focus on a wide range of cultural debates from a variety of critical perspectives." Journal policy is given as: "*Sites* will serve as a forum to encourage and develop understanding of cultural questions from socialist, feminist, anti-racist, popular—democratic and other critical perspectives. The only collective editorial policy is to promote broadly radical perspectives on culture. Within this general project we invite contributions from a plurality of positions. We encourage: adaptation of overseas theory to the New Zealand context; original theoretical work on New Zealand culture; indigenous qualitative work; work in progress as well as finished statements; work on non-New Zealand cultural questions with direct relevance to the New Zealand situation."

9. A major three-day international conference—"Pacific Spaces/Global Marketplaces: Cultural Studies in Pacific Contexts"—took place at Victoria University of Wellington on July 13–14, 1998. The conference had seminar sessions on "Contested Identities," "New Cultural Formations and Deformations," "Consuming, Performing and Producing Culture" and "Situating Culture Studies in Aotearoa/New Zealand."

10. Markley describes the affair thus: "Alan Sokal, the NYU physicist . . . hoodwinked the editors of *Social Text* by publishing an article full of scientific gibberish in their journal and then revealing his hoax (Sokal 1996a)." In a recent article Sokal (1996b: 339) addresses himself to the question of why he perpetrated the hoax in the first instance:

I confess that I'm an unabashed Old Leftist who never quite understood how deconstruction was supposed to help the working class. And I'm a stodgy old scientist who believes, naively, that there exists an external world, that there exist objective truths about that world, and that my job is to discover some of them. . . . But my main concern isn't to defend science from the barbarian hordes of lit crit. Rather, my concern is explicitly political: to combat a currently fashionable postmodernist/poststructuralist/social-constructivist discourse—and more generally a penchant for subjectivism—which is, I believe, inimical to the values and future of the Left.

See Sokal's own web page on the affair, which includes all his papers and those written by others: http://www.physics.nyu.edu/faculty/sokal/index.html.

REFERENCES

Abrams, M. H. (1997) "The Transformation of English Studies." *Daedalus* (Winter): special issue devoted to *American Academic Culture in Transformation: Fifty Years, Four Disciplines.*

Barradori, G. (1994) *The American Philosopher*, trans. R. Crocitto. Chicago: University of Chicago Press.

Barry, Andrew, Osborne, Thomas and Rose, Nickolas (eds.). (1996) *Foucault and Political Reason: Liberalism, Neo-Liberalism and Rationalities of Government.* London: UCL Press.

Bender, Thomas. (1997) "Politics, Intellect, and the American University, 1945–1995." *Daedalus*, 126(1) (Winter): 1–38.

Bernstein, Basil. (1990) *The Structuring of Pedagogic Discourse*, vol. 4: *Class, Codes and Control*. London: Routledge.

Bolter, Jay David. (1991) *Writing Space: The Computer, Hypertext, and The History of Writing*. Hillsdale, NJ: Erlbaum.

Burchell, Graham, Gordon, Colin and Miller, Peter (eds.). (1991) *The Foucault Effect: Studies in Governmentality*, with two lectures and an interview with Michel Foucault. Hemel Hempstead, England: Harvester Wheatsheaf.

Caputo, John and Yount, Mark. (1993) *Foucault and the Critique of Institutions*. University Park, PA: Pennsylvania State University Press.

Clark, Timothy and Royle, Nicholas. (1995) "Editorial Audit." In Timothy Clark and Nicholas Royle (eds.), *The University in Ruins: Essays on the Crisis in the Concept of the Modern University*, Special issue, *Oxford Literary Review*, 15: 3–14.

Davidson, Arnold. (1997) "Structures and Strategies of Discourse: Remarks Towards a History of Foucault's Philosophy of Language." In Arnold Davidson (ed.), *Foucault and His Interlocutors*. Chicago: University of Chicago Press, 1–20.

Delany, Paul and Landow, George, P. (1993) "Managing the Digital Word: The Text in an Age of Electronic Reproduction." In George P. Landow and Paul Delany (eds.), *The Digital Word: Text-Based Computing in the Humanities*. Cambridge, MA: The MIT Press, 3–30.

Dyke, Chuck. (1993) "Extralogical Excavations: Philosophy in an Age of Shovelry." In John Caputo and Mark Yount (eds.), *Foucault and the Critique of Institutions*. University Park, PA: Pennsylvania State University Press.

Elam, Diane. (1994) *Feminism and Deconstruction*. London: Routledge.

Foucault, Michel. (1973) *The Order of Things: An Archaeology of the Human Sciences*. New York: Random House, Vintage Books edition. [Originally published as *Les Mots et les choses*. Paris: Editions Gallimard, 1966; and first published in English in the World of Man series, Editor R. D. Laing. London: Tavistock Publications, 1966.]

———. (1992) *The Archaeology of Knowledge*, trans. A. M. Sheridan Smith. London: Routledge. [Originally published as *L'Archéologie du savoir*. Paris: Editions Gallimard, 1969; and first published in English in the World of Man series, Editor R. D. Laing. London: Tavistock Publications, 1972.]

———. (1994) "La Philosophie analytique de la politique." In Daniel Defert and Francis Ewald, with Jacques Lagrange (eds.), *Dits et écrits, 1954–1988*, vol. 3. Paris: Gallimard, 540–41.

———. (1997) *Ethics: Subjectivity and Truth*. In Paul Rabinow (ed.) and Robert Hurley et al. (trans), *The Essential Works of Michel Foucault*, vol. 1. London: Allen Lane, The Penguin Press.

Frow, John. (1990) "The Social Production of Knowledge and the Discipline of English." *Meanjin*, 49: 358–359.

———. (1992) "Beyond the Disciplines: Cultural Studies." In K. K. Ruthven (ed.), *Beyond the Disciplines: The New Humanities*. Canberra: Australian Academy of Humanities, 22–28.

Gibbons, Michael et al. (1994) *The New Production of Knowledge: The Dynamics of Science and Research in Contemporary Society*. London: Sage.

Giroux, Henry, Shumway, David, Smith, Paul and Sosnoski, James. (1994) "The

Need for Cultural Studies: Resisting Intellectuals and Oppositional Public Spheres." *Dalhousie Review,* 64: 472–486.

Gray, Herman. (1996) "Is Cultural Studies Inflated? The Cultural Economy of Cultural Studies in the United States." In Gary Nelson and Dilip Parameshwar Gaonkar (eds.), *Disciplinarity and Dissent in Cultural Studies.* New York: Routledge, 203–216.

Grossberg, Lawrence. (1996) "Toward a Genealogy of the State of Cultural Studies: The Discipline of Communication and the Reception of Cultural Studies in the United States." In Gary Nelson and Dilip Parameshwar Gaonkar (eds.), *Disciplinarity and Dissent in Cultural Studies.* New York: Routledge, 131–148.

Guha, Ranajit (ed.). (1982–1992) *Subaltern Studies.* Delhi: Oxford University Press, vols. 1–7.

Guha, Ranajit and Spivak, Gayatri Chakravorty (eds.). (1988) *Selected Subaltern Studies.* New York: Oxford University Press.

Hall, Stuart. (1988) *The Hard Road to Renewal: Thatcherism and the Crisis of the Left.* London: Verso.

———. (1990) "The Emergence of Cultural Studies and the Crisis of the Humanities." *October,* 53: 11–25.

———. (1992) "Cultural Studies and Its Theoretical Legacies." In L. Grossberg et al. (eds.), *Cultural Studies.* New York: Routledge.

———. (1996) "Culture and Power." Stuart Hall interviewed by Peter Osborne and Lynne Segal. *Radical Philosophy,* 86 (November–December): 24–41.

Hall, Stuart and Jefferson, T. (eds.). (1976) *Resistance through Rituals: Youth Subcultures in Post-War Britain.* London: Hutchinson.

Hall, Stuart, Critcher, Chas, Jefferson, Tony, Clark, John and Roberts, Brian (eds.). (1978) *Policing the Crisis: Mugging, the State, and Law and Order.* London: Macmillan.

Hall, Stuart et al. (eds.). (1980) *Culture, Media, Language: Working Papers in Cultural Studies, 1972–79.* London: Hutchinson; Birmingham: Centre for Contemporary Cultural Studies, University of Birmingham.

Hindess, Barry. (1995) "Great Expectations: Freedom and Authority in the Idea of the Modern University." *Oxford Literary Review,* 17: 29–50.

Hunter, Ian. (1994) *Rethinking the School: Subjectivity, Bureaucracy, Criticism.* St. Leonards, NSW: Allen and Unwin.

———. (1995) "The Regimen of Reason: Kant's Defence of the Philosophy Faculty." *Oxford Literary Review,* 17: 50–86.

Jantsch, Eric. (1972) "Towards Interdisciplinarity and Transdisciplinarity in Education and Innovation." In *Interdisciplinarity: Problems of Teaching and Research in Universities.* Paris: Organization for Economic Cooperation and Development, 97–121.

Kerr, Clark. (1994) *Higher Education Cannot Escape History: Issues for the Twenty-First Century.* Albany, NY: State University of New York Press.

Klein, Julie Thompson. (1993) "Blurring, Cracking, and Crossing: Permeation and the Fracturing of Discipline." In E. Messer-Davidow, D. R. Shuman, and D. J. Sylvan (eds.), *Knowledges: Historical and Critical Studies in Disciplinarity.* Charlottesville: University Press of Virginia, 185–214.

———. (1998) "Notes Toward a Social Epistemology of Transdisciplinarity." Communication at Premier Congrés Mondial de la Transdisciplinarity, Convento da Arrábida, Portugal, November 2–6, 1994.

Landow, George P. (1992) *Hypertext: The Convergence of Contemporary Critical Theory and Technology*. Baltimore: The John Hopkins University Press.

Landow, George P. and Delany, Paul (eds.). (1993) *The Digital Word: Text-Based Computing in the Humanities*. Cambridge, MA: The MIT Press.

Lanham, Richard A. (1993) *The Electronic Word: Democracy, Technology and the Arts*. Chicago: University of Chicago Press.

Lee, Alison and Green, Bill. (1997) "Pedagogy and Disciplinarity in the 'New University.' " *UTS Review*, 3(1) (May): 1–25.

Lefebvre, Henri. (1991) *The Production of Space*. Oxford: Blackwell.

Lyotard, Jean-François. (1984) *The Postmodern Condition: A Report on Knowledge*, trans. G. Bennington and B. Massumi. Minneapolis: University of Minnesota Press.

———. (1993) *Political Writings*, trans. B. Readings and K. P. Geiman. Minneapolis: University of Minnesota.

———. (1994). *Political Writings*, trans. Bill Readings and Kevin Paul Greiman. Minneapolis: University of Minnesota Press.

Mahon, Michael. (1992). *Foucault's Nietzschean Genealogy: Truth, Power, and the Subject*. Albany: State University of New York Press.

Messer-Davidow, Ellen, Shunway, David R. and Sylvan, David, L. (eds.). (1993) *Knowledges: Historical and Critical Studies in Disciplinarity*. Charlottesville: University Press of Virginia.

Morris, Meaghan. (1992). "Cultural Studies." In K. K. Ruthven (ed.), *Beyond the Disciplines: The New Humanities*. Canberra: Australian Academy of Humanities, 1–21.

Nandy, Ashis. (1988) *Science, Hegemony and Violence: A Requiem for Modernity*. Oxford: Oxford University Press.

Nelson, Cary and Gaonkar, Dilip Parameshwar (eds.). (1996) *Disciplinarity and Dissent in Cultural Studies*. New York: Routledge.

Nicolescu, Basarab. (1998a) "The Transciplinary Evolution of the University: Condition for Sustainable Development." Talk at the International Congress, "Universities' Responsibilities to Society," International Association of Universities, Chulalongkorn University, Bangkok, Thailand, November 12–14, 1997.

———. (1998b) *Transciplinarity: A Manifesto*, trans. Karen-Claire Voss. Lexington, KY: Watersign Press.

Nietzsche, Friedrich. (1956) *The Genealogy of Morals*, trans. Francis Goffling. Harmondsworth, England: Penguin [1887].

Odlyzko, Andrew, M. (1994) "Tragic Loss or Good Riddance? The Impending Demise of Traditional Scholarly Journals," *Surfaces*, 4(105): 1–44.

Okerson, Ann (1994) "Oh Lord, Won't You Buy Me A Mercedes Benz: Or, There *Is* a There There." *Surfaces*, 4(102): 1–13.

Palmeri, Anthony, J. (1997) "On Cultural Studies and Radical Politics: Movements, Critique of Capitalism, and Rhetoric." *Journal of Communication Inquiry*, 21(2) (Fall): 35–45.

Peters, Michael. (1989) "Technoscience, Rationality and the University: Lyotard on the 'Postmodern Condition.' " *Educational Theory*, 39(2): 93–105.

———. (1992) "Performance and Accountability in 'Post-Industrial Society': The Crisis of British Universities." *Studies in Higher Education*, 17(2): 123–139.

———. (ed.) (1995) *Education and the Postmodern Condition*. Foreword by Jean-François Lyotard. Westport, CT: Bergin & Garvey.

———. (1996) *Poststructuralism, Politics and Education*. Westport, CT: Bergin & Garvey.

———. (1997) (ed.), *Cultural Politics and the University*, Palmerston North, NZ: Dunmore Press.

———. (ed.) (1998) *Naming the Multiple: Poststructuralism and Education*. Westport, CT: Bergin & Garvey.

Peters, Michael and Roberts, Peter. (1999) *University Futures and the Politics of Reform*. Palmerston North, New Zealand: Dunmore Press.

Peters, Michael and Roberts, Peter (eds.). (1998) *Virtual Technologies and Tertiary Education*, Palmerston North, New Zealand: Dunmore Press. (Forthcoming)

Poster, Mark. (1990) *The Mode of Information: Poststructuralism and Social Context*. Cambridge: Polity Press.

Rabinow, Paul. (1997) "Introduction: The History of Systems of Thought." In Michel Foucault, *Ethics: Subjectivity and Truth*, in Paul Rabinow (ed.) and Robert Hurley et al. (trans), *The Essential Works of Michel Foucault*, vol. 1. London: Allen Lane, The Penguin Press, xi–xlii.

Readings, Bill. (1993) "For a Heteronomous Cultural Politics: The University, Culture and the State." *Oxford Literary Review*, 15: 163–200.

———. (1995) "Towards a Heteronomous Politics of Education." In M. Peters (ed.), *Education and the Postmodern Condition*. New York: Bergin & Garvey.

———. (1996) *The University in Ruins*. Cambridge, MA: Harvard University Press.

Roberts, R. H. and Good, J. M. M. (eds.). (1993) *The Recovery of Rhetoric: Persuasive Discourse and Disciplinarity in the Human Sciences*. Charlottesville: University Press of Virginia.

Rodman, Gilbert B. (1997) "Subject to Debate: (Mis)reading Cultural Studies." *Journal of Communication Inquiry*, 21(2) (Fall): 56–70.

Rorty, Richard. (1982) "Professionalized Philosophy and Transcendentalized Culture." In *Consequences of Pragmatism: Essays, 1972–1980*. Minnesota: University of Minnesota, 60–72.

Ruthven, K. K. (ed.). (1992) "Introduction." In *Beyond the Disciplines: The New Humanities*. Canberra: Australian Academy of Humanities, vii–ix.

Said, Edward. (1994a) *Culture and Imperialism*. New York: Vintage.

———. (1994b) *Representations of the Intellectual: The 1993 Reith Lectures*. New York: Pantheon Books.

Shumway, David and Messer-Davidow, Ellen. (1991) "Disciplinarity: An Introduction." *Poetics Today*, 12: 201–225.

Sokal, Alan. (1996a) "Transgressing the Boundaries: Towards a Transformative Hermeneutics of Quantum Gravity." *Social Text* 46/47 (Spring–Summer): 217–252.

———. (1996b) "Transgressing the Boundaries: An Afterword." *Philosophy and Literature*, 20(2): 338–346.

Sosnoski, James J. (1995) *Modern Skeletons in Postmodern Closets: A Cultural Studies Alternative*. Charlottesville: University Press of Virginia.

Storey, John. (1997) "There's No Success Like Failure: Cultural Studies; Political

Romance or Discipline?" *Journal of Communication Inquiry,* 21(2) (Fall): 98–110.

Wittrock, Björn. (1993) "The Modern University: The Three Transformations." In Sheldon Rothblatt and Björn Wittrock (eds.), *The European and American University Since 1800: Historical and Sociological Essays.* Cambridge: Cambridge University Press.

Chapter 1

The Political Economy of "Studies"

RUTH BUTTERWORTH

The term "political economy" is usually understood to propose an analysis of the relationship between economic and political processes and of the relationship of social structures and power. It applies to all aspects of relations between the economy—defined as the way production is organized—and the political and social institutions of society. Such analysis can proceed at different levels; global, regional, the state or polity, locality or community.

If we are to understand the shift from "discipline" to "studies," we need to analyze both relations within the academy and the relations between the academy and its social and political environment. Both sets of relations are illuminated if we conceptualize education as a system of production. This system or industry is characterized by its development and application of rites of passage and its dependence on state and corporate godfathers. At its extremity, we can define the process as the industrialization of professionalism.

The modalities of the shift from "disciplines" to "studies" may be characterized in a political economy model as opportunity structures. Analyzing the opportunities within the nexus of both the internal and external relations of the academy provides a way of suggesting how structural changes may be connected with shifts in group behaviors. There are, that is to say, feedback loops between the institution, its denizens and recruits and various social, political and economic modifications.

What happened to political economy provides a paradigm of sorts. In the eighteenth and nineteenth centuries political economy was a part of moral philosophy. David Hume (1711–1776), David Ricardo (1772–1823) and Adam Smith (1723–1790) were all part of the Edinburgh School of Moral Philosophy, leading players in the Scottish Enlightenment. Both Ricardo and Smith were professors of moral philosophy in the University of Edinburgh. It was this Edinburgh tradition which landed in Otago, New Zealand and in other sites of Scottish settlement where academies were established in the Americas.

The tradition informed but ultimately failed to fully shape the degrees offered by the University of New Zealand. The form rather than the substance survived in further migrations and among burgeoning numbers of academic establishments in the anglophone world. It is relevant to observe that no one ever refers to an English Enlightenment and there were more of the English in the colonial diaspora than there were Scots.

In New Zealand, political economy gave way to political philosophy, and political philosophy soon enough was reincarnated as political theory drawing further away from its moral philosophy roots. Political theory texts were those which served a polity more anxious to establish property rights and the duties of the state in regard to private property than they were concerned with other relativities. Meanwhile, on the one hand, political economy fell into bad odor where it was associated with the "wickedness" of Marxism. On the other, it was parcelized into the three "disciplines" of politics, philosophy and economics; the modern greats of twentieth-century Oxford.

The content, nomenclature and even location within the academy of what subsequently emerged as political science remained fluid even while the "disciplines" and disciplinary boundaries were being established in the dominant academic institutions of the West. In anglophone establishments, though not in continental Europe, the boundaries were narrowed progressively in company with academic bureaucratization. A classical education as the preferred grounding for public service in England was inapt for the dominions.

Nevertheless, we are talking about relatively small entities; content in student courses and the academic product was as much a function of who was recruited and where their interest and expertise lay as of anything else. Adam Smith was no more locked up in departments of economics than were Marx and Weber in sociology. Marx, after all, revolutionized the proceedings of historians, and sociology was long confused with social work.

The modern history of western universities is at its base grounded in the Enlightenment; this was the rationale for their establishment, for state as well as private support. The other part of the modern academies' development is, however, to be found in more concrete realities. For what purposes were the redbrick and land grant colleges of Britain and America set up and supported by the establishments of their time? Their basis in civic pride is one thing, but there is also the question of what was to be taught and to whom? How were both teachers and taught to be financed? How was what research provided for and organized; and was it a central or peripheral activity?

The foundations of the nineteenth century answered to the needs of the state for larger cadres of educated and professionally qualified people; senior teachers, doctors, lawyers, soil scientists, nutritionists, auditors, civil servants. Well into the twentieth century there was a great deal of "sitting next to Nellie" involved in this process; pupil-teaching, local and state service cadetships, law and accountancy clerkships. Degrees came hard for poorer students by way of part-time and evening study. The "disciplines" were subdivided or modularized for the purpose of graduating cadres of educated adults.

Why were they not simply to be trained? Support for universities as such (i.e., as centers of learning), was sustained because in the settlements of Australasia and America, progressive and democratic thinking was sustained. It was necessary to civilization that citizens should be thinking participants in a rational society; and scientific learning was key. Moreover, the nation-state no less than the imperial project demanded educational socialization and the means to address those discontents which threatened both. As access to secondary education was broadened, which was a necessary response to small populations, so entrance to universities could filter a wider number of people into professional and subprofessional occupations. As well as this, while professional organizations firmly maintained their hierarchies and grew their specialisms, the civic society of the burgomasters, museum directors and newspaper proprietors decreed the necessity of support for and access to the arts and humanities which they, in turn, controlled in the interests of a species of civility.

Until the end of the First World War the emphasis in universities in the Anglo-American orbit was on undergraduate teaching and production, on the one hand, and on graduating professionals, on the other. Research was a professorial function in the social sciences and the humanities, and such work was as likely as not to be undertaken outside the academy by scholars of independent means or alternative occupations. Within the wealthier colleges, scholars were easily sustained, but they were not accompanied by a buzzing congeries of graduate students competing for patronage, advancement and research grants. Scientists and engineers worked within companies or for state entities as well as in universities with or without graduate assistants. The Ph.D. and higher research degrees were the invention of continental Europe. In Germany in particular the doctorate was part of an internal qualification system which ensured the professorial succession. Truly a rite of passage, the German doctorate was in direct line of descent from the medieval system. It was German scientific and technological progress which moved President Woodrow Wilson to urge upon American and British Commonwealth universities the necessity for comparable programs after 1918.

After 1918, Ph.D. programs were established in anglophone universities to enhance scientific research. The collaboration of industry and the academy was a growth area; the clear motive was the competitive advantage of nations in war or peace. Other parts of the academy necessarily entered the competition for market share. The social sciences were beefed up through the scholarly diaspora of the 1920s and 1930s. The Ph.D. industry was extended to the social sciences; their direction and methodologies were borrowed from Germany. Thereafter, as is the case with all wars, opportunities for profit multiplied and hence opportunities for graduates and for more research. Waging total war, moreover, involved engaging the expertise of the recently strengthened social sciences.

Anthropologists, sociologists and political scientists were called in to advise on, even design, electoral systems for postwar Europe and Japan. In the 1940s and through the 1950s, the term "idiot-savant" gained an entirely new meaning, as the spawn of the new graduate industries, uneducated in much other than narrow methodologies, applied their expertise to the problems of rationing and maldistribution. The first coming of "trickle-down" was upon us, together with the first signs of "media studies," from the shallows of which it was seriously opined that television would surmount the obstacles of third world illiteracy by a species of direct selling which would rapidly monetarize the rural majorities.

Meanwhile, back in the metropolitan centers of anglophonia, a rapid expansion of higher education followed from the G.I. Bill of Rights and a general determination to avoid the horrors of the previous postwar demobilization and unemployment. Methodology as disciplinary core to the Ph.D. program—met up with new technologies, on the one hand, and new opportunities in the consumer society, on the other. Increasing numbers of graduate students found new machines for counting things and, necessarily, sought out more things and different ways to count. Ironically enough, the industrial period of universities coincides with the development of the postmodern. The advertising and marketing industry, together with corporate and political public relations, developed vast data banks providing further opportunities for graduate research while public bodies came rapidly to the belief that data constituted knowledge. Sociology and political science continued, of course, to examine and analyze and to purvey perfectly useful matters. The industry of which they were a part, however, was being financed for rather different reasons.

Total war, postwar reconstruction, a prolonged baby boom and the burgeoning affluence which accompanied these provided the opportunity structures that governed university expansion. Two sets of demands affected the universities. The student/consumer demanded "relevance" and "voice." The state/corporate consumer demanded that the academies produce more of their higher value postgraduate line. The entry of large numbers of undergraduate students provided for larger numbers to be hired to teach. New classes of students in the context of expanded hirings forced diversification in the mass undergraduate product. Niche market modules grew into whole departments as turf wars were settled by way of separate provision and additional opportunity hierarchies. Hence both the will and the capacity to produce black studies, women's studies, media studies.

The struggle of the different for voice and status within the WASP establishments that forced the provision of separate programs resulted at best in existing disciplines and research being tuned up by an infusion of new perspectives. Scholarship was vastly enriched as new groups made claims upon the academy. More history was revised faster than ever before, providing more history for more researchers to re-revise. It was a highly satisfactory indeed "virtuous" reproductive cycle. The scramble for higher places in the academic sun involves, however, perverse competition, hyperdifferentiation. It is about contesting tribes and lolly chases. Here I encounter cultural studies and its gurus: Althusser, Foucault, Derrida, Lyotard. Their catchphrases resonated with the new times and the new generation of would-be scholars. They declared the end of history, the failure of the Enlightenment project, the end of grand narrative, war on modernity. Cultural studies, their not entirely legitimate offspring, has involved the rejection of emancipatory theory. Its afficionados dismiss the Enlightenment belief in the possibility of the rational scientific understanding of the natural and social world. Universalism is declared to be Eurocentric and, by definition, racist. This is a species of pessimism that licenses the thugs and seeks to cast out from the temple the liberal humanist along with great books and grand narrative.

In examining the economy of cultural studies, I place three pieces on the chessboard: the gurus, mainly Franco-German, but including the converted marxists of the Birmingham School; forty years of mass market academia; and the market in baby boomers.

For Althusser and the Frankfurt School the question was why the workers did not revolt against post–World War II capitalism in the way Marx said they would. The Frankfurt School said it was the mass media which turned workers into helpless and passive subjects of capitalist totalitarianism. A stone's throw away these helpless workers were negotiating job security, health insurance, holidays and pensions. No matter; Althusser taught that the "ideological state apparatuses," which were the education system, trade unions, churches and mass media, were all in support of the capitalist status quo. Indeed they were; they were part of the "historical compromise" of the welfare state and mostly benefited mightily. They were important agents of socialization, legitimated in statute and by custom and practice, shackled for the time being in good behavior bonds and by the electoral systems invented by social science hirelings. So to this point, all was well and good and mainstream even. Althusser, however, imported structuralist theory from Ferdinand de Saussure. Thus did we acquire "the world as text" and "the media as villain."

Et voilà, and not entirely coincidentally in the academic validation stakes, a whole new series of job opportunities and connections for all those Eng.-

Lit. et al. graduates. In the academic marketplace, the paradigm case of political science methodology—appropriated from and developed for the sale of consumerism in political life—is a forerunner to the growth in cultural studies. The textual analysis of language and culture elevated methodology into "high science." It claimed an esoteric parity with the denizens of royal societies for its practitioners. Forget the virtual absence of forms of validation; these were frowned on as being necessarily in the service of the hegemonic state and capitalism.

In the 1960s, under pressure from the mass media market served by social science, Lit.-crit. was on a declining market. Cultural studies in the shape of textual analysis enabled literary critics to move in on media studies, psychology, sociology, legal studies, bits of political theory and history. This latter was defined by the afficionados of cultural studies as a sort of movable feast of fictions. Notwithstanding which, and while the disciplinary core held together, textual analysis invigorated legal studies in particular but also underpinned what historians had, in fact, already been into.

On the cultural studies side, however, there was a distinct "wobble." In essence the notion of "deep structure" communication signals lodged in the unconscious enabled the cultural studies protagonists to evade the payment of traditional scholarly dues. The unconscious can hardly be tested so anyone in this neck of the woods could get away with the statement that "identity under capitalism is constituted by advertising." Until, that is, psychology deserted Freud and Jung and ploughed into its own version of deep structure in the actual brain.

Regrettably none seem to have offered an opinion about how identity under communism was constituted. Pity about that; culturalists might have saved us the trouble of working through the connections between, say, oil pipelines and conflicts in the Caucasus. Culturalists have indeed provided a blanket explanation. It is all down to ethnicity, identity politics, the politics of difference. Identity politics is a sanitized descriptor for killing people. Lethally, a central part of the Althusser analysis is the location of academics as being on sanitary detail in the socialization corps. For all its contributions to the mainline, the linguistic obfuscations of cultural studies have underwritten twenty years of establishment obscurantism. Careful abstention from commitment has become the hallmark of the academic classes in the mass market era.

Cultural studies provided academics with a defense-in-depth; it has declared a plague on analysis and substituted deconstruction. These Mrs. Grundys of the postmodern obfuscate the real; a necessary exercise given that their epistemologies equate claims to knowledge with the exercise of power.

The promotion of individualism which is at the heart of the postmodernist message is also central to the uses of communications technology in the marketplace. What began with a Marxist conundrum escalated with Foucault into antihumanism. Foucault claimed that all analyses of society are arbitrary and fictitious and that human consciousness and free will have no significance for social life and history. Which takes care of Marx and leads on to Derrida and the Gulf War that did not happen. He had a point, as did Foucault. There was little to choose between the electronic battlefield purveyed to the world in General Schwartzkopf's media briefings and Nintendo zapping games. Save that Nintendo games "work," whereas not a lot of the realtime electronics in Iraq did. But if we are or have been rendered into helpless fragments, should this grand pessimism not be in some way countered?

Deconstruction, understood in its popular sense of demolition, *is* a central effect of capitalist technologies and an intended one. Television in particular operates to privatize what were hitherto social or civic lives. It is a technology that carries the virus that plasticizes the social environment. By the same token and technology, however, some people may have dimly apprehended that the Gulf War did happen to other people who got killed realtime. And Homer Simpson exposes a thousand lies. Fragmentation, disintegration and disaggregation do indeed proceed apace, and these are processes that demand analysis. Counterintelligence is also the business of the academies, "going with the flow" means accommodating the enemy.

The academic market in the last thirty years has become a mass and globalizing one. It has been subject to internal competition that produced new learning. Its component academies competed for students and scholars and for the state and corporate dollar. The devices and mechanisms that developed were those familiar in other parts of the capitalist system: expansion, both horizontal and vertical; hostile takeover battles and strategic amalgamations; loss leaders and phoney come-ons. In colleges where journalism had been taught as a craft, for example, credentialism and program inflation took over. The search for academic validation and respectability met up with postmodernism and the world-as-text. Inter- and intradepartmental competition for rewards and fairies encouraged cultural entryism.

It should be acknowledged that all of this is fun; academic playtime and painting by numbers has many serendipitous outcomes. But games are not what intellectuals should spend all their time on.

To be sure, such games are less poisonous than those played on and in the stock exchanges and the bond markets. We are accustomed in the privacy of our halls to encouraging, applauding even, the spectacle of very clever people playing with themselves like little boys totally absorbed in watching sticklebacks and oblivious to all around them. And some boys [*sic*] never grow up, will never go out and get "a proper job." It is appropriate to a point that the academy be their sandpit, their adventure playground, and none of this would have much consequence in the scheme of things except that the deconstructions of the cultural studies followers play powerfully to the New Right. Objective conditions provided the opportunity for the progress of neo-liberal economics and the emancipation of finance capital. Its political triumphs, however, result from the bizarre coalitions produced out of the social dislocations that accompanied demographic change. Hence the baby boom piece on my chessboard.

It is commonplace to say that the children of the "historical compromise" grew up in security only to turn and rend the whole thing asunder, bringing on rampant individualism and unleashing capital from state bondage. Althusser would say that the youth culture of the 1960s was a construct of the forces of capitalism, but the security of the welfare state was equally salient. The baby boomers singularly lacked a context for their good fortune: no Great Depression; an abundant choice of occupations; a world of places to travel to be the same in. Their internationalism was electronically bred, ideologically disconnected. While the unaffluent went to war, the new affluents went to Wall Street and enjoyed the fruits of the virtual empire. Whatever brief chance there might have been of worker-student alliance in 1968, the heart of the matter was closer to a Paris placard: "I take my desires for reality because I believe in the reality of my desires." This was group rebellion, but it had subjectivity at its heart. As did the feminist slogan "the personal is the political," which set off a whole stream of affirmationist studies.

Eric Hobsbawm (1994) says of the rebellious multitude and their adult selves that what they were doing constituted a rejection of the long-established and historical ordering of human relations in society that social conventions and prohibitions expressed, sanctioned and symbolized. That rejection was not in favor of an alternative ordering of society such as had characterized previous uprisings and, for that matter, contemporary ones in the colonial world. Their rebellion was made in the name of the unlimited autonomy of individual desire, a world of self-regarding individualism.

These boomers backward somersaulted into the arms of Friedrich Hayek (b. 1899), guru of the "free" market and saint of neo-liberalism. The emancipation of capital on the back of new, unregulated technologies represents the triumph of the individual over society. It was underwritten in the academic mass market. At a critical time key academics fled into "discourse," "deconstruction" and "representation," retreating into culturalism and ethnicism. Cultural studies, which is not expensive, was the ideal loss-leader in the window of the academic supermarket. Its representations too accurately "represent" the helpless discontents of the postmodern.

The deconstructionists reduce society to the accidental interaction of individuals. Their "anything goes" theory of meaning admits of no commensurabilities which, in the beaten way of academic competition, was the position taken by the protagonists of black and women's studies, which, in academia-turned-supermarket, turns into the popularized esoterica whereby the privileged yet again find their places in the academic sunshine.

In an excoriating condemnation of culturalism, Sivanandan (1996) wrote that "the notion that everything is contingent, fleeting, evanescent is the philosophical lodestar of individualism, an alibi for selfishness, a rationale for greed." These notions, he said, are "the cultural grid on which global capitalism is powered and the post-modernist intellectuals have helped keep it in place, lent it their skills, their ideas . . . [they are] usurers in the temple of knowledge" (11).

These things matter. What is carelessly purveyed in a two-semester minor turns up in the mouths of junior advisers, policy analysts and public relations officers. Postmodernism as underwritten in cultural studies is not a liberatory movement. In "studies" programs the ghetto is reinforced in the cause of "identity" and "difference." It is a symbol of proud separation, a "racialized space." As someone once said, those who express contempt for economic determinism are those whose lives are not economically determined. Such privileged beings it is who under the rubric of communication studies preach the noncommunication of unshared nonmeanings in assemblages of programs to which is attached some species of academic imprimatur (Malik 1996).

By this imprimatur the graduates of "studies" teach in schools, develop and administer school curricula and persuade local authorities to set up "ethnicity units." One such, in the East End of London, quoted by Sivanandan (1996:8) recently asserted that "the lethal aspect of racial harassment is not the material damage [i.e. killing people] done, but the hidden wound inflicted as it sets in motion the ancient regression from room to womb and turns the womb into a kind of tomb." The antidote proposed was "cultural work" which would enable the thugs to construct "a white working class ethnicity," to which there would seem to be only one possible response: something along the lines of "get off the grass." But then the culturalists would reply in turn with some version of Lyotard's attack on modernity. It should, he said, be erased because it had failed to abolish ignorance, prejudice and the absence of enjoyment.

Academics' playtime finished sometime around 1990. As the low birth rate years cut into traditional sources of finance and capital squeezed the academies, reality came out to bite the culturalists. Writing on postmodernity, David Harvey (1989) has made the point that all groups have a right to speak for themselves and that the acceptance of their voices as authentic and legitimate was essential to the pluralistic stance of postmodernism. Advocates of this plurality claimed that it undermined the grip of dominant groups over social and political discourse. It is an error reiterated by protagonists of the Internet's web sites and chat rooms; not one that Althusser would have made. As authenticity spat from the Serbian guns in Bosnia, rape and pillage legitimated a rather older version of womb, tomb and lebensraum.

The insights, the new ways of looking from postmodernist scholarship have long since fertilized the mainstream of the "disciplines." The academies, however, are touting for custom alongside UC and McDonalds in the international student bazaar. Repackaging continues apace in the service of the current market dominants.

REFERENCES

Harvey, David. (1989) *The Condition of Postmodernity*. Cambridge: Blackwell.

Hobsbawm, Eric. (1994) *Age of Extremes: The Short History of the Twentieth Century*. London: Michael Joseph.

Malik, Kenan. (1996) "Universalism and Difference: Race and the Postmodernists." *Race and Class*, 37(3): 13–24.

Sivanandan, A. (1996) "Heresies and Prophecies: The Social and Political Fallout of the Technological Revolution: An Interview." *Race and Class*, 37(3) (April–June): 1–12.

Chapter 2

After the Science Wars: From Old Battles to New Directions in the Cultural Studies of Science

ROBERT MARKLEY

The conflicts that have erupted since 1994 over the cultural study of science seemed to have reached the point of self-parody. Several universities in the United States have staged "debates" between various defenders of cultural studies and Alan Sokal, the NYU physicist who hoodwinked the editors of *Social Text* by publishing an article full of scientific gibberish in their journal and then revealing his hoax (Sokal 1996a, 1996b). These debates, and similar exchanges in venues ranging from *Dissent* to the *New York Review of Books*, give Sokal and his antagonists opportunity after opportunity to talk past each other and preach to the converted. At best, they allow the participants to describe incommensurate philosophical positions in radically different languages; at worst, they reinforce conventional disciplinary boundaries by displacing conflicts within fields, such as literary study and evolutionary biology, into conventional restatements about the "essential" differences between the sciences and the humanities. The real problem, though, with the so-called "science wars" is that they are least a decade behind the times. In setting "realists" against "constructivists," these spectacles obscure the important work of scientists and cultural critics, who have jettisoned the terms of this debate, and ignore the significant contributions that the cultural study of science has made to the development of postdisciplinary programs of study.[1] My purpose in this chapter, then, is to signal an end to the science wars, at least as they have been staged and perpetuated by both sides, by suggesting some of the way in which scientists and cultural critics can work toward finding common idioms to describe the pedagogical, political, and intellectual problems that now confront researchers and educators.

Having been drawn into the science wars by Sokal's misreading of my work, I make no pretense to offer an objective battlefield dispatch; however, because his approach typifies the ways in which the cultural study of science has been travestied by Paul Gross, Norman Levitt, Martin Lewis and Jean Bricmont, my response gives me two opportunities hard to resist: to demonstrate the intellectual shoddiness of their attacks and to counter the dead-end political and philosophical assumptions that motivate their misreadings (Gross and Levitt 1994; Gross, Levitt and Lewis 1996; Sokal and Bricmont 1997). In the first section of this chapter, then, I examine the methodological failings of their work to demonstrate that their manichean view of a world divided between good realists and bad constructivists perpetuates what Richard Lewontin, Alexander Aggasiz Professor of Biology at Harvard, characterizes as the "depauperate view that scientists have of science" (Lewontin 1991: 141). Gross and Levitt's critique of the cultural study of science fails to make much headway because the task they set for themselves, for a start, would have to take seriously a vast range of material and then refute its values, assumptions, and conclusions historically and philosophically. In the second section, I outline what these scientific exceptionalists would have to do in order to cordon off science and its procedures for producing objective descriptions of the universe from interpenetrations by culture, politics, and religion.[2] The exceptionalist position, I suggest, even when it is articulated by a Nobel Laureate such as Steven Weinberg, represents a lapse from the methodological rigor and scepticism that traditional defenders of science explicitly invoke as two of their field's defining characteristics. In the final section, I try to bring the mountain to Mohammed by indicating what scientists have to gain from the cultural study of science.

THE SCIENTIFIC EXCEPTIONALISTS AND THE FLIGHT FROM METHOD

> Scientific fraud is always a transgression against the methods of science, never purposely against the body of knowledge. Perpetrators always think that they know how the experiment would come out if it were done properly.
>
> —David Goodstein, "Conduct and Misconduct in Science" (1996: 33)

Sokal's hoax in *Social Text* followed in the wake of Gross and Levitt's *Higher Superstition*, a sci-tech version of the neo-conservative assault against feminists, multiculturalists and theory-mongers launched by Dinesh D'Souza, Roger Kimball and Allan Bloom, and a successor volume, *The Flight from Science and Reason*, which Gross and Levitt coedited with Martin Lewis (D'Souza 1991; Kimball 1990; Bloom 1987). Both volumes conjure into being a manichean universe of scientists defending the ramparts against

Marxists, feminists, and constructivists, then invest this battle with quasi-apocalyptic significance. Gross and Levitt defend a view of science that Lewontin calls "something out of a high school textbook" and demonize any deviations from their ideological program as "relativistic" (Lewontin 1995: 262). They attack fringe characters, such as Dave Foreman and Jeremy Rivkin, while remaining silent on the work of scientists who share the political and epistemological views of the so-called "academic left," and they ignore the scientific credentials of many of the feminists they attack, including Evelyn Fox Keller and Donna Haraway. To put it bluntly, *Higher Superstition* is abysmally researched. Gross and Levitt provide a bibliography that is long enough for Edward O. Wilson on the dust jacket of the book to declare that their study is "documented with surgical precision." But as Roger Hart demonstrates, there is no evidence that Gross and Levitt have read more than a few pages of any of the works that they cite; their analyses typically focus on no more than one or two paragraphs taken out of context. They do not write a single coherent precis of the works they attack: they ignore the central arguments of Steven Shapin and Simon Schaffer's *Leviathan and the Air Pump* and get wrong the salient points of the one section that they do discuss; their attack on Sandra Harding is based on two sentences that are clearly marked in context as questioning the point that they allege she is making; they denounce Katherine Hayles for the opposite of what she is saying, then rephrase her argument as their own; and they criticize Haraway on the basis of a single interview, conflating her comments with the editors' summaries to misrepresent her position (Hart 1996: 261–277; see also Hayles 1995). Imagine this scenario: suppose a cultural theorist were to criticize the work of a prominent scientist based solely on a single interview, without reading any of his or her published works; Gross, Levitt, Sokal or anyone else would have ample reason to ridicule such an indefensible methodology.

Sokal's method mimics Gross and Levitt's. In his self-styled "satire," Sokal quotes passages out of context from two of my articles to prove that I am a "postmodernist" attacking the notion that there is a real world; his recent study, coauthored with Bricmont, apparently repeats this criticism.[3] He does not realize that my ironic title—"The Irrelevance of Reality"—introduces a critique not of "reality" but of the realist philosophy of science and its penchant for uncritical reflection theories of representation. Sokal ignores the first four sections of the article in which I argue that descriptions of reality are always historically contingent and that therefore, given what Bakhtin calls the dialogic nature of all systems of understanding, realist and constructivist philosophies of science are, at bottom, disputes about the nature of representation (Markley 1992: 249–263; Markley 1993: 1–33).

As far as I can tell, I earn Sokal's wrath because I call attention to the contested nature of quantum physics in order to demonstrate the problems of realism when it confronts probabilistic theories of the subatomic realm.

Sokal quotes a passage where I admittedly go wrong in lumping together "[q]uantum physics, hadron bootstrap theory, complex number theory, and chaos theory" as nondeterministic. Complex numbers do not belong in this list; they have been around since the nineteenth century and are reasonably simple to grasp as combinations of real and imaginary numbers (see Peat 1988: 185–191). Quantum theory, I noted, calls forth different interpretations, but I did make clear that, for many physicists, it operates on two levels: its mathematical laws are deterministic, but its observable phenomena follow Heisenberg's uncertainty principle (Pesic 1991: 971–974, 975–978). While Bricmont and Weinberg insist on the epistemological coherence of a deterministic quantum mechanics, their dreams of a final theory are treated sceptically by other scientists (Bricmont 1996: 131–175; Weinberg 1992). For David Lindley, "quantum mechanics denies the existence of any absolute reality, denies that there is a mechanical world of particles and forces existing independently of us. The world is what we measure it to be, and no more than what we measure it to be" (Lindley 1993: 76). In an article devoted to the argument that descriptions of reality are irrevocably dialogic, it would have made more sense for me to emphasize debates about the implications of quantum mechanics rather than the epistemological affinities between Heisenberg's interpretation and cultural theory. Nevertheless, my key point (slightly updated) stands: the disagreements between Bricmont and Ilya Prigogine, in an important sense, concern the adequacy of representations of quantum theory and therefore impinge on the territory of the cultural study of science (Bricmont 1996: 131–175).

There is a significant difference, most of us would agree, between casual mistakes (which have no effect on my critique of philosophical realism) and deliberate misrepresentations that verge on Goodstein's (1996) definition of fraud. I introduce the section of the article from which all of Sokal's quotations are taken by indicating that I am offering a heuristic analysis based on "an overlay of two metaphors: Bakhtin's notion of the dialogical nature of all utterances, all human understanding, and Geoffrey Chew's version of hadron bootstrap theory" (Markley 1992: 266). Repeatedly, Sokal confuses representation and reality, and ignores my crucial point that all semiotic systems are historically situated.[4] For example, before the sentence in which I assert that quantum mechanics and chaos theory are nondeterministic, I describe a precise context for my argument:

In quantum physics, reality, as Leibniz, Laplace, or even Marx would have defined it, is no longer 'real,' that is, no longer susceptible to authoritative description, as Heisenberg notes: the language of quantum physics 'is not a precise language in which one could use the normal logical patterns; it is a language that produces pictures in our mind, but together with them the notion that the pictures have only a vague connection with reality, they represent only a tendency toward reality.' [Heisenberg 1958: 181] (Markley 1992: 264).

My description of "reality," as this quotation makes clear, refers explicitly to my historical analysis of the differences between Newton's natural philosophy and Leibnizian determinism and subsequent misinterpretations (including Bricmont's and Sokal's) of Newton's science as deterministic (Bricmont and Sokal 1997b: 17). By omitting the quotation from Heisenberg, Sokal eliminates the standard account of quantum mechanics—one that challenges notions of the representational adequacy of Laplacean determinism.

Similarly, when he quotes a passage in which I suggest that hadron bootstrap theory provides a metaphor for the contested narratives we use to describe reality, he cuts Geoffrey Chew's account of this theory to make it seem as though I am discussing "reality" itself rather than epistemological problems of representation: "the question [of describing accurately subatomic particles]," according to Chew, "will become clearly posable only at the moment when the answer to the question becomes apparent. The finding of appropriate language is the essence of the game" (Chew 1974: 94). My point is not, as Sokal implies, that theory choice is the simple-minded result of "ideology," but that scientific theories, including quantum mechanics, are shaped by the narrative and conceptual expectations "into which data are placed and by which they are interpreted" (Markley 1992: 269). I state explicitly that I am not promoting one theory over the other in the following sentence, which Sokal does not quote: "My claim, then, is not that bootstrapping provides a 'true' description of reality but that it redefines the ways in which we conceive of our methods of describing the universe" (Markley 1992: 269). The scare quotes around "true" indicate my focus on problems of representation. Within this context, then, it makes sense to say that " 'Reality,'—note the scare quotes—finally, is a historical construct" (Markley 1992: 270) because statements that one makes about nature are irrevocably historical and contextual. Had Sokal read—or understood—the first thirteen pages of my article, or had he looked at my 1994 article, which he footnotes but obviously has not read (he misidentifies its subject: the role of boundary mathematics in the programming of virtual reality systems, not the boundary conditions of quantum mechanics) he would see little, if any, difference between my assessment of realist accounts of representation and those offered by Lewontin, Chew, and a host of historians and philosophers of science (Markley 1994).[5]

My claim, like theirs, is not that the cultural studies of science offers a means to reduce science to its ideological contexts but that any attempt to isolate science from culture is predicated on monological views of language that are epistemologically suspect and historically uninformed. Sokal is free to disagree with me; more power to him if he can meet the methodologically rigorous conditions for an internalist description of science that I outline in section two. But to distort my arguments by selective (mis)quotation into a mirror image of his own naive dualism ironically makes him the butt of his own jokes about the "decline in the standards of rigor in certain precincts of the academic humanities" (Sokal 1996b: 62). Based on what they have published, Gross, Levitt and Sokal could not pass a rigorous undergraduate course in critical theory let alone in the history and philosophy of science.

There are two—and only two—possibilities that explain the methodological failures of Sokal, Gross and Levitt: the first is that they see themselves as noble polemicists combating the inroads of the "academic left" (notwithstanding Sokal's claim that he is a "leftist"). In such a fundamentalist worldview, all's fair in their battles against feminism, socialism and environmentalism, including polemics that strive to outdo the nightmarish excesses that they claim to find in their antagonists. Lewis, for instance, tries to discredit environmentalists who criticize the practices of multinational capitalism by claiming that "the most concerned Greens" believe that "the very survival of human civilization, if not life itself, depends on a wholesale rejection of science and reason" (Lewis 1996: 209). This rejection, he alleges, supposedly entails "total decentralization, deurbanization, economic autarky, a ban on most forms of high technology, and the complete dismantling of capitalism" (Lewis 1992: 7). Such absurdist caricatures can be defended only by assuming that the ends—defending "reason"—justify irrational means.

This possibility, however, is less worrisome than the alternative: suppose that *Higher Superstition* and *The Flight from Reason and Science* represent the best efforts of Gross, Levitt and their contributors to understand contemporary cultural theory. Suppose that their readings of Hayles, Haraway, Shapin and Schaffer, or Sokal's use of my work, indicate the research protocols that they practice in their own fields. What they offer is a bad parody of the scientific method: rather than rigorously isolating key variables, they abandon any sort of methodological scepticism, not to mention any sort of critical reading skills, and seize arbitrarily on terms which they wrench out of context to fit preconceived notions. When Gross, Levitt and Sokal find scientific terms used in unfamiliar (and often clearly metaphoric) contexts, they assume that cultural critics have misunderstood unambiguous concepts that can be represented unproblematically and, therefore, they are justified in claiming that such "errors" invalidate entire critical enterprises, even though they do not understand the arguments they are attacking and are often ignorant of the controversies and principles to which such critics are alluding. Quite simply, their monological view of representation in science admits of no epistemological—let alone political—variations; their commitment to an unexamined dualism leaves them unable to recognize the legitimacy of other areas of inquiry, other specialized languages (Smith 1997). Their defenses of rigor and the scientific method, in short, do not call forth rigorous demonstrations of that method, but polemical defenses of what I shall argue below are ahistorical dualisms and naive, progressivist accounts of the history of science.

HOW TO CRITIQUE THE CULTURAL STUDY OF SCIENCE: SEVEN IMPERATIVES

The exceptionalists' attack on critical theory indicates the extent to which the realist philosophy of science must invoke seemingly fundamental dualisms to justify its tenets: reason versus superstition, science versus culture, authoritative descriptions versus jargon, truth versus fiction, objectivity versus subjectivism and so on. However, as I have demonstrated, because the defenders of scientific exceptionalism have misrepresented the positions that they attack, they have not produced a sustained critique of the cultural study of science, but merely created straw men to bolster their claims to social and intellectual authority. Because cultural critics can only benefit from a dialogic exchange on the theory and practice of science studies, I want to outline in this section what such a critique would entail. I have two purposes in mind: to show how far exceptionalists have to go to live up to their own declared principles and to suggest what lies beyond prepackaged contests between realism and constructivism.

1. *Learn the Field.* For a start, exceptionalists need to identify major works in the cultural study of science and develop sustained critiques of them. They need to summarize accurately the arguments that they attack, then demonstrate why these approaches are less plausible than internalist accounts. For example, suppose they were to try to counter the theses of Philip Mirowski's *More Heat Than Light,* a classic study of the inaccurate application of scientific theories (the conservation of energy) to social activity (economics). Mirowski argues that the principle of the conservation of energy was appropriated by nineteenth-century economists as the cornerstone of their efforts to legitimate the objectivity of their discipline. By misinterpreting and misapplying this principle, they devised economic theories predicated on misunderstandings of physical laws, then argued that their theories were as objectively true as scientific facts. In turn, these economic "truths" later helped to shape theories that applied an inaccurate view of the conservation of energy to fields as diverse as biology and sociology (Mirowski 1989; see also Porter 1995). To counter Mirowski's argument, the exceptionalists would have to go back to the original sources in nineteenth-century physics and economics and show that (a) physicists' understanding of the conservation of energy either did not change over time or that Mirowski misinterprets the changes that did occur; (b) the law of the conservation of energy was not adopted by economists; (c) economists did adopt the law but understood its principles correctly and that therefore it is Mirowski who misinterprets the conservation of energy; or (d) economic "laws" derived from the conservation of energy had no reciprocal effects on scientific understanding. Because Mirowski demonstrates that appeals to "reason" can be deployed carelessly in economics and physics in mutually reinforcing ways, an exceptionalist would have a difficult time trying to

prove any of these alternatives. For Sokal, undertaking such a critique might prove eye-opening, because the exploitative, laissez-faire capitalism to which he, as a self-proclaimed leftist (Sokal 1996b), presumably is opposed invokes the same principles of "reason" and "objectivity" that he claims as the foundation of science.

2. *Defend Your Methodology.* Scientific exceptionalists are insufficiently sceptical about their ability to separate science from culture. When exceptionalists zero in on what they consider the "purely" scientific validations of a deterministic viewpoint, they frequently have to ignore or distort other scientists' accounts of the implications of their theories. Bricmont, for example, invokes David Bohm's pilot wave theory as one of his crucial points in arguing against Heisenberg's interpretation of quantum mechanics (Bricmont 1996: 133–134, and 161, n.13). Because he does not actually footnote Bohm but only others' accounts of this physicist's work, he seems unaware that Bohm explicitly rejects mathematical determinism and maintains that the pilot wave theory cannot be used to reduce nature to deterministic laws: "People are going to talk about the theory of everything, but that's an assumption, you see, which has no basis. At each [subatomic] level we have something which is taken as appearance and something else is taken as the essence which explains the appearance. But then when we move to another level essence and appearance interchange their rules" (quoted in Horgan 1996: 87–88; see also Bohm 1980). Bohm's interest in this "implicate order" leads him to make explicit connections between pilot wave theory and Indian mysticism. Bricmont's commitment to an unexamined reductionism leads him to base his argument on evidence which undermines the very principles he is trying to assert.

To defend their methodology, exceptionalists would have to rescue a prominent scientist from contextualist interpretations of his or her work by demonstrating that an internalist approach offers a higher threshold of explanation than a historicist account. In the case of Isaac Newton, for example, they would have to demonstrate that (a) Newton believed he had discovered deterministic mathematical laws to explain the operations of the known universe; (b) his experimental practice followed or developed a rigorous research protocol that led to deductive insights in optics and matter theory; (c) he rejected externalist—specifically theological—accounts of physical phenomena; (d) therefore his work in alchemy, biblical prophecy, ancient history and theology (a mass of manuscripts that dwarfs his mathematical work, published or unpublished) had no effect on his "purely" scientific theories; and (e) Newton was a Newtonian (as that term is commonly misused); that is, that he believed in the postulates of a deterministic science. Because Newton occupies such a crucial position in traditional histories of modern science, they would have to demonstrate—by analyzing a large body of published and unpublished evidence—that secular notions of objectivity and method emerged from within his practice of science.

To accomplish this task, exceptionalists would need to familiarize themselves with the work of Charles Bazerman (1988) on the rhetorical development of Newton's optical papers, Betty Jo Dobbs (1991) on the interpenetration of alchemy, mathematics, and matter theory in Newton's thought, and my work (1993) on Newton's theology as an integral aspect of his work in natural philosophy. More specifically, they would have to explain the different manuscript drafts of the observations and theoretical postulates that predated the 1672 publication of "A New Theory of Light and Colours" and demonstrate that Bazerman's account of Newton's creation of a "closed text" is historically inaccurate (Bazerman 1988: 83–127). Exceptionalists would have to show either that Newton shaped rhetorically "the sequences of thoughts and experiments" that constitute his scientific methodology without reference to the philosophical and scientific disputes in which he was embroiled or that he practiced a rigorous scientific method for the better part of ten years without indicating anything about it in his laboratory or lecture notes (Bazerman 1988: 95). To challenge Dobbs' interpretation of the foundational role of alchemy in Newton's scientific thought, exceptionalist historians would have to work their way through thousands of pages of material, as she did, to define precisely the differences between his science methods and his alchemical procedures. They would have to demonstrate that Newton's concept of gravity, for example, does not derive from his alchemical work. In the case of Newton's theology, they would have to demonstrate that Newton's lifelong defense of induction and his fervent attacks on scientific systematizers such as Leibniz were separate concerns from his theological beliefs. They would have to explain why Newton insisted in the *Principia* that gravitation could not be the result of "mere mechanical causes" and that a voluntaristic God had to intervene at unpredictable intervals to keep the solar system in order; and they would have to explain what Newton and Leibniz argued about for decades if not about radically different theocentric interpretations of science (Newton 1934: 544). In brief, exceptionalists cannot simply assume that internalist explanations are sufficient without considering the historicist views that now are widely accepted among historians and philosophers of science.[6]

3. *Acknowledge Scientists Who Disagree with You.* The glaring weakness in the exceptionalists' argument is their refusal to acknowledge, let alone debate, those scientists who disagree with them. They would have to demonstrate that those scientists, such as Lewontin, Ruth Hubbard and Richard Coyne, who rely explicitly on feminist and cultural theory to describe their work, are wrong in claiming that insights drawn from these fields have reshaped their scientific practice (Coyne 1995; Hubbard 1993). Lewontin, for example, offers precisely the kind of historicist argument that Gross, Levitt and Sokal dismiss: "If one examines science as it is actually carried out, it becomes immediately clear that the assertion that it consists of universal claims as opposed to merely historical statements is rubbish" (Lewontin

1991: 142). Lewontin and Hubbard, among other scientists, argue that our access to that world is culturally and historically situated, and that consequently truth-claims about reality have complex internal structures and complex networks of external affiliations. If one accepts their views, then no gulf appears between the practice of science and the claims of much recent critical theory. To counter Lewontin and Hubbard, exceptionalists would have to make a reasoned argument to indicate precisely how scientists move from historical statements to universal truths.

Because they assume a one-to-one correspondence between representation and reality, realists can deal with competing views of the universe only in terms of inadequate or incomplete data, error or corruption. When confronted by conflicts within science, many of the exceptionalists simply ignore points of view with which they disagree. Weinberg dismisses Heisenberg's *Physics and Philosophy* as "wanderings," footnotes Bricmont's response to Prigogine on the philosophical significance of nonlinear dynamics, and then declares, "So much for the cultural implications of discoveries in science" (Weinberg 1996a: 12). Rather than trying to paper over conflicts within science, scientific exceptionalists would have to demonstrate that cultural theory is irrevocably hostile or irrelevant to the practice of science by doing an in-depth study of, say, Lewontin's work and making a convincing case that he is revealing universal truths without realizing it or that his scientific work is distinct from his political and cultural views. To make such claims, they would have to presuppose a metastandpoint from which to tell Lewontin that he is wrong about what he is doing and show convincingly that evolutionary biology does not depend on metaphors of development or these metaphors are not artifactual but are "just the way the world is" (Weinberg 1996b: 56).

4. *Defend Your Epistemology.* In an important sense, the difference between Lewontin and Weinberg reflects a profound disagreement about the nature of representation in science: the cultural study of science calls attention to the dialogic nature of all systems of representation, including mathematics (Markley 1993; Rotman 1993; Woolgar 1988). The realist program presupposes the adequacy of its own languages—as Weinberg puts it, "our statements about the laws of physics are in a one-to-one correspondence with aspects of objective reality" (Weinberg 1996a: 14). For Weinberg, this "correspondence" comes without any cultural or metaphysical baggage. In contrast, Lewontin argues that "[f]acts in science do not present themselves in a preexistent shape. Rather it is experimental or observational protocol that constructs facts out of an undifferentiated nature" (Lewontin 1991: 147). "Constructs" in this sentence does not mean, as Sokal assumes, "make up out of whole cloth"; it implies instead that representational schemes do not inhere in nature but mediate our apprehensions and measurements of nature through sociohistorical technologies. The crucial difference, then, between cultural analysis and exceptionalism rests on the

rhetorical force of such statements about the natural world: "[I]n biology there may be general statements, but there are no universals, and . . . actual events are the nexus of multiple causal pathways and chance perturbations" (Lewontin 1991: 147). Lewontin's comments, like Hubbard's work, indicate the resistance within science itself to universalizing assumptions and deterministic metaphors that try to deny their historical and cognitive status.

Realists are hardly wrong in emphasizing the instrumental utility of dealing with the world as we perceive and measure it, but they run into epistemological problems when they try to elevate Weinberg's reflexive view—"the correct answer when we find it is what it is because that is the way the world is" (Weinberg 1996a: 14)—to a transhistorical absolute. It should be obvious by now that Weinberg's and Lewontin's views of "the way the world is" are incommensurate. Realist ontology offers no means to assess the plausibility of such claims when scientists hold competing models of phenomena and, as Weinberg admits, no way to discuss the cultural implications of particular theories and findings.

Because, for exceptionalists, determinism inheres in the impersonal structure of the universe rather than in consensualist systems of representation, they can claim that "the results of research in physics . . . have no legitimate implications whatever for culture or politics or philosophy" (Weinberg 1996a: 12). They must take as an article of faith, then, that they can distinguish between "the direct logical implications of purely scientific discoveries" and their "use as metaphor," or, in Lewontin's terms, between universal and historical statements (Weinberg 1996a: 12; 1996b: 55). But as in Bricmont's attempt to claim that Bohm's pilot wave theory is a victory for mathematical reductionism, realists usually have to deny the theological, philosophical and cultural implications that scientists claim for their own work.

Weinberg, for example, invokes the "profound cultural effect of the discovery, going back to the work of Newton, that nature is strictly governed by impersonal mathematical laws" (Weinberg 1996a: 12) but tries to restrict that effect to an endorsement of his realist philosophy. Depending on how one defines "strictly," one could argue that Weinberg, to echo his own language, is wrong. Neither Newton nor any of his followers—including William Whiston, Samuel Clarke, J. T. Desaguliers, Colin Maclaurin and Benjamin Martin, all of whom wrote extensively about the political, cultural and theological implications of the *Principia*—believed that mathematics was the be-all and end-all of scientific explanation (M. Jacob 1976; Markley 1993: 178–256). Newton never claims that his mathematics, in and of itself, provides a true, accurate, or complete description of an objective reality; objectivity in natural philosophy is guaranteed only by his religious faith, only by identifying the viewpoint of the mathematician, historian or alchemist with a transcendent theological perspective (Markley 1993: 95–177; Peterfreund 1991). In fact, one of the great intellectual controversies of the early eighteenth century between Newton and Leibniz concerned the sociopolitical and theological conflicts that arose from their very different interpretations of what is meant by "strictly governed" and "impersonal" (Hall 1980; Shapin 1981: 187–215). In claiming, then, that "as far as culture or philosophy is concerned the difference between Newton's and Einstein's theories of gravitation or between classical and quantum mechanics is immaterial," Weinberg confuses instrumental claims about what mathematics can do with ontological beliefs about what it is (Weinberg 1996a: 12). This distinction, in an important sense, describes the territory of science studies.

Thus, in their eagerness to defend their investments in "objective" reality, exceptionalists conflate social negotiations over what count as "facts" in specific historical and cultural contexts and what they defend as a mind-independent reality. This distinction between scientific "facts" and "reality," however, is crucial to the cultural study of science: neither Lewontin nor Latour, who criticizes both constructivists and deconstructivists (Latour 1993), claims that the world is a hodgepodge of subjective impositions but that because all systems of representation are contingent there can be no unmediated access to "reality."

Ironically, when exceptionalists try to defend their ontological views or explain the comprehensibility of the universe, they have to fall back on the metaphysically laden language of aesthetics to describe the physical world and their means of understanding it: "the beauty in our present theories," Weinberg claims, "may be 'but a dream' of the kind of beauty that awaits us in the final theory" (Weinberg 1992: 17). Weinberg describes "scientific explanation" as "a mode of behavior that gives us pleasure, like love or art," and then relies on an experiential analogy to explain deductive knowledge: "The best way to understand the nature of scientific explanation is to experience the peculiar zing that you get when someone (preferably yourself) has succeeded in actually explaining something" (Weinberg 1992: 26). Like anyone else, Weinberg has to invoke an embodied and historical experience to "explain" science as "the deduction of one truth from another" (Weinberg 1992: 27) That is, in borrowing metaphors from art and psychology, he does precisely what he condemns cultural critics for doing—appropriating a specialized language to serve his own ends. "Peculiar zing," after all, is not an objective description but a culturally, biologically and historically specific rendering of an experience. For Weinberg, this experience may be a hedge against a "pointless" universe, but for Newton this aesthetic component of mathematical description is an incontestable proof of God's existence.[7] To suggest that Weinberg must rely on contested or dialogic languages of explanation is not an attack on his work but a means to historicize it.

5. *Defend Your Concept of History.* Exceptionalists are unabashed apologists for progressivist interpretations of science. Weinberg claims that "the Whig interpretation of history is legitimate in the history of science in a way

that it is not in the history of politics or culture, because science is cumulative, and permits definite judgments of success or failure" (Weinberg
1996a: 15). These "definite judgments," however, can be asserted only with
the advantage of twenty-twenty hindsight, and have to be reinforced continually by narratives that focus solely on post-hoc assessments of what is
relevant to a transhistorical conception of science. The Whiggish history of
science has fallen into disfavor among historians because it is epistemologically suspect, even tautological; it encourages present-day writers to see
themselves as the products of a coherent tradition, then to construct tele-
ological narratives whose ends are encoded in "depauperate" views of the
object of their study. For exceptionalists, the history of science becomes a
series of deductive leaps—an erasure of the historical experiences of controversy, indecision and debate.

Given its tendencies to decide in advance what is "relevant" or "irrelevant" to its progressivist narratives, Whiggish history of science is often
poorly researched. The neglect of Newton's alchemy before the 1970s—
despite his readily accessible accounts of its scientific and theological significance—demonstrates the weaknesses of "cumulative" histories of science.
Because such histories enforce a strict chain of cause and effect that assumes
rather than demonstrates the existence of a historically distinct set of practices that can be defined as science, they end up having to claim, implicitly
or explicitly, that Newton cannot be trusted to give an accurate account of
the development of his natural philosophy. By excluding Newton's volun-
tarist theology from discussions of his scientific work, internalist histories
are at a loss to explain why, within a half-century of his death, "Newtonian"
science came to mean precisely the opposite of what Newton himself intended—the strict determinism of mathematical laws which Weinberg invokes (Markley 1993). Newton's mathematics was not purged of its
sociocultural excrescences; it was misread and shoehorned into the deterministic views that Newton struggled against throughout his life.

The self-confirming logic of internalist history, then, results in a basic
paradox: Newton (or Heisenberg) cannot describe the significance of his
own work but exceptionalists can. Although exceptionalists may imagine a
past from which they would like to be descended, their Whiggish principles
are next-to-useless in describing contemporary controversies because they
imply that scientists would have to be able to distinguish accurate descriptions of nature as they came into being from dead ends. Consequently, the
challenge for an internalist history of science is indeed daunting: identify a
method for deciding which statements Bohm made are "science" and which
are "merely" historical by writing a history of the proliferating candidates
for a grand unified theory in the last twenty years.

6. *Learn Something about the Enlightenment.* Gross, Levitt, Lewis and
Sokal all claim to be defending "the Enlightenment foundation of modern,
secular, and liberal society" (Lewis 1996: 221). But none of them dem-

onstrate any firsthand knowledge of what natural philosophers in the eighteenth century actually said. Here, then, is a quick test:

As the whole is a plenum, which means that the whole of matter is connected, and
because in a plenum every movement has some effect on distant bodies in proportion
to their distance, so that each body not only is affected by those which touch it, and
is in some way sensitive to whatever happens to them, but also by means of them is
sensitive to those which touch the first bodies by which it is itself directly touched;
it follows that this [gravitational] communication stretches out indefinitely. Consequently every body is sensitive to everything which is happening in the universe, so
much so that one who saw everything could read in each body what is happening
everywhere, and even what has happened or will happen, by observing in the present
the things that are distant in time as well as in space.[8]

Is this passage based on empirical, verifiable results? Is it scientifically
sound? Does it make a contribution to a "cumulative" history of science?
Or is it metaphysical nonsense that meanders from empirical facts to un-
warranted speculation? Can we attribute any lasting scientific influence to
the views articulated by the author? Can we even decide if this passage is
"science" or "philosophy"? Does it articulate Enlightenment values of reason? It is difficult to respond intelligently to any of these questions without
a sense of the historical context in which this passage was composed. But
since exceptionalists claim that statements about the real world are objectively true or false, they should be able to distinguish scientific propositions
from metaphysical excess baggage. Also, because they perceive the history
of science as cumulative, they should be able to identify what contributions,
if any, the author's view have made to "science."

It would have come as news to most of the major figures in the seventeenth and eighteenth centuries that intellectual inquiry was founded on
secular standards of "reason" and "objectivity" because both terms were
bitterly contested during the period in theological rather than in "purely"
scientific arenas. The "Enlightenment" criteria for distinguishing science
from culture, politics and religion, which exceptionalists celebrate uncritically, do not arise organically from within a self-consistent experimental or
mathematical practice but are imported consciously from other fields, notably theology (Markley 1993; Shapin 1993). More generally, accounts of
the "rise" of "secular" and "liberal" values during the long eighteenth
century have been challenged by historians across a wide array of disciplines;
both Whiggish interpretations of the period and its radical, Marxian off-
shoots have been questioned by historians such as Jack Goldstone and John
Brewer (Brewer 1990; Goldstone 1991). Even if exceptionalists reject such
socioeconomic and cultural histories, they need to provide coherent accounts of why notions of "secular" reason emerge from attacks directed
against the scientific and technological practices of the time (J. Jacob 1983).

7. *Lose the Paranoid Narratives of Recent Intellectual History.* Because realists divide the intellectual world into champions of truth and purveyors of error, they are inclined to adopt self-serving narratives of recent intellectual conflicts. The exceptionalist view, as it is represented in *The Flight from Reason and Science*, approaches unintentional self-parody in its depictions of postmodern barbarians storming the citadels of reason and science. Beginning in the 1970s, many of the contributors claim, entrenched ideals of reason and modernity came under assault from feminists, deconstructionists, and leftists who somehow promulgated their own views and soon were monopolizing tenured positions, grants and cultural capital within the humanities and critical social sciences. Although there is little attention paid to the question of why traditional defenders of reason lost battle after intellectual battle, Gross, Levitt and others allege, without evidentiary support, that liberal professors abdicated their responsibility out of either misplaced concerns for social justice or mere self-hatred, thereby allowing "postmodernism" to triumph.

Stephen Cole's account of the rise of constructivism in the sociology of science illustrates the weaknesses of this one-sided view. Cole blames the rise of the strong program in the sociology of science on the leftist politics of young sociologists, their resentment of authority, and their lack of philosophical training, but he provides no history of the changes that have occurred within his field, no analysis of why he finds himself on the wrong side of a paradigm shift (Cole 1996: 274–277). His critique of constructivism boils down to his contention that it fails to demonstrate "how a specific social variable influences a specific cognitive content" (Cole 1996: 278). In his earlier study (Cole 1992), he tries to impose on science studies a deterministic causal logic which Latour and other constructivists are at pains to contest. Ironically, by reducing constructivism to simplistic notions of cause and effect—ideology determines the form and content of science—and then attacking this straw man, Cole ends up lending unintentional support to the nondualistic approaches that he wants to attack.

Without resorting to conspiracy theories of intellectual change, we can explain the science wars, like the culture wars which preceded them and then faded from view, straightforwardly: critical theory won; naive realism and internalist history lost. The point that Cole and other exceptionalists can neither accept nor deny is that the views that they denounce won out in the marketplace of ideas. Almost without exception, the scholars who Gross, Levitt and Sokal attack have questioned and transformed intellectual traditions from within institutional standards designed to enforce rigor and reason; and they have been rewarded by systems of professional validation that—at the start—were indifferent or hostile to the revisionist approaches they advocated. The reasons are not mysterious. If one takes the history of science in the seventeenth and eighteenth centuries, for example, the revisionist work I have cited above transformed the field because it proved more rigorous and convincing than internalist accounts: it considers a wider array of sources; explains far more anomalies in the natural philosophy of the period; spends far more time and attention discussing what scientists actually wrote as opposed to restating principles gleaned from textbooks; develops fuller contexts for understanding the relationship among scientific and sociopolitical, economic and cultural history; avoids the reductionism of deterministic accounts; and, in general, offers a higher threshold of explanation than the internalist accounts they have replaced.

The tone of wounded malice that creeps into the exceptionalists' jeremiads stems ultimately from the recognition that they are fighting rearguard actions in a battle that already is lost. But their dualistic views of history, philosophy and science lead them to exaggerate the importance of the very intellectual conflicts in which they are engaged. There is nothing apocalyptic in the current ascendancy of critiques of dualistic thinking. In fact, the dominant paradigm of science studies already is shifting to accommodate new analyses of information and genetic technologies, historical ecology, and socioecological analyses of the impact of technologies on human populations. In the next section, I try to assess where the cultural study of science will be when the smoke from the science wars clears.

WHY SCIENTISTS NEED THE CULTURAL STUDY OF SCIENCE

One of the inadvertent effects of the science wars has been to underscore the need for scientists and cultural critics to forge working relationships across disciplinary divisions in order to comment intelligently on matters beyond the confines of their areas of specialization. If my analysis demonstrates how inept most exceptionalists are in trying to read cultural theory and history, Sokal's hoax shows the limitations of a narrow constructivism that imagines distinct entities called "society," "politics" or "patriarchy" which determine the practices of science and technology. In this respect, the science wars illustrate the basic paradox that "an observer who is not immersed in the practice of a particular scholarship and who wants to understand it is at the mercy of its practitioners. Yet those practitioners are themselves mystified by a largely unexamined communal myth of how scholarship is carried on" (Lewontin 1991: 140).[9] Crossdisciplinary study, then, demands a reflexive examination of the "communal myth[s]" of one's home discipline, an examination that can be furthered by colleagues who have transgressed disciplinary boundaries, bringing with them their own assumptions, values, and questions." While the approaches that constitute science studies have been developed and contested within existing disciplines (such as history), the revisionist critiques they offer become fair game for ongoing reassessments when they are examined from different vantage points (those of anthropology). To avoid falling into new forms of disciplinary one-upmanship, however, these ongoing efforts at crossdisciplinary analysis need to be guided by an ethical and methodological injunction—study other disciplines with the diligence that you would be studied by them. Needless to say, this is an injunction that both sides in the science wars often fail to heed.

At the beginning of this chapter, I suggested that scientists as well as cultural critics stand to benefit from such a reflexive commitment to the cultural study of science. These benefits fall into three categories: a means to theorize technology and its effects; a pedagogical restructuring that will attract students to both science and science studies; and ways for progressive scholars to link their efforts to redefine disciplinary boundaries to larger social and political concerns. Taken together, they form the beginnings of a new heuristic.

In the last decade, electronic environments have reshaped the humanities and critical social sciences, redefined the nature of literacy and posed challenges that traditional disciplines—and traditional notions of interdisciplinarity—often fail to meet. One of the crucial issues facing scholars in all disciplines is to theorize the changes that have occurred and continue to occur in humankind's relations to these technologies. Without a sophisticated metacritical account of new media, it is difficult to cut through the promotional hype about cyberspace, hypertext, virtual technologies, and the World Wide Web and to analyze critically the ways in which these technologies are reshaping educational institutions and society at large (Bolter and Grusin 1996; Hayles 1995; Markley 1996). Paradoxically, many exceptionalists have little to say about technological development; their rejection of Latour's and Haraway's efforts to question the seemingly fundamental distinction between nature and culture can be read, in one sense, as a refusal to theorize the technological transformations which have radically altered perceptions of these terms (Haraway 1991; Latour 1993). This repression of technology invites staid views of the history and philosophy of science that render "nature" and "society" as distinct entities. Such approaches relegate technology to secondary status: exceptionalists characteristically remain silent on the division of labor which has persisted since the seventeenth century between conceptual knowledge obtained by "gentlemen" and the practical knowledge of artisans, workers and engineers (Shapin 1994), and they give short shrift to discussions of humankind's technological and sociocultural responses to conditions of scarcity (Goldstone 1991; Harris 1977).

In contrast, cultural critics of science, in a variety of ways, suggest that technology is not simply a tool employed by coherent subjects to preconceived ends but an integral part of emergent cyborg identities constantly assimilating technological interventions—from aspirin to implants—as part of their "natural" experience (Cronon 1995). In practice, contextualist histories of science recognize that knowledge is technologically constituted; in the seventeenth century, Newton and Boyle could not search for the seeds of gold in base metals without significant investments in expensive chemical equipment; at the beginning of the twenty-first century, particle physicists will not be able to find the Higgs boson without a new generation particle accelerator. If the science wars are being fought, in part, over contrasting visions of human subjectivity—bourgeois selves versus cyborgs—this debate needs to be reframed within larger discussions of the ways in which technology is redefining who we are and what our physical and socioeconomic environments are becoming. In turn, this ongoing process of redefinition has significant implications for what we teach our students.

Although exceptionalists lament what they perceive as ongoing crises in scientific education, their rejection of cultural analyses closes off potentially valuable avenues to attract and retain students who want to know more than the answers found at the back of the book. A view of science predicated on internalist models leads to a "depauperate" pedagogy. To make this statement is not to criticize individual teachers but to suggest that students will respond more enthusiastically and responsibly to historicist approaches— "with this technology, at this time, we achieved these results, which we interpret as follows"—than to universalizing assertions. In this regard, one of the crucial lessons that the contextualist history of science teaches is the prominent role of induction—often trial and error painstakingly practiced— in processes of invention and discovery. Internalist accounts of science as an ever-lengthening chain of deductive truths de-emphasize contextualist narratives that call attention to the complex processes by which innovations occur. Richard Westfall, to take only one example, calls attention to Newton's characteristic erasure of the steps by which he proceeded in his mathematical and experimental work by removing from the *Principia* all traces of the concept of inherent force which he had to work through and discard to arrive at his first law (Westfall 1980: 417). To teach the narrative structure of scientific discovery does not entail a surrender to relativistic views but an awareness of a self-reflexive historical method that focuses on experiments as complex matrices of cultural and scientific negotiation.

A pedagogical emphasis on technology and induction thus offers the opportunity to have students investigate critically the boundaries between "science" and "culture" as a way to supplement and extend traditional methods of teaching. As opposed to having students wait for a "peculiar zing" in order to understand underlying mathematical and scientific principles, such an approach provides incentives to students to motivate themselves to learn crucial concepts. Those readers who assume that I am describing idealistic thought experiments may want to look closely at programs such as the science, technology and culture (STAC) major at Georgia Tech (Knoespel 1994: 1996). Undergraduate students in this program learn, for example, that scientists must rigorously control all experimental parameters in order to isolate key variables, but they also are taught that such experiments depend on significant investments of money, labor, computing equipment, software, hardware and expertise and that such projects take place within complex networks that require intelligent scrutiny. The STAC program, in this regard, is an important step toward institutionalizing the cultural study of science along lines that appeal to wide constituencies in a prominent university that emphasizes technological innovation and applied science. Rather than enforcing disciplinary biases, programs such as this offer opportunities for students to learn the care and rigor required for scientific investigation as well as the virtues of open-ended inquiry; to develop the healthy scepticism of the critical social sciences toward the very techniques of modeling and quantification that are integral to the program as well as a methodological commitment to cultural and natural ecologies as complex systems; and to practice the critical readings skills of humanities as well as to consider broader sociocultural issues.

Some exceptionalists may balk at the idea of having to address, even tangentially, sociopolitical concerns. But to retreat from the study of science in its cultural contexts is itself a political act. Sokal presents his hoax as an in-house dispute among progressives, but his fellow travelers' response to science studies—denounce the academic left and attack feminism—discloses an ideological agenda which motivates their discourse. Despite their disclaimers, exceptionalists reveal an anxiety that ultimately seems misplaced. Neither Gross and Levitt nor their cohorts provide any empirical evidence to back up their bizarre claim that the cultural study of science is undermining public confidence in science itself (Gross and Levitt 1994; Gross, Levitt and Lewis 1996). There are no woman-in-the-street interviews that I know of in which Haraway is invoked as a reason to condemn the super conducting super collider to oblivion. If the debates of the science wars often boil down to the semantic difference between culture shaping science and culture constructing science, the nature of this rhetorical argument itself should suggest something of the narrowness of an approach that pushes aside questions of the consequences of science and technology. Whatever philosophical differences may exist between leftist realists and leftist constructivists, they are far less important than what we might presume are their shared political commitments to do something about environmental racism, air and water pollution, disappearing rain forests, rising cancer rates and the prospect of global warming. In frankly political terms, the cultural study of science offers an ongoing commitment to consider the consequences of scientific, technological, economic, and political practices that traditionally have been parceled out to different domains of professional expertise.

Cultural studies has had some far-reaching effects within universities because it challenges a variety of disciplinary claims to transhistorical knowledge and cultural authority. To participate in such challenges is not to surrender to relativism but to remain open to what have always been ongoing reformulations of how we represent and think about the world. For scientists to think through the implications of cultural theory is not, as Lewontin, Hubbard, Coyne and others recognize, to abandon the practice of science for anthropology or literary criticism but to expand that practice to consider the socioeconomic values that underlie our lived experience of science and technology in the 1990s. Like the rest of us, scientists are forced to operate within an econometric realm in which the human and environmental costs of population increases, resource degradation and the gulf between industrialized and developing nations are routinely, even brutally, externalized. Any analysis of the practices of science and technology in the 1990s has to begin by recognizing that locally, nationally and internationally the costs of environmental cleanup, the degradation of air and water quality, wage losses and increasing divisions between rich and poor know no disciplinary boundaries (Hawken 1993). Beyond the science wars, then, lie opportunities to ask some fundamental questions about a planetary future that resists being confined to single ways of knowing.

NOTES

1. On crossdisciplinary scholarship and pedagogy see Knoespel (1994, 1996).

2. Exceptionalism may be defined as the belief that science remains distinct in theory and practice from other cultural and cognitive practices. In philosophy, exceptionalism generally takes the form of realism, the belief in a mind-independent reality that be can be expressed in totally adequate languages of description. Because realists believe in a one-to-one correspondence between the external world and the semiotics that describe it, their view of reality, as I shall suggest below, elevates it to the status of a transhistorical absolute. In historical study, exceptionalism takes the form of internalist history, the belief that scientific development is progressive and effectively independent of culture, politics, religion and economics.

3. Sokal and Bricmont obtained permission from *Genre* to do bad translations of these passages by subterfuge. His publisher wrote a letter, originally dated June 30, 1997, to claim that they wanted "to reproduce the texts 'The Irrelevance of Reality' " for a volume entitled "Essaie sur la philosophie postmoderne." Several transatlantic faxes have failed to produce a copy of the book, which has created a significant controversy in France. The first chapter is available on-line at http://www.liberation.com/chapitre/sokal.html.

4. Sokal quotes a passage from my 1991 introduction to a special issue of *New Orleans Review* in which he conflates the distinction between my comments on "[n]arratives of scientific progress" (1991: 6) and scientific practice. The sentences that follow refer clearly to these narratives, which have been challenged—indeed discredited—on historical and epistemological grounds (Bazerman 1988; Porter 1995; Rouse 1991).

5. This article and my 1993 book have been on reading lists for discussion groups of scientists and social scientists at UCLA and the University of Washington.

6. See Westfall 1980 and the essays collected in Force and Popkin (1998).

7. Contrast as well Weinberg's statement that "[t]he more the universe seems comprehensible, the more it seems pointless" (Weinberg 1977: 154) to John Bar-

row's and Frank Tipler's discussion of the anthropic cosmological principle (Barrow and Tipler 1986; see also Barrow 1992).

8. Since this is a test, no citation.

9. On communication problems within science, see the argument by Jared Diamond, a distinguished physiologist at UCLA and a recipient of a MacArthur Foundation "Genius" Grant, who demonstrates that "even scientists can't possibly understand most articles written by scientists" (Diamond 1997: 49). Although, as Diamond notes, scientists demand that the public understand, appreciate and fund their work, they often retreat to the disciplinary confines of specialization and respond with "widespread indifference, hostility, and penalties, such as honors and promotions delayed or even denied" to scientists such as Carl Sagan who seek to make science accessible (Diamond 1997: 46).

REFERENCES

Barrow, John. (1992) *Pi in the Sky: Counting, Thinking, and Being*. New York: Oxford University Press.

Barrow, John and Tipler, Frank. (1986) *The Anthropic Cosmological Principle*. New York: Oxford University Press.

Bazerman, Charles. (1988) *Shaping Written Knowledge: The Genre and Activity of the Experimental Article in Science*. Madison: University of Wisconsin Press.

Bloom, Allan. (1987) *The Closing of the American Mind: How Higher Education Has Failed Democracy and Impoverished the Souls of Today's Students*. New York: Simon and Schuster.

Bohm, David. (1980) *Wholeness and the Implicate Order*. New York: Routledge.

Bolter, Jay David and Grusin, Richard. (1996) "Remediation." *Configurations*, 4: 311–358.

Brewer, John. (1990) *The Sinews of Power: War, Money and the English State, 1688–1783*. Cambridge, MA: Harvard University Press.

Bricmont, Jean and Sokal, Alan. (1997a) *Impostures Intellectuelles*. Paris: Odile Jacob.

———. (1997b) "What Is All the Fuss About? How French Intellectuals Have Responded to Accusations of Science-Abuse." *Times Literary Supplement*, October 17: 16–17.

Chew, Geoffrey. (1974) "Impasse for the Elementary-Particle Concept." *The Great Ideas Today 1974*. Chicago: Britannica.

Cole, Stephen. (1992) *Making Science: Between Nature and Society*. Cambridge, MA: Harvard University Press.

———. (1996) " 'Voodoo Sociology': Recent Developments in the Sociology of Science." In Paul Gross, Norman Levitt and Martin W. Lewis (eds.), *The Flight from Reason and Science*. New York: New York Academy of Sciences, 274–287.

Coyne, Richard. (1995) *Designing Information Technology in the Postmodern Age: From Method to Metaphor*. Cambridge, MA: MIT Press.

Cronon, William. (1995) "Introduction: In Search of Nature." In William Cronon (ed.), *Uncommon Ground: Rethinking the Human Place in Nature*. New York: Norton, 23–56.

Diamond, Jared. (1997) "Kinship with the Stars." *Discover*, 18: 44–49.

Dobbs, Betty Jo Teeter. (1991) *The Janus Faces of Genius: The Role of Alchemy in Newton's Thought.* Cambridge: Cambridge University Press.

D'Souza, Dinesh. (1991) *Illiberal Education: The Politics of Race and Sex on Campus.* New York: Free Press.

Force, James E. and Popkin, Richard (eds.). (1998) *Newton and Religion.* Dordrecht: Kluwer Academic Publishers.

Goldstone, Jack. (1991) *Revolution and Rebellion in the Early Modern World.* Berkeley: University of California Press.

Goodstein, David. (1996) "Conduct and Misconduct in Science." In Paul Gross, Norman Levitt and Martin W. Lewis (eds.), *The Flight from Reason and Science.* New York: New York Academy of Sciences, 31–38.

Gross, Paul and Levitt, Norman. (1994) *Higher Superstition: The Academic Left and Its Quarrels with Science.* Baltimore: Johns Hopkins University Press.

Gross, Paul, Levitt, Norman and Lewis, Matthew W. (eds.). (1996) *The Flight from Reason and Science.* New York: New York Academy of Sciences.

Hall, A. Rupert. (1980) *Philosophers at War: The Quarrel between Newton and Leibniz.* Cambridge: Cambridge University Press.

Haraway, Donna. (1991) *Simians, Cyborgs, and Women: The Reinvention of Nature.* New York: Routledge.

Harris, Marvin. (1977) *Cannibals and Kings: The Origins of Cultures.* New York: Vintage.

Hart, Roger. (1996) "The Flight from Reason: Higher Superstition and the Refutation of Science Studies." In Andrew Ross (ed.), *Science Wars.* Durham, NC: Duke University Press, 259–292.

Hawken, Paul. (1993) *The Ecology of Commerce: A Declaration of Sustainability.* New York: Harper Business.

Hayles, N. Katherine. (1995) "Simulated Nature and Natural Simulations: Rethinking the Relation between the Beholder and the World." In William Cronon (ed.), *Uncommon Ground.* New York: Norton, 409–425.

———. (1996) "Consolidating the Canon." In Andrew Ross (ed.) *Science Wars.* Durham, NC: Duke University Press, 226–237.

Heisenberg, Werner. (1958) *Physics and Philosophy: The Revolution in Modern Science.* New York: Harper and Row.

Horgan, John. (1996) *The End of Science: Facing the Limits of Knowledge in the Twilight of the Scientific Age.* New York: Addison-Wesley.

Hubbard, Ruth. (1993) *Exploding the Gene Myth.* Boston: Beacon.

Jacob, James R. (1983) *Henry Stubbe: Radical Protestantism and the Early Enlightenment.* Cambridge: Cambridge University Press.

Jacob, Margaret C. (1976) *The Newtonians and the English Revolution, 1689–1720.* Ithaca, NY: Cornell University Press.

Kimball, Roger. (1990) *Tenured Radicals: How Politics Has Corrupted Our Higher Education.* New York: Harper and Row.

Knoespel, Kenneth. (1994) "Technology and the Status of the Human Sciences." Plenary address. Interface Conference, Atlanta, Georgia.

———. (1996) Forum, *PMLA,* 111: 304–305.

Latour, Bruno. (1993) *We Have Never Been Modern.* Cambridge, MA: Harvard University Press.

Lewis, Martin W. (1992) *Green Delusions: An Environmentalist Critique of Radical Environmentalism.* Durham, NC: Duke University Press.

———. (1996) "Radical Environmental Philosophy and the Assault on Reason." In Paul Gross, Norman Levitt and Martin W. Lewis (eds.), *The Flight from Reason and Science,* New York: New York Academy of Sciences, 209–230.

Lewontin, Richard. (1991) "Facts and the Factitious in the Natural Sciences." *Critical Inquiry,* 18: 140–153.

———. (1995) "A la recherche du temps perdue: A Review Essay." *Configurations,* 3: 257–265.

Lindley, David. (1993) *The End of Physics: The Myth of a Unified Theory.* New York: Basic Books.

Markley, Robert. (1992) "The Irrelevance of Reality: Science, Ideology, and the Postmodern Universe." *Genre,* 25: 249–276.

———. (1993) *Fallen Languages: Crises of Representation in Newtonian England, 1660–1740.* Ithaca, NY: Cornell University Press.

———. (1994) "Boundaries: Mathematics, Alienation, and the Metaphysics of Cyberspace." *Configurations,* 3: 485–507.

———. (ed.). (1996) *Virtual Realities and Their Discontents.* Baltimore: Johns Hopkins University Press.

Mirowski, Philip. (1989) *More Heat than Light: Economics as Social Physics, Physics as Nature's Economics.* Cambridge: Cambridge University Press.

Newton, Sir Isaac. (1934) *Principia,* Andrew Motte (trans.); Florian Cajori (ed.). Berkeley: University of California Press.

Peat, E. David. (1988) *Superstrings and the Search for the Theory of Everything.* New York: Contemporary Books.

Pesic, Peter. (1991) "The Principle of Identicality and the Foundations of Quantum Theory I, II." *American Journal of Physics,* 59: 971–974, 975–978.

Peterfreund, Stuart. (1991) "Saving the Phenomenon or Saving the Hexameron? Mosaic Self-Presentation in Newtonian Optics." *The Eighteenth Century: Theory and Interpretation,* 32: 139–165.

Porter, Theodore M. (1995) *Trust in Numbers: The Pursuit of Objectivity in Science and Public Life.* Princeton, NJ: Princeton University Press.

Rotman, Brian. (1993) *Ad Infinitum: The Ghost in Turing's Machine. Taking God Out of Mathematics and Putting the Body Back In.* Stanford, CA: Stanford University Press.

Rouse, Joseph. (1991) "Philosophy of Science and the Persistent Narratives of Modernity." *Studies in History and Philosophy of Science,* 22: 141–169.

Shapin, Steven. (1981) "Of Gods and Kings: Natural Philosophy and Politics in the Leibniz-Clarke Disputes." *Isis,* 72: 187–215.

———. (1994) *A Social History of Truth: Civility and Science in Seventeenth-Century England.* Chicago: University of Chicago Press.

Smith, Barbara Herrnstein. (1997) "Microdynamics of Incommensurability: Philosophy of Science Meets Science Studies." In Barbara Herrnstein Smith and Arkady Plotnitsky (eds.), *Mathematics, Science, and Postclassical Theory.* Durham, NC: Duke University Press, 243–266.

Sokal, Alan. (1996a) "Transgressing the Boundaries: Toward a Transformative Hermeneutics of Quantum Gravity," *Social Text,* 46/47 (Spring–Summer): 217–252.

————. (1996b) "A Physicist Experiments with Cultural Studies." *Lingua Franca*, 6(4) (May–June): 62–64.

Sokal, Alan and Bricmont, Jean. (1998) *Fashionable Nonsense: Postmodern Intellectuals' Abuse of Science*. New York: Picador.

Weinberg, Steven. (1977) *The First Three Minutes: A Modern View of the Origins of the Universe*. New York: Basic Books.

————. (1992) *Dreams of a Final Theory: The Search for the Fundamental Laws of Nature*. New York: Pantheon.

————. (1996a) "Sokal's Hoax." *New York Review of Books*, 43(13) (August 8): 11–15.

Weinberg, Steven et al. (1996b) "Sokal's Hoax: An Exchange." *New York Review of Books*, 43(16) (October 3): 54–56.

Westfall, Richard. (1980) *Never at Rest: A Biography of Isaac Newton*. Cambridge: Cambridge University Press.

Woolgar, Steve. (1988) *Science: The Very Idea*. London: Tavistock.

Chapter 3

Going to Cyberschool: Post/Trans/Antidisciplinarity at the Virtual University

TIMOTHY LUKE

In this brief critical discussion, I want to express some thoughts about taking higher education into cyberspace. More specifically, how suitable are networked computing environments for tertiary-level learning, and in what ways will existing academic disciplines be challenged or changed by integrating cyberspatial sites into university teaching? As the domains of the World Wide Web, or the multimedia-based regions of the Internet, have expanded in terms of their overall absolute numbers and relative growth rates, private and public plans for using cyberspaces as educational sites have proliferated at a heart-pounding pace.

Yet very few of these plans, and even fewer of the actual experiments with cyberspace-based teaching methods, have considered their longer-run cultural implications for the existing structures of any university or every academic discipline as they confront the prospect of such total transformations. Cyberspace in the "second media age" is quite interesting at this juncture inasmuch as so much of it appears to be extradisciplinary in its forms and functions (Poster 1995). Of course, the servers that sustain it may still be located in departments of English, or computer science, or biology, or political science and their disciplinary dedication may even prop up some seemingly fixed epistemological divides between today's various disciplines. Nonetheless, in disembedding academic discourses and cultural practices from existing built environments, in bridging canons of knowledge from many fields of endeavor and in flowing within the hypertextuality of net-centered communication, many existing cyberspatial domains with "educational" intentions/origins/underpinnings now mostly have post/trans/antidisciplinary tendencies coevolving with them. In cyberspace, the world no longer needs to be "naturally divided" into the conventional units of traditional university-defined disciplinarity. Transdisciplinary collisions ride along with postmodernistic antidisciplinary subversions, creating auras of postdisciplinarity in entirely extradisciplinary pools of data, flows of facts, rushes of images. What will cultural studies become when schools and universities go on-line? Could the study of culture simply stop as cyberspace displaces face-to-face interactions?

POSTMODERNITY AND THE NEW WORLD ORDER

Following Lyotard, we might connect the crisis of disciplinarity with the postmodern. Postmodernity arises with the decline of modernity's grand narratives, which have until quite recently embedded Western capitalist society's economic, political, scientific and technological practices in deeper metaphysical projects of *Bildungsphilosophie*. Such metanarratives, or the fables of reason and freedom that postulate a gradual, but inevitable, progress will come to both individuals and societies through the unfolding of history, once legitimated many less grand, albeit no less important, operational narratives of everyday theory and practice in every individual discipline. These metanarratives in learned disciplinary institutions justified gradual policy advances and centered individual decisions in moral registers anchored to improving the condition of mankind in general.

With the global transition to postindustrial flexible specialization during the 1960s and 1970s, however, Lyotard now sees this historical era closing. The postmodern is based

upon the perception of the existence of a modern era that dates from the time of the Enlightenment and that now has run its course: and this modern era was predicated on the notion of progress in knowledge, in the arts, in technology, and in human freedom as well, all of which was thought of as leading to a truly emancipated society: a society emancipated from poverty, despotism and ignorance. But all of us can see that the development continues to take place without leading to the realization of any of these dreams of emancipation. (1984: 39)

Alongside this expanding distrust in metanarratives of truth, reason or progress and the disciplines that stick with these myths, Lyotard sees science and technology falling under the sway of "another language game, in which the goal is no longer truth, but performativity—that is, the best possible input/output equation" (1984: 46).

Following Jameson, postmodernity represents the rise of "a new social system beyond classical capitalism" emerging from "the world space of multinational capital" (1992: 59, 54). More specifically, this new social system of multinational capital is developing its own world spaces by disintegrating the Fordist regime of industrial production, capital accumulation and state intervention formed during the 1930s through the 1970s in national welfare

states. In its place, a new regime of flexible accumulation, technical specialization, and state deregulation has emerged in loosely coupled transnational
alliances of market centers, factory concentrations, technology generators,
capital suppliers and government regulators that have been managed from
cyberspace since the 1970s. From out of this mix comes the "new world
order." Transnational firms produce world cars, global hamburgers, planetary pants, or earth shoes from nowhere and anywhere to sell everywhere,
making a travesty both of nationalist campaigns to "Buy American" and
xenophobic reactions to resist "Americanization."

Like Chernobyl, "America," as postmodernity's most typical economic
formation, mass culture or ecological system, is now everywhere. It is no
longer simply a nation-state or one ethnonational population; it becomes
the sign of how the human and nonhuman are being collectivized into new
global networks that frame a new consciousness as well as a mode of production at the nucleus of a worldwide chain reaction (Latour 1993: 4). And,
as it melts down, the fallout of this quasi-ecological event is changing all
life forms everywhere. Spatial barriers and time zones collapse in the com-
pression dynamics of multinational capital's acceleration of global production. As Harvey observes, "flexible accumulation typically exploits a wide
range of seemingly contingent geographical circumstances. . . . The result
has been the production of fragmentation, insecurity, and ephemeral uneven
development within a highly unified global space economy of capital flows"
(1989: 294, 296). Under the horizon of flexible accumulation, Lyotard's
vision of performativity is what anchors those structures and agents inhabiting the new postmodern social regime. Today, every learned discipline is
in crisis inasmuch as

the State and/or company must abandon the idealist and humanist narratives of
legitimation in order to justify the new goal: in the discourse of today's financial
backers of research, the only credible goal is power. Scientists, technicians, and instruments are purchased not to find truth, but to augment power. (Lyotard 1984:
46)

From these bearings taken on postmodernity, we might map the postmodern era as: (1) a historical-geographic condition; (2) a political-
economic mode of production; or (3) a cultural-ethical regime of
representation. A complete survey would take more time and energy than
can be expended from this brief aside here and now. Nonetheless, one special quality of postmodernity might be addressed, namely, its uniquely spatial
characteristics. Jameson argues that with the postmodern, "we are back in
the spatial itself," and postmodern theory

infers a certain supplement of spatiality in the contemporary period and suggests that
there is a way in which, even though other modes of production . . . are distinctively

spatial, ours has been spatialized in a unique sense, such that space is for us an existential and cultural dominant, a thematized or foregrounded feature or structural principle standing in striking contrast to its relatively subordinate and secondary . . . role in earlier modes of production. (1992: 365)

This primacy of postmodern spatiality is seconded by Soja, who sees this new range of space as a domain of performativity. Like cyberspace it now becomes so flexibly produced that its forms are "never primordially given or permanently fixed" (1989: 122).

Bill Readings could be right about the development of the contemporary academy. That is, "the history of the modern university can be crudely summarized by saying that the modern university has had three ideas: the Kantian idea of reason, the Humboldtian notion of culture, and now the technological idea of excellence" (1993: 165). However, in a global economy where the shape and substance of space are never primordially given or permanently fixed, the sites of cyberspace mirror these basically fluid conditions. Amidst this flux of forms, the agendas of excellence, culture and reason are being hard pressed by the logics of performativity, or the best possible input/output equations, as Lyotard frames the imbrication of scientific disciplines and university institutions, in the augmentation of power. So in a world now riven by cyberspace, the shape and substance of once stable disciplinary practices in the academy are beginning to be pushed and pulled by the emergent structures of cyberschooling. As a result, the problematic agendas of performativity now can assail the existing disciplinary divisions of the university in the guise of worries about the cost of higher education as well as the market-driven usefulness of its products. In this environment of fluid spaces, cultural studies may have to get in-line with performative expectations or be tagged as being totally out-of-line in the on-line academy.

Therefore, this chapter examines how and why cyberschooling may become such a pervasive reality in higher education that we might see disciplinarity dissipating entirely within many of its practices. On-line, it appears, the medium would be the message, providing the ultimate parameters for the ordered production, circulation, interpretation and regulation of truth-like statements. To make the techniques of cyberschooling more attractive to the many, fields of enquiry will be redrawn, boundaries between fields could be busted apart and socializing practices may become recentered. Webcrawling might well privilege the personal, the specific, the oral and the local against the collective, the universal, the written and the global as the multimedia of electronic communication swamp the monomedia of print. The exhaustion of classic metanarratives becomes fully apparent in the local/ global intertextuality of cyberspace where proprietary operating systems and corporate software applications now frame discourse. Indeed, the particularities of the World Wide Web reveal much about the intertwined coevolution of postmodernity and the new world order, which now contextualize the possible workings of cyberschool in the larger frames of world political economy and cybernetic cultural practice.

CULTURES OF PERFORMATIVITY

These reminders about postmodernity are important when we recognize how thoroughly the proliferation of performativity, or rationalized productivity codes, often are a side-effect of a more general social movement being masterminded, to a significant extent, by elements of the digiterati, or those professional-technical workers whose identities, careers, communities and livelihoods depend upon the use and growth of new computer/network/telecom technologies. Working for and/or owning business enterprises that produce such informational goods and services, these groups tout the inexorable necessities of an informational revolution. From telecommuting, virtualizing offices, or dematerializing enterprises to computer voting, internetworking, or digitized entertaining, the digiterati incessantly repeat the claims of their cybernetic ideologies: the system is the solution, the power of networks, applications for a small planet. They believe our question is already answered: "Of course cyberspace is a suitable environment for education!" And, then, they maneuver to sell colleges and universities the goods and services needed to realize this belief as fact. Such forces are at work, and we must be aware of their different, and often contradictory, agendas for informationalization, because in some ways the theoretical prospect and practical project of cyberschooling, or a net-centered mode of education using these new instructional technologies, is just one more facet of existing late-industrial society.

My sense of the situation, however, is that most colleges and universities still are not running at the same speed as the digiterati. In fact, most disciplines have not yet started addressing the problems posed by cyberschooling very systematically at all. Instead, one sees incredible transdisciplinary intramural battles over smaller concerns, like the decision to adopt an Apple-based or a Wintel-based PC operating system. Often after many years of building either an Apple or a Wintel desktop-centered environment, any given university has a major investment in one hardware/software combination as it contemplates moving full tilt into local or wide-area networking. Some will want to change, some will not want to change; almost all are very confused about the implications of this decision. As a result, a coordinated initiative by all disciplines about rethinking how to teach on new networks breaks down into fights over different operating systems or network architectures, which makes any effort to systematically mobilize new instructional technologies in teaching more difficult rather than more efficient.

Nonetheless, many colleges and universities can show evidence of innovative computer-based instruction in the departments of English, music, philosophy, sociology, mathematics, as well as chemistry, statistics, physics, engineering or geology. This suggests some independent in-house innovators are making significant progress toward meeting the expectations of various outside publics who want universities to use new instructional technologies. Most of these already existing experiments, however, do not alter the "credit for contact" model as their applications are captured almost totally by established patterns of classroom interaction. Many faculty members, for example, are testing different variants of what already prevails within each of their disciplines, namely, "credit for contact *plus* computers." In some instances, students come to special computer-equipped lecture halls to see computer-generated graphics, outlines, or image displays supplementing the lecture format in traditional large-enrollment classes. In other instances, students come to special computer-equipped classrooms to work in realtime and physical co-location with their instructors to perform computer-mediated math problems, music exercises or composition assignments.

All of these innovations are exciting and important but, at the same time, we must ask if they really do push interdisciplinarity or alter "the credit for contact" model? Typically, students and faculty still meet physically in realtime on a standard academic calendar at the same specific site in one of the university's or college's classroom buildings to study a single disciplinary field. Televisions and/or computers here only extend/amplify/improve the display of information ordinarily mediated by the instructors' speaking voices, chalkboard diagrams, overhead projectors, slide presentations or technical demonstrations. In each of these applications, however, even when personal computers are used in truly multidisciplinary experiments in cultural studies or ecological analysis, they often do not fully exploit the technical potential that outside interests hope educational institutions can realize from instructional technologies.

PRACTICES AND PRACTICALITIES

What is this "technical potential" for cyberschooling? One obvious answer is rethinking the use of personal computers in terms of Internet-based connections to promote a "virtualization" of the classroom. Networks of computers generate alternate sites for interaction, or fixed spaces, where many forms of work, leisure or educational activity can be conducted. Like labor performed in telecommuting links, education can be provided at cyberschooling sites. And these simulated sites of educational interaction will alter the personal and social discourses that have been developed for teaching and learning in realtime at the same physical co-location at one built environmental site on a fixed calendar. Telecom networks and personal computers can be redeployed in combinations of instructional technics that construct "infostructures" (linking software packages, hardware servers and telecommunication networks). Here is "where" post/trans/antidisciplinarity might run free, upending completely our current containers of knowledge and the knowledgeable.

These changes would break what has been called the "credit for contact" model, but they would, at the same time, require the invention of new "credit for interaction" models tied to accepting/experiencing/validating new instructional performances mediated through the infostructures of these virtual universities. Still, why make this move at all? How would disciplinarity operate within these infostructures? And, would the transdisciplinary practices of cyberschools have any practical benefits?

On Cost Controls/Correspondence Principles

The key reasons for shifting to virtual instruction are familiar ones: "cost control" and the "correspondence principle." On the one hand, the pervasiveness of global neo-liberalism now directs the inhabitants of many societies to rethink what they paid for collectively and how they benefit from it. Consequently, any large, publicly-financed program, like secondary or tertiary education, is under increased fiscal scrutiny. Traditional educational services presume large systems with high personnel costs, major physical plant investments and fixed curricular programming. Cyberschooling, like telecommuting's dematerialization of fixed work sites, promises to reduce costs by moving educational activity into cyberspatial infostructures, dumping access costs (computers and network time) to users, downsizing administrative and teaching staffs, eliminating many physical plant needs by constructing flexible infostructures and keeping curricula more fluid. While it remains to be proven in practice as true in fact, cyberschooling is believed by many to be highly cost-effective inasmuch as it reduces some of the many ways that educational funds are spent by public authorities now. In turn, any major future investment in such systems could be off-loaded on to the private sector (telecom, computer, network firms as well as entrepreneurial blocs from the digiterati) for the delivery of allegedly more rational solutions without the impediments of disciplinary boundaries.

On the other hand, the notion that we now live in an "Information Age" society is seen as dictating an "Information Age" school system; hence, the future of labor via telecommuting or leisure through webcrawling must be brought into more a complete coincident correspondence with education as cyberschooling. While this expectation would match teaching techniques to whatever alluring reflections the myths of an informational society are casting over the general public, it also ironically begins to embed education in the instabilities of global flexible specialization (Harvey 1989). If labor is going to be increasingly outsourced by production units, and if workers will be expected to operate as independent entrepreneurs who will surf the whirlpools and eddies of Internet data flows seeking business by themselves, then

cyberschooling might indeed begin to capture some "correspondence" with
the real world, particularly if much of it occurs within privatized infostruc-
tural domains on a for-profit basis. Now this truly is a transdisciplinarity
with real postdisciplinary qualities. In pursuit of these principles, and in light
of the yet to be fulfilled predictions of cost-effectiveness we now also often
see elements in the digiterati maneuvering to control how and why these
correspondences will be drawn between school class sites and business work
sites in a yet-to-be-attained netcentric world.

Some Practical Issues

Nonetheless, college and university faculty should not dismiss the practical
implications of new instructional technologies. These technologies can totally transform the existing discourses and practices of education; once they
become more common, it would mean teaching on TV, instructing through
computers, performing on CD-ROM—perhaps in post/trans/antidiscipli-
nary registers. Seeing this as disruptive, many faculty argue that the virtualization of instruction should not happen, and they pledge these changes
shall not pass. This stance, however, is under fire. Because of the lobbying
efforts of the digiterati, who wish to profit from and direct the virtualization
process, and because of dwindling support for costly public goods, such as
the existing systems of "contact" teaching in public universities, these narrow points of faculty faith are being thoroughly questioned by many state
authorities and some members of the public. The "virtual university" can
be constructed; and, in being built, it might prove to be highly performative.
There are no serious technological barriers preventing it from developing.
And there are reasons to believe, again mostly promoted by the digiterati
and information service industries, that cyberschooling "fits" the cultural
sensorium of today's students. If the obliteration of disciplinarity is part of
the cost of admission to cyberspace, then universities may well be forced to
pay this price. Consequently, we should begin considering the implications
of this stubborn resistance, lest these important choices about educational
practices get made elsewhere, producing perhaps less favorable outcomes for
college and university faculty.

Virtualized courses of instruction are becoming identified as the mythic
payoff for "instructional technologies" because a virtualized college or university could address three important concerns identified as critical to larger
publics: breaking the credit for contact paradigm of teaching, expanding the
options for distance-learning and realizing new efficiencies in service delivery. If, however, these publics are serious about such transformation, then
these changes will mean, in the final analysis, creating entirely new spaces
and styles of instructional interaction that could: (1) reorder the entire
discipline-based mode of education with its existing systems for informing/
testing/credentialing students; (2) shift the basic disciplinary understandings

of scholarship/teaching/service for faculty; (3) change the meaning of management/off-campus extension/instruction for administrators; (4) cost a great deal of money/time/energy on an order of magnitude not fully appreciated by all concerned; and (5) threaten the survival of all existing disciplinary communities.

Cyberschools most likely may structure themselves, like universities have for over a century, within the still existing disciplines to organize their delivery systems of instruction, assemble knowledge relations and reproduce their objects of analysis. However, the diversity of production sites, the flexibility of reproduction routines and the dematerialization of embodied interactions will undoubtedly change how and why any single discipline must operate, and upon whom it individually must exert its effects, in order to fabricate disciplinarity. Because the disciplines we know today are so much a product of cultures for learning at the "contact" university, it seems likely that they will change, weaken or disappear to the extent that institutionalized cyberschool formations lose their "sitedness" in previrtualized university settings. Virtualizing education, and taking it into cyberspace, will revamp the infrastructures of teaching, service and research so thoroughly that many disciplinary discourses and practices may not survive. In fact, the virtualization of higher education most likely must run on a platform of post/trans/antidisciplinarity to gather momentum and allies for its revolutionary projects.

PROFESSIONAL PRACTICES AND POLITICAL ECONOMY

Enacting the collective decision to construct cyberschooling systems, then, will necessitate major changes in our professional practices as educators as well as in the political economies of each university as a public enterprise. These concerns are on the horizon, and there are no easy answers on how to respond to them. Still, they need to be raised.

From a professional practices standpoint, the virtualization of instruction shifts us into entirely new post/trans/antidisciplinary registers of action. Much of what we do is rooted to tacit disciplinary understandings grounded in print culture, industrial training, hierarchic structure and guild values that run at cross purposes with netcentric modes of operation. Consequently, the disciplinarities of many existing professional practices may not stand up in this new teaching/learning environment.

First, and particularly now until standards for software/hardware applications get more firmly fixed, the instructor is responsible for minding his/her own "little silicon schoolhouse." All of the infostructures of instruction must be designed, built, maintained, renovated and used by "someone." At this juncture, that "someone" is the instructor, or small teams of instructors, mobilized to pursue some teaching enhancements from these changes. This role for the educator is a major sociological displacement to worry about as he/she is shifted into a new division of labor where many unknown or unexpected demands will be made on everyone's time and energy. Being a software troubleshooter, hardware expert, network manager, or CD-ROM maker in addition to working as a teacher is a radical shift.

Second, cyberschooling, like telecommuting, recenters control in the educational experience. Many describe cyberschooling techniques as "student-centered." Hence, it also might be seen as "teacher-decentered." To embark upon this path of development, professional practice will need to refocus the "education product." Instead of fixating upon credentialing students through time-limited/context-dependent tests, successful training may shift more toward training students to cooperate in small groups to process new information, create new informational findings or construct new networked sites. Autonomy, responsibility and discipline could be key expectations in such student-centered systems of instruction. So educators may lose contact with students, get closed out of old built environments, find themselves disempowered and have less control over students and learning as webcrawling redefines how students learn.

Third, cyberschooling presumes new disciplinary discursive canons. What literacy means, how writing will be done, what education may represent and how any existing discipline could change are all open questions. Inasmuch as books, written work, oral presentations or lab work is replaced by CD-ROMs, e-mail, desktop video interactions or laboratory simulations, one will find the rhetoric and reason behind learned/disciplined disciplinary thinking changed. New postdisciplinary audiovisual representations may overwhelm traditional disciplinary print presentations in these multimedia worlds. Print literacy will not disappear, but it plainly may not be as privileged as it is now. A new aesthetics of educational performance, a new taste culture about correct modes of argument and a new preference set for proper communication will displace existing ones tied to the industrial-era, print culture–centered, middle class–based higher education institutions that have evolved over the past century.

Looking at the nuts and bolts issues of political economy, cyberschooling will totally upend many political practices and economic choices that have been settled by educating people at closed physical sites with personnel from closed disciplinary guilds paid for by closed political entities within closed territorial spaces. Cyberschooling infostructures are, for the most part, the total antithesis of all these once tightly closed domains and practices inasmuch as they assume a great deal of post/trans/antidisciplinarity. Easy access via netcentric modes of interaction essentially opens up all of the these once tightly closed domains with serious questions of political economy: who, whom?

First, who owns and controls cyberschool sites? If territorial and disciplinary boundaries are not respected in cyberschool learning, then the control of access to education radically changes. Who deals with admissions into and graduations from cyberschool courses of study? Who measures, evaluates, issues and registers credits, degrees and courses? Who recruits students, trains teachers, finds administrators? What will local authorities do about netcentric academic credentials? Will credits and degrees from cyberschools be certified/approved/endorsed in the marketplace or by governments? Will it be teachers, students, networks, businesses, governments or some subset of all them?

Second, what happens to disciplinarity in the flux of cyberspace? Who certifies teachers, accepts students, operates infostructures, and where? Can anyone gain access anywhere anytime? Will employers and educators recognize cyberschooling as legitimate? Can other public entities become virtual free riders and close down their own educational services—real or virtual—once some course of cyberschool study is up on the net somewhere? And, more importantly, in any single political domain one must consider how building a cyberschool might make some, or even many, "contact" campuses redundant. Getting an education in cyberspace could be worked into any one person's individual career such that fewer people would devote one to four years of their life to moving somewhere else "to go to school." Their schooling could come to them over the net. Hence, a Thatcher-style rationalization of campuses could occur on a subnational, national or international scale. The potential for new inequalities in access, dependencies on monopoly providers, or oligopolistic domination of cyberschooling services is considerable.

Third, who will set prices, fees, costs at cyberschool? Does this educational innovation simply represent the intervention of commodity-production logics into education, obliterating one of the last bastions of feudalistic in-kind production and consumption systems with a cash-on-the-barrelhead logic? Will more private businesses start producing education in netcentric markets, like a Microsoft University, a Compuserve Academy, or America On Line College, displacing the authority now held by nonprofit institutions, governments and professional educators? One can see cyberschooling as the operational means whereby transnational flexible specialization could invade the institutionalized disciplines at universities as they have infiltrated many factory environments over the past twenty years. Virtualizing universities may well mean that many disciplines will be eradicated; and, in turn, jobs will be lost, underemployment will rise, the scholarly community will be disrupted and academic life will, in general, suffer significantly. New quasi-imperial inequalities of access and exchange could emerge if early innovators close out second-wave providers, especially if some public contact institutions were closed down to "save money." Who then defines, owns, uses or profits from education: Will it be teachers, students, networks, businesses, governments or some subset of them all?

Obviously, these post/trans/antidisciplinary changes raise even bigger issues of identity, community and nationality for cultural studies. Schooling is intimately entwined with defining who a person is politically, what a community is culturally and where a nation is socially. A netcentric world is a nation-decentered world in which intensely-felt community ties can and will form around interests articulated at web sites rather than geographic sites. Will CyberNewZealand exist, and can it compete with CyberJapan, CyberAmerica, or CyberBritain? "Who is us?" becomes a major question of personal/group identity in a world where webcrawling may begin to displace nationalistic civil rituals as a means of self-understanding. Certainly, the anglocentricity of operating systems, the technoscientifics of network and the hardware constraints of access all guarantee that many of today's existing systems of privilege and prejudice will continue to be found in these cyberspaces. But will they work in the same ways through the same spaces? The prospect for new cultural imperialisms, but now all the way down to the level of wired/wireless telecom networks, operating system chauvinisms or information service disutilities, crops up immediately for anyone advocating the proliferation of cyberschooling options.

Cyberschools may work well, but as they work one may see them exerting new corrosive pressures on prevailing systems of political community, economic autonomy and cultural identity (Luke 1989). Such issues may not seem apparent to cultural studies at first glance, but a thorough-going evaluation of their possibilities soon must face these implications for training political subjects anywhere anytime anyway in a netcentric world. As the cyberporn shutdown of Compuserve in Germany illustrates, does Cyber-NewZealand want CyberNewZealanders cybersurfing around elsewhere, and how will it control or code what they do, see or hear when they are speeding through foreign-based servers? Likewise, who does CyberNewZealand want interviewing cyberspatially in its domains, and how will imagine-learned disciplines train its own citizens to cope with such informatic co-operators or hyperreal coaccelerants within this cybernation?

CONCLUSIONS

To conclude, the key educational issue for cyberschooling arguably will be how it actually valorizes instruction on such virtual campuses. Will it lower or raise the value of the education being provided? "Managed care" innovations in many health care systems in the United States basically cash out by rewarding doctors for *not providing medical treatment*. Cyberschool experiments should not be structured to reward professors *for not teaching students*. Unless and until cyberschool instruction enhances and enriches the education we now provide, it will be counterproductive to advance in these directions. Netcentric instruction systems will be seen by faculty and students, on the one hand, as techniques for degrading and displacing academic labor as well as, on the other hand, maneuvers leading to the degradation of degree credentials and the displacement of academic status.

Cyberschools need not provide a devalued product, but it is clear how virtual instruction can be designed to greatly increase faculty workloads, decrease student interactions, shortchange certain disciplines, overemphasize particular skills, scatter institutional resources and reduce the value of academic services. In turn, many people—both inside and outside of the university—should see this set of outcomes as disastrous rather than as economical. Whether or not it is either the insidious planned intention of cost control–conscious state authorities or the inevitable unfortunate outcome of misapplied correspondence principles, proponents of cyberschooling must guard against this destructive downside in all of their initiatives.

Will cyberschooling save money? Most experience thus far suggests that they probably will not. In fact, unless cyberschooling is turned into another broadcast medium, these educational environments appear to cost much more money inasmuch as they are supplements to what now exists. Where once the university only invested in buildings, faculty and various supplies to teach students, it must continue to spend money in this fashion for its streams of "contact" instruction plus pay now to build and maintain infostructures. Moreover, keeping on the cutting edge of this technology will mean reequipping faculty with new PCs every three to four years, installing more bandwidth to carry more traffic and hiring additional support staff to simply maintain everything in good working order. At best, it might save some money for students and their families because learners need not "move away" to "somewhere else" in order to "get educated." But, for the most part, the answer now is fairly clear: "No!" Cyberschooling does *not* save money, although it allows us to develop new post/trans/antidisciplinary learning communities, tap into now unserved student markets and teach very differently by going on-line.

Will cyberschool prepare students for an Information Age society? My sense here is again mostly no, but then, ironically, maybe yes. After all, what is an Information Age society? Is it secure employment in virtual factories and firms via telecommuting? Is it perpetual underemployment for workers subcontracting out to flexibly specialized hollow corporations as "permanent temporaries? Is it coping with unemployment in low-wage, low-skill jobs centered upon data entry, word processing, boilerplate code writing? Obviously, it can be all of these alternatives, depending on what are one's nationality, race, class, gender, age or income (Luke 1994). Cyberschool may prepare students for coping with the culture of such environments, but there will undoubtedly be a good deal of slack in the correspondence principle as the gap between what "the real world" really is and what "the school" actually can be probably will remain as large as it is now. At the same time, cyberschools may mimic the inequalities of Information Age societies as they train the informationally competent elite, which makes up "the symbolic analysts" or "successful fifth" of any informational system, how to manage the affairs of the "failed four-fifths" or informationally obsolete who get left behind (Reich 1991). In fact, all cyberschoolers may even get some serious exposure to the new material inequalities of an informational order—slow operating systems, restricted bandwidth, limited memory, narrow net access, inaccessible data bases, crude web sites.

Consequently, if more cyberschools are to be built, then they should be designed by their users as an open-ended transdisciplinary experiment to change (but not increase) faculty workloads, to enhance (but not decrease) student interactions, to equalize (but not shortchange) the resources, prestige and value of all disciplines, to balance (and not overemphasize) the transmittal of certain vital skills, to concentrate (and not scatter) the investment of institutional resources and to strengthen (and not reduce) the value of all academic services. New technologies, like those used in cyberschooling, do not have only one or two univalent structural possibilities locked up within them, awaiting their right use or wrong misuse. Cultural studies would show that they have multiple polyvalent potentials, which are structured by the existing social relations guiding their control and application. We can construct a cyberschool's virtual spaces and classrooms so that they will help actualize a truly valuable (and innovative) new type of higher education, which escapes the limits of traditional disciplinary education, while not obliterating what has been valuable in disciplinary forms of learning. Yet this can happen only if some key initial intradisciplinary decisions steer cyberschooling down operational post/trans/antidisciplinary paths that are truly service-enhancing instead of plainly service-degrading as we all struggle to apply and interpret the ironic outcomes of the correspondence principle in this neo-liberal era of global cost control.

REFERENCES

Harvey, David. (1989) *The Condition of Postmodernity*. Oxford: Blackwell.

Jameson, Fredric. (1992) *Postmodernity, or the Cultural Logic of Late Capitalism*. Durham NC: Duke University Press.

Latour, Bruno. (1993) *We Have Never Been Modern*. London: Harvester Wheatsheaf.

Luke, Timothy W. (1989) *Screens of Power: Ideology, Domination, and Resistance in Informational Society*. Urbana: University of Illinois Press.

———. (1994) "Placing Power/Siting Space: The Politics of Global and Local in the New World Order." *Environment and Planning D: Society and Space*, 12: 613–628.

Lyotard, Jean-François. (1984) *The Postmodern Condition: A Report on Knowledge*, trans. G. Bennington and B. Massumi. Minneapolis: University of Minnesota Press.

Poster, Mark. (1995) *The Second Media Age*. Oxford: Blackwell.

Readings, Bill. (1993) "For a Heteronomous Cultural Politics: The University, Culture, and the State." *The Oxford Literary Review*, 15: 163–200.

Reich, Robert B. (1991) *The Work of Nations: Preparing Ourselves for 21st Century Capitalism*. New York: Knopf.

Soja, Edward. (1989) *Postmodern Geographies*. London: Verso.

Chapter 4

Fragmented Visions: Excavating the Future of Area Studies in a Post-American World

RAVI ARVIND PALAT

There are many maps of one place, and many histories of one time.
—Julie Fredrickse, *None But Ourselves*

Though the institutionalization of "area studies" in professional associations, scholarly journals and academic programs since the end of the Second World War has had a transformative impact on comparative studies of societies and histories outside the privileged arena of Europe and North America, there has been little, if any, questioning of its conceptual underpinnings and continuing relevance as we stand at the threshold of the twenty-first century.[1] Even the occasional survey of particular areas of study habitually seeks only to identify topics that are underrepresented in order to target these fields for future growth, or to plead for greater resources claiming the actual or potential strategic significance of a particular segment of the globe. The most penetrating of such surveys have merely bemoaned the lack of inclusion of the findings of area specialists in the received canon of disciplinary departments—especially in economics (Amsden 1992; Johnson 1988)—or the decline in linguistic competence among contemporary practitioners when compared to pioneer scholars (Anderson 1992). None have questioned, or even examined, the continuing relevance of the segmentation of the globe enshrined in the various programs of area studies in the context of the enormous sociopolitical and economic changes of the last decade. Moreover, given the geographical focus and disciplinary orientation of most practitioners, it is hardly surprising that the only surveys of the development of area studies as an academic enterprise over the last four decades have been those commissioned by private foundations and the U.S. Departments of Defense and Education.² The very terms of reference of these reports, and their methods of investigation, precluded an examination of the intellectual foundations of area studies programs. Hence, apart from making pious declarations on the need for greater global awareness, they are silent on the *type* of awareness that is required as we stand at the cusp of the twenty-first century.

If it is true that every piece of knowledge, every work of human creation, is heavily tinged by the conditions of its production, then a refusal to submit the intellectual enterprise represented by the area studies project to the protocols of a rigorous scrutiny is doubly egregious since its constitution as a field of study was directly related to the rise of the United States to a hegemonic position in the capitalist world economy in the aftermath of the Second World War. Originating in specialized military training programs devised to train soldiers and civilians assigned to administer occupied territories in Europe and the "Far East,"³ area studies was constituted as a field of inquiry on the U.S. ascension to a position of global hegemony.⁴

Born in the throes of the most widespread and destructive war ever known to this planet, area studies is, I shall argue, thoroughly impregnated with the geopolitical conditions of its conception. My concern here is neither with a depiction of the nature of U.S. hegemony, nor with a detailed inventory of the evolution of programs of area studies in the last forty-odd years, though I will have occasion to touch on aspects of both these issues. Rather, my focus is on how the geopolitical imperatives of U.S. hegemony conditioned the institutional underpinnings and substantive content of area studies programs. I seek, in particular, to excavate the unexamined intellectual assumptions underlying these programs and to assess their validity.

In this endeavor, the first section of this chapter locates the emergence of area studies programs in the context of the bipolar rivalry between the United States and the USSR and the restructuring of the global flows of trade and investments after the Second World War. I argue that these processes involved a shift from colonial control to monopoly control over peripheral raw materials and labor which was reflected in a new geopolitical segmentation of the globe, and to a consequent redefinition of the units of analyses, institutionalized in universities as area studies programs. Moreover, though these programs were envisaged as multidisciplinary assemblages of scholars to study broad geocultural areas—"to breed a new kind of academic amphibian," as an enthusiastic proponent once put it, "the scholar whose habitat is in one medium but who is fully at home in another" (Gibb 1963: 14)—the mode of their insertion within universities has meant that despite pretensions to catholicity, area studies scholarship has tended towards microlevel analyses. Hence, though area studies scholarship has considerably increased the pool of empirical information on the peoples of Africa, Asia, Latin America, the Middle East and the Pacific, it has not contributed to an assimilation of their distinct historical experiences and contemporary realities into our theoretical categories, which continue to remain mired in their narrow Euro–North American referential bases.

The unraveling of the geopolitical ecology of U.S. hegemony—due to an increase in competitive pressures in the core with the reconstruction of the economies of Western Europe and Japan, the exhaustion of import-substituting industrialization policies in most low- and middle-income states and the structural crises of centrally-planned economies—undermined the partitioning of the globe on which area studies programs had been based. Consequently, the second section of this chapter examines the implications of the continued segregation of programs of area studies from studies of "postindustrial," postmodern economies in an era when material and cultural production have become increasingly globalized. It is argued that, despite the explicit repudiation of post-European Enlightenment rationality by several new academic specializations, they continue to perpetuate and reinforce the series of binary oppositions between an essentialized and totalized West and its equally essentialized and totalized other(s).

If the units of analysis in comparative studies are framed by the structures of hegemonic control over peripheral material and human resources—colonial control during the era of British hegemony, monopoly control during US hegemony, transnational control in the contemporary period of capitalist restructuring—the final section of this chapter suggests that the onset of an era of transnational integration of networks of finance, production and trade makes a reformulation of our inherited categories of analysis imperative. In particular such a reformulation must seek to integrate the distinctive experiences of non-Western peoples into the conceptual frameworks of the humanities and the social sciences, rather than blithely assume that Euro–North American patterns of capitalist development and state formation will be diffused across the globe. This implies a fundamental excavation of the theoretical categories framing the various disciplines and hence entails the forging and deployment of procedures of conceptualization that are resolutely *antidisciplinary* in orientation.

Despite scattered references to area studies in other parts of the world, and to the work of scholars from a variety of "areas," the focus of this chapter will be on the institutionalization of area studies in universities in the United States. While it is true that the development of area studies elsewhere—particularly in the former European colonial powers—was not identical to the U.S. pattern, a reorganization of the academic universe denoted by the institutionalization of area studies in the hegemonic power has had a profound impact everywhere. This is primarily because, as we shall see, the contemporary partitioning of the globe into several distinct areas was a consequence of the reconstitution of the world market under the leadership of the United States. The acceptance of these divisions as adequate units for analysis, debate and research has had an inordinate influence on the study of non-Western societies even in those states with a long tradition of such scholarship. Finally, as the organization of knowledge in Western universities has been replicated in institutions of higher learning elsewhere on the planet, the ethnocentric biases inherent in the basic organizing principles of the Western academy has had, and continues to have, a pervasive influence.

IMAGINATIVE GEOGRAPHIES OF U.S. HEGEMONY

> Prophesy now involves a geographical rather than historical projection; it is space not time that hides consequences from us.
>   —John Berger, *The Look of Things*

The end of the Second World War marked a radical shift in the global balance of power. The devastation of the industrial economies of Western Europe and Japan had made the United States unquestionably the first industrial power on earth; the occupation of Eastern Europe by the Red Army signaled the rise of the Soviet Union as a world power and foreshadowed the Cold War; the initial Japanese defeat of colonial forces in Asia had stoked fires of national and liberation movements all across Africa and Asia that European colonizing powers were increasingly unable to restrain. These geopolitical conditions—particularly the haunting fiction of the spread of communism on a world scale—provided the substantive and ideological justifications for a reconstitution of the capitalist world market under U.S. hegemony (Wallerstein 1992).

A key element in the U.S. strategy to reintegrate the world market under its auspices was the restructuring of global flows of trade and investment (see Arrighi 1982, 1990, 1994; Palat 1993a, 1996). The exponential increase in the productive capacities and technological capabilities of U.S. industries during the war had created a demand for new sources of minerals and other industrial raw materials. Simultaneously, as peripheral exports of raw materials to the United States grew at a lower rate than imports of manufactured goods from the hegemonic power, it created inflationary pressures and thereby threatened U.S. industrial expansion. These pressures could only be resolved by expanding U.S. access to peripheral resources at a pace greater than the rate at which markets for its industrial products was growing. However, the acquisition of peripheral resources was constrained by colonial structures of control—restrictions on trade, patterns of land tenure, metropolitan state ownership of mineral rights, control over foreign exchange, regulations on investment, etc. The United States was successfully able to break down these barriers by threatening to withhold reconstruction assistance to European colonial powers, and by manipulating the nationalist aspirations of peripheral states, eager for foreign investment (Bunker and O'Hearn 1993). In contrast to the era of British hegemony, when core capitalists had sought access to peripheral raw materials through colonial controls, access to these materials was now being increasingly sought through monopoly control—patents, exclusive contracts between resource-rich peripheral states and large, vertically-integrated corporations domiciled in the core. On the other side of the ideological divide, the establishment of Soviet dominance over Eastern Europe led to a parallel, though more spatially circumscribed, reconstitution of relational networks orchestrated by Moscow. The consequent reorientation in the flows of trade and investments remapped the political geography of the world.

The origins of area studies as a field of academic inquiry can be traced to this vast expansion in the scale and scope of the activities of the U.S. state and business corporations and the outbreak of the Cold War.[5] As the acute dearth of expertise on the peoples and institutions of most parts of the world had been made painfully evident during the Second World War, a series of reports commissioned by learned societies to study the wartime programs[6]— most notably the Committee on World Area Research set up by the Social Science Research Council (Hall 1947) and the Commission on Implications of Armed Services Educational Programs of the American Council of Education (Fenton 1947)—advocated the creation of multidisciplinary assemblages of scholars specializing on specific geocultural regions to provide accurate information useful to policymakers. Corporate interests were particularly involved in this project, and private foundations were the main underwriters of area studies programs in universities until 1958, when the U.S. federal government, shaken by the Soviet launch of the Sputnik, assumed primary responsibility.[7]

While this project promised to transcend the disciplinary partitioning of knowledge and to provide an integrated and holistic perspective on the peoples and institutions of the world, its integral link with the foreign policy objectives of the hegemonic power, and the rise of contract research, pervades every aspect of area studies as currently constituted. It infects, violates and contaminates all area studies scholarship, not only in the social sciences, but also in the humanities; not only economics and political science, but also the performing arts and philosophy. Most importantly, U.S. hegemony impresses upon, and pervades, all area studies scholarship by redefining the units of analysis, and then by reifying them. By thus projecting the strategic geopolitical ecology of the immediate postwar period into the past, I shall argue, it distorts our comprehension of long historical processes, and inhibits our projections of future possibilities.

Respatializing Comparative Studies

After forty-odd years of area studies scholarship, we are so accustomed to the segmentation of the globe into several regions—Western Europe, Soviet Union (now the Commonwealth of Independent States, Georgia and the

Baltic republics) and Eastern Europe, the Middle East and North Africa, sub-Saharan Africa, South Asia, Southeast Asia, East Asia, Australasia, the Pacific, North America, Latin and Central America, the Caribbean—that we noddingly accept this divisioning of the world as obvious and natural. When few terms appear as self-evident as these, it is instructive to wonder why "East Asia" and "Southeast Asia" are not called "West Pacific" and "Southwest Pacific" (Emmerson 1984: 4; Issacs 1980). Once we pose such questions, it immediately becomes obvious that the contemporary designations, for all their apparent normality, are historical constructions, that there is nothing natural or self-evident about the segmentation of the globe on which area studies scholarship is based, that it is not the inert physical features of cartography but the activity of human beings that structure regions as coherent units of analysis (Dirlik 1992).

The sheer arbitrariness of the geopolitical segmentation of the globe institutionalized by the development of area studies programs can easily be illustrated by a few examples. The term "Southeast Asia," for instance, gained widespread currency only during the Second World War, when Lord Mountbatten's command of the Allied forces in that theater was designated as such in 1943 (Emmerson 1984: 7). Prior to that time, while it may have been convenient to describe the zone between India and China as "Southeast Asia," it seldom occurred to anyone to view the peoples living between Assam and the Philippines, and between Indonesia and China—professing a number of different faiths, speaking a multiplicity of languages, and administered by several colonial powers—as inhabiting a cohesive geocultural region. Indeed, the fact that there were no roads or communication links connecting Burma, Thailand, Malaya, the Netherlands' East Indies, French Indo-China or the American Philippines should caution us not to assume that locational proximity necessarily engenders the growth of relational linkages between politico-juridical units. Instead, reflecting colonial control over raw materials and peripheral markets, these territories were linked directly to the colonial metropoles or, in the case of Thailand, to the then hegemonic power, the United Kingdom (Dixon 1991: 86–121).[8]

Though forged in war, the current demarcation of Southeast Asia as a distinct region was equally shaped by the strategic concerns of the Cold War and the restructuring of the patterns of trade and investment under U.S. hegemony. U.S. plans to stem the tide of communism in Asia were rooted in an attempt to reconstruct Japan as a second-rank economic power. This policy entailed a reorientation of preexisting patterns of trade and investment since a resource-poor Japan could act as a U.S. surrogate only if assured supplies of raw materials, particularly since its earlier sources—in Manchuria and North Korea—were inaccessible. Thus, using its reconstruction assistance as a leverage against European colonial powers, the United States compelled them to loosen their controls over trade and investment in their remaining colonies in Asia (Cumings 1987: 61–62).

These strategic imperatives led to the extension of the term "Southeast Asia" to French Indo-China and the Philippines which were never part of Mountbatten's command. At the same time, the partitioning of the British Indian Empire into several independent states gave currency to the term "South Asia," which included Sri Lanka, where Mountbatten's headquarters had been located. These changes are reflected not only in the contemporary demarcation of Southeast Asia as a distinct geocultural zone, but also in the change in nomenclature from the "Far East" to "East Asia" and in the subsequent reorganization of the Far Eastern Association as the Association for Asian Studies.

Similarly, the occupation of Eastern Europe by the Red Army and the onset of the Cold War determined the creation of the Soviet Union and Eastern Europe as a region separate from, and opposed to, Western Europe. It was, after all, this redivisioning of Europe that led to the (perhaps temporary) political obsolescence of the designation "Central Europe." Before this extension of the Soviet "sphere of influence," as Milan Kundera (1981: 230) once remarked, Bohemia, Poland and Hungary had historically been a part of Western culture and the fount of some of the greatest "impulses" of "modern culture," including "psychoanalysis, dodecaphony, Bartók's music, Kafka's and Musil's new esthetics of the novel." Likewise, the decolonization of Africa and the "Near East" was paralleled by the creation of the "Middle East and North Africa," and "sub-Saharan Africa" as distinct regions. These geopolitical imperatives also led to the demise of "Central Asia" as a cartographical designation. Only the geopolitical partitioning of the Americas, where the Second World War had not been waged, remained unchanged.

This redivisioning of the world represented a significant reorganization in the study of the peoples and institutions of the globe. Prior to the end of the Second World War—with the exception of some investigations in anthropology, comparative philology and linguistics—comparative studies of non-European peoples tended to be examinations of similarities and contrasts between different colonial structures of control: examining the differences between French and British colonies in Africa, or between the British Indian Empire and the Netherlands' East Indies, or between the British colonies in Africa and India. Significantly, this tradition of scholarship— traces of which still linger on in journals like the *Journal of Imperial and Commonwealth History*—had little correspondence to the contemporary segmentation of the world because it reflected the colonial control over peripheral resources that was superseded by the geopolitical conditions of U.S. hegemony.

The redefinition of the units of analysis under U.S. hegemony also denoted a major change in the substantive nature of studies on the non-Western world since boundaries exclude as much as they include. Since units of analysis determine the framework of research, defining the range of significant relational networks, the arbitrary projection of current regional designations to the past circumscribes the historical imagination and distorts the internal structuring of these areas. It imposes a unity on peoples who were never unified in this way before. At the same time, it fractures the unities of preexisting networks of social relations.

Once we begin to constitute courses on the history of "South Asia" or "Southeast Asia" from the mists of antiquity to the present day, for instance, we begin to posit these entities as enduring realities, when they were in fact creations of the post–World War II era. Relationships falling outside the boundaries of these areas are treated as inessential and inconsequential to the formation and reformation of their internal structuring. At best, there is an acknowledgment of the transmission of religious beliefs, political institutions, writing systems and trade across the Bay of Bengal in the first millennium A.D. Even if the importance of such relationships is recognized, the eastern coasts of India figure only in the background, while the Philippines, which had no similar pattern of linkages, is considered an integral part of Southeast Asian history. By what logic is an area that had a formative influence on the peoples and institutions of the eastern Indian Ocean archipelago considered an inessential aspect of its history, while another area that was marginal at best is considered a constitutive element of the region? Similarly, the separation of "Asian" studies from "Middle Eastern" and "African" studies marginalized the historical and contemporary relationships between the peoples inhabiting these regions.

Triumph of Microperspectives

Even if the areas of study derived from the post–Second World War divisioning of the world are accepted as adequate units of analysis, the enormous diversity of languages within each geocultural zone quickly puts to rest any pretensions to comprehensive scholarship. In fact, quite paradoxically, the creation of area studies programs in universities has accentuated the difficulties of acquiring the linguistic competence and research skills necessary to produce in-depth analyses integrating the various disciplinary competencies and synthesizing trends within broad cultural regions by shifting the locus of work away from the areas of study to metropolitan centers of instruction. Bereft of the institutional support that academics now take for granted, it was inevitable that the bulk of scholarly work on the non-Western world prior to the end of the Second World War be produced by colonial bureaucrats and missionaries.[9] These pioneer scholars were able to produce exemplary works in the absence of large libraries, research assistants and grants, primarily because their lifelong association with particular locales familiarized them with local customs and reflected a mastery of at least the current vernaculars, while their insertion within the colonial enterprise ensured easy access to research materials, native informants and archival sources (Anderson 1992: 25–27).

In contrast, the requirement that scholars spend much of their time teaching and publishing has meant that they no longer command either the linguistic competence or the familiarity with indigenous sources that their predecessors once did. After all, a field trip or a year or two at the beginning of their academic careers collecting material for their dissertations and the odd sabbatical is no substitute to residing in the area of study for the entire course of their professional careers. The consequences of this are nicely captured by Benedict Anderson's interesting observation that although sexual relations between area specialists and peoples from their locales of study have persisted, the implications of these relationships have been reversed from those of the colonial era. Thus, "rather than the scholar-bureaucrat being creolized by these relationships, out there in the colony, it is the spouse or significant other, moved to California or Massachusetts who is likely to be Americanized" (Anderson 1992: 28).

As a result, though the intellectual project that led to the creation of area studies programs promised integrative scholarship on broad cultural regions, the highly diversified linguistic environment and the institutionalization of area studies programs in universities has produced a rapidly accumulating collection of country-specific studies rather than analyses integrating trends spanning jurisdictional frontiers within geocultural regions.

Of course, the trend towards country-specific studies cannot merely be attributed to the institutional structures of metropolitan academies. It was reinforced by the strategies deployed by state bureaucracies and dominant elites in the former European colonies in Africa and Asia to promote national integration.[10] Formal independence inevitably led to a vigorous involvement of the state apparatus in curricular matters, ostensibly to correct the distortions of colonial education, but designed as well to assimilate ethnic minorities by obliterating their distinct identities and to obscure the *comprador* role played by indigenous elites in the colonial enterprise. Thus, attempts to create a national culture and a national history inevitably entailed a series of selections, annotations, displacements and silences to serve the interests of dominant elites.

Yet, in many former European colonies in Africa, Asia and the Middle East, jurisdictional frontiers provided unviable units of analysis since the arbitrary determination of jurisdictional boundaries by colonial powers split ethnic and linguistic groups between different colonial possessions, or between the equally arbitrarily formed internal administrative units within colonies. The familiarity and ready acceptance of jurisdictional entities like "India" and "Nigeria" and their depiction in distinct colors on world maps obscures that their constitution as states involved a violent reorganization of preexisting patternings of social relationships;[11] that maps are, in essence, the very symbols of possession and instruments of plunder (McClintock 1988: 151). Indeed, the etymological derivation of terms associated with cartography—region, province, field—from the vocabulary of aggression should alert us that mapmaking, far from being an inert politically-neutral scientific exercise, is an integral element of colonialism (editors of the journal *Hérodote* in Foucault 1980: 69; see also Mudimbe 1988).

A recognition of this fact neither implies that no social systems existed in these spaces before they were incorporated into the capitalist world economy nor that the agencies of capitalism were free to reshape the global map at will. Rather, it is to insist that while peoples have interacted with one another for millennia, their consciousness of these relationships differed from the nomenclatures that now dominate maps of the world. Indeed, Arthur Whitaker's perceptive observation about the Americas, has equal validity for all areas outside Europe: "The idea that America possessed a unity of any kind . . . was one which, before the arrival of the Europeans had never occurred to anyone in all the agglomeration of atomistic societies that inhabited America from Alaska to the Tierra del Fuego" (quoted in Dirlik 1992: 64). Moreover, even when the continent was named after Amerigo Vespucci, the set of relational networks we currently associate with the term— Canada being the single largest trading partner of the United States, Central and Latin America being insultingly labeled its "backyard," and even the existence of the states of the Americas as currently constituted—did not exist. The thirteen colonies that were to become the nucleus of the United States were more closely connected to England than to the Pacific coasts on the west, and the colonial possessions of Spain and Portugal were more tightly integrated with the European metropoles than with their northern neighbors. The same can clearly be said about Asia—a term unknown to any indigenous language of that quarter of the globe—and Africa, while the limits of the Pacific were only traced by Europeans and their transplants in the Americas (see Dirlik 1992; Spate 1979). Finally, even a cursory glance at historical maps will reveal that the boundaries of the various empires of China fluctuated widely.

The trend towards compartmentalized, microlevel studies rather than country-specific analysis was reinforced by the diversity of source material within multilingual and multiethnic states. These sources ranged from oral traditions and lithic inscriptions to palm-leaf manuscripts and printed texts which were organized by categories, orders of concepts and discourses rooted in a multiplicity of indigenous systems of knowledge (see Dirks 1987; Errington 1989; Vansina 1961). Since the acquisition of the skills required to recover the cultural contexts that invested specific symbols, classes of events and particular juxtapositions of episodes with meaning in multilingual, multiethnic states varied widely according to the linguistic and ethnic configurations of each locality, studies were largely of particular localities rather than of the country as a whole—studies of the Punjab or Bengal rather than of India, or of Bali or Java rather than of Indonesia. In the absence of a broad theoretical framework synthesizing the various microlevel investigations, these analyses either tended to inappropriately generalize their findings on a statewide or areawide scale, or to emphasize the unique particularities of their region of expertise to the detriment of a broader comparative framework (Munck 1993: 481).

In this context, the arbitrary encapsulation of each geocultural area of study as a closed, self-validating arena of research and debate has meant that area studies specialists are largely unaffected by the disputes and theoretical approaches employed by scholars investigating similar themes in other segments of the world, apart from occasional one-off references. This is particularly true of Asian studies scholarship. Though other programs of area studies frequently divide their region of study into smaller segments—"anglophone" and "francophone" states in Africa and in the Caribbean, or the "southern cone" and the Andean regions of Latin America, for instance—the marginalization, decimation and sometimes even the total annihilation of indigenous peoples (particularly in Australasia and the Americas) has meant that records, at least since European contact, are almost exclusively maintained in a handful of metropolitan languages.[12] Similarly, though the Levant and northern Africa have had a long history of contact with the peoples of the northern Mediterranean, the spread of Islam and its universal language, Arabic, as well as the political hegemony long exercised by the Ottoman empire has contributed to create a relatively unified research environment for studies on the Middle East. In all these cases, the relative homogeneity of a linguistic environment for research has promoted a certain degree of genuinely comparative approaches, as witnessed for instance by the influence of the *dependencia* tradition or the bureaucratic-authoritarian model in Latin American studies. Whatever errors of archaeology-like misconstructions these paradigms may contain, they have nevertheless stimulated widespread debate and discussion and have left an indelible imprint on country-specific analyses conducted within the rubric of area studies scholarship on these regions.

That no similar paradigm pervades Asian studies scholarship, that it remains a constellation of country-specific and microregional studies isolated in relatively impermeable, compartmentalized bodies of research and debate, is a function of the significant historical differences in the encounters between the peoples of Europe and Asia. Even more than Islam, Asia was constitutively constructed as Europe's "other"—its chief cultural contestant, its exemplar in the arts, sciences and even in practical craftsmanship. Even after the reversal of the positional superiority between Asian and European states between the mid-eighteenth and the mid-nineteenth centuries, there could be no question of marginalizing, decimating or exterminating the peoples of Asia. The very magnitude of populations in that cartographic space ensured that the European presence would be confined to a few insertions along the coasts and at administrative seats. These factors entailed a qualitatively different research environment—the diversity of source materials and languages, value systems and artistic styles, all contributed to an almost exclusive concentration on country-specific or microregional studies, loosely grouped together by the geopolitical divisions of the post–Second World War era (e.g., China, Japan, Southeast Asia, etc.). As a result, they have remained stubbornly resistant to a variety of theoretical approaches that have fundamentally transformed the study of, say, Latin America or sub-Saharan Africa, over the last few decades. This is perhaps best illustrated by noting that though the work of the subaltern studies group, influential in modern Indian history, share convergences, similarities and parallels with the work of scholars investigating "everyday forms of resistance" in Southeast Asia, there has been little or no cross-fertilization of ideas, concepts and research strategies between the two schools.

Imperialism of Departments

If the diversity of languages, ethnic groups, value systems and sociohistorical conditions in the broad geocultural divisions of the post–Second World War era frustrated the promise of integrated macroregional investigations, the institutionalization of area studies programs in universities has also meant that the promise of an integrated, multidisciplinary perspective, a new synthesis of knowledge, on the peoples of the various segments of the globe has remained largely unfulfilled, as William Nelson Fenton foresaw in his prescient 1947 report. Such programs faced fierce resistance from the "imperialism of departments" since they challenged the fragmentation of the human sciences by disciplinary departments, each endowed with a particular methodology and a specific intellectual subject matter (Fenton 1947: 26, 81). Responding to this departmental imperialism, university administrations ensured that most area studies programs had a weak institutional base and that most, if not all, of their faculty depended on disciplinary departments for tenure and promotion. As a result, in contrast to pioneer scholars who ranged freely across several fields of study, most "areaists" (to use Fenton's felicitous term) work within disciplinary boundaries, and interdisciplinarity in area studies merely denotes the marriage of a modicum of linguistic competence with the policy sciences (Said 1985: 106–107, 290).

In a sense, the continued fragmentation of knowledge by arbitrary departmental and jurisdictional boundaries admirably suited the interests of the two communities of scholars involved: disciplinary and area studies specialists. This arrangement absolved disciplinary specialists from the responsibility of testing their theories against the experiences of the vast majority of humanity, and of familiarizing themselves with the work of their colleagues in cognate academic specialties. Disciplinary specialists also tended to believe that their colleagues in area studies programs were not equipped to provide insights relevant for the nomothetic social sciences as they spent inordinate amounts of time in particularistic investigations which detract them from the study of "theory." This abrupt refusal to attend to the findings of area studies scholarship has thwarted attempts to develop a genuinely comparative approach (Pletsch 1981: 582–583, 586). Mainstream economists, politicians and journalists, for instance, routinely ignore detailed investigations of the Japanese, South Korean and Taiwanese economies which reveal the central role of the bureaucratic apparatus in their strategies for upward mobility in the global divisioning of labor (e.g., Amsden 1989; Johnson 1982; Wade 1990) and attribute the remarkable rates of growth registered by these states over the last few decades to their firm adherence to laissez-faire policies. Similarly, those who attribute the problems of political integration/fragmentation in contemporary Africa to the tenacious resilience of primordial tribal allegiances ignore the findings of historians that the "tribal concept was in fact an expression of the first stage of amalgamation resulting from colonial rule" (Oliver 1991: 185).[13]

Conversely, "areaists" faced with the awesome task of learning a difficult language and alien culture were absolved from simultaneously mastering a vast theoretical literature (Hough 1977: 2; Pletsch 1981: 587).[14] The strong idiographic thrust of these programs is evident in a basic postulate shared by most practitioners: linguistic homogeneity creates an enduring field of analysis, immune to geopolitical and epistemological shifts. Or as Pierre Ryckmans (Simon Leys) was to assert in a hostile response to Edward Said's *Orientalism*:

The sinological field is defined linguistically. . . . [N]o specialist, whatever his area of expertise, can expect to contribute significantly to our knowledge of China without first mastering the Chinese literary language. In order to be able to read classical and modern Chinese, it is necessary to undergo a fairly long and demanding training that can seldom be combined with the acquisition and cultivation of another discipline. For this reason, sinology is bound to survive in fact, if not necessarily in name, as one global multidisciplinary humanistic undertaking, solely based upon a specific language prerequisite. (1984: 20)

The insularity which flows from such a conceptualization ensures that most "areaists" are unaffected by the theoretical and epistemological debates being conducted in the disciplines. This is amply evident from another hostile response to Said—this time from David Kopf who, in accusing Said of "distorting historical reality" and of shirking from "the hard work of discovering and ordering the data of past human experience," goes on to state his own epistemological premise: "that a primary responsibility of the historian is to allow the past to speak for itself" (1980: 499). That the premier U.S. journal on Asian studies could even publish a piece based on so anachronistic a premise—one that ignores practically *all* the important theoretical work done in this century, from Marc Bloch and Fernand Braudel to Thomas Kuhn and Michel Foucault—is testimony enough to the wide chasm that separates "areaists" from their colleagues in the disciplinary departments.

Consequently, despite an exponential increase in information about non-Western peoples, the persistent fragmentation of knowledge into discrete disciplinary tributaries has continued to exoticize the peoples of the various geocultural regions of the globe. The emphatic idiographic nature of area studies programs has permitted a reductionism of the "cultures and civilizations" of the inhabitants of these regions—particularly of Africa, Asia and the Middle East—to a few simplistic axioms which, with what Said (1985: 176) terms "the restorative citation of antecedent authority," has acquired the status of unquestionable truth. Thus, Confucianism is said to represent the "essence" of Chinese culture, the caste system the essence of Indian culture, tribalism the essence of African culture, etc. This reductionism, biased towards patriarchy and the elites, has no vocabulary to encompass the vibrant belief systems of women, subordinate social groups and ethnic minorities. Heterodox challenges to the orthodoxy in each geocultural area are simply dismissed as unruly, discontented, noisy voices, not meriting the attention of metropolitan scholars.

This reductionism of the cultures of non-Western peoples to a few simple axioms, was reinforced by the institutionalization of comparative studies of the peoples and institutions of the world in area studies programs, set off against each other in hermetically quarantined politico-jurisdictional and disciplinary compartments. Whereas most disciplinary specialists in America and Europe are acquainted with another metropolitan language besides their own, few among them know a single non-European language. Additionally, the very frequency of translations back and forth between European languages ensures that even those with a limited command of languages other than their own are at least familiar with the broad patterns of sociohistorical conditions in the West. Conversely, though most scholars working in Asia and Africa are comfortable in at least one European language, only a few would know another non-European language besides his or her own; and translations to and from these languages are extremely limited and woefully inadequate (Ahmad 1992: 97). In the absence of a complex grid of scholarly exchanges—translations, comparative analyses, collaborative research—the enclosed, self-referential character of area studies has reinforced Japanese, Zulu, Islamic, Tamil and other exceptionalisms rather than produced a unified and coherent body of knowledge about each presumed geocultural macroregion.

In these conditions, comparative historical studies tend to compare and contrast developments in a particular segment or subsegment of the globe with the Western European experience—examining the causes for the periodic withering away of the emerging "sprouts of capitalism" in China (Balazs 1960; Grove and Esherick 1980), or the "potentialities of capitalistic development in Mughal India" (Habib 1969), or whether there was an "Indian feudalism" (Mukhia 1981). All these exercises implicitly or explicitly accept the Western European pattern of sociohistorical transformation as the norm, against which the "Chinese" or "Indian" experiences are cast as deformed, travestied and imperfect models, failing to evolve autonomously towards the universal goal of capitalist development due to a variety of structural impediments. By generalizing a model of long-term, large-scale social change derived from the particular experience of northwestern Europe, these studies are unable either to perceive the possibility of alternate trajectories of historical transformation or to recover the specific sociohistorical dynamics of different historical social systems before capitalism englobed the world. Or as Francesca Bray persuasively argues: "if the dynamics of change differ from those we have identified as operating in European history, then it is not surprising that our traditional models fail adequately to interpret change in non-European societies, or even acknowledge its existence" (1983: 4).

Since reigning procedures of comparative inquiry do not involve an examination of the patterns of sociohistorical evolution in different parts of the globe—of social systems in peninsular India and southern China, or patterns of urbanization in the "Middle East" and the Indo-Gangetic plain—without reference to the West European experience, they inhibit our comprehension of long-term, large-scale processes of change, both within these antiseptically sealed compartments, and of Europe and North America as well.

Perhaps the best indication that the creation of area studies programs has not resulted in a new synthesis of knowledge transcending the partitioning of intellectual labor by disciplinary enclosures, has not led to a truly holistic and interdisciplinary project,[15] is that despite four generations of scholars having received training in area studies, the content of such programs remain embarrassingly fluid. This is most tellingly illustrated in the curricula of area studies programs that have *never* sought to validate, theoretically or methodologically, their field of study—justifications for the creation of new academic programs in area studies, or for enhanced funding of existing ones, being typically couched in terms of their potential utility for the formulation of policies (see Gourevitch 1989: 9). Indeed, the very claim to comprehensive study of large geocultural areas inherently precludes the development of a common set of methodological tools or theoretical perspectives. After all, what do students of Sanskrit poetry, fifteeenth-century Khmer statecraft and the impact of economic liberalization in contemporary Guangdong province share in common except an interest in the same cartographic sector of the globe?

Contract Research and the Link with Policy Objectives

Since area studies programs were constituted to provide information on the peoples and institutions of the world useful to corporate managers and political leaders, the overriding importance of the link between scholarship and policy concerns pervades every aspect of area studies as currently constituted. As a result, unlike pioneer scholars who had primarily been concerned with precolonial history, epigraphy, archaeology and philology, in keeping with the strategic political and economic interests of the United States, area studies research has been concentrated in the fields of modern history and contemporary political, social and economic conditions.[16]

The structural dependence of area studies programs on corporate foundations, and increasingly on the U.S. federal government, for funding transformed the study of non-Western peoples in two additional respects. First, the rise of contract research in the social sciences has meant that the level of funding for each segment of the globe is determined by its perceived strategic or potential importance for the United States. Consequently, the distribution of resources between areas of study were allocated unevenly and tended to vary enormously over time, reflecting changing geopolitical imperatives. In the field of Asian studies, for instance, reflecting the Cold War opposition between a "democratic" India and a "communist" China, there was a disproportionate allocation of resources to the study of these two Asian giants in the fifties and sixties. The increasing involvement of the U.S. in the Vietnam war spurred an equally dramatic rise in the allocation of funds for Southeast Asian studies. However, the U.S. withdrawal from Vietnam and the onset of detente, as well as the sluggish rates of growth registered by the Indian economy, has led to a precipitous decline in resource allocations to these regions. Simultaneously, the economic resurgence of Japan and the "four dragons" (Hong Kong, Singapore, South Korea and Taiwan) has witnessed an equally disproportionate allocation of resources to the study of states strung along the Pacific perimeters of Asia since the late seventies and early eighties. Similarly, though the implementation of market reforms and the possibility of tapping the enormous markets of the People's Republic of China has ensured continued high levels of funding for Chinese studies, detente and a thawing of the Cold War has resulted in a rapidly falling interest in sovietology.[17]

The intimate relationship between policy considerations and area studies scholarship has also had a more invidious ideological influence, though an examination of this second characteristic must necessarily remain more speculative given the impossibility of any one scholar examining the burgeoning corpus of work conducted under the rubric of area studies in its entirety. On the one hand, where large domestic constituencies deeply concerned with the implications of U.S. foreign policy exist, a tradition of scholarship has emerged that is strongly critical of American policy objectives and has sometimes successfully challenged its orientations and the foreign policy establishment's definitions of "national interest." Thus, for instance, the civil rights movement and the struggle against apartheid contributed to a radicalization of African studies and to the imposition of sanctions against South Africa, while the increasing presence of migrants and refugees from—and their compelling testimony regarding oppression in—Central and Latin America eventually forced the U.S. government to withdraw support from its client-dictators like Anastasio Samoza and Augusto Pinochet. On the other hand, where no similar constituency exists, a critical tradition of scholarship has rarely emerged. This is true, not only of South Asian Studies, but of studies on the Soviet Union as well. Indeed, as Michael Burawoy (1992: 774) has recently noted, "Western Marxists . . . were often much more critical of state socialism than Sovietologists." Equally significantly, despite the ascendance of Japan as an economic powerhouse, a radical critique of the Japanese state and society is conspicuous only by its absence within mainstream currents of area studies scholarship.

In short, the creation of area studies programs was a reflection of the changed patterning of relational networks caused by the reintegration of the world market under the leadership of the United States in the context of the Cold War. Since the resultant configuration of economic and political linkages was profoundly different from those prevalent during the epoch of British hegemony, area studies programs were envisaged to provide a broad, catholic perspective on the peoples and institutions of the world organized by the segmentation of the post–World War II globe. However, in the context of a highly diversified linguistic and research environment, rather than the promised integrative analyses of broad geocultural regions, area studies scholarship has produced a rapidly accumulating collection of narrow, localized studies. At the same time, since the institutionalization of these programs in universities did not challenge the disciplinary partitioning of intellectual subject matter, they perpetuated the fragmentation of knowledge within departmental enclosures. Finally, the policy-driven allocation of resources between the different areas of study has meant that serious imbalances—in intellectual foci and ideological orientation—exist among the various areas of study.

And yet, despite its failure to deliver the promised multidisciplinarity, despite the flawed intellectual assumptions informing it, despite its failure to understand the Euro–North American "other," area studies is not simply a monument of lies. It reflects the very real reorientation of commodity trade, investment flows and labor migrations forged during the period of U.S. hegemony in the context of the Cold War—the creation of new core-periphery relations in previously incorporated zones of the world, in Pacific-Asia, in southern Africa, in the Soviet Union and Eastern Europe, in Western Europe.[18] For a hegemonic power with extremely limited prior experiences of relationships with peoples outside its own hemisphere and Europe, the pronounced idiographic thrust of these programs served cognitively to map constellations of local pressure groups, factional alliances and animosities, and cultural sensitivities in strategically important arenas. The importance of this delineation of the diverse patternings of economic arrangements, political institutions and value systems in the several regions of the planet can hardly be overestimated as they, at least theoretically, enabled policy-makers to deploy their resources more optimally by adopting strategies adapted to local conditions to better manipulate peripheral elites to further the objectives of the United States in an era of bipolar rivalry.

However, as I shall endeavor to show in the next section, these relational linkages have been rendered anachronistic with the transnational integration of production and the consequent decline in the regulative capacities of states. Additionally, while the abysmal state of education in most colonies—with educational institutions designed primarily to train clerks, apothecaries and subordinate staff required for the colonial enterprise, and their curriculum rarely reflecting social realities within the colonies—provided a certain rationale for area studies as a corrective measure, this has been undermined with the creation of impressive educational infrastructures in many former colonies. The rapid development of an intelligentsia among formerly colonized peoples, as well as their deep immersion in local cultures, their greater familiarity with local languages and their easier access to source materials precisely when metropolitan scholars of Africa, Asia, Latin America and the Middle East are increasingly distanced from their locales of study has radically transformed the terrain of scholarship. In these conditions, the work of indigenous scholars is often superior to that being produced in metropolitan academies, even if they remain trapped by theoretical categories developed for the study of Euro–North American societies. Consequently, the current segmentation of the globe is increasingly unable to provide an understanding of contemporary conditions and future possibilities, and we may plausibly expect that chairs in area studies will progressively become as anachronistic as chairs in colonial studies and imperial history became after the end of the Second World War.

CONCEPTUALIZING A POST-AMERICAN WORLD

As we have seen, area studies programs derived their legitimacy in large part from the reconstitution of the world market under the Bretton Woods system and the bipolar rivalry between the United States and the Soviet Union. The Bretton Woods system had created a mechanism for the international settlement of the balance of payments while preserving the autonomy of each state to maintain a social policy responsive to its particular needs. At the same time, the installation of a "free enterprise" system enabled large U.S. corporations to expand their operations across national borders to exploit wage and cost differentials within different territorial jurisdictions, particularly in the Americas and Western Europe. The collapse of this system due to the reconstruction of West European and Japanese economies and the consequent diminution of the industrial and financial lead of the United States, the growth of a supranational money market which could not be policed by state-centered regulatory mechanisms and the increasing prominence of transnational corporations (TNCs) with the growing fragmentation and dispersal of manufacturing operations has considerably eroded, though not eliminated, the ability of states to set social policy within their jurisdictions.[19] This is evident by the deregulation of economic activities in the core, the "structural adjustments" imposed on severely indebted low- and middle-income states by the International Monetary Fund and the World Bank, and the recent ratification of a wide-ranging agreement on world trade at the conclusion of the Uruguay Round of negotiations. The escalating transnational integration of production in fact required a progressive dismantling of state-centered regulatory mechanisms since the task of coordinating a vast web of manufacturing and service operations spread over an increasing number of jurisdictions made the TNCs extremely vulnerable to political interventions from a variety of actors—ranging from recalcitrant officials to militant trade unions—holding diverse ideologies and responding to a wide array of local pressures (Picciotto 1990: 38).

On the other side of the ideological divide, the exhaustion of an extensive model of economic growth in the Soviet Union, Eastern Europe and the People's Republic of China led to an erosion of the hitherto-impermeable walls between the two competing ideological blocs. In both cases, given the decline of state-centered regulatory mechanisms, the unique characteristics of particular configurations of sociohistorical forces in jurisdictional entities are accorded less significance. This was most visible in the field of Soviet studies where the numbers of students enrolled in Russian language classes in the United States were almost halved during the seventies and were fewer than those studying Latin![20] While other area studies programs—with the notable exception of South Asian studies—did not suffer declines of similar magnitudes, their rates of growth have slowed dramatically.[21]

Though the bipolar rivalry between the two superpowers postponed a recognition of the emergence of a "new world order" till the collapse of the Berlin Wall in 1989, the increasing transnational integration of global networks of production, trade and investment by huge conglomerates, facilitated by the exhaustion of import-substituting industrialization strategies in many low- and middle-income states, has led to an increasing homogenization of the conditions of accumulation. In addition, the availability of vast pools of highly trained, relatively cheap and politically docile labor with the end of "actually existing socialism" in the former Soviet Union, Eastern Europe and China presents the TNCs with an unprecedented opportunity to expand the scale of their operations. Simultaneously, the implementation of a series of innovations—the automation, computerization and robotization of production; the lowering of freight costs through containerization; and the development of satellite communications systems—has freed production from resource constraints to such an extent that there is a virtual denial of the validity of alternate patternings of economic arrangements, political institutions and social relationships—a denial, in short, of the very rationale on which area studies programs were based. Finally, the "footloose" character of contemporary production also implies that areas where the infrastructure has been so devastated that local networks can no longer be reconstituted under the aegis of the TNCs and the coterie of global institutions led by the World Bank—as is the case over large swathes of sub-Saharan Africa, for instance—are being marginalized, simply declared redundant to the processes of capital accumulation and left to sink into chaos as their infrastructures are relentlessly destroyed by internecine warfare.

Old Wine in New Bottles

These fractures in the geopolitical partitioning of the globe on which area studies programs had been based have been accompanied by the creation of new regional designations. Reflecting the high rates of growth registered by economies along the Pacific perimeters of Asia and the eclipse of trans-Atlantic trade by that across the Pacific, the term "Asia-Pacific" is gaining wide currency. The very catholicity of this term and the ease with which we can locate the dynamic economies and plot their complex economic and political relationships on maps endows it with an aura of obviousness. However, its popularity masks a profound redefinition of both "Asia" and the "Pacific": that discussions habitually exclude most of "peasant" Asia (Afghanistan, interior regions of China, India, Myanmar, etc.), as well as Australia, New Zealand, the Pacific islands and all of Central and Latin America (e.g., Borthwick et al. 1992; Drakakis-Smith 1992; Gibney 1992).

Surprisingly, this redrawing of the boundaries of Asia has been fiercely contested, not by states that had previously been included within that designation, but by states in Australasia and in Latin America. Denied their preferential access to markets in the United Kingdom since the seventies, Australia and New Zealand have been compelled to shed their identities as European outposts in the South Pacific and pose as the "white tribes" of Asia due to the changed geopolitical ecology of the contemporary world. Similarly, Latin American countries—even Brazil which fronts the Atlantic—attempting to attract investments from the "miracle" economies of East Asia, are seeking to be included in a "Pacific" region that excludes the islands in its center. Finally, the dissolution of the Soviet Union has prompted calls for the reconstitution of "Central Asia" as a distinct unit of analysis encompassing the breakaway Muslim republics of that once awesome behemoth, particularly since the totalitarian monolithicity ascribed to the former superpower concealed the abysmal ignorance among U.S. scholars and policymakers of a raft of minority nationalities (the Abkhazis, Azeris, Chechens, Kirgizis, Ossetians, Tajiks, etc.) which are becoming increasingly assertive.

These attempts to reconstitute geopolitical units of analysis in the aftermath of the Cold War on the basis of the area studies paradigm ignore the hallmarks of the current phase of capitalist restructuring. The globalization of the circuits of exchange and investment and the fragmentation of production has undermined the regulatory competencies of nation-states to such an extent that states can no longer be taken as self-evident units of analysis. This is indicated by the progressive shift of macroeconomic policymaking to interstate negotiations and the consequent diminution in the political influence of domestic factions and alliances in all states. From these optics, any attempt to create new programs of study based on the contemporary spatialization of sociopolitical and economic relations (as, for instance, on "Asia-Pacific," the European Union, "Central Asia," etc.) would be futile. Linguistic diversity within each of these regional units would once again lead to a proliferation of microlevel studies, while the continued fragmentation of knowledge by disciplinary boundaries ensures that the promise of interdisciplinary studies will remain unfulfilled.

Additionally, in the context of the large-scale diasporic movement of peoples, particularly the tremendous increase of Asian and Hispanic immigrants to the United States after the removal of discriminatory immigration restrictions in 1965,[22] the intellectual segregation of the study of non-Western peoples from the study of ethnic minorities in the West denoted by the institutional separation of area studies from ethnic studies fails to provide an adequate understanding of race relations in the core. This bifurcation, as Kristin Ross notes, tends to promote "a form of American exceptionalism . . . by leading students to conceive of issues like ethnicity, race, or gender, in a merely parochial or local way, as uniquely American experiences" (1993: 675), and serves to disempower them by obscuring connections between their conditions of existence and those of peoples elsewhere on the globe. At the same time, the ghettoization of socially disadvantaged minorities in programs of ethnic studies perpetuates their marginalization within the university. Similarly, the cultures of indigenous peoples are conceptually refrigerated as narratives of authenticity, as repositories "for some more genuine or organic lived experience" (Ross 1993: 673), once again denying them agency and history. In all these cases, the resultant exoticization of non-Western cultures inhibits a study of these experiences as essentially contested, historically contingent processes. Instead, classic texts of the East (the *Analects of Confucius*, the *Bhagavad Gita*, etc.) are accorded a monumental status that severs them from their historical contexts and reifies them as timeless "truths" about the Chinese and the Indians.

Consequently, the cultural legacies of newer groups of migrants to the

United States, especially of Asians, are reified, essentialized and exoticized. Thus, for instance, Confucianism and the caste system are often caricatured as the irreducible essences of the Chinese and the Indians respectively, rather than as cultural resolutions of historical processes of change and conflict, including colonialism. Moreover, the reification and exoticization of these cultural legacies tends to accept the *weltanschauung* of dominant, patriarchal elites and neglects the voices of women, subaltern classes and ethnic and religious minorities in these states. These considerations are particularly significant as the riots following the verdict in the Rodney King case has made the continued framing of race relations within a black/white dichotomy patently untenable (see Gooding-Williams 1993).

While area studies scholars, eddying in self-referential ghettos seek to constitute new programs of study on "Central Asia," and "Asia-Pacific," the inability of these paradigms to explain emerging sociopolitical and economic trends is becoming increasingly apparent to corporate sponsors. An early, if striking, indication of their recognition of the untenability of the partitioning of the globe into several antiseptically sealed compartments is provided by the Andrew W. Mellon Foundation's decision in February 1994 to replace its "support for area studies as they are traditionally defined" with seminar programs

on such themes as nationalism and the shaping of national identities, the resurgence of ethnic and religious rivalries, new varieties of democratization, the role of violence in settling—or exacerbating—disagreements, the spread of mass culture and Western economic values as well as countermovements emphasizing tradition, fundamentalism, and desecularization. (quoted in Heginbotham 1994: 36–37)

This decision indicates that the insularity of area studies programs renders them unable to analyze the consequences of the globalization of networks of material and cultural production just when such information is vital for the policymakers and corporate managers. Precisely when distances are being reduced on a variety of scales—physical distances through the development of satellite communications, containerized transportation and long-haul aircraft, cultural distances through the globalization of American mass culture through satellite television broadcasts and the circulation of audio and video cassettes—the continued acceptance of the post–Second World War geopolitical divisions as autonomous units of analysis precludes the study of the consequences of these phenomena. If the area studies paradigm is increasingly seen to be inadequate to provide politicians and "captains of industry" with the information they require to formulate national policies and investment decisions, can it be any more serviceable for those subject to the punishing rigors of "structural adjustments" imposed by the World Bank, or subject to the wave of micronationalisms and the resurgence of ethnic conflict?

Globalization, Multipolarity and the Postmodern *Angst*

The implications of the changed geopolitical ecology of the contemporary world have been equally ominous for the nomothetic social sciences, though their seriousness has been partly camouflaged by the rhetorical triumph of laissez-faire economics and the installation of elected governments in many low- and middle-income states. The failure of enfranchised modes of inquiry to adequately analyze the seismic transformations in the material conditions of life occasioned by the transnationalization of the circuits of capital—including the erosion of state sovereignty, an apparent decline in the salience of social class as a political category and the rapidly changing configurations of ethnic identity—is evident in the progressive corrosion of disciplinary boundaries, the creation of a host of new academic specialties which de-center subject positions to highlight the multiple, complex, fluid character of identities, and in the postmodernist "incredulity towards metanarratives" (Lyotard 1989: xxiv).

Since the pronounced idiographic, self-referential character of area studies programs have largely insulated them from the winds of change sweeping across the disciplinary departments, I will not attempt any detailed dissection of these trends here. Instead, I seek to explore some of the implications of the continued segregation of area studies programs in the context of the broader socioeconomic and political changes during the current phase of capitalist restructuring and the epistemic changes they have occasioned in the disciplines.

Reflecting the determining influence of their link to policy objectives and their deeply entrenched insularity from contemporary theoretical and epistemological debates in the humanities and the social sciences, "areaists" have responded to the challenges posed by geopolitical changes in recent decades by reasserting their unique abilities to understand and interpret the region of their expertise. This instrumentalist advocacy of the utility of their training ignores a considerable body of work and argument that demonstrate the untenability of separating the "knower" from the "known," of "objective" knowledge (see Dutton and Jeffreys 1993). It is also historically myopic since those who attribute the economic dynamism of states strung along Asia's Pacific perimeters to their Confucian heritage (Berger and Hsiao 1988; Morishima 1982) conveniently forget that at least till the sixties, this very tradition was castigated for the stagnation of the Qing Empire.

A secondary strand in the response of area specialists to changes in the geopolitical ecology of the contemporary world and the greater diversity and increasing assertiveness of ethnic minorities in the core has been to advocate the inclusion of their voices within the disciplinary curricula. Under the banner of "multiculturalism," this approach to "mainstreaming" the experiences of subaltern classes, women, indigenous peoples and ethnic and religious minorities typically involves the introduction of texts by non-

Western authors and women into the canon. However, since these attempts rarely entail a fundamental questioning of the epistemological status and theoretical categories of the different disciplines, they often tend to perpetuate the exoticization and essentialization of women and the non-Western "other(s)," particularly since the chrestomatic procedures that present *certain* texts and not others as the authentic voices of these diverse constituencies are rarely specified.

In this context, while the impetus towards the constitution of multicultural curriculums stems from the increasing presence of migrants from Africa, Asia, the Caribbean, Latin America and the Middle East in Europe and North America, the continued isolation of the study of their regions of origin from the conditions of life faced by ethnic minorities in the core forecloses at the very outset the possibility of teaching texts by nonwhite authors, as well as by "women of color," in a nonexoticized manner. Cultural forms and genres then emerge not as symbolic resolutions to historically contingent political and social contradictions but as the invariant characteristics of essentialized, exotic cultures: the patriarchal value system as an intrinsic ingredient of the Confucian heritage of East Asians, the hierarchical caste system of the Hindus, the religious fanaticism of the Muslims, etc.

The idiographic, self-referential character of area studies programs and their continued anchoring in an anachronistic, postitivist epistemology has also had an adverse impact on the humanities and social science disciplines. The fragmentation and widespread dispersal of manufacturing operations by the TNCs, the emergence of major nodes of capitalist accumulation along the Asian perimeters of the Pacific and the globalization of even the networks of cultural production render analytical categories of the several disciplines increasingly inadequate as they embody the theoretical encapsulation of West European and North American patterns of large-scale social transformation. A widespread recognition of these inadequacies, evident in Jean-Francois Lyotard's "incredulity towards metanarratives," has spawned a variety of new academic specialties and perspectives privileging local, plural and heterogeneous identities and interactions over global, monolithic, and homogeneous structures and practices.

However important this recuperation of a politics of location and difference may be from other points of view, as far as comparative studies are concerned, the postmodernist movement has reinforced the watertight separation between a postmodernist West, and a modernizing postcolonial, non-West (Anderson 1992: 34; Said 1989: 222).[23] Thus, despite the differences that otherwise divide them, both Lyotard and Fredric Jameson agree that they seek to investigate the "conditions of knowledge in the most highly developed societies" (Jameson 1991: x; Lyotard 1984: xxiii). Similarly, in his magisterial survey of the "condition of postmodernity," David Harvey (1989) pointedly ignores what used to be called the "second" and "third" worlds. This segregation of "highly developed societies" from "developing" ones ignores a very considerable body of work stemming from the *dependencia* tradition—if not from Marx, given his well-known account of "primitive accumulation"—in the social sciences which demonstrates that metropolitan socioeconomic structures are so integrally linked to their peripheral opposites that it is impossible to study either one as an internally coherent, bounded whole. Even for those who have a particular antipathy for economic and political analysis, how is it possible to ignore the influence of the projection of racial hierarchies in the United States—particularly the negative depictions of African Americans in films and television programs, the distorted caricature of America as a meritocratic "land of opportunity" and the deliberate silence on the history of oppression and exploitation of Native Americans and other peoples of color—through Hollywood films, video cassettes and satellite television broadcasts on the waves of new migrants and their implications for race relations, an influence so pervasive that travelers to remote villages in the Himalayas record children pestering them for tapes of Michael Jackson and Madonna?

The postmodern emphasis on ephemeral, multiple, de-centered identities and subjectivities, in fact, may be taken to reflect the changes in the forms of industrial organization and social life being implemented in the current phase of capitalist restructuring. The transformation of industrial production occasioned by the integration of the most backward forms of industrial organization with most advanced forms of capitalist organization—the integration of patriarchal, family-based sweatshops through extensive subcontracting networks and small-batch "just-in-time" production processes to large TNCs—has spawned a variety of positions of subordination to capital, while cutting the ground from under class-based organizations. In this context the postmodern discursive emphasis on multiple subject positions can be read as a bourgeois metaphor for contemporary industrial relations—that is, as the metaphor of the dominant class rather than the combative metaphor of the dispossessed masses, indeed as "the fetishization of alienation" (Dirlik 1994b: 111–112).

Viewed in this light, it is striking that the positive revaluation of the Confucian tradition corresponds to the reappearance of family-based sweatshops both in the newly industrializing regions and in the older industrial heartlands in Western Europe and North America. While the Protestant work ethic was the ideological expression of production relations in an earlier era, the Confucian ethic corresponds more closely to the relations of production in an era when capitalism has transcended its origins in Europe to become "an authentically global abstraction . . . [as] non-European capitalist societies now make their own claims on the history of capitalism" (Dirlik 1994a: 350). It is hence quite appropriate that the most vocal advocates of Confucianism as a modernizing, developmentalist ideology are mainstream establishment intellectuals in and of East Asia.

To recapitulate, an increase of competitive pressures in the core with the rebuilding of the Japanese and West European economies, the limits imposed on import-substituting industrialization strategies by narrow domestic markets and the realization of the limits of extensive growth in centrally planned economies all combined to dissolve the post–Second World War geopolitical segmentation of the globe into "three worlds." The consequent expansion of the networks of production, exchange and investment, along with associated changes in the patterns of labor migration, have severely undermined the regulatory competence of nation-states. Simultaneously, the collapse of "actually existing socialism" in the Soviet Union and Eastern Europe and the installation of market-oriented reforms in the People's Republic of China have signified the irrelevance of an earlier orthodoxy that stressed the central role of the state in economic affairs. Given the apparently increasing homogeneity of the conditions for investment and production, area studies programs are progressively becoming irrelevant as the Cold War partitioning of the globe rapidly unravels as a consequence of the current phase of capitalist restructuring. The inability of currently enfranchised modes of inquiry to account for the seismic changes in the material conditions of life caused by the current phase of capitalist restructuring has spawned a host of new academic specialties which, despite their explicit claims to challenge the Eurocentricity of dominant conceptions of knowledge, have tended to reinforce and perpetuate the axiomatic distinction between Europe and its others.

ANTIDISCIPLINARITY AS PRAXIS

> Can one divide human reality, as indeed human reality seems to be genuinely divided, into clearly different cultures, histories, traditions, societies, even races, and survive the consequences humanly?
> —Edward Said, *Orientalism* (1985)

If the massive dislocations caused during the "long" nineteenth century by the French and industrial revolutions and the spectacular expansion of the capitalist world economy to englobe the planet led to the current institutional partitioning of knowledge into discrete disciplinary tributaries, the emergence of major nodes of accumulation in Asia and the simultaneity of the globalization of circuits of material and cultural production in the contemporary era with the implosion of a variety of ethnic and religious particularisms call for an equally sweeping reorganization of the academic universe. Put differently, the terminal crisis of area studies programs indicates a far deeper malaise: the fundamental untenability of the nineteenth century institutionalization of knowledge as non-European societies make their own distinctive contributions to the history of capitalism.

Though there is a widespread acknowledgment of the inadequacy of en-franchised modes of inquiry—manifested by the progressive corrosion of disciplinary boundaries and the postmodern repudiation of post–European Enlightenment rationality—the conceptual and analytical categories forged over the last century have rarely been excavated or challenged. By way of illustration, consider reigning conceptions of economic development. Since the industrial revolution transformed England into the "workshop of the world," industrialization has been so inextricably linked to development that most studies take the form of tracing the rise of urban-industrial complexes in individual states and ranking them by the extent of industrial activities within their jurisdictions. Correspondingly, the growth of an industrial pro-letariat is charted and conceptually distinguished from the mass of rural workers, often termed "traditional peasants" (cf. Bergquist 1986; Martin 1994; Ward 1990).

The fundamental premise underlying these inquiries is the assumption that the European narrative of capitalist development and state formation will gradually be diffused across the globe, the very modernist assumption that present day peripheral societies represent the past of core states. Yet the evidence against this foundational premise of the modern social sciences is compelling. A rapidly accumulating collection of studies have shown that the expansion of capitalism and consolidation of state structures in Europe was predicated on the economic underdevelopment—"the development of underdevelopment" in André Gunder Frank's marvelously adequate phrase—and the unraveling of state structures elsewhere; that much of what is commonly perceived as "traditional" structures in Asia and Africa are, in fact, the results of European expansion and colonial structures of rule rather than pristine survivals from a precapitalist past; that capital accumulation in sixteenth-century northwestern Europe resulted in an intensification of "feudal" ties in Eastern Europe and the creation of slave plantations in the "New World"; that the industrialization of England caused the forced dein-dustrialization of India in the nineteenth century; that the decolonization and creation of nation-states in nineteenth-century Europe was paralleled by the colonization and violent rupturing of governance structures in Asia and Africa.

The virtual identity between industrialization and development is, how-ever, so tenaciously ingrained in contemporary conceptual frameworks that even the *dependencistas* who forcefully refute the axiomatic distinction be-tween "modern" and "traditional" sectors in a comparative context often recuperate this binary opposition within peripheral societies. Thus, by pos-iting that a delinking from metropolitan structures of accumulation could lead to the creation of autonomous urban-industrial structures within pe-ripheral areas, they continue to operate within the framework of a "dual economy" thesis that they otherwise reject. However, as feminist scholars have demonstrated, the dichotomous opposition between a "modern in-

dustrial proletariat" and a "traditional" sector merely reinforces the gendered biases of "productive" waged work even in the core by divorcing
wage-labor from the wider social networks of reproduction (Scott 1988: see
also Ward 1990). If the distinction between "productive" waged work and
"unproductive" unwaged work provided an inadequate understanding of
the heartlands of industrial capitalism itself, it is increasingly evident that it
produces grotesque caricatures when blithely applied to other regions where
substantial populations remain outside the waged sector altogether.

The synonymity between industrialization and development is especially
invidious in the current phase of capitalist restructuring, since the progressive fragmentation of production into part-processes implies that the benefits
that had accrued during earlier historical phases of industrialization no
longer accrue to the "newly industrializing" states. The implementation of
selective labor recruitment policies—manifested by the femininization of the
workforce, particularly in the low-skilled, assembly-line processes in a number of industries ranging from garments and footwear to consumer electronics—as well as the pervasive growth of a variety of subcontracting
arrangements not only led to a progressive shift of the costs of reproduction
to households and to the "subsistence" sector but also transformed the
terrain of class struggle. Thus, as Harvey (1989: 153) observes, "struggling
against a father or uncle who organizes family labor into a highly disciplined
and competitive sweatshop that works to order for multinational capital" is
very different from struggling against managers of large, vertically integrated
corporations. To put it another way, the transformation of the family into
a highly disciplined, low-wage labor force working to order for multinational
capital in farms and small subcontracting units

operates against the tendency toward empowerment of workers in advanced sectors
of capital and, at the limit, neutralizes the politico-economic consequences that Marx
associated with the generalized increase in capital intensity of production and that
more recent analysts have associated with large, vertically integrated firms. (Sassen
1991: 31–32)

Approaching the issue from another angle, studies on proletarianization
are dominated by a set of assumptions derived from the European experience that typically endows the working class with "a (potentially) uniform,
homogenized, extrahistorical subjectivity" (Chakrabarty 1989: 223). Built
into this central, "extrahistorical," theoretical category are the cultural legacies of the "free-born Englishman"—("the remembered village rights, of
notions of equality before the law, of craft traditions" [Thompson 1966:
194])—where the worker appears in "dot-like isolation" as Marx (1973:
472) once put it. The mechanical transfer of the set of expectations that
flow from this extrahistorical conceptualization of the working class to places

marked by inegalitarian, hierarchical structures of power and community—as in the case of India—where identities based on language, religion and place of origin habitually override class solidarities has been shown to be seriously flawed (Chakrabarty 1989). Similarly, in the case of South Korea, though there was an extraordinary degree of ethnic homogeneity, a mere application of a dehistoricized notion of a "working class" has proved to be grossly inadequate since there was an absence of the artisanal traditions which were so important in the formation of class consciousness in the paradigmatic case of England (Koo 1990).

In the context of the contemporary globalization of the networks of material and cultural production, it is also clear that these anomalies cannot be addressed by simply adding the history of the "peoples without history" to the narrative of Euro-American history. Eric Wolf's (1982) survey of the global circuits of commodities, labor exchanges and capital flows illustrates, for example, the limitations of such attempts as they do not forge any new theoretical categories to integrate the distinctive experiences of non-Western peoples into the conceptual arsenal of the modern social sciences (Martin 1994: 151). Similarly, the inadequacies of the conventional comparative-historical method are shown by Charles Tilly's (1990: 92) contention that it is "not utterly stupid to suppose that non-Western states would undergo some of the same experiences as their Western counterparts and end up looking much more like them"—a contention that is all the more startling as it comes precisely when we witness a consolidation of structures of governance in the core (European Union, greater intergovernmental coordination through the G-7 meetings, etc.) and the unraveling of state structures in much of sub-Saharan Africa. Moreover, even when the "nation" is presented, not as a "natural" development of a universal human rationality but as an "imagined community" (Anderson 1991), the historical experiences of non-European peoples continue to be denied since they are still condemned to follow the trails blazed by Europeans and their transplants in the Americas (Chatterjee 1993: 5).

These observations indicate that the consequences of the expansion of capitalism cannot be tracked by uncritically employing the conceptual tools forged by a century of core-centric social science, but require a radical reconceptualization of our analytical frameworks. Indeed, if we are right in seeing the postmodern disenchantment with metanarratives, despite its explicit repudiation of post–European Enlightenment rationality, as reinforcing the binary opposition between the "highly developed societies" of the core where the "modernization process is complete" (Jameson 1991: x) and the non-Western peripheries, a strategy to transcend this dichotomy must perforce begin not with the fragmentation of social life, but with the underlying singularity of the historical processes of capitalism.

CONCLUSION

The insistence on the fundamental unity of continual capitalist (re)structurings of the world does not license a recuperation of reigning metahistorical analytical categories and the current institutional partitioning of intellectual subject matter by a theoretical sleight of hand. Rather, as suggested by the preceding sketches illustrating the inadequacy of applying categories of analysis encapsulating a false understanding of the Euro-American experience to other regions, the challenge is to contextualize dense narratives of local processes within larger global forces of transformation. For instance, instead of unproblematically transposing the trajectories of the rise and fall of labor movements in the core to the "newly industrializing countries" on the Pacific perimeters of Asia or in Latin America, these procedures of inquiry will seek to locate workers in export-processing zones within local structures of labor control and networks of social reproduction which are integral elements of a global divisioning of labor (Martin 1994: 171–174; Ward 1990).

Proceeding from both ends of the nomothetic-idiographic spectrum—as the rubric of programs called world-systems analysis and "world literature and cultural studies" (Ross 1993) indicate—the dual insistence on locating phenomena within their historically specific contexts and on the singularity of large-scale, long-term processes of capitalist expansion implies a transcendence of the binary Western/non-Western, postmodern/modern(izing) oppositions inscribed in our inherited theoretical categories. An essential aspect of such forms of inquiry is a repudiation of a synecdochical model of knowledge, whereby parts represent the whole. Instead of transhistorical, meta-theoretical categories, the emphasis on the relational nature of historical processes dictates that analytical categories represent theoretical encapsulations of temporally and spatially specific processes to conceptually encompass the local processing of global forces, to investigate the consequences of the interpenetration of world-relational processes of accumulation and commodification with local structures of power and community.

In both cases, the word "world" signifies a stubborn refusal to delineate in advance the object of inquiry. Since the complacent acceptance of units of analysis that are given to the analyst rather than being constructed during the course of inquiry reduces relationships that transcend the boundaries of these units to the status of epiphenomena and thereby distorts causal explanations within these units themselves, this strategy offers a means to locate our analyses within the widest informational range. A refusal to accept a priori units and tools of analysis implies an erasure of these hermetically sealed partitionings of knowledge while the contextualization of relational processes within the widest possible frame of reference endows analysis with a deeper time-and-space specificity than more narrowly focused, spatially and temporally circumscribed modes of inquiry.

Immanuel Wallerstein's (1974: 67–129) creative reconceptualization of the so-called "second serfdom" in Poland, for example, indicates how local processes of change can be integrated within a wider relational matrix. By situating different forms of labor exploitation within a larger organizational nexus, this analysis is able to provide a more precise conceptual context without diluting their concrete historical specificity. Similarly, as Said (1993) and others have insisted, we cannot study the blossoming of cultural production in the core without studying the conditions in the periphery, that wider relational processes were deeply imbricated in the production of that which the nineteenth-century institutionalization of knowledge had cast as decidedly local and particular.

The emphasis on embedding richly textured historical narratives within wider relational networks entails two further propositions. First, the coincidence of the emergence of critiques of Eurocentric diffusionist models with the unraveling of U.S. hegemony indicates that conceptual categories are determined by the geopolitical location of researchers. Thus, the diffusionist model provided a workable framework during the fifties and sixties as decolonization and the global spread of industrialization proceeded apace. Its inadequacies were revealed only during the phase of global economic contraction beginning in the late sixties, a contraction that was marked by the corrosion of disciplinary boundaries and the emergence of radical critiques to post–European Enlightenment rationality. The critique of metahistorical theoretical categories also entails that conceptual tools be forged in relation to the object of inquiry, that analytical procedures for the study of forms of labor control during the "long" sixteenth century may be quite inadequate to investigate the global divisioning of labor during the current phase of capitalist restructuring marked by the fragmentation of production into part-processes and the revival of patriarchal family-based sweatshops even in the core (see Martin 1994: 170–171). Or, as George Marcus and Michael Fischer (1986: 81) note, "[R]ather than hardening into dogma or a 1950's-style paradigm, the so-called world-systems theory survives today primarily as a general orientation."

Second, the construction of new theoretical and conceptual tools, and of constructing genuine world-scale sets of data poses formidable challenges. Constrained as individual researchers are by their abilities, resources and training much of the most important work has involved densely structured local or regional studies that attempt to place these developments as moments within wider relational processes (e.g., Bergquist 1986; Tomich 1990). The more challenging task of devising truly world-relational datasets, as indicated by the work of the Research Working Group on World Labor (1986) at the Fernand Braudel Center at Binghamton University, involves a quite different procedure. While it is increasingly being recognized that states are inadequate as units of analysis, they remain units of observation. However, since national datasets are decidedly not world-relational in their construction, the creation of world-relational datasets necessitates the combination of individual research with the efforts of collective teams of researchers, merging their different competencies to tackle large, collaborative projects as is increasingly the case in the natural and physical sciences and in the entrepreneurial world. This again implies that scholars in the humanities and the social sciences repudiate the long tradition of individual research and begin to participate in truly crossdisciplinary, collaborative investigations.

The creation of such crossdisciplinary—or, better yet, *antidisciplinary*—clusters of knowledge will of course face the "imperialism of departments" that area studies programs faced, as we have seen. However, in the present conjuncture, the very proliferation of a multiplicity of fragmented bodies of knowledge and the increasing erosion of disciplinary boundaries perhaps provides an opportune moment to create new paradigms of knowledge. Such paradigms must, initially at least, emerge from the initiative of small groups of faculty and graduate students spread across several disciplinary departments and/or area studies programs facing similar intellectual concerns and frustrations at having to devise ad hoc solutions in isolation and fighting a series of separate curricular battles. Indeed, since the current phase of capitalist restructuring—with the emergence of major nodes of accumulation in East Asia, the diasporic movement of peoples and the downgrading of industrial production in the global divisioning of labor—represents a climacteric at least as profound as the nineteenth-century "age of revolutions," it is imperative that such groups spearhead a move to break the shackles imposed by the nineteenth-century partitioning of knowledge production as we forge towards a brave new world.

Briefly put, despite its claims to provide a holistic analysis of the peoples and institutions of the non-Western world by transcending the disciplinary divisioning of knowledge, the area studies project has reinforced the axiomatic distinction between Europe and the "peoples without history." The inability of "areaists" to challenge the disciplinary partitioning of knowledge has meant that the conceptual categories of the various disciplinary departments continue to remain theoretical encapsulations of the Euro–North American narrative of capitalist development, state formation and social change. The inadequacies of these inherited conceptual categories have been cast in stark relief with the globalization of the networks of material and cultural production, the declining salience of states and the downgrading of industrialization in the global divisioning of labor. These limitations can only be overcome if we can transcend the nineteenth-century fragmentation of knowledge into discrete disciplinary tributaries and reconceptualize our analytical categories in world-relational terms. Finally, in the context of the widening disparities in income and wealth between the core and the periphery, and the resultant imbalances in library facilities, computer facilities and the like, scholars located in the core have a special responsibility to aid their colleagues in less-favored locales resist the deepening commodification of everyday life by providing them the information to locate particular configurations of social relations within larger contextual frameworks.

NOTES

Earlier versions of this chapter were presented at conferences at the University of Hawaii at Manoa and at the University of Wisconsin at Madison. I am grateful to participants at these conferences, and to Giovanni Arrighi, Cristina Bacchilega, Charles Crothers, Arif Dirlik, Mike Forman, Patricia Lane, Peter Manicas, John Rieder, Faruk Tabak and Rob Wilson for detailed comments, some of which I have incorporated, others I have recklessly ignored, and yet others I am still pondering.

1. While the debates surrounding Edward Said's *Orientalism* underscore the Eurocentric biases of area studies discourse, they do not address the broader issues involved in the geopolitical segmentation of the world. Though world-historical studies, in contrast, provide the most sustained and comprehensive critiques of the current partitioning of the globe (see Pletsch 1981; Wallerstein 1974, 1991c; Wolf 1982), they are primarily concerned with the fragmentation of the social sciences within arbitrary disciplinary enclosures, or with the division of the globe into "three worlds." Hence, they impinge only tangentially upon the intellectual underpinnings of the area studies project.

2. The most comprehensive survey to date is the one commissioned by the Department of Defense, see Lambert, et. al. (1984). The 1991 study by the National Council of Area Studies Associations (NCASA) commissioned by the Department of Education focuses solely on the prospects for hiring new faculty within the area studies programs and not on the substantive intellectual content of the programs (NCASA, 1991). Represented on this council are the Association for Asian Studies (AAS), the American Association for the Advancement of Slavic Studies (AAASS), the African Studies Association (ASA), the Latin American Studies Association (LASA), and the Middle East Studies Association (MESA).

3. Recognizing that the United States was ill-equipped to administer occupied territories in the two major theaters of the Second World War—the "Far East" and Europe—due to the relative ignorance about the peoples living in these areas, the Provost Marshal General established the Army Specialized Training Program in 1943 to train officers and enlisted men of the occupying forces in the cultures of the regions they were assigned to administer. Supplemented by other programs such as the Foreign Area Language Study and the Civil Affairs Training Schools, these programs were eventually instituted in 227 universities and colleges and had a peak enrollment of 13,185 by December 1943. For an overview, see Angiolillo (1947: 29–34); Fenton (1947); Lambert et. al., (1984: 5–6).

4. There were, of course, some exceptions to this generalization. By the turn of the twentieth century, Yale and Columbia Universities had begun to lay the foundations for their programs in East Asian Studies, and the Oriental Institute for the study of the Middle East and South Asia was established at the University of Chicago in 1923. The mid-1930s saw the creation of several programs. Among the more prominent of these were the University of Michigan's Programs in Oriental Civilizations (dealing primarily with China and Japan), and in Latin American studies; the

Latin American Studies Programs at the Universities of California at Berkeley and Los Angeles; and the Far Eastern Department at the University of Washington (Hall 1947: 17, 55; Lambert et. al. 1984: 3). Most of these pre–Second World War programs, however, had no autonomous status within the universities and depended on individual faculty members volunteering their time in addition to their normal assignments.

5. The first national "area studies" association to be formed in the United States was the Far Eastern Association in 1943, subsequently reorganized as the AAS in 1956. This was followed by the creation of the AAAASS in 1948, the ASA in 1957 and MESA in 1966 (NCASA 1991). It is emblematic of the marginal significance of Australasia and the Pacific Islands to the strategic concerns of the United States that there is no professional association to foster the study of these societies as yet.

6. Though the experience of training military and civilian personnel in the languages and cultures of the areas they were assigned to administer provided a model for the creation of integrated area studies programs, it was recognized that the urgencies of war had meant that the courses of instruction had very limited objectives. Or, as William Fenton wryly puts it: "Although general education admits of varying views, training demands the right answer" (1947: 5; see also Hall 1947: 18).

7. The Rockefeller Foundation had helped create the Oriental Institute at the University of Chicago in the 1920s. Additionally, in 1946, the Foundation provided substantial assistance for the creation of the program in Far Eastern and Russian Studies at Yale, the Far Eastern Institute at the University of Washington and the Russian Institute at Columbia. The Carnegie Corporation's grant of $740,000 to Harvard University in 1948 for the establishment of its Russian Research Center was the largest endowment of its kind at that time. To enable their state universities to compete with private East Coast institutions, the state legislatures of Michigan and California also appropriated substantial grants for international and area studies in the late forties and early fifties. Between 1953 and 1966, the principal private funding agency for area and language studies was the Ford Foundation which disbursed over $270 million to 34 universities for this express purpose (Hall 1947: 52, 55–56, 60; Lambert et al. 1984: 8–9).

8. In fact, taking cognizance of these geopolitical realities, Mountbatten's command was originally designated the American-British-Dutch-Australian (ABDA) Command (Emmerson 1984: 7).

9. In the United States, studies on the Soviet Union between the Bolshevik Revolution and the outbreak of the Second World War were largely confined to the works of journalists, missionaries and fellow-travelers, see Filene (1967).

10. These points are conveyed telegraphically here since their full elaboration falls beyond the purview of this chapter.

11. Roland Oliver notes that it "was quite normal for a single one of the newly defined [European] colonies [in Africa] to comprise two or three hundred earlier political groupings, even after discounting those societies which recognized no authority wider than that of the extended family" (1991: 185).

12. This is particularly important since many of the indigenous inhabitants of these areas had nonliterate cultures prior to the arrival of European "discoverers"—indeed in many cases it was the European missionaries who devised alphabets and compiled dictionaries for the indigenous languages in these regions as a part of their evangelizing endeavors. Hence, the source material for the reconstruction of their histories

are almost exclusively compiled in metropolitan languages (e.g., travelogues and accounts of explorers, missionaries, colonial administrators and journalists).

13. Or as John Iliffe observed of colonial Tanganyika: "Africans wanted effective units of action just as officials wanted effective units of government. . . . Europeans believed Africans belonged to tribes; Africans built tribes to belong to" (quoted in Ranger 1983: 252).

14. While Hough and Pletsch were primarily concerned with the impact of this divisioning of intellectual labor for the nomothetic social sciences, it had an equally significant impact on the idiographic humanities as evident, for example, by the fact that "philosophy" typically refers to the traditions of knowledge and inquiry derived from Greco-Roman antiquity, while other ways of thinking and knowing are *always* qualified by an adjective (e.g., "African," "Chinese" or "Indian" philosophy) (see Mudimbe 1988).

15. "To do something interdisciplinary," as Roland Barthes once put it, "it's not enough to choose a 'subject' (a theme) and gather around it two or three sciences. Interdisciplinarity consists in creating a new object that belongs to no one" (quoted in Clifford 1986: 1).

16. It should be noted that one important reason for the pioneer scholars to neglect contemporary issues was due to the fact that such research would inevitably have highlighted their location within the colonial enterprise.

17. For an indication of the fluctuating distribution of resources between the different areas of study compare Bennett (1951) with Lambert (1973), Lambert et al. (1984) and NCASA (1991).

18. I have developed these arguments at greater length elsewhere (see Palat 1993a, 1996); for southern Africa, see Martin (1986; 1991); for the Soviet Union and Eastern Europe, see (Wallerstein 1991a, 1991b: 90).

19. Since I have discussed the geopolitical conditions that led to the unraveling of the relational networks constituted under U.S. hegemony and their consequences at length elsewhere (see Palat, 1993a, 1993b, 1996), I repeat them here only in order to make the present argument intelligible.

20. By the beginning of the seventies, 40,000 students were enrolled in Russian language classes in the United States, while only 24,000 were enrolled by the early eighties (Atkinson 1991: 20–21).

21. Though the incompatible methods of estimation utilized by different area studies associations make an accurate assessment impossible, an indication of the declining interest in such programs is provided by projections of anticipated loss of area studies faculty in the nineties. NCASA (1991: 79), for instance, estimates that the AAASS will lose 42.7 percent of its faculty, AAS 41.2 percent, MESA 36.7 percent, LASA 34.5 percent and the ASA 33.7 percent. For an assessment of the changing patterns of funding for Fulbright Programs see Koppel (1995).

22. While Europeans had accounted for over 50 percent of immigrants to the United States as recently as 1960, migrants from Europe accounted for only 11 percent of all legal immigrants in 1985. Correspondingly, Asian migrants rose from 9 percent in 1960 to 47 percent in 1985 (Sassen 1990: 62–63). Other core locations experienced a similar pattern in the influx of migrants from low- and middle-income states—from Africa, the Middle East and Eastern Europe to Western Europe, from East and Southeast Asia and the Pacific Islands to Australasia, from continental Asia

and the Philippines to Japan—though the magnitudes of these inflows were much smaller.

23. Studies on Japan prove a rare exception to this generalization, but then Japan is considered a modernized economy and does not challenge the ethnocentricity of the postmodern project. For Japan, see Miyoshi and Harootunian (1989).

REFERENCES

Ahmad, Aijaz. (1992) *In Theory: Classes, Nations, Literatures.* London: Verso.

Amsden, Alice. (1989) *Asia's Next Giant: South Korea and Late Industrialization.* New York: Oxford University Press.

———. (1992) "Otiose Economics." *Social Research*, 59(4) (Winter): 781–797.

Anderson, Benedict R. O'G. (1991) *Imagined Communities: Reflections on the Origin and Spread of Nationalism.* London: Verso.

———. (1992) "The Changing Ecology of Southeast Asian Studies in the United States, 1950–1990." In Charles Hirschman, Charles F. Keyes and Karl Hutterer (eds.), *Southeast Asian Studies in the Balance: Reflections from America.* Ann Arbor, MI: Association for Asian Studies, 25–40.

Angiolillo, Paul F. (1947) *Armed Forces' Foreign Language Teaching: Critical Evaluation and Implications.* New York: S. F. Vanni.

Arrighi, Giovanni. (1982) "A Crisis of Hegemony." In Samir Amin et al., *Dynamics of Global Crisis.* New York: Monthly Review Press, 55–108.

———. (1990) "The Three Hegemonies of Historical Capitalism." *Review*, 13(3) (Summer): 365–408.

———. (1994) *The Long Twentieth Century: Money, Power, and the Origins of Our Time.* London: Verso.

Atkinson, Dorothy. (1991) "Soviet and European Studies." In the National Council of Area Studies Associations, *Prospects for Faculty in Area Studies: A Report from the National Council of Area Studies Associations.* Stanford, CA: American Association for the Advancement of Slavic Studies, 19–34.

Balazs, Etienne. (1960) "The Birth of Capitalism in China." *Journal of the Economic and Social History of the Orient*, 3(2) (June): 196–216.

Bennett, Wendell C. (1951) *Area Studies in American Universities.* New York: Social Science Research Council.

Berger, Peter L. and Hsiao, H.-H. Michael (eds.). (1988) *In Search of an East Asian Developmental Model.* New Brunswick, NJ: Transaction Books.

Bergquist, Charles. (1986) *Labor in Latin America: Comparative Essays on Chile, Argentina, Venezuela, and Columbia.* Stanford, CA: Stanford University. Press.

Borthwick, Mark et al. (1992) *Pacific Century: The Emergence of Modern Pacific Asia.* Boulder, CO: Westview.

Bray, Francesca. (1983) "Patterns of Evolution in Rice-Growing Societies." *Journal of Peasant Studies*, 11(1) (October): 3–33.

Bunker, Stephen G. and O'Hearn, Denis. (1993) "Strategies of Economic Ascendants for Access to Raw Materials: A Comparison of the United States and Japan." In Ravi Arvind Palat (ed.), *Pacific-Asia and the Future of the World-System.* Westport, CT: Greenwood Press, 83–102.

Burawoy, Michael. (1992) "The End of Sovietology and the Renaissance of Modernization Theory," *Contemporary Sociology*, 21(6) (November): 774–785.

Chakrabarty, Dipesh. (1989) *Rethinking Working Class History: Bengal, 1890–1940.* Princeton, NJ: Princeton University Press.

Chatterjee, Partha. (1993) *The Nation and Its Fragments: Colonial and Postcolonial Histories.* Princeton, NJ: Princeton University Press.

Clifford, James. (1986) "Introduction: Partial Truths." In James Clifford and George E. Marcus (eds.), *Writing Culture: The Poetics and Politics of Ethnography.* Berkeley: University of California Press, 1–26.

Cumings, Bruce. (1987) "The Origin and Development of the Northeast Asian Political Economy: Industrial Sectors, Product Cycles, and Political Consequences." In Frederic C. Deyo (ed.), *The Political Economy of New Asian Industrialism.* Ithaca, NY: Cornell University Press, 44–83.

Dirks, Nicholas B. (1987) *The Hollow Crown: Ethnohistory of an Indian Kingdom.* Cambridge: Cambridge University Press.

Dirlik, Arif. (1992) "The Asia-Pacific Idea: Reality and Representation in the Invention of a Regional Structure." *Journal of World History*, 3(1) (Spring): 55–79.

———. (1994a) "The Postcolonial Aura: Third World Criticism in the Age of Global Capitalism." *Critical Inquiry*, 20(4) (Winter): 328–356.

———. (1994b) *After the Revolution: Waking to Global Capitalism.* Hanover, NH: Wesleyan University Press.

Dixon, Chris. (1991) *South East Asia in the World-Economy: A Regional Geography.* Cambridge: Cambridge University Press.

Drakakis-Smith, David. (1992) *Pacific-Asia.* London: Routledge.

Dutton, Michael and Jeffreys, Elaine. (1993) "The Humanities, Humanism and Asian Studies." *Asian Studies Review*, 26(3) (April): 2–9.

Emmerson, Donald K. (1984) " 'Southeast Asia': What's in a Name?" *Journal of Southeast Asian Studies*, 25(1) (March): 1–21.

Errington, Shelley. (1989) *Meaning and Power in a Southeast Asian Realm.* Princeton, NJ: Princeton University Press.

Fenton, William N. (1947) *Area Studies in American Universities: For the Commission on Implications of Armed Services Educational Programs.* Washington, DC: American Council on Education.

Filene, Peter G. (1967) *Americans and the Soviet Experiment, 1917–1933: American Attitudes Toward Russia from the February Revolution until Diplomatic Recognition.* Cambridge, MA: Harvard University Press.

Foucault, Michel. (1980) *Power/Knowledge: Selected Interviews and Other Writings.* Colin Gordon (ed.). New York: Pantheon.

Gibb, Hamilton A. R. (1963) *Area Studies Reconsidered.* London: School of Oriental and African Studies.

Gibney, Frank. (1992) *The Pacific Century: America and Asia in a Changing World.* New York: Charles Scribner's Sons.

Gooding-Williams, Robert. (1993) *Reading Rodney King/Reading Urban Uprising.* New York: Routledge.

Gourevitch, Peter. (1989) "The Pacific Rim: Current Debates." *The Annals of the American Academy of Political and Social Science*, 505 (September): 8–23.

Grove, Linda and Esherick, J. W. (1980) "From Feudalism to Capitalism: Japanese

Scholarship on the Transformation of Chinese Rural Society." *Modern China*, 6(4) (October): 397–438.

Habib, I. (1969) "Potentialities of Capitalistic Development in the Economy of Mughal India." *Journal of Economic History*, 29(1) (March): 32–79.

Hall, Robert B. (1947) *Area Studies: With Special Reference to Their Implications for Research in the Social Sciences*. Washington, DC: Committee on World Area Research.

Harvey, David. (1989) *The Condition of Postmodernity: An Enquiry into the Origins of Cultural Change*. Oxford: Basil Blackwell.

Heginbotham, Stanley J. (1994) "Rethinking International Scholarship: The Challenge of Transition from the Cold War Era." *Items*, 48(2/3) (June–September): 33–40.

Hough, Jerry F. (1977) *The Soviet Union and Social Science Theory*. Cambridge, MA: Harvard University Press.

Issacs, Harold. (1980) *Scratches on Our Minds: American Images of China and India*. White Plains, NY: M. E. Sharpe.

Jameson, Fredric. (1991) *Postmodernism, or the Cultural Logic of Late Capitalism*. Durham, NC: Duke University Press.

Johnson, Chalmers. (1982) *MITI and the Japanese Miracle: The Growth of Industrial Policy, 1925–1975*. Stanford, CA: Stanford University Press.

———. (1988) "Study of Japanese Political Economy: A Crisis in Theory." In The Japan Foundation, *Japanese Studies in the United States: I. History and Present Condition*. Ann Arbor, MI: Association for Asian Studies, 95–113.

Koo, Hagen. (1990) "From Farm to Factory: Proletarianization in Korea." *American Sociological Review*, 55(5) (October): 669–681.

Kopf, David. (1980) "Hermeneutics versus History." *Journal of Asian Studies*, 397(3) (May): 495–506.

Koppel, Bruce M. (1995) *Refugees or Settlers? Area Studies, Development Studies, and the Future of Asian Studies*. Honolulu: East-West Center.

Kundera, Milan. (1981) *The Book of Laughter and Forgetting*, trans. Michael Henry Heim. Harmondsworth: Penguin.

Lambert, Richard D. (1973) *Language and Area Studies Review*. Philadelphia: American Academy of Political and Social Science.

Lambert, Richard D. et al. (1984) *Beyond Growth: The Next Stage in Language and Area Studies*. Washington, DC: Association of American Universities.

Lyotard, Jean-François. (1984) *The Postmodern Condition: A Report on Knowledge*, trans. Geoff Bennington and Brian Massumi. Minneapolis: University of Minnesota Press.

Mafeje, Archie. (1971) "The Ideology of Tribalism." *Journal of Modern African Studies*, 11(2) (August): 353–361.

Marcus, George E. and Fischer, Michael J. (1986) *Anthropology as Cultural Critique*. Chicago: University of Chicago Press.

Martin, William G. (1986) "Southern Africa and the World-Economy: Cyclical and Structural Constraints on Transformation." *Review*, 10(1) (Summer): 99–119.

———. (1991) "The Future of Southern Africa: What Prospects After Majority Rule?" *Review of African Political Economy*, 50 (March): 115–134.

———. (1994) "The World-Systems Perspective in Perspective: Assessing the Attempt to Move Beyond Nineteenth-Century, Eurocentric Conceptions." *Review*, 27(2) (Spring): 145–185.

Marx, Karl. (1973) *Grundrisse: Foundations of the Critique of Political Economy (Rough Draft)*, trans. Martin Nicolaus. Harmondsworth: Penguin.

McClintock, Anne. (1988) "Maidens, Maps, and Mines: The Reinvention of Patriarchy in Colonial South Africa." *South Atlantic Quarterly*, 87(1) (Winter): 147–192.

Miyoshi, Masao and Harootunian, Harry D. (eds.). (1989) *Postmodernism and Japan*. Durham, NC: Duke University Press.

Morishima, Michio. (1982) *Why Has Japan "Succeeded"? Western Technology and the Japanese Ethos*. Cambridge: Cambridge University Press.

Mudimbe, V. Y. (1988) *The Invention of Africa: Gnosis, Philosophy, and the Order of Knowledge*. Bloomington: Indiana University Press.

Mukhia, Harbans. (1981) "Was There Feudalism in Indian History?" *Journal of Peasant Studies*, 8(3) (April): 273–310.

Munck, Geraldo L. (1993) "Between Theory and History and Beyond Traditional Area Studies: A New Comparative Perspective on Latin America." *Comparative Politics*, 25(4) (July): 475–498.

National Council of Area Studies Associations (NCAS). (1991) *Prospects for Faculty in Area Studies: A Report from the National Council of Area Studies Associations*. Stanford, CA: American Association for the Advancement of Slavic Studies.

Oliver, Ronald. (1991) *The African Experience*. London: Weidenfeld and Nicolson.

Palat, Ravi Arvind. (1993a) "The Making and Unmaking of Pacific-Asia." In Ravi Arvind Palat (ed.), *Pacific-Asia and the Future of the World-Economy*. Westport, CT: Greenwood Press, 3–22.

———. (1993b) "Transnationalization of Capital and the Paradox of Democracy: Free Markets, Decline of States, and Ethnic Conflicts." Paper presented at the conference on "The State in Transition: Reimagining the Local, National, International," La Trobe University, Melbourne, Australia, August 6–8.

———. (1996) "Pacific Century: Myth or Reality?" *Theory and Society*, 21(3): 303–347.

Picciotto, S. (1990) "The Internationalization of the State." *Review of Radical Political Economics*, 22(1) (Spring): 28–44.

Pletsch, Carl E. (1981) "The Three Worlds, Or the Division of Social Scientific Labor, circa 1950–1975." *Comparative Studies in Society and History*, 23(4) (October): 565–590.

Ranger, Terence. (1983) "The Invention of Tradition in Colonial Africa." In Eric Hobsbawm and Terence Ranger (eds.), *The Invention of Tradition*. Cambridge: Cambridge University Press, 211–262.

Research Working Group on World Labor. (1986) "Global Patterns of Labor Movements in Historical Perspective." *Review*, 10(1) (Summer): 137–155.

Ross, Kristin. (1993) "The World Literature and Cultural Studies Program." *Critical Inquiry*, 19(4) (Summer): 666–676.

Ryckmans, Pierre. (1984) "Orientalism and Sinology." *Asian Studies Association of Australia Review*, 7(3) (April): 18–20.

Said, Edward W. (1985) *Orientalism*. Harmondsworth: Penguin.

————. (1989) "Representing the Colonized: Anthropology's Interlocutors." *Critical Inquiry*, 15(2) (Winter): 205–225.

————. (1993) *Culture and Imperialism*. New York: Alfred A. Knopf.

Sassen, Saskia. (1990) *The Mobility of Labor and Capital: A Study in International Investment and Labor Flow*. Cambridge: Cambridge University Press.

————. (1991) *The Global City: New York, London, Tokyo*. Princeton, NJ: Princeton University Press.

Scott, Joan W. (1988) *Gender and the Politics of History*. New York: Columbia University Press.

Spate, Oskar Hermann Khristian. (1979) *The Pacific Since Magellen: I. The Spanish Lake*. Minneapolis: University of Minnesota Press.

Thompson, Edward Palmer. (1966) *The Making of the English Working Class*. New York: Vintage.

Tilly, Charles. (1990) *Coercion, Capital, and European States, AD 990–1990*. Oxford: Basil Blackwell.

Tomich, Dale W. (1990) *Slavery in the Circuit of Sugar: Martinique and the World-Economy, 1830–1848*. Baltimore: Johns Hopkins University Press.

Vansina, Jan. (1961) *Oral Tradition: A Study in Historical Methodology*. Chicago: Aldine.

Wade, Robert. (1990) *Governing the Market: Economic Theory and the Role of Government in East Asian Industrialization*. Princeton, NJ: Princeton University Press.

Wallerstein, Immanuel. (1974) *The Modern World-System: I. Capitalist Agriculture and the Origins of the European World-Economy in the Sixteenth Century*. New York: Academic Press.

————. (1991a) "The Cold War and Third World: The Good Old Days?" *Economic and Political Weekly*, 26(17) (April 27): 1103–1106.

————. (1991b) *Geopolitics and Geoculture: Essays on the Changing World-System*. Cambridge: Cambridge University Press.

————. (1991c) *Unthinking Social Science*. Cambridge: Polity Press.

————. (1992) "Geopolitical Strategies of the US in a Post-American World." *Humboldt Journal of Social Relations*, 18(1): 217–223.

Ward, Kathryn (ed.). (1990) *Women Workers and Global Restructuring*. Ithaca, NY: Cornell University Press.

Wolf, Eric. (1982) *Europe and the Peoples Without History*. Berkeley: University of California Press.

Chapter 5

Geography and Area Studies

WARREN MORAN

In the last decades of the twentieth century, geography has had its place in the sun. All of the social sciences and many of the humanities have incorporated geographic thinking and metaphor into their rhetoric. Images from geography have infiltrated the spectrum of writing from the scientific to the popular. Globalization is the vogue word. Virtually everything is being metaphorically mapped against other things. Scholars from across the social sciences frequently have space and place at the center of their analyses. Palat, a sociologist, begins his seminal paper on area studies with the provocative quote from Fredrickse—"There are many maps of one place, and many histories of one time" (Palat 1996: 269; also this volume). Such powerful spatial metaphors demonstrate how discourse, power and knowledge come together in language.

Much of the colorful spatial imagery derives from French scholars who take geography seriously, notably Braudel (1980), Lefebvre (1991) and especially Foucault (1980, 1982) who reified space and material and social stratigraphy, although mostly at finer resolution. The continental origins of this thinking reminds us that knowledge is itself geographic. And the boundaries of disciplines vary through space and time, like national boundaries. What is regional economics in France may be geography in New Zealand or the Netherlands. What is area studies in the United States at one time is regional geography in the United Kingdom at another. But I would also argue, as Molloy (this volume) does, that disciplinary knowledge itself makes special and distinctive contributions to interdisciplinary knowledge. Without it the interdisciplinary project is likely to be much less influential or enlightening, if only because it will not be able to confront on their own terms some of the other powerful disciplines such as economics.

Although it has the flavor of determinism, I wish to argue that geography shapes what the discipline geography is and what geography does. Livingstone (1992) makes similar arguments for the influence of history on the geography that is practiced at any particular time. New Zealand, my own country, is the beginning point for the discussion. Its location, physical and social geography, colonial history and intellectual connections, bicultural and multicultural society, and recent economic restructuring have resulted in a distinctive niche for geography in New Zealand. Geography, as a discipline, has always been much more important in New Zealand than in countries such as the United States, whereas area studies, has had much less impact. After discussing the changing real and intellectual context for area studies, I turn to the recent history of geography, especially the emphasis on theory within human geography, and pose the question of the role of geography as a discipline in the enhancement of local and international understanding through an area studies for the twenty-first century.

THE EARLY NEW ZEALAND EXPERIENCE

New Zealand has a distinctive experience from which to contribute to the debate on area studies. Marshall's *The Geography of New Zealand* (the first book of this title published in New Zealand) begins with the provocative statement that "the fortunate inhabitants of these islands should be geographers by instinct" (Marshall 1905: 1). Marshall was a geologist, and his assertion was based on the diversity of terrain and physical environments that excited natural scientists who visited the country. But he, or rather someone else, could equally well have been referring to the way in which the country's geographical situation establishes an instinctive geographical context for any attempt by New Zealanders to understand themselves through literature or social science, or the way overtly geographic processes such as migration and international trade and investment have inscribed themselves on such identities. A first step towards an understanding of New Zealand should be taken with maps in hand, including one plotting the history of geography as a discipline in New Zealand.

Geography was an important component in New Zealand's colonial school curricula of the nineteenth century. The colonial nature of the project is strongly apparent in the curricula of the Native Schools where geography retained its position (Barrington and Beaglehole 1974; Simon et al. 1997). The photographic images of the time capture the ironies of a global but Empire geography being taught to the indigenous inhabitants (Figure 1). This use of geographic teaching in New Zealand was an extension of what Livingstone (1992: 166) has called "The Imperial Impulse." As late as the 1950s the main textbooks used in the senior geography classes in New Zealand were of British origin by authors such as Dudley Stamp. Not surprisingly, they continued to reflect the British colonial view of the world.

Figure 1
Open Air Geography Class, circa 1910

Source: Northwood Brothers Collection, Alexander Turnbull Library, National Library of New Zealand, Te Puna Mātauranga o Aotearoa (negative number PA1-o-394-05).

New Zealand is not without its indigenous geography. Almost totally neglected until recently is the finely-honed geographic knowledge and attitudes of Maori that has been demonstrated by archaeologists and social anthropologists (see Firth 1929; Schwimmer 1966). But it was not this knowledge which influenced the geography curricula of secondary schools as geography emerged as a strong subject after the Second World War. I have argued elsewhere that academic geography in New Zealand is a distinctive blend of local interest and initiative with the British and American academic traditions (Moran 1984). The local interest is first seen in the work of geomorphologists and geologists in the nineteenth century.

The formal emergence of academic geography in New Zealand came with the establishment of departments of geography from the late 1930s. Scholars from these departments (initially mainly of United Kingdom origin) were influential in the emergence of a new geography in the secondary schools. It was based on the emerging paradigms of the time and especially the strong emphasis on regional geography—the interpretation of the patterns of human activities within natural environments. A perusal of the geography curricula of the universities in the 1950s and 1960s shows that these decades were the apogee of geography as area studies in New Zealand. These perspectives were strongly influenced by Hartshorne's ideas as perpetrated by K. B. Cumberland who held the first chair in geography at the University of Auckland from 1949. A generation of secondary school students were brought up on this mesolevel regional approach using textbooks such as *New Zealand: A Regional View* (Cumberland and Fox 1958) and similar interpretative descriptions of Asia, Africa, Latin America and Europe. Alternative and distinctive views of geography were perpetrated, most strongly from the Department of Geography at Victoria University of Wellington where Keith Buchanan (the notable Chinese scholar) and Harvey Franklin influenced a generation of students by bringing wider intellectual experience from the social sciences and humanities into the geographical spotlight. They had a direct impact on students who disseminated their ideas in teaching and elsewhere, although their immediate influence on the curricula of area studies through secondary school syllabuses was less.

From the 1950s, and increasingly from the 1960s, a higher proportion of geography departments were staffed by New Zealanders who had received higher degrees in geography from universities in the United Kingdom or, more commonly, from those in Canada and the United States. From then on New Zealand geography experienced a similar sequence of paradigms as the rest of the world, although often with different emphases than elsewhere. I do not have time to explore these recent developments here although I return to the strong recent engagement with theory later in the chapter.

THE CONTEXT FOR AREA STUDIES

As geographers contemplate their involvement in area studies for the twenty-first century the changed real and intellectual environment in which all social scientists are working must be recognized. Two interrelated sets of ideas are useful as a context. First, are the changes that are taking place in the world economy and society. These are often encapsulated in the single word "globalization," a process that is proving much more nuanced and diverse than it is sometimes painted. The interpretations of globalization differ according to the discipline that is analyzing it. My second theme, the practice of area studies, is one prism from which to view globalization. Different disciplinary perspectives and the contestation of intellectual territory are in sharp relief in the long-term and recent history of area studies. I conclude this section with some examples of the way global processes are influencing New Zealand and its relationships with some countries of Asia.

In one sense globalization is a reality. People are traveling much more than ever before; while the phenomenon of the transnational corporation has been developing for several decades. GATT, the WTO and the EU and other groups of nations and individual nations are making it easier for goods and people to move globally. These initiatives and altered spatial practices are inextricable from a second reality of globalization, its incorporation into political discourse. The primary intellectual arguments supporting globalization come from economics, and one branch of economics in particular. Neo-liberal theory suggests that barriers to competition and free movement of goods and services should be reduced or eliminated, and that this will generate greater wealth for all (Friedman 1982; Hayek 1960). Since 1984, governments of different political persuasions in my own country have embraced these ideas as comprehensively as in any other and used them as the basis of their policy. The financial instability of many countries of Asia in late 1997 reminds us of the fragility of the global capitalist economy and the need for intervention and regulation by international agencies like the World Bank and International Monetary Fund to sustain it.

In reality the process of globablization is much less homogeneous, as sociologists, political scientists and geographers have been demonstrating. McMichael (1996) urges us to remember that the globalization we refer to is not a new concept, but the latest reconstruction of a global socioeconomy. Philip Cerny elegantly captures the paradoxes of this latest round of globalization in a recent paper.

The central paradox of globalization is that rather than creating the big economy in one big polity it also divides, fragments and polarizes. Convergence and divergence are two sides of the same coin. Globalization is not even a single discourse but a contested concept giving rise to several distinct and intertwined discourses, while national and regional differences belie the homogeneous vision as well. (Cerny 1997: 273)

He emphasises that the transnational companies that are articulating the globalization, and are its most obvious symbols, have adopted global strategies precisely because they seek to exploit difference. He adds that economic and cultural globalization are matched by counterforces and indeed unleash others. And he is unconvinced that globalization is ultimately an homogenizing force.

Even more problematic are the subnational, transnational, and supranational ethnic cleavages, tribalism and other revived or invented identities and traditions—from local groups to the European Union—which abound in the wake of the uneven erosion of national identities, national economies and national state policy capacity characteristic of the "global era." Globablization can just as well be seen as the harbinger not simply of a "new world order" but a new world disorder, even a "new medievalism" of overlapping and competing authorities, multiple loyalties and identities, prismatic notions of space and belief and so on. (Cerny 1997: 256)

These different readings of globalization are evident in two contexts that I wish to consider here—the recent experience of Maori in New Zealand

and the changed relationship between New Zealand and Korea. New Zealand's current legal status was established in 1840 by a treaty between indigenous Maori and the British Crown. Over the last two decades, new legislation, the Treaty of Waitangi Act (1975) and its later amendments, has allowed the grievances of Maori over the illegal confiscation and taking of their land to be addressed as a claims process. Large settlements have been made in the form of capital, land and interests in economic enterprises including rights to commercial resources such as forests and fish. One settlement has included a controlling interest in a major fishing company—Sealord—for Maori. A recent development has been an offer to return New Zealand's highest mountain, Mt Cook (now to be known as Aoraki), to the South Island tribe Ngai Tahu as part of a major settlement. Maori have become implicated directly in the globalization process by using their new capital to make their own arrangements with trading partners in a variety of countries. Strong direct relationships have also been established with First Nations people in Canada, the United States and elsewhere. Maori scholarship, invigorated by the research for the treaty claims, is becoming an essential literature in the understanding of indigenous people internationally. Such tribal and personal relationships transcend national boundaries.

The interest of Korea in New Zealand and New Zealand in Korea has been stimulated by economic associations. Trade between the two countries has grown rapidly with Korea now being New Zealand's fourth or fifth largest trading partner with a volume of trade approaching that of the United Kingdom. Korean investment in New Zealand is now substantial, notably in forests and in forest processing and increasingly in other industries and in urban real estate. From a very small base in the late 1980s over 15,000 Koreans are now living in New Zealand. Tourism has grown rapidly. In some years in the 1990s over 135,000 people from Korea have visited New Zealand—more than ten percent of New Zealand tourists. These associations have meant many more Koreans coming in contact with New Zealanders. The connection also has a strategic and institutional foundation. As Tremewan (1996:21) points out, "[W]e are both partners in the Asia-Pacific region with shared interests in the region's security and prosperity. We are both founding members of APEC, joint participants in the ASEAN Regional Forum for discussion of regional security, both are dialogue partners of ASEAN and now both are members, or soon to be, of OECD."

AREA STUDIES, GEOGRAPHY AND NEW ZEALAND

Palat (1996) sees the rise of area studies as a post–Second World War phenomenon very much tied to the dominance and needs of the United States. He relates the interest in, and funding of, area studies to the power of the United States during the Cold War and the need for it to have detailed knowledge, including expert language knowledge, of a variety of regions where it had strategic interests. It is not surprising that area studies, as it developed in the United States, was dominated by studies of an idiographic nature (the study of particular cases). The interests in detailed knowledge of regions and the type of knowledge which it sought, when combined with the disciplinary hierarchy in the United States, resulted in many of the participants in area studies coming from the languages, sociology and political studies.

The origins and nature of area studies in the United States has received much attention in the 1990s as the content of programs and their funding have been under intense debate (Heilbrunn 1996; Palat 1996; Wallerstein 1996). In the academic literature, the area studies that developed in the United States has more recently revived a strong cultural studies component. The countries being studied, it is argued, are best approached through their literature and culture but approached in a way that is more akin to the social sciences (Wallerstein 1996). The paradox is evident. Although the original motive may have been strategic, many of the individuals who were involved in area studies were sympathetic to the cultures and countries that they were studying and teaching. It is unlikely that these courses themselves changed the American view of the world and its regions, but as the area studies programs have recently come under scrutiny, the nature of the knowledge embodied in them has been questioned.

There is little doubt that the imperatives now driving area studies are different from the period of the Cold War. Economic interests, in the real and theoretical senses, have become more powerful, even though from the beginning they were central issues, although strategically expressed. The reasons for doing area studies are now different. Informal area studies is part of the daily experience of the transnational corporations. Knowledge of place, although usually from a particular perspective, is more and more necessary for doing business. Formal area studies for corporations is carried out by internal research teams, international business consultants or schools of international business. Not surprisingly, the powerful, perhaps unparalleled, dominance of neo-liberal economics, which has colonized the discourse of globalization and defines many of the research questions of corporate area studies, is reflected in the knowledge produced by it. But one could argue that for corporations to be really successful the knowledge that they need is a deep and rich one of the places where they are investing.

These contradictions expose the vulnerability of area studies. Heilbrunn (1996: 52) argues that "the old antagonism . . . was heightened by the new prominence of rational choice theory, which seeks to replace ethnographic study with an economics-based explanation of human behavior." Wallerstein (1996: 2) conceptualizes this conflict in the idiographic-nomothetic distinction, which he argues forms the basis of the separation of history from what he calls the "hard" social sciences in the late nineteenth and early twentieth century. Intriguingly, this same distinction was the foundation of intense debates within geography in the 1950s and 1960s when theory and quantitative testing of ideas were becoming dominant at the expense of the areal differentiation advocated in Hartshorne's (1939, 1959) two books. To geographers who, as Livingstone (1994) has admirably documented, have always responded to the needs of the time, this interdisciplinary upheaval all sounds a little old hat.

This United States experience is quite different from countries like my own where area studies of an interdisciplinary nature has emerged more recently. It is tempting to argue that in small countries, or those not central to the major global alliances, there was no strategic need for a specific focus on area studies. Thus, the traditional disciplines were sufficient to maintain knowledge of the world. Any reading of the syllabi taught in secondary and tertiary institutions in New Zealand illustrates this point. As with any other nation, they show strong emphases on certain parts of the world and periods of history that reflect the geography and history of the nation. Indeed, the United States too had its own geography, history and economy to deal with before becoming a dominant power and turning its attention to the strategic production of knowledge. The New Zealand experience reflected the centrality of geography rather than strategy, and placed geography at the heart of area studies.

THE GEOGRAPHER'S CONTRIBUTION TO AREA STUDIES

Close engagement with social science theory and philosophy has undoubtedly characterized geography in the last thirty years. The works of Foucault (1982) and Lefebvre (1991) in particular have established a central place for space in social theory that has opened serious debate in geographic literature (see Gregory 1994); while at the same time geographers such as Harvey (1969, 1989, 1996), Soja (1989) and Castells (1991) have been powerful contributors to the wider debates. Alongside the emphasis on global processes, geographers have been exploring at the level of place, locality and individual activity precisely the contradictory forces of convergence and divergence that Cerny (1997) refers to. However, in so doing, I feel that the discipline has become characterized by an uneasy sense that something has been lost. This sense of unease and the unresolved tensions between the recent flowering of theory and the discipline's traditional imperatives underlie my comments on the potential contribution we might expect geography to make to area studies in the first decades of the next century. In a provocative introduction to *Justice, Nature and the Geography of Difference*, Harvey (1996: 2) expresses a more profound disquiet, quite at odds with much recent theory, when he suggests that "[T]he task of critical analysis is not, surely to prove the impossibility of foundational beliefs (or truths), but to find a more plausible and adequate basis for the foundational beliefs that make interpretation and political action meaningful, creative, and possible."

I suggest that to maximize its contribution geography must continue to provide the following:

* explicit consideration of space and place as essential components of understanding;
* an explicit recognition of people-environment interaction, which encompasses a focus on cultural processes in the understanding of geographic difference;
* a continued close engagement with theory;
* empirical testing of theoretical ideas through direct observation and collection of information;
* an explicit consideration of the role of the organization and control of production on the geographic distribution of wealth; and
* a strategic approach to the disciplinary imperative in education.

Place and Space

Regardless of paradigm, the distinctive contribution of geography to area studies is clearest when place and space are in the forefront of the questions being asked. Their centrality is clear even when it is place-names themselves (the bane of the lives of all academic geographers) that are being probed. Palat (1996) and in earlier papers severely criticizes the categorizations within which area studies is conducted. He sees these categories as an imposition from the Western centers of power. Such a point of view resonates with many New Zealand geographers. Even the treatment of the nation on world maps is disconcerting. In almost all atlases the Southern Hemisphere is truncated at about 60 degrees south, making New Zealand appear much more distant from the equator and the old and emerging centers of power. Maps of the world are seldom centered on the Pacific as Figure 1 showed. When they are realigned, a totally new perspective emerges (Figure 2). If we widen the discussion in the way that Palat intended to our regional categorization among the other Pacific islands, the situation becomes more revealing. Geographers of the 1960s placed New Zealand in the "Southwest Pacific" with other Pacific islands but, not surprisingly, did not include Southeast Asia. The names that assume real authority in the Pacific are the linguistic and ethnographically imposed Polynesia, Melanesia, Micronesia and Austronesia.

The recent debates, of course, center around the extent to which New Zealand can be considered as part of Asia. But the Pacific Rim doughnut needs investigation at all sorts of levels. I found it enlightening at a recent conference to be greeted by a Chilean colleague whom I had not met previously as, "Ah! My Pacific neighbor." I am sure Korean geographers can

Figure 2
The World from New Zealand

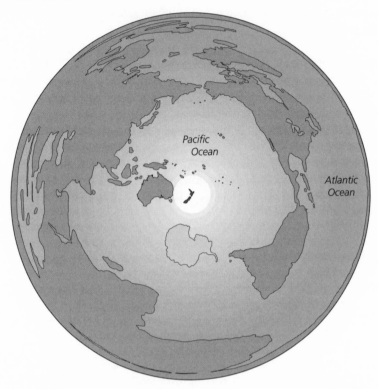

Based on great circle azimuths and distances from Wellington to all parts of the world.

quote similar examples from their own experience. At a quite different resolution, Yoon has demonstrated the distinctiveness of the place-names of
New Zealand in regionally retaining a very high proportion of Maori names.
Indeed, as I understand it, the Korean classical tradition in geography, as
practiced by such scholars as Kim Chong-ho, has involved a close attention
to the details of place through field observation and mapping (Yoon 1995),
a point that also relates to the need I identify for empiricism informing
theory.

The Preoccupation of Geography with Theory and Environment

While other social sciences have recently begun to focus on space and
place, geographers have been directing little of their energy into area studies
(other than at the local scale). Two reasons are apparent. First, as I sug-

gested, many geographers have been concentrating the theoretical debates of social science. Their work is now fully imbedded in the mainstream literature of social science. Second, geographers have had the environment on their agenda. Both physical and human geographers have had almost too many opportunities to teach and to research all manner of environmental issues and concerns. This environmental imperative for geographers and other natural scientists has similarities with the interest of all social sciences in space and place. All of the natural and physical sciences, and many of the social, have seen a place for themselves in investigating the environmental concerns of the late twentieth century. One of the central and long-standing interests of geographers—the environment—now has many other protagonists, although for many of these disciplines it remains subsidiary. Their core business is often elsewhere.

Much of the recent environmental emphasis in geography is disappointing for its limited perspective. Like many of the other disciplines claiming the environment as territory, the overwhelming emphasis in geographic research that is labeled as environmental has been on human impact on the natural environment rather than in attempting to understand the environment as milieu for human activity. Although understandable from the threats that many scientists claim are posed to planet earth, this emphasis seems like a reversion to the environmental interest of the 1950s and 1960s when the rallying point was the volume edited by Thomas and with a title fitting to the time—*Man's Role in Changing the Face of the Earth*. The current emphasis could be paraphrased as *People's Role in Changing the Atmosphere and Its Impact on the Earth*. The resolution of such work is often very coarse, a characteristic that it shares with the literature on globalization. At finer resolution, whether it be regional or local, people-environmental interaction (and especially the influence of natural environments on people) is culturally mediated. Indeed, the separation of people from nature or environment is not helpful. As Harvey (1996: 435) so forcibly argues, "[T]he distinction between *environment* as commonly understood and the *built, social, and political-economic environment* is artificial and that the urban and everything that goes into it is as much part of the solution as it is a contributing factor to ecological difficulties."

Geography needs to reintegrate the environmental turn into the traditional strengths of the discipline. In New Zealand, there are signs that this may be occurring, in part through tying environmental debates to a traditional geographical definition of the most elusive, yet dominating, term "sustainability." For example, in a current study of the Northland region funded in order to investigate "sustainability" (the central concept of New Zealand's environmental legislation) the investigatory framework is the boundaries of a single river catchment. Geographical frames of reference and themes such as land use, water, studies of communities in situ, the mechanics of place and ethnic identity have been used to explore the catchment and its resources (Blunden et al. 1996; Kaipo 1997; Scott et al. 1997). And the traditional methodologies of geography, including the new GIS technologies, have been married with ethnographic techniques and perspectives. Thus, this example also illustrates the need for a reinsertion of cultural processes into studies of geographic difference. Certainly, it is no longer possible to study almost any theme in New Zealand without recognizing the bicultural and multicultural elements that pertain to it.

Empirical Testing of Theory

Molloy (this volume) argues that all social sciences need to engage in empiricism if only to provide evidence to question the unsubstantiated assertions of economics. Geographers roundly rejected the dominance of a singularly economistic and theory-dominated approach to understanding after the intense attempts of the 1950s and 1960s to model spatial social and economic processes quantitatively. While the exclusivity of the approach was rejected, the need for convincing information of the sort provided by that period is necessary if the empirically unsubstantiated claims of the rational choice models of economics are to be debated effectively.

In all parts of the discipline geographers have been struggling to relate the local to the regional to the national to the global. To understand the influence of the global on place many human geographers have returned to detailed studies of small areas in cities and rural areas, often through qualitative analysis. They have been successful in exposing and clarifying some of the complexities of globablization discussed by Cerny (1997). Whether these microstudies can be replicated effectively at the mesoscale, and a similar level of understanding emerge, is far from clear.

The Geography of Organizations

One of the unresolved debates of the recent decades is concerned with establishing a deeper understanding of the relationships between environmental degradation (and people-environment interactions in general) and the uneven distribution of wealth. The major debates of the 1992 Rio conference centred on this issue as something of a standoff developed between the nations and groups of the North and South. It is clear that the same sorts of issues are emerging within nations and among different sets of nations as more international pressure is being placed on everyone to be more environmentally responsible, particularly the firms and farms involved in production. The North-South division and its attendant development issues remained intense during the debates at the Kyoto conference of late 1997 over greenhouse gas emissions. The vitriolic exchanges ended in a modest reduction in emissions by the European Union, Japan and the United States.

Often the degradational effects of the actions of major corporations are treated in an oversimplified way by attempting merely to find ways to enforce more responsible action. As has happened in the past, the debate will shift, I believe, to more fundamental issues that revolve around the organization of production and the nature of our cities (see Harvey 1996). In rural areas, for instance, the real issue that is emerging is the relationship between the property rights of land owners and the powers that local, regional and national governments have to limit or change these rights. This interplay is locally and regionally differentiated as well as strongly influenced by the make-up of the local population, their culture and their involvement in the political economy. It is not difficult to see debates intensifying over the organization of industrial production in relation to its total environmental effects. Without a continuing research and teaching agenda on the geography of the material conditions of production, and the forms of production around which they are organized, geographers will not be able to make the interconnections necessary to maximize their contributions to these people-environment issues.

A Strategic Approach to Disciplinary Self-Interest

Williams (in Pinkey 1989: 160) identifies the influence of the inclusion of work experience in the curriculum on the opportunities for cultural studies. On one level it limits the opportunity for other offerings by holding out powerful material incentives. On another level it introduces the "routines of the foreseen formations of the new industrial capitalism." Meanwhile, the opportunities to enhance the human and social knowledge of individuals will be reduced. Harvey (1996: 433) makes a similar observation when he writes, "One of the strong objections to capitalism is that it has produced a relatively homogeneous capitalist person. This reductionism of all beings and all cultural differences to a common commodified base is the focus of strong anti-capitalist sentiments."

Such arguments are relevant to geography in the school curriculum for the twenty-first century. While the need for geographic education is increasingly being recognized, often as a result of the global and environmental interests already discussed, the curriculum as a whole is often dominated by subjects that are perceived as offering a more certain path to employment. The controversy and delays surrounding the introduction of a new high school curriculum in social studies in New Zealand during the 1990s illustrates the manner in which the curriculum is becoming a more overt site for social contestation of knowledge. The intense debates over constructivism in science in many countries is an even better example. In such an environment of competition the geographic community must have its case for inclusion coherently developed and closely argued.

There are indications that within the national and international geographic communities progress is being made. In the last five years various of the national and international professional geographic organizations have assessed their current position in research and education. I commend the impressive work of the Commission on Education of the International Geographical Union, and its charter, to any group that is planning its curricula or wishes to have an international perspective on geographic education. Such globalization of knowledge must also be informed by national and regional attempts to evaluate and publicize the discipline. Intense debates are in progress, for instance, in South Africa on the shape of the geographic curriculum beyond apartheid. From such distinctive local perspectives these discussions are questioning the geographic curricula that have been developed in other parts of the world, notably their emphasis on the didactic teaching of values and on limited case studies at the expense of more comprehensive understandings of place. Contemporaneously, the U.S. National Research Council's recent publication on geography (National Research Council 1997) has been developed to capitalize on the reemerging concern in the United States about the geographic illiteracy of the population. Given the earlier discussion of area studies, one cannot help recognize the distinctive international, temporal and chronological circumstances for the revitalization of geography in the elementary and secondary schools in many parts of the United States. Geographic education and contact between peoples is one of the ways of achieving a culturally sensitive globalization.

CONCLUSION

To be successful the area studies of the future will require strong contributions from both the social sciences and from cultural studies. Geography has an important role to play within area studies, but to be effective, it must recapture its own discourse. It must use the insights derived from the intense theorizing and emphasis on the nomothetic of the last twenty years to produce a more nuanced and empirically established understanding of place that makes its own distinctive contribution to area studies. At the same time, it must continue to engage fully with the other social and environmental disciplines, as it has done in the recent past.

Certainly the knowledge created must be culturally informed. It is quite insufficient to assume that any association among countries be based only on economic interests and the implied knowledge that derives from limited and prescriptive approaches to understanding. It may be that what we see emerging in area studies, as envisaged by Wallerstein, is a closer drawing together of the humanities and social science through a reintegration of cultural studies with social science theory. For geographers any such package must be informed by a people-environment emphasis and the recognition that place makes a difference.

NOTE

I gratefully acknowledge the assistance of Linda Smith, Kathryn Lehman and Hong-key Yoon in guiding me to some literature. Greg Blunden and Nick Lewis as always provided fruitful discussions, good words and other help in getting this chapter together.

REFERENCES

Barrington, J. M. and Beaglehole, T. H. (1974) *Maori Schools in a Changing Society: A Historical Review.* Wellington: New Zealand Council for Educational Research.

Blunden, G., Cocklin, C., Smith, W. and Moran, W. (1996) "Sustainability: A View from the Paddock." *New Zealand Geographer,* 52(2): 24–34.

Braudel, F. (1980) *On History.* Chicago: University of Chicago Press.

Castells, M. (1991) *The Informational City: Information, Technology, Economic Restructuring, and the Urban-Regional Process.* Oxford: Basil Blackwell.

Cerny, P. (1997) "Paradoxes of the Competition State: The Dynamics of Political Globalisation." *Government and Opposition,* 32(2): 251–274.

Cumberland, K. and Fox, J. (1958) *New Zealand: A Regional View.* Christchurch: Whitcombe and Tombs Limited.

Firth, R. (1929) *The Primitive Economy of the New Zealand Maori.* Wellington: Government Printer.

Foucault, M. (1980) "An Interview with Michel Foucault Conducted by Michael Bess." *History of the Present,* 4: 1–13.

———. (1982) "Spatialisation of Power: A Discussion of the Work of Michel Foucault." *Skyline* (March): 21–23.

Friedman, M. (1982) *Capitalism and Freedom.* Chicago: University of Chicago Press.

Gregory, D. (1994) *Geographical Imaginations.* Oxford: Blackwell.

Gulbenkian Commission on the Restructuring of the Social Sciences. (1996) *Open the Social Sciences: A Report of the Gulbenkian Commission on the Restructuring of the Social Sciences.* Stanford, CA: Stanford University Press.

Hartshorne, R. (1939) "The Nature of Geography: A Critical Survey of Current Thought in the Light of the Past." *Annals of the Association of American Geographers,* 29(3, 4): 73–469.

———. (1959) *Perspective on the Nature of Geography.* Chicago: Association of American Geographers, Rand McNally and Company.

Harvey, D. (1969) *Explanation in Geography.* London: Edward Arnold.

———. (1989) *The Condition of Post-Modernity: An Enquiry into the Origins of Cultural Change.* Oxford: Basil Blackwell.

———. (1996) *Justice, Nature and the Geography of Difference.* Cambridge, MA: Blackwell.

Hayek, F. (1960) *The Constitution of Liberty.* London: Routledge and Keegan Paul.

Heilbrunn, Jacob. (1996) "Everywhere Does Global Thinking Threaten." *Lingua Franca* (May–June): 49–56.

Kaipo, S. (1997) *Te Tangi a te Iwi (Why our people cried): Mangakahia Irrigation from a Tangata Whenua Perspective.* Occasional Publication 35, Department of Geography, The University of Auckland.

Lefebvre, H. (1991) *The Production of Space.* Oxford: Basil Blackwell.

Livingstone, D. (1992) *The Geographical Tradition: Episodes in the History of a Contested Enterprise.* Cambridge, MA: Blackwell.

Marshall, P. (1905) *The Geography of New Zealand: Historical, Physical, Political and Commercial.* Christchurch: Whitcombe and Tombs.

McMichael, P. (1996) "Globalisation: Myths and Realities." *Rural Sociology,* 61(1): 25–55.

Moran, W. (1984) "Time, Place and New Zealand Human Geography in the 1980s." In I. F. Owens et al. (eds.), *Proceedings of the Twelfth New Zealand Geography Conference.* Christchurch, 18–27.

National Research Council. (1997) *Rediscovering Geography: New Relevance for Science and Society.* Washington, DC: National Academy Press.

Palat, R. (1996) "Fragmented Visions: Excavating the Future of Area Studies in a Post-American World." *Review,* 19(3): 269–315.

Pinkey, T. (ed.) (1989) *The Politics of Modernism: Raymond Williams.* London: Verso.

Schwimmer, E. (1966) *The World of the Maori.* Wellington: Reed.

Scott, K., Park, J., Cocklin, C. and Blunden, G. (1997) *A Sense of Community: An Ethnography of Rural Sustainability in the Mangakahia Valley, Northland.* Occasional Publication 33, Department of Geography, The University of Auckland.

Simon, J. (ed.). (1997) *The Native Schools System.* Auckland, NZ: Auckland University Press.

Soja, E. (1989) *Postmodern Geographies: The Reassertion of Space in Critical Social Theory.* London: Verso.

Tremewan, C. (1996) "Reform and Democratisation in the Asia-Pacific: Korea and New Zealand in the Post-Cold War Era." Keynote address at the launch of The Korea Public Policy Forum, Seoul, November 6. Unpublished.

Wallerstein, I. (1996) "Open the Social Sciences." *Items,* 50(1): 1–7.

Watts, M. (1996) "Development III: the Global Agrofood System and Late Twentieth Century Development (or Kautsky Redux)." *Progress in Human Geography,* 20(2): 230–245.

Yoon, H. (1995) "Kim Chong-ho." *Geographers Bibliographical Studies,* 16: 37–44.

Chapter 6

Women's Studies/Cultural Studies: Pedagogy, Seduction and the Real World

MAUREEN MOLLOY

When Mike Peters asked me to write a chapter on women's studies as part of his seminar series on interdisciplinarity in the university, I was more than pleased to participate. I felt it was important that women's studies, as one of the earliest and, I would argue, most formative of the interdisciplinary fields of research and teaching, be represented at such a series. However, when I received the preparatory material, I must confess to being a little nonplussed. The title of the series was "Disciplinarity: The University and the Emergence of Cultural Studies." The suggestions to presenters explained the model for the series as follows:

Since the late 1960s, both internationally and locally, we have witnessed the growth of subject areas outside the traditional liberal arts curriculum and disciplinary structure of the university curriculum: Maori (or Black) Studies, Feminist or Women's Studies, New Zealand (or American Studies), Critical Legal Studies, Film and Media Studies, Asian Studies, Gay Studies. . . . This course of seminars is designed to examine the emergence of "cultural studies" (a generic term used to cover the newly emergent field of study).

Hold on, I thought. Women's studies is not simply a subset of cultural studies, nor as I understand them, are many of the "studies" listed under that rubric by our esteemed host. Women's studies, as I understand it, is in part interdisciplinary, but also has strong disciplinary bases. In many universities women's studies is still constituted only by crosslisted papers contributed by discipline-based scholars from traditional discipline-based departments. Even in the women's studies program at the University of Auckland, although it has staff appointed to women's studies and a strong core of interdisciplinary papers, the majority of papers offered in the program are taught within disciplines and with strong disciplinary theoretical and methodological foci. The interdisciplinarity of women's studies teaching, one might argue, often occurs more in the student's experience of the program, than in the pedagogy within specific papers. This is not the whole picture, of course, but certainly it is possible to take a minor in women's studies at this university and take only strongly discipline-based papers at each stage except the first.

Nor is all interdisciplinary research and teaching done in the name of women's studies cultural studies. I can think of a number of interdisciplinary research projects and could certainly envisaged teaching an interdisciplinary paper which would use readings and tackle problems in women's studies that would bear little resemblance to the body of work usually associated with "cultural studies" and increasingly located in doorstop sized books entitled variously *Cultural Studies* (Grossberg et al. 1992), *A Cultural Studies Reader* (Munns and Rajan 1995) or *Contemporary Literary Criticism: Literary and Cultural Studies* (Davis and Schleifer 1994). So, I thought, he's got it wrong. It seemed to me that what Mike was focusing his seminar series around might more accurately fall under what Gayatri Spivak has called "marginality studies"—encompassing as it does those subjects or objects of knowledge which have been marginal to either the canon, as in film studies, or to the proper Western subject—women, Maori, blacks, gays, colonial nation-states—and whose marginality is so central to the construction of that subject. This left me with the question of whether I wanted to focus on the relationship of women's studies to interdisciplinarity or to its most popular contemporary manifestation—cultural studies.

My decision to focus on cultural studies came from my niggling suspicion that if Mike wasn't right about women's studies and cultural studies on one level, he was very close to being right on another. And this "rightness" was at the core of a set of problems I have been trying to work through since becoming involved in women's studies at this university—a set of problems that has, I think, dogged tertiary level women's studies and academic feminism for a long time. That set of problems might be variously articulated around the oppositions theory and practice, academia and "the real world," cultural studies and social policy. It is not my intention in this chapter to canvass the historical interactions or current overlaps between women's studies and cultural studies. Those tasks have been more than adequately covered in a number of articles by those central to the development of both fields internationally (see, for example Brunsdon 1996; Franklin, et al. 1991; Long 1996; Lovell 1995; Stimpson 1988). What I want to do in this chapter instead is to explore some of the tensions underpinning this shift in women's studies towards cultural studies, in order to map out some of its implications for effective teaching at university level.

This set of problems has been brought home to me in two specific ways.

The first has been the three exercises in appointing junior staff that we have been involved in since women's studies was set up. Each time we have included social policy as one of our preferred areas of expertise. Despite receiving close to 100 applications through these ads we have never had a viable candidate whose area of academic expertise was social policy, however broadly conceived. For one of the ads I could have written the prototypical application (perhaps eighty percent of appointable applicants). The applicant had just completed or was completing a Ph.D. in English or film studies. If majoring in English she was writing a thesis on a canonical male figure—Lawrence, Shakespeare, Browning, etc., etc., and examining narrative spaces, power/knowledge, hybridity, feminine ambiguity, etc., etc., with the aid of Derrida, Foucault, Lacan, or less commonly Irigaray, Kristeva . . . you can fill in the blanks. She had one article in a local journal and perhaps another in press—a group of undoubtedly bright women scholars virtually indistinguishable from each other in the academic pack. This raised questions for me about the current state of feminist graduate education and about how we could design our graduate program to give our students some advantage in this difficult job market.

The second time this issue was brought home to me with particular force was in April 1996 when I, along with about 2,000 other women, attended the Sixth International Interdisciplinary Conference on Women at the University of Adelaide. This United Nations–sponsored conference is held every two years and brings together academics, researchers and policymakers from around the world. It was a large conference, the book of abstracts an inch thick; the papers, as is generally true of these kinds of conferences, genuinely mixed in the degree of their coherence, theoretical and methodological sophistication and subject matter. For me the conference was marked by two quite noticeable features—the absence of any of Australia's poststructuralist feminist stars and the first world/third world split in the kinds of papers offered and the attendance at these sessions. I will focus principally on the last of these features, although I suspect the first is a symptom of the kinds of problems I am attempting to explicate.

I chaired a session on the family and the economy. There were five papers presented by researchers from Bangaladesh, Malaysia, Turkey, Hong Kong and Italy. They were, respectively, on violence against women and children (Zaman 1996), structural constraints on women's labor force participation (Tiun and Abdad 1996), division of labor within the family (Kasnakoglu et al. 1996), gender and class mobility and attitudes to women, work (no refeerence available) and childrearing (Palomba 1996). The results of each of these studies was, depressingly, entirely predictable. Domestic violence, even wife murder, often goes unpunished in Bangaladesh; lack of affordable child care is the biggest constraint on women's labor force participation in Malaysia; men of all classes and education levels in Turkey do little housework, regardless of whether their wives work outside the home or not; men absorb family resources as they try to improve their class mobility in Hong Kong, while women respond by tighter domestic budgeting and increasing their own hours of work; Europeans, generally, regard children as important, as a burden and as principally the responsibility of the wife to care for and tend to. One is tempted to say that the name of the country in which the research was done had minimal impact on the results. There were few "first world" women at this session, not, I think, because they do not care about or are not aware of these issues, but because these kinds of studies have already been done repeatedly in first world countries; they have been re-done ten or twenty years after; the results are known; the patterns proving much harder to change than anyone would have predicted in those first heady days of the women's liberation movement. In a first world academic climate emphasising "difference" these studies pose an empirical threat to the argument that women are not also marked by "the same."

Like many of my colleagues I attended a mix of sessions, including one on the history of second wave feminism in Australia (Borrett et al. 1996), a performance by a Filipino scholar/writer/poet about the ambiguities of going/coming/leaving home when home is both metropolitan Australia and a rural Filipino village (Bobis 1996) and a session in which a colleague from Canada explicated the sophisticated attempts at redefining the Canadian nation by Pauline Johnson (Strong-Boag 1996). Johnson, who was the daughter of a Mohawk father and English mother, was a feminist, nativist romantic poet whose poems every Canadian child of my generation and my mother's, memorized in primary school and whose Edwardian sentimentalism had led to her dismissal by a younger, more modern, more hard-edged, more political (?) generation of nationalist poets and literary critics. These were innovative rereadings of history, migration and the politics of poetry with hardly a hint of violence, poverty or washing the dishes. Good scholars, publishable papers, each located comfortably within the cultural studies paradigm.

My responses to these quite different sets of papers bothered me. I felt horrified, depressed and ineffectual in the face of the empirical studies of domestic politics. I enjoyed and was challenged by the some of the cultural studies papers. I felt uneasy about my responses and about what seemed to me to be the pattern of papers. If my definition of women's studies does not map as easily onto cultural studies as Mike's does, it seems nevertheless that in practice cultural studies is increasingly the dominant research paradigm within first world academic women's studies. Although I myself work principally within that paradigm, this trend makes me uneasy. I want to ask what is being left out or lost? There are serious issues about pedagogy and politics here that mandate a careful attempt to think through the relation between the realities of many women's lives and academic practice, particularly pedagogical practice, a thinking through which avoids the pitfalls of name-calling, easy oppositions and simplistic politics.

FEMINIST STUDIES/CULTURAL STUDIES

Simon During in his article "Professing the Popular" (During 1990) locates the rise of the teaching of popular culture in the humanities in Australia (compared to its virtual absence from Oxbridge) to a number of cultural and political economic factors: the fact that Australian students tend to get their undergraduate education "at home," still embedded in familial and peer communities, a population less tolerant of class distinction and more committed to (on some level) an egalitarian ethos, Australia's less hierarchical tertiary education system, and a move to student-based funding, which has resulted in disciplines competing for students. He attributes its rise in the United States to the affirmative action programs of the 1970s and the commitment to and funding of social justice and diversity in American universities. The rise of cultural studies in New Zealand is attributable, I think, to some combination of these two factors, the political economy of tertiary training and a social justice agenda, plus one other which During misses, New Zealand's status as a self-consciously decolonizing nation.[1] For During that which distinguishes academic teaching of popular culture from the position of "fan" are two features: (1) the representational analysis which inevitably reads the popular as symptom of something else; and (2) the political commitment underlying that symptomatic reading. During leaves out those features of academic practice that (we hope) distinguish it from any form of nonprofessional appreciation: a critical approach to the material and a commitment to rigor.

Overt political commitment has always been at the core of cultural studies, at least in Britian and Australasia.[2] Cultural studies' genealogy can be traced back from Stuart Hall and the Birmingham Centre, on the one hand, through the Marxist scholarship of Raymond Williams, E. P. Thompson Antonio Gramsci, György Lukács and the Frankfurt school and, on the other, through Richard Hoggart and F. R. Leavis. Is there a matriline? Sadly, cultural studies, according to some of its historiographers (Easthope 1991; Inglis 1993), seems to be no exception to the rule that cultural births are the result of male parthenogenesis. Fred Inglis (Inglis 1993), for example, footnotes one article by Queenie Leavis and cites Janet Radcliffe-Richards' *The Sceptical Feminist* (Richards 1980, 1994) as his guide to second wave posthumanist feminism in single paragraph that is overly generalized and takes no account of the depth and breadth of feminist cultural studies. Marxist mothers had to fight for any recognition of their role in its birth, much less the legitimacy of trying to give the child a feminist cast. Charlotte Brunsdon, for example, cites with obvious pain and anger Stuart Hall's description of feminist students in the Birmingham Centre who disrupted the cosy socialist consensus and "crapped on the table" (Brunsdon 1996: 279).

While feminist cultural studies also grew initially out of that attempt to insert women into the Marxist version of culture, its more dominant matriliny comes, curiously enough, via film studies. Analyses of the psychoanal-ytics and politics of film and film viewing by Laura Mulvey, Teresa de Lauretis and, in Australasia, Meaghan Morris would seem to me to be that which most firmly put feminist cultural studies on the agenda in Australasia, at least. Each of these three is, of course, highly influenced by Sausurrean semiotics, Lacanian psychoanalytic theory and Foucault's formulations of power/knowledge. Current output in feminist cultural studies follows suit and suggests that the old Marxist patriliny has lost custody of its child to a set of smooth-talking Frenchmen. Jane Gallop (Gallop 1982: 26) has argued that in the early 1980s feminism was been seduced by Lacanian psychoan-alytics and has indeed located this seduction formally within the oedipal metaphor. It has, however, given rise to an amazing range of research and writing.

Now seduction, in these terms, is a easy word. But in terms of theory, and by one of those who has most bravely put issues of the erotics of ped-agogy on the agenda, it seems to me to be a cop out. Seduction implies duping, lack of sense, lack of agency on the part of the seduced, which hardly seem to give credit to the amount of careful and insightful analysis which has been enabled by the translation of poststructuralist French the-orists into English. It also belies a lack of responsibility on the part of the seduced feminists that puts them right back into the category of victim, a category hardly merited.

The other, and perhaps less acknowledged, matriarchal line in women's studies is via political philosophy. I am thinking here specifically of the work that perhaps reached its culmination in Carole Pateman's *The Sexual Con-tract* (Pateman 1988b). This gendered reading of the pale male contract theorists whose work underpins so much of European popular and academic thinking has enabled a vast range of feminist cultural studies work, and is a genre by which I myself, somewhat sceptical of psychoanalysis, am partic-ularly influenced. And of course the French feminists, particularly Irigaray and Kristeva whose works transverse the psychoanalytic and the political, continue to be extremely influential.

THE REAL WORLD

The enormous influence of poststructuralism in feminist cultural studies has undercut the principal ground on which earlier versions if Anglo-American feminism stood—experience—and indeed has imposed a third term into the uneasy alliance between cultural studies and feminism.[3] Within feminism the "real world" has often been coded as experience. Women's experience has been taken to be a ground that both constitutes and validates knowledge. This privileging of experience has been eroded over the past years by scholars working with Foucaultian or poststructuralist theories who have argued that experience must be explained and cannot be taken to be either self-evident or in itself a validating mechanism. Joan Scott (Scott 1991, 1992), for instance, has caused a furor in the historical world for by arguing that gender is a useful and necessary category for historical analysis, one which problematizes the social and renders experience as something which needs to be explained.

However, the repudiation of "experience" as the real ground of knowledge has left a gap in how we understand what we do, and perhaps also, why we do it. This is a gap which Elspeth Probyn attempts to bridge. Probyn is one of the more interesting theorists working within a cultural studies paradigm that includes both the older Marxist tradition as developed by Williams and French tradition represented by Foucault (who are not as far apart as they might appear). Probyn can be read in some sense as retrieving cultural studies for the social sciences and as retrieving "the social" from the hegemonic grasp of the psychoanalytic for cultural studies. In *Sexing the Self: Gendered Positions in Cultural Studies* (Probyn 1993: 21) she argues that it is premature and counterproductive to jettison experience as a valuable tool in cultural studies. She argues that experience can stand in relation to "the social" in three ways: (1) that experience itself speaks of the composition of the social formation; (2) that experience can be overwhelming and work to conceal the connections between the different structures; and (3) that the critic's own experience can impel the analysis of his or her differentiated relations to levels of the social formation.

It is principally the latter, the "use of the critic's self for cultural studies work," on which she focuses. She draws on Williams' description of "those specific and definable moments when very new work produces a sudden shock of recognition" and argues further that "[w]e are drawn to recognize and research certain experiences . . . because we have at some level lived and experienced them ourselves." Williams' "shock of recognition" attests to this, and in a feminist framework we can extend this term to talk about the shock of recognition of gendered experiences (Probyn 1993: 23). Probyn argues that the cultural critic must make experience work in two registers, the ontological and the epistemological:

[A]t an ontological level, the concept of experience posits a separate realm of existence—it testifies to the gendered, sexual and racial facticity of being in the social; it can be called an immediate experiential self. At an epistemological level, the self is revealed in its conditions of possibility; here experience is recognised as more obviously discursive and can be used overtly to politicise the ontological. (Probyn 1993: 16–17)

In considering, again, how this might work, I want to reflect on student response to two lectures I give at Stage One. I have been teaching the bulk of one of our Stage One papers, "Women, Gender and Society," for four years. This paper was conceptualized as an introduction to the "social science" side of women's studies. It includes an introduction to theories of power, knowledge and language and a review of the major popular and sociological conceptions of class, race, ethnicity, sexuality, etc., and how they are gendered. It has a section on "the body" and one that considers the recent history of work and politics with regard to women. I have been struck each year that I have taught it by the students' response to two of the lectures I give. Each of us who has taught big classes knows what the feeling is like when our lectures "click," when they hit something in the class that engages the mind and or the passions of the student, with the result that they are either unusually quiet and attentive or unusually noisy and exuberant as they leave the lecture theater.

The two lectures that most consistently get this response are one on housework and one on the citizen. It seems to me, on reflection, that these lectures engage the students at quite different levels of experience, perhaps homologous to Probyn's notions of the epistemological and the ontological. The response to the housework lecture is in some sense not surprising. In it we review the history of housework in the context of rising class differentiation during the industrial revolution and its embeddedness in the pedagogy of the working class associated with the rise of professional social work and the welfare state. We go on to explore the contemporary research on division of labor within the home, pausing to reflect on the relatively meager increase in the time men spend doing housework relative to the increase in women's involvement in the paid work force, the ways in which housework is divided between the sexes and how some tasks (cleaning toilets, wiping the bench, putting away the laundry) are surprisingly resistant to male involvement. It gives rise to what the tutors call the "I hate my father" or "I am going to leave my husband" tutorials. We know that, statistically, it touches on the lived experience of virtually every woman who has ever lived with a man and experienced the almost maniacal workload of the double shift or the maddening frustrations of trying to change what are perceived to be trivial matters.

The second lecture that invokes a surprisingly intense response is one on citizenship. Each year I have reconsidered whether this lecture belongs at Stage One because it is one of the more abstract lectures in an already overly abstract paper. In it we consider Carole Pateman's (Pateman 1988a) argument that the citizen is fundamentally a (European) male, both historically and currently. Pateman bases her argument on what she identifies as three defining characteristics of the citizen: the capacity to own property, including property in one's own person, the capacity to bear arms and the capacity for governance of self and others. Students tend to respond to this lecture with a kind of intensity which I have never been able to explain and to leave volubly discussing its contents. It seems to me that this lecture invokes a somewhat different response: the "shock of recognition" which says not "that is me," "that is my experience," as does the housework lecture, but more complexly "that is us": we are gendered, we are racialized. This response is what Teresa de Lauretis calls the "aha" of feminism—those precious times when theory articulates experience, often experience that we did not even know we had, when theory somehow makes the world more and not less real, when it is seen in a different light, one which cannot be turned off.

The ontological "shock of recognition" is relatively easy to achieve in women's studies. Women's studies is not a particularly pretty field. Misogyny, sexual abuse, rape, emotional and physical violence, discrimination, dismissal and erasure are easy to find and form almost our daily bread. It would be relatively easy to use this "real world" to hook students emotionally into the discipline without ever confronting the complexities of theory, and there are indeed those who believe that this is women's studies task. A sense of outrage can be very seductive. The epistemological "aha" of feminism is more difficult, I think, because at one level it is countercultural. It involves reading against the culture and reading against the easily tapped emotionality of violence.

If our pedagogy has a politics then that gap between the ontological and the epistemological must where it is practiced. And that, it seems to me, is the strength of cultural studies. The study of culture, whether as conceived within the anthropological tradition, or in its more recent focus on contemporary Western culture or the culture of colonialism, is about reading between the lines, against the grain, within the everyday. It is the necessary critical step from experience to the real world, a real world that is not the self-evident world.

In trying to think about the relation of feminist pedagogy to cultural studies I have been struck by how little has been written on this topic, either within feminism or without.[4] Books on feminist pedagogy often focus on teacher/students relations, problems of authority and equality, and interpersonal processes. Books on feminist research commonly focus on the methodology of traditional disciplines, but little has been written on the teaching of cultural studies. Stuart Hall, despite being the most successful cultural studies pedagogue of our times, has written nothing, as far as I can tell from a bibliography of his written work, on the pedagogy of cultural studies (Morley and Chen 1996).

The grand exception to this rather surprising chasm in the literature is Gayatri Chakravorty Spivak, whose work over the past five years has revolved implicitly and explicitly around the politics of teaching and the place, if any, of cultural studies within that politics, culminating in her most recent book *Outside in the Teaching Machine* (Spivak 1993). Spivak seems to be unique, not only for her focus on pedagogy, but also for her deeply unapologetic commitment to tertiary teaching, to locating her politics and her political identity in what she calls "the institutional appellation 'teacher'," and for her almost nonchalant, undefensive and taken-for-granted feminism. I like the way she is always present in the texts, and how her texts are always contextualized by place, time and audience, while at the same time she refuses to validate her work through any easy or nominal identities.

Spivak's context does not map neatly onto ours. She is writing within a precise set of debates in the United States about "cultural literacy," on the one hand, and decanonization, on the other, a debate that tried to surface here a few years ago in the context of the inclusion of Maori in the English curriculum, but that, mercifully, has for the most part died, or at least gone underground. Neverthless, it seems to me that she has something to offer those of us engaged in tertiary teaching in marginality studies. For Spivak, what we as academics are engaged in is negotiating a politics within the teaching machine. In a Marxist reading of Foucault she renders his power/ knowledge into the seemingly ontological pouvior/savoir, "the ability to know," "lines of knowing constituting ways of doing and not doing." Ahead of these, she argues, "making their rationality fully visible, are the great apparatuses of *puissance/connaisance*," including the teaching machine, that "space one cannot (not) wish to inhabit" (Spivak 1993: 37). Much of her work is focused on how from within that apparatus one can persistently critique it, to halt, displace or disrupt the formation of "a new orientalism" growing out of the emphasis on and interest in postcolonial theory. Her work is significant not because she tells us how to do cultural studies (although she does occasionally drop hints) but because she shows us how to do it, through the extraordinary range of her knowledge and reading and her ability to make connections between, for example, the constitutive position of "we the people" in a new reading of the American Constitution, recent Turkish history, the relative ethical positions of intellectuals in France and Europe in the aftermath of World War II and the teaching of an internationalized cultural studies in American tertiary institutions (Spivak 1993: 255–284).

To do cultural studies well is not simply to seduce students into our departments and programs to win the numbers game. More than any other field, cultural studies requires breadth of knowledge about the "real world" and the ability to make or see connections between seemingly unrelated or dissociated cultural artifacts or events. This requires concrete knowledge and theoretical depth and range. It requires an intellectual division of labor which retains both strong disciplinarity and the flexibility to range across disciplines. Without this we are relegated to the banality of much of what passes for cultural studies, those "thousands of versions of the same article about pleasure, resistance and the politics of consumption which are being run off under different names with minor variations," the master copy of which, Meaghan Morris suggests, is kept on a disk in some English publisher's vault (Morris 1994: 648).

Moreover, this kind of cultural studies demands that we reclaim the social scientific heritage of cultural studies. A great deal of "cultural theory" teaching and writing is located in or comes out of the humanities, especially English departments. It is ironic that Williams, the literary scholar who wrote the great methodological work on the sociology of culture, should find his brainchild has moved back home (Williams 1981). Popular culture has come increasingly to mean "low culture" produced for mass consumption, such as comic books, television, film, the Internet. It is far less likely these days to invoke its anthropological heritage and to involve the meanings people give to their own lives or to involve ethnographic fieldwork, such as forms the basis for Bob Connell's *Masculinities* (Connell 1995) or even interviews, as did its early Marxist versions. A good cultural studies means that we cannot afford to lose the skills for either producing or reading empirical social science. Despite all that has been written about the death of the grand narratives there is a grand narrative that has in a frightenly short time become the received truth and it is called monetarist economics. It has produced, as well as a raft of polemics that have been read and deconstructed, a new emphasis on empirical, statistical research, accountability and, supposedly, transparency. We must structure our pedagogy so that our students are not limited to deconstructive readings of the polemics, for they are limited, boring and repetitive. We have to be able to tackle this other material as well and be able to produce our own facts and figures.

It seems to me if there is a point in all of this it is that we must guard against collapsing these categories. We cannot afford to view interdisciplinarity as coincident with cultural studies as it is defined by those doorstop books. We lose too much that is valuable in other ways of knowing, and we hobble ourselves and our students in our/their abilities to read, think and act politically. Furthermore, we need to reclaim the concept of culture in its broader, more anthropological version. When "cultural studies" is increasingly defined as literary, film or media studies and when the mantra "there is nothing outside the text" becomes "only written or filmed or otherwise recorded texts are worthy subjects of academic inquiry," we are in grave danger of losing an extremely valuable set of analytical tools and skills, necessary for both the creation of new knowledges and the critique of received truths. On the other hand, cultural studies, as an enterprise that continually transgresses and undercuts traditional disciplinary boundaries and that has, so far at least, resisted the efforts of some of its proponents to define and contain it, has not yet seemed to exhaust its possiblities for surprising, informing and giving pleasure.[5]

And what does feminism offer to cultural studies? I suppose that my answer has to be that it offers everything—that without the systematic consideration of the gendered-ness of culture, in all of its mainfest forms, cultural studies can only repeat the existing masculinist hegemonies. That is, it can only be symptomatic of that which it is trying to analyze. Further, without that consideration, the academic study of culture fails in its prime requirement—that is, the requirement of rigor. It loses one of the features that distinguishes the academic from the fan—the ability to convincingly read the popular as symptomatic and to reveal its political implications.

NOTES

1. John Frow and Meaghan Morris make a similar argument for Australia (Frow and Morris 1996).
2. Ellen Rooney argues that American cultural studies does not have a similar association with a particular political postion (Rooney 1996: 210).
3. See Terry Lovell's 'Introduction' to the two volume *Feminist Cultural Studies* for a mapping of this tension by a scholar who is not entirely happy with this shift (Lovell 1995).
4. For exceptions see Brunsdon 1991, Downing 1994, Giroux et al. (1996). There is also now a number of books about research methods for cultural studies which are implicitly pedagogical—i.e. written for research methods teaching (Alaasutari 1995, Downing 1994, Storey 1996, Thwaites et al. 1994).
5. There is certainly a piece of research to be done on the pleasure of consuming cultural studies.

REFERENCES

Alaasutari, P. (1995) *Researching Culture: Qualitative Method and Cultural Studies*. Thousand Oaks CA: Sage.
Bobis, M. (1996) "Beyond Ethnicity: Cultural Representation as Personal Choice" (a performance paper). Paper presented at the Sixth International Interdisciplinary Congress on Women, Adelaide, Australia.
Borrett, K. et al. (1996) "Can We Have a Rave About Difference—Or Not? Difference in the Australian Women's Movement in the 1970s." Paper presented at the Sixth International Interdisciplinary Congress on Women, Adelaide, Australia.
Brunsdon, C. (1991) "Pedagogies of the Feminine: Feminist Teaching and Women's Genres." *Screen*, 32(4): 364–381.
———. (1996) "A Thief in the Night: Stories of Feminism in the 1970s at CCCS." In D. Morley and K.-H. Chen (eds.), *Stuart Hall: Critical Dialogues in Cultural Studies*. New York: Routledge, 276–286.
Connell, R. (1995) *Masculinities*. St. Leonards, NSW: Allen and Unwin.
Davis, R. C. and Schleifer, R. (eds.). (1994) *Contemporary Literary Criticism: Literary and Cultural Studies*. New York: Longman.
Downing, D. B. (ed.). (1994) *Changing Classroom Practices: Resources for Literary and Cultural Studies*. Urbana, IL: National Council of Teachers of English.
During, S. (1990) "Professing the Popular." *Meanjin*, 49(3): 481–491.
Easthope, A. (1991) *Literary into Cultural Studies*. London: Routledge.
Franklin, S., Lury, C. and Stacy, J. (1991) "Feminism and Cultural Studies: Pasts, Presents, Futures." In S. Franklin, C. Lurie and J. Stacey (eds.), *Off-Centre: Feminism and Cultural Studies*. London: Harper Collins Academic, 1–20.
Frow, J. and Morris, M. (1996) "Australian Cultural Studies." In J. Storey (ed.), *What Is Cultural Studies? A Reader*. London: Arnold, 368–380.

Gallop, J. (1982) *The Daughter's Seduction*. London: MacMillan Press.

Giroux, H., Lankshear, C., Mclaren, P. and Peters, M. (1996) *Counternarratives: Cultural Studies and Critical Pedagogy in Postmodern Spaces*. New York: Routledge.

Grossberg, L. et al. (eds.). (1992) *Cultural Studies*. New York: Routledge.

Inglis, F. (1993) *Cultural Studies*. Oxford: Blackwell.

Kasnakoglu, Z., Cayioglu, M. and Erdil, E. (1996) "Time Use and Household Production by Gender." Paper presented at the Sixth Annual International Interdisciplinary Congress on Women, Adelaide, Australia.

Long, E. (1996)"Feminism and Cultural Studies." In J. Storey (ed.), *What Is Cultural Studies? A Reader*. London: Arnold, 197–207.

Lovell, T. (1995) "Introduction." In T. Lovell (ed.), *Feminist Cultural Studies*, vol. 1. Aldershot, England: Edward Elgar, xiii–xxix.

Morley, D. and Chen, K.-H. (1996)"A Working Bibliography: The Writings of Stuart Hall." In D. Morley and K.-H. Chen (eds.), *Stuart Hall: Critical Dialogues in Cultural Studies*. New York: Routledge, 504–514.

Morris, M. (1994) "Banality in Cultural Studies." In R. C. Davis and R. Schleifer (eds.), *Contemporary Literary Criticism: Literary and Cultural Studies*, 3rd ed. New York: Longman, 642–666.

Munns, J. and Rajan, G. (eds.) (1995) *A Cultural Studies Reader: History, Theory, Practice*. New York: Longman.

Palomba, R. (1996) "Women's Attitudes on Marriage, Children, Labour Force Particpation and Social Policies in Europe." Paper presented at the Sixth Annual International Interdisciplinary Congress on Women, Adelaide, Australia.

Pateman, C. (1988a) "The Patriarchal Welfare State." In A. Gutmann (ed.), *Democracy and the Welfare State*. Princeton, NJ: Princeton University Press.

———. (1988b) *The Sexual Contract*. Stanford, CA: Stanford University Press.

Probyn, E. (1993) *Sexing the Self: Gendered Positions in Cultural Studies*. London: Routledge.

Richards, J. R. (1980, 1994) *The Sceptical Feminist*. London: Penguin.

Rooney, E. (1996) "Discipline and Vanish: Feminism, the Resistance to Theory and the Politics of Cultural Studies." In J. Storey (ed.), *What Is Cultural Studies? A Reader*. London: Arnold, 208–220.

Scott, J. (1991) "The Evidence of Experience." *Critical Inquiry*, 17 (Summer): 773–797.

———. (1992) "Experience." In J. Butler and J. W. Scott (eds.), *Feminists Theorize the Political*. London: Routledge, 22–40.

Spivak, G. (1993) *Outside in the Teaching Machine*. London: Routledge.

Stimpson, C. (1988) "Nancy Reagan Wears a Hat: Feminism and Its Cultural Consensus." *Critical Inquiry*, 14: 223–243.

Storey, J. (1996)*Cultural Studies and the Study of Popular Culture: Theories and Methods*. Athens, GA: University of Georgia Press.

Strong-Boag, V. (1996) "Red Girl's Reasoning: E. Pauline Johnson Constructs the New Nation." Paper presented at the Sixth International Interdisciplinary Congress on Women, Adelaide, Australia.

Thwaites, A., Davis, L. and Mules, W. (1994) *Tools for Cultural Studies: An Introduction*. South Melbourne: Macmillan Education.

Tiun, L. T. and Abdad, M. (1996) "Child Care and Participation of Women in the

Labour Force in Peninsular Malaysia—With Reference to Penang Island." Paper presented at the Sixth Annual International Interdisciplinary Congress on Women, Adelaide, Australia.

Williams, R. (1981) *Culture*. London: Fontana.

Zaman, H. (1996) "Victims of Globalisation: Women and Children." Paper presented at the Sixth International Interdisciplinary Congress on Women, Adelaide, Australia.

Chapter 7

Disciplined Absences: Cultural Studies and the Missing Discourse of a Feminist Politics of Emotion

MEGAN BOLER

In this chapter I examine two absences which impoverish the interdisciplinary studies of culture—ideology and lived relations. Feminist contributions to theorizing subjectivity and politically informed, historicized analyses of emotion as a central feature of subjectivity are frequently overlooked and ignored in critical theory and cultural studies. This Chapter distills several ideas that I explore in much greater detail within my larger project,[1] in which I offer a cultural history of emotions as both a site of social control and political resistance within education. Systematic studies of discourses of emotion are crucial to interdisciplinary studies of culture because emotions appear to be one of the least understood sites of power relations. Further, emotions are increasingly recognized as central to knowledge construction in the modern domains of cognition, morality and aesthetics which constitute Western cultural practices and relations. Feminist theories have most consistently contributed to the study of emotions and power, and these contributions need to be taken on board rather than representing an "add-on" to cultural studies.

I begin this chapter by offering an example from the 1930s of social scientists' and educators' recognition of the "emotional student" as the target of educational control. I will then examine two contemporary examples of educational encounters that cannot be adequately explained through the lens of critical theory and ideology critiques. With a sense of how and why cultural studies and critical theory need a systematic theory of emotions and power, I will examine two glaring absences within cultural studies and critical theory: what I call the missing discourses of feminisms and the missing discourses of emotion. I conclude by outlining how two recent feminist theorists contribute to a politicized theory of emotions as related to power and hegemony.

BEYOND THE SUBJECT AND POWER: ACCOUNTING FOR EMOTIONS

Why do we need a systematic theory of emotions to augment our study of power and lived relations? Cultural studies and critical theory both profess a central fascination with the "subject and power." The schools of thought that constitute cultural studies and critical theory—namely, neo-Marxism, cultural anthropology, psychoanalysis and poststructuralism—increasingly seek to understand power as a two-way process: subjects are not simply "victims" of social forces (e.g., of capitalist ideologies) but redefine dominant discourses of power through their resistances.[2]

In the early decades of this century social scientists and educators founded a crusade known as the "mental hygiene movement."[3] The key target of this medicalized discourse was the "improperly emotional" or "labile" student, whose lack of correct adjustment to social conditions (e.g., industrialization, immigration and urbanization) produced stress within the individual. The child was seen as the primary cause of all social problems due to its emotional maladjustment. Historical phenomena such as the mental hygiene movement need to be understood through our contemporary analyses of education and liberation. Cultural studies and critical theories of education are, in a sense, one step behind the conservative social scientists of the 1930s. For all of cultural studies talk about understanding the interrelationship of the subject and power, we haven't yet developed a systematic theory to understand specific historical discourses regarding emotions in relation to power relations and social forces. The need for an interdisciplinary analysis of discourses of emotion is especially urgent, as my research on contemporary popularity of "emotional intelligence" and "emotional literacy curricula" suggests that these represents a new version of the mental hygiene movement.[4]

I first encountered the term "labile" in a 1938 text, *Emotion and the Educative Process*, written following the Depression and marking the rise of fascism and the Second World War. Daniel Prescott, the central author of this commissioned study, funded by the American Council of Education and reprinted ten times between 1938 and 1961, recognized the "labile" student as the challenge to the modern educational system. In the text, labile means "overemotional." *Emotion and the Educative Process* combines Dewey, American readings of Freud and Darwinian concepts of self. Lability, the authors surmise, is a response to the stress of civilization. The text explicitly acknowledges that a central motive for "disciplining" emotion is to balance discrepancies between desires produced within capitalism, on the one hand, and the "reality" of unfulfilled needs that cause "frustration," maladjustment and conflict. Nationalism and capitalism hence reveal their dependence on emotional equilibrium. This book articulates a rule of industrial capitalism, namely, that *the school should not set up expectations that will not be fulfilled within the society.*

[T]he existence of conditions which drive large blocks of the population to hold attitudes too sharply antagonistic . . . can only cause conflict, lowered efficiency, and ultimate disintegration in a society. . . . Not only is affect important in connection with the formation of attitudes, but attitudes themselves are important sources of affect when the behavior they imply is obstructed or penalized. *If certain factors in society such as the school, advertising, or the teachings of the church develop attitudes favorable to types of behavior made impossible by prevailing social conditions, then tension, disappointment, and feelings or frustration are inevitable. Either the attitudes must be replaced, or social changes must come about, or the individual must compartmentalize his thinking and submit to permanent dissociation due to the lack of harmony between his beliefs and his actions.* (Prescott 1938: 43, emphasis added)

I cannot spend as much time as I would like on this history and the shifting discourses about emotions in education here. What is significant about this example is that the focus on the labile student reflects a brief *explicit* attempt in the history of education to predict and measure emotion.

"Labile" is a post-Enlightenment term first used in the seventeenth century. It is defined by the *Oxford English Dictionary* in five central ways: (1) liable; prone to lapse; (2) liable to fall from innocence into error or sin; (3) slippery, unstable; (4) prone to undergo displacement; and (5) in reference to woodworking—as in a "labile construction material"—it resonates with John Dewey's description of the mutability and complexity of subjectivity as "plasticity."[5] These meanings contradictorily suggest both a passive material that can be shaped and tendencies to "lapse or degenerate" as a result of physiological, social or internal factors. Montaigne, referring to Pythagoras, recapitulates that "everything of matter is labile." Jeremy Taylor's philosophic use of this term during the early eighteenth century noted: "Sensibility and Intelligence, Being by their Nature and Essence free must be labile, and by their lability may actually lapse, degenerate. All creatures, being finite and free must necessarily by their nature be labile, fallible, and peccable." Lability is opposed to "impeccability," which refers to the code of Euro-American and Christian character, class, manners and dress. To be impeccable is not only to be well-dressed and mannered, but "not liable to sin; free from fault, blemish, or error." That these lapsing "tendencies" defy social control reflects the complicated story of Western fears of emotion's threat to rationality and self-control. The notion of a pliable material that can also degenerate or mutate connects with the history of education. Histories of education in Western and colonized countries reflect the religious and class-based values that determine what counts as stability and wholeness for the student/worker/citizen. These imposed models of the "good self" include proscriptions about emotional behavior, which are largely unstated cultural mores. The term "lability" continues to be used in the fields of social work, social sciences and special education today.

The 1984 collection entitled *Changing the Subject: Psychology, Social Regulation, and Subjectivity* (Henriques et al.) invaluably attempts to bridge Marxism and psychoanalysis (a bridge representative of much work in cultural studies and some critical theory) as it addresses the need for critical analyses of social scientific discourses. The following quote summarizes what I see as an unresolved tension within cultural studies and suggests a conceptual as well as linguistic overlap between the labile student and the requirement for compliance with dominant cultural norms:

The concept of resistance itself . . . includes both conscious opposition and the mute automatic resistance of that which is in the process of being shaped. Indeed the material to which we refer, namely particular individuals, is notably *pliable*: the success of a normalizing power also depends on the willing *compliance* of the subject who is the target of the technologies of normalization. *It is precisely this fact which largely remains to be explained.* (Henriques et al. 1984: 115, emphasis added)

The etymology of "pliable" has an uncanny resonance with a unique term, "lability." The concern with the labile student suggests an interesting site for understanding how emotions and hegemony overlap. Lability provides an alternative to the jumbled confusion over the terms "feeling," "affect" and "emotion," which are used disparately and inconsistently within and across disciplines, and the overused terms of "consciousness" and "desire" as they are invoked in cultural studies to reference the psychic site of ideology. Lability suits our need for a term that suggests the unpredictability of the subject within modern life and structural forces. Lability might allow us to begin thinking of affect in relation to power and social relations. The challenge in theorizing emotions continues to be that in both popular and scholarly discourses we think of emotions as natural and idiosyncratic, and therefore private and individualized. Lability's definitions as the tendency to "lapse, degenerate, to fall into error and sin" describes key modes of resistance to what Foucault (1983) calls "pastoral power," the insidious modes of power encountered in administratively governed democracies.[6]

CONTEMPORARY EXAMPLES OF THE LABILE STUDENT

Let me provide two examples of educational encounters that reflect different forms of "resistance." A recent Calvin and Hobbes cartoon depicts a quandary faced by radical educators which I call "refusal." In the first frame, Calvin hands a book back to his mother and says, "I read this library book you got me." She responds, "What did you think of it?" Scratching his head, he answers "It really made me see things differently. It's given me a lot to think about." In the last frame, Calvin's mother says, "I'm glad you enjoyed it" and Calvin, walking away, says, "It's complicating my life. Don't get me any more."

How might critical theory, for example, explore the phenomenon of a student's refusal? In the neo-Marxist, Freirean tradition Calvin's refusal would likely be read as reflecting his ideological investment in the dominant culture, his "fear of freedom." Calvin doesn't want to rock the boat or "see things differently." He doesn't want to complicate his comfortable life.[7]

However, let me provide an example of Calvin's sister which requires a different explanatory account. During a recent course I taught in educational sociology, a young female schoolteacher who is married and lives in the upper-class neighborhood of Remuera articulated her version of Calvin's refusal. During our discussions of feminism in this third-year course in education she proclaimed, "I never thought of myself as female. It has never held me back in any way. Maybe that's because we've come such a long way since our mothers' time." Her narrative states that she has never thought of herself as "female," that being female "has never held her back," and she accounts for lack of a consciously gendered experience by saying, "Maybe it's because we've come such a long way since our mothers' time." Her position is quite different from the female student who says women should be happy staying at home, being denied privileges granted to men. One doesn't have to be a feminist scholar to notice how remarkable it is that she refuses to identify with a particular gender, when she comes from a culture in which gender is one of the centrally defining features.

In explaining her refusal to identify she actually gives us clues that she is aware of the centrality of gender and its impact on power relations through her allusion to historical changes. We might read her as follows: The refusal to identify as woman can be understood as a form of intelligent resistance: Why should I want to be a woman if woman occupies the historically powerless side of the binary—significantly, in a culture where woman is synonymous with victim or lack of power? So she aspires to the ultimate goal of liberal individualism—a free and mobile human unfettered by constructions of gender. Calvin's sister is resisting and complying at the same time—complying with her own subjugation because she's accepted the dominant ideology's appropriation of feminism: namely, that women had it bad but they don't have it bad anymore.

These refusals need to be analyzed not only in terms of ideology but in terms of the emotional investments that characterize how and when we are embedded in culture and ideology. By and large, it has been feminist theorists from different disciplines who most persistently theorize not only the gendered particularities of our subjective positioning but who theorize emotions as a site of social control and of political resistance. While cultural studies and critical theory offer valuable theoretical tools, they are impoverished by their ongoing lack of recognition of feminist contributions to the study of culture, ideology and subjectivity.

The particularities and intricacies of refusal as they manifest in different contexts by different persons distinguished in terms of race, class, gender and culture are particularities that matter a great deal as we attempt to provide a genealogy of what I call "economies of mind." To study Calvin's sister as a way to study emotion is not a coincidence, since femininity and emotion have been powerfully conflated in Western cultures. But Frantz Fanon's (1967) study of the consciousness of black men in colonized histories similarly reflects black men's exclusion from the club of rationality. Thus, I argue that a politicized theory of emotion suggests a framework in which to think about emotion and power relations. Students' refusal to "see things differently" provides a launching point, ultimately, towards a politicized theory of emotions.

THE MISSING DISCOURSE OF FEMINISMS IN CULTURAL STUDIES

Let me very crudely summarize what cultural studies contributes to the study of Calvin's "refusal." Stuart Hall in 1980 characterizes cultural studies as a tension between the "culturalists" and the "structuralists."[8] The culturalists, like Raymond Williams, are primarily interested in the lived experience of culture, the very particular instances of how individuals and communities play out and manifest the larger structural forces and ideologies. The structuralists, on the other hand, are much more interested in the forces of ideology, in the nation-state or economy, or in language as political determinants of what counts as meaningful. Each side faces its own version of the very problematic question of how agency and structure, or individual and society, are interrelated. Hall credits a few thinkers for bridging agency and structure. Following his tribute to Althusser, Gramsci and Laclau, Levi-Strauss is named as Hall's big hero for having introduced semiotics and psychoanalysis. Levi-Strauss fills the gap in structuralism: "[By] way of the Freudian concepts of the unconscious and the Lacanian concepts of how subjects are constituted in language . . . [he] restores the decentered subject, the contradictory subject, as a set of positions in language and knowledge, from which culture can appear to be enunciated" (Hall 1994: 536).

Cultural studies generally provides us with the language to speak basically from one of two directions. Either we adopt the Marxist language of ideology, consciousness and false consciousness, or we adopt the psychoanalytic language of desires and the unconscious. Even Foucault (1976), in his early work *Mental Illness and Psychology*, waffled between the two accounts; existential psychology that mutates into Marxist humanist psychology or psychoanalysis. Yet despite these two dominant accounts of subjectivity we still have dozens of radical social theorists perplexed by the problem of agency versus structural determination.

So what gets left out? There are two glaring absences in radical social theory and cultural studies. First are the countless feminist interventions into these master narratives, which commence in the 1970s and continue to this day to be largely ignored by cultural studies. The second absence is a politicized theory of emotion that would allow us to speak systematically about the particulars that underlie such terms as consciousness and unconscious. For example, instead of speaking broadly about "subjugation," we need to develop a vocabulary to talk about how positions of powerlessness,[9] victimization and silencing are constructed and about the role of specific emotions related to subjugation such as resentment, bitterness, anger, shame, fear and despair. Similarly, instead of speaking broadly of "resistance" and empowerment, agency and action, we need to understand emotions such as hope, anger and excitement.[10] The space I want to fill in I call "economies of mind," a concept that describes the global and local processes through which subjugation and resistance are enacted. The relation between culture and ideology, between lived experience and the determining structures of economy and the state, are a collaborative process between the self and the social. Economies of mind offer a means of tracing the ethical relations between subjects through an analysis of the genealogies of emotion.

While I cannot summarize all of the feminist theories that are overlooked, let me signal just a few. One of the earliest feminist contributions to cultural studies is Gayle Rubin's essay "The Traffic in Women: Notes on the Political Economy of Sex" (1975). Rubin's essay marked a turning point for feminist theories and socialist feminisms. She analyzes Marx, Levi-Strauss and Freud and persuasively demonstrates the ways in which the sex/gender system relies on women as an object of exchange. Donna Haraway notes that Rubin's essay sparks an "explosion of socialist and Marxist feminist writing indebted to Rubin" (Haraway 1991: 128). However, Rubin's essay is rarely mentioned within the largely androcentric traditions of cultural and critical studies. I think as well of the work of anthropologist Margaret Mead; while Claude Levi-Strauss holds an exceptionally esteemed place in cultural studies, Mead's (1963) pioneering work on cultural differences in gender roles is rarely mentioned. Michelle Rosaldo offered groundbreaking analyses in 1974 and later in such essays as "Towards an Anthropology of Self and Feeling" (1984). Since the 1980s, feminist theories that contribute to rethinking subjectivity in relation to gender and Marxist accounts, for example, have been innumerable. Political philosopher Sandra Bartky (1990) draws on the work of Sartre and Fanon to theorize "psychological domination" specifically in relation to gender and alienation. Ann Ferguson (1991) theorizes the sex/affective production, which extends Rubin's analysis of women and family as central sites of capitalist production. Sociologist Arlie Hochschild in 1983 wrote *The Managed Heart: Commercialization of*

Human Feeling, in which she argues that "emotional labor" contributes a undertheorized feature of capitalist production. And what of feminist psychoanalysts? In *The Bonds of Love*, Jessica Benjamin (1988) theorizes relations of domination and subordination in her study of Freud. Benjamin's work has been so influential that international conferences dedicated to analyzing her work have occurred in her lifetime.

Examples of the erasure and ignorance of feminism abound; I select an example here which is quite random. With respect to the contemporary work in educational theory, it is important to point out that feminist theories in education also fail to offer systematic theories of emotion.[11] Elsewhere, I explore the phenomenon throughout educational theories of a tendency to privilege; for example, Freire's theories of developing critical consciousness over feminist pedagogy and consciousness-raising.[12]

I select as a random example the introduction to *Culture/Power/History* (Dirks et al. 1994). In fact, I find the work of the editors of the volume I quote from below useful and valuable. My point is simply to offer one example of a repeated erasure, neglect and ignorance of feminist contributions. In point of fact, nine of the twenty chapters in this volume are written by women. I am not arguing that cultural studies neglects feminist contributions entirely, but that feminism often functions as an add-on and that, as a result of being marginalized, accounts of subjectivity and power are impoverished.

In their introduction the editors of *Culture/Power/History* focus on the tensions between "agency" and "structure." According to their history of this tension, poststructuralism perpetuates the structuralist bias (Claude Levi-Strauss, they assert, doesn't even "nod" to the agent) against the notion of the free and willing agent with intentionality (Dirks et al. 1994: 12). The only recognized subject in their narrative is the Lacanian subject: the decentered and fragmented self which has now become watered down into such language as multiple/contradictory subjectivity.

These editors then address the "ambiguity" of all the possible terms we might use for this "actor." A main problem is that all of the terms indicate either passivity or activity: the editors list "person, self, actor, individual and consciousness" (Dirks et al. 1994: 13). They then quote Michel Foucault's characterization of the subject from "The Subject and Power" as the most extreme representation of the "subjected" self. Less extreme they say is Bourdieu, who focuses again on the cultural practices that show how the "structures" seep into the dailiness that makes up what we embody and call identity. Briefly they characterize through Dick Hebdige and Frederic Jameson the postmodern critique of the overly celebrated "fragmented decentered self."

Finally, midway through their introduction, the editors of *Culture/Power/History* mention one of their included essays and therefore mention feminism. However, feminism doesn't get full credit even in its granted paragraph. The topic sentence transitions from Jameson and Hebdige: "Central to such discussions is the point that a theoretical position constructed around a depthless subject with no sense of history cannot generate a coherent political actor." The next sentence secondarily adjoins feminist theorist Linda Alcoff's work to the cultural studies project: "This point is also taken up by Linda Alcoff in considering the implications of poststructuralism for feminist theory and practice" (Dirks et al. 1994: 14). Alcoff's contribution is syntactically positioned as an "add-on" to a project already theorized by Jameson and Hebdige. To read her contribution as an "add-on" is ironic given their apparent accolade to feminist theory in the next sentence: "More than perhaps anywhere else, it is in feminist theory that the problem of rescuing the subject from both poststructuralist dissolution and Foucaultian overconstructionism has been—and is being—confronted" (Dirks et al. 1994: 14). I ask the reader to tolerate my irony as I read the tone and passive construction of this sentence. The first clause offers a wonderfully vague positioning feminist theory's legitimized place: "more than perhaps anywhere else." What a place to be situated, as the "more than perhaps anywhere else"—a dissociated place, floating and anchorless, without even clear reference to the idea in the previous sentence! As a result feminism is "more than" (ostensibly a quantifiable and discernible amount), which is then modified by "perhaps" to instill doubt and qualify feminism's contribution, dubiously relegating it to the distinctive place of "anywhere else."

However, perhaps the editors have uncannily summarized feminism's place in cultural studies with respect to developing theories of subjectivity. In the eyes of cultural studies writ large, feminism offers an unidentifiable, unquantifiable vague contribution—a "perhaps" kind of contribution, that is located "perhaps" in those spaces not included in the space of "anywhere else." The clarity of feminism's esteem in their eyes continues as the passive construction is used to communicate feminism's particular contribution: "It is in feminist theory that the problem of rescuing the subject from both poststructuralist dissolution and Foucaultian overconstructionism, has been—and is being—confronted" (Dirks et al. 1994: 14). First, it is comforting to see that in the eyes of cultural studies, proponents of the antimaster narrative school, use the singular to refer to "feminist theory" rather than the vastly more appropriate "theories." Then ironically, the activity characterizing the contribution of feminist "theory" represents another version of the nurturing female as feminists "rescue" the subject. But actually, there is no direct action of feminists rescuing. Rather, "[I]t is in feminist theory that the problem of rescuing the subject . . . has been—and is—confronted." The passive voice works well to capture the vagueness of the opening clause: somewhere "in feminist theory" is this somewhere-place that the "problem of rescuing has been—and is—confronted."

This vagueness about the contributions of feminist theories to cultural studies has numerous adverse effects. First, it reflects an unabashed igno-rance of a vast terrain of three decades of feminist theories that in part constitute, as we near the millennium, what we call cultural studies. Second, this ignorance and dismissal through silence thereby overlooks—if we are to believe these authors—the fact that feminist theory contributes "more than any other theory" to the challenge of theorizing the subject within male-defined paradigms that either dissolve the subject entirely or construct it so heavily as structurally-determined that we cannot speak of political volition.

The Missing Discourse of Emotions in Cultural Studies

The absence of systematic study of emotions in cultural studies and critical theory impoverishes our analyses of the subject and power. Raymond Wil-liams, one of the "fathers" of cultural studies, coined the term "structures of feeling" and it is in his discussion that one finds the most sustained analyses of feelings as a significant aspect of our cultural experience and consciousness (1977). Larry Grossberg (1992) has also explicated two con-cepts—"mattering maps" and "affective epidemics" to describe approaches to theorizing emotions in cultural studies.

However, the feminist theories I summarized earlier, as well as many oth-ers, have offered pioneering analyses of emotion and power which are largely unmentioned in androcentric cultural studies and critical theories. Given time, I would like to look more closely at how educational theorists such as Elizabeth Ellsworth (1989) and Valerie Walkerdine (1985) draw on Marx-ism and psychoanalysis, and I would investigate how these accounts are and are not helpful in analyzing Calvin's sister's lability. Sandra Bartky's work *Femininity and Domination* offers one of the most concise analyses of "psy-chological domination" drawing on the work of Fanon and Sartre. I want to briefly note the contribution of Frantz Fanon here, whose text *Black Skin, White Masks* (1967) offers a brilliant example of applying existentialist psy-chology and psychoanalysis in turn to explain, in the project of what he calls a "sociodiagnostic," the processes by which "the black man" sees himself through the eyes of others and how he is able to act in the world either in subjugation or resistance. He writes, "[I]f there is an inferiority complex [as white psychologists had termed it] it is the outcome of a double process:— primarily, economic;—subsequently, the internalization—or better, the ep-idermalization—of this inferiority" (Fanon 1967: 11). To refer to this sub-jugation as an "epidermalization" uncannily foreshadows Foucault's call to think of power as "inscribed," and this seems apt since Fanon sees no need to speak of the trauma of colonization as buried in the unconscious. Rather, he says, "Since the racial drama is played out in the open, the black man has no time to 'make it unconscious' " (150). The repeated traumas of contact with a racist world, and not the domesticated oedipal complex, explain the contradictory consciousness—perceptive and emotional—of being black. Fanon finds that both existentialism and psychoanalysis fail to explain black man's consciousness and the psychic experience of colonization. Fanon is preceded by a philosopher and historian whose work I would argue far predates the genre we now call cultural studies: W.E.B. Du Bois's *The Souls of Black Folk* (1903/1989). Du Bois's description of black men coming to an awareness of the "veil" that hangs between them and the rest of the world, he calls a "double-consciousness." Du Bois draws neither on existentialism nor psychoanalysis to describe the genealogies of oppression, a phenomenon that appears to occur within any society defined through social hierarchies and power differentials foundationally articulated through race, class and gender. In the 1980s, Gloria Anzaldúa writes of this phenomenon in terms of the experience of being a lesbian Chicana, and she outlines this psychic territory as the "borderlands."

These texts offer politicized accounts of consciousness, and in each there are examples of emotions of "self-evaluation": shame, guilt, self-esteem, etc. Missing from these texts is both a full analysis of emotions as the particular manifestation of "consciousness," and with the exception of Anzaldúa, any thorough analysis of gender.

A great deal more might be said about psychoanalysis and Marxist existentialism as explanatory frameworks for the phenomenon of lability that I've sketched out here. But for now, I'll just say that while these traditions may contribute to aspects of this project, I think both have limitations and I want to push us into new directions for exploring emotions and power.

FEMINIST THEORIES OF EMOTION, POWER AND IDEOLOGY

Not all or even most feminist theories address economies of mind: I find myself frustrated with many texts that I entirely respect which tend to use the catch-all terms "consciousness," the "unconscious," and "desire" without either full invocation of the psychoanalytic or Marxist notions that lay behind these terms. Also, these umbrella concepts "let us off the hook" from developing greater histories of emotions.[13] However, there is much promise in some specific strands of feminist theory.

Let us return to Calvin's sister and the question: How do we understand and explain her refusal to identify as a woman? I provide a sketch of two feminist politicized theories of emotion that move beyond the binaries of rational/irrational, and also beyond the traditional conception of the individual that usually underpins discourses of emotion. We saw with Calvin's sister how her refusal was both a rejection of identification with a class she perceived as powerless and simultaneously a compliance with her subjugation. Rather than view this as a binary contradiction, I want to read her lability as neither rational nor irrational. My purpose is to sketch an analysis in which the apparent contradictions of her refusal are not located primarily in the individual, but are seen as socially dynamic, the substance of my "economies of mind."

Feminist philosophies of emotion can be characterized in part by the following: (1) They challenge the traditional separation of emotion and cognition; (2) Emotions are not private, but rather must be understood as collaboratively constructed; and (3) Emotions are viewed not as gender-specific, but gender related (e.g., it's not that women don't get angry in public or that men don't feel shame, but there are gendered and culturally specific patterns to emotion that can be identified).

Feminists usually appeal to cognitive and/or evaluative theories of emotion. Let me situate these cognitive theories within the history of philosophy. Philosophers have viewed emotions very differently over the centuries, but by and large—especially under the influence from the Stoics to Plato, Descartes and Kant—emotions have been seen as an obstacle to knowledge and reason, rather than as a contributing partner to knowledge. However, more recently philosophers have argued for the cognitive/evaluative theory of emotions, in which emotions are understood as essentially tied to beliefs (these cognitive accounts frequently are traced back to Aristotle and Dewey). According to evaluative theories, emotions are judgments: To be angry at someone is to *believe* that this person has wronged you in some way.

Such theories are a vast improvement over other philosophical traditions that dismiss emotion altogether. However, I have always been frustrated even with feminist versions of cognitive theories, because emotions are granted epistemological status only by virtue of their association with rationality. For example, if I am wrong to be angry, it is because there is a problem with my belief that so-and-so wronged me. In sum, according to these theories emotions are *rational* responses to the beliefs that one holds. Thus emotions are valued only by twisting the picture and granting emotional reactions as having rational origins. Such a portrait leaves us still in a model that privileges rationality. This problem stems in part from the deeply entrenched binary either/or concepts in our language.

In her study of shame and gender, socialist feminist and political theorist Sandra Bartky reveals the ways in which the language of rationality is at least an impoverished if not an inadequate way to assess emotions. Bartky's book *Femininity and Domination* appeared in 1990, and her analysis of shame and gender challenges the cognitive theory of emotion. I begin with Bartky's compelling example from an educational setting. Upon handing in papers, her mature female students' demeanor and words consistently expressed shame over their work. She writes, "My students felt inadequate without really believing themselves to be inadequate in the salient respects: They sense something inferior about themselves without believing themselves to be generally inferior at all" (Bartky: 1990: 93). This example resonates with the work of Fanon, who writes, "Shame. Shame and self-contempt. Nausea. When people like me, they tell me it is in spite of my color. When they dislike me, they point out that it is not because of my color. Either way, I am locked into the infernal circle" (Fanon 1967: 116). Later he writes, "A feeling of inferiority? No, a feeling of nonexistence. Sin is Negro as virtue is white. All those white men in a group, guns in their hands, cannot be wrong. I am guilty. I do not know of what, but I know that I am no good" (139).

DuBois and Fanon both speak of this contradiction between how one wants to and should feel about oneself versus what the world says about you. Bartky uses the term "double-ontological shock" to describe the messy contradictions feminists face in explaining the phenomenology of the world: for example, is my reserve and silence at a staff meeting my own personality trait, or a symptom of internalized sexist self-doubt? These uncertainties, she says, "make it difficult to decide how to struggle and who to struggle against" (Bartky 1990: 14).

Shifting and slippery lability is how I would describe this female self-awareness, which is founded on a "contradiction between appearance and reality . . . the presumption of equality on the part of all actors in this drama, and on the other hand, its actual though covert and unacknowledged absence" (Bartky 1990: 94). This describes Calvin's sister's lability perfectly: "the presumption of equality"—i.e., her acceptance of the ideology that we are all equal now—alongside her reluctant awareness of its (at least historical) absence.

Bartky, drawing on the existentialist philosophy, argues for shame as an example of how emotions are differently engendered "attunements" that disclose information about how we are situated in the world. Shame is not "merely an effect of subordination, but . . . a profound mode of disclosure both of self and situation" (87).

It is not the case that shame is a privately constructed experience. Quite to the contrary, one's self-perception is constructed through the eyes of the other. Bartky defines shame as "the distressed apprehension of the self as inadequate or diminished: it requires if not an actual audience before whom my deficiencies are paraded, then an internalized audience with the capacity to judge me" (86).

Shame signals a loss of self-determination: for example, a woman modeling nude for a portrait may feel entirely safe and powerful, but when she realizes that the painter is seeing her as a sexual object she reexperiences herself through shame that is not "self-chosen": she did not freely choose to be ashamed.

Bartky concludes:

In sum, then, the 'feelings' and 'sensings' that go to make up the women's shame . . . do not reach a state of clarity we can dignify as belief. [Nonetheless] they are

profoundly disclosive of women's 'being-in-the-world,' far more so than many of the
fully formed beliefs women hold . . . such as . . . that they enjoy like men 'equality
of opportunity' or that school and workplace is meritocratic in character. What gets
grasped in the having of such feelings is nothing less than women's subordinate status
in a hierarchy of gender, their situation *not in ideology but in the social formation as
it is actually constituted.* (95)

In my reading of Bartky, she is critiquing the limits of "ideology" as an
explanation for women's contradictory self-perceptions. She does not invoke
a theory of the unconscious. Rather, I think, her description evokes what I
am calling "lability." She points out that the rhetoric of equality that is part
of ideology does not account for women's shame; that shame is constituted
through social formation. I believe Bartky's analysis of shame successfully
shows the inadequacy of the terms consciousness and ideology to describe
how power relations are formed. She also shows how the analytic philosophical theories of emotion cannot account for shame's persistence: even
if there is no evidence on which to found a belief that I am inferior, I can
feel ashamed. Perhaps most importantly, she demonstrates that shame is not
an idiosyncratic or an individualized phenomenon, but is socially formed.

More recently, philosopher Sue Campbell has extended the politicized
theory of emotion, building on Bartky, Marilyn Frye and Lynne McFall's
important feminist essay "What's Wrong with Bitterness?" (1991). Campbell (1994) emphasises an expressivist theory of emotion: that public expression and "uptake" of the emotion are what construct our emotional
life. Campbell also challenges the language and implications of "rationality."
In order to grasp Campbell's argument, I need to take a moment here for
a couple of definitions. First, Marilyn Frye's (1983) concept of "social uptake," an interaction which she defines as "necessary to the *success* of emotions" (Campbell 1994: 480). Social uptake refers for example to a woman
who gets angry watching her mechanic mess up the successful adjustment
she herself had made to her carburetor. When she gets angry at him he calls
her a "crazy bitch" and changes the subject. In other words, not only does
he refuse to "uptake" her anger, but he displaces it and frames her as crazy.
Her emotional expression is successfully "blocked." Frye's analysis exemplifies the social formation of emotions.

Now I turn to bitterness, which is an important emotion for these theorists to explore precisely because, they argue, it is formed only through a
collaborative interaction. Bitterness is commonly believed to be a "bad"
feeling, one that should be avoided: it eats at she who feels it and is also a
symptom of refusing to forgive. McFall (1991), who I mentioned earlier,
argues that those who are bitter (about systematic injustices, for example)
may have legitimate and rational reasons for feeling bitter.

Sue Campbell, like Bartky, questions the appropriateness of McFall's language of rationality to emotional assessment. One effect of framing bitter-

ness in terms of its "legitimate reasons" is that the "burden of proof" is thrust onto the bitter individual to validate her expression. Campbell shows that bitterness is more complicated. Someone is angry. She expresses her anger. Someone else tells her she's bitter. Not only does the accusation "you're bitter" demand that you then justify your reasons. To be told "you're bitter" is also a dismissal, and a silencing, so that even if you then articulate your reasons for being bitter the other is no longer listening. Campbell uses Marilyn Frye's concept of "uptake" to describe the phenomenon of emotions: an expression of anger, for example, is limited in its meanings and productivity by whether "uptake" occurs, whether or not it is "heard"—taken up—or dismissed. The dismissal, through not listening and other means, functions to individualize an emotion—to throw it back on the speaker, constructing it as her problem. Discourses around "feminism" are a classic example of this dynamic: women stand, yet again, to recite the litany of inequalities and violences perpetrated against them. Backlash is precisely about dismissal: the anger is not "uptaken," and it is not uptaken through such accusations as "You are bitter." Today the accusation of bitterness is founded on the ideology of achieved equality: "Are you still angry about that?! You're just bitter!" Feminists are then in the position of justifying their position, but simultaneously the accusation of bitterness is a silencing through dismissal.

What we learn from Campbell is that bitterness is collaboratively formed. She says, "bitterness is publicly formed rather than privately formed before being revealed to others" (1994: 51). It is not that I knew I felt bitter and then happened to decide to express it. Rather, I expressed my anger and was told, "You're just bitter." In this collaborative manner the feeling of bitterness was shaped and becomes part of my consciousness. If bitterness is collaboratively formed, then why should the burden of proof rest on the bitter person? Campbell's brilliant twist here is to argue that the individuation of feelings—the commonly held conception that my feeling is my own private experience—is actually a collaborative undertaking. Thus, to tell someone that her expression has failed actually requires not that the speaker justify her reasons for her expression, but rather a full social accountability for the interpretive context.

Let me try to tie these politicized theories of emotion back into lability and education. Campbell outlines several features of a theory of affect that seeks to understand the public formation of feelings. I conclude with two of her points: that the expression of feeling which has an important public role can be articulated only through socially acquired resources such as language, action and gesture. The interpretation of the meaning and significance of these expressions requires that we all "have an adequate range of resources to make clear the significance of things to us and . . . that we secure uptake or response frequently enough that this meaning can actually be formed or individuated, even for ourselves, in ways that neither distort our intentions nor leave them opaque" (Campbell 1994: 454–455).

I believe that educational environments can do both of these things: provide shared resources to learn to articulate feelings as expressions of what is important and provide uptake and response frequently enough that collaborative and individuated meanings can take shape. (Of course, schools and classrooms can as easily be sites where the absences and silences are perpetuated and exacerbated.) But the pedagogy of lability gives me hope as a crucial alternative to the capitalist manifesto, that *the school should not set up expectations that will not be fulfilled within the society.* One direct route to challenging the reproduction of docile workers is to provide students with paradigms and environment to encourage our slippery and unstable lability so that, precisely, we *do* develop expectations that far exceed what the existing system offers us.

A final note about Calvin and his sister: I want Calvin to want to go to the library himself to find more books that will challenge him; and as for Calvin's sister, I want so many things for her, not the least of which is an educational setting in which she can take emotional and intellectual risks and explore the experience—in her words—of "not being held back in anyway," and, in my vision, without having to refuse the possibilities of being a woman. To create education as a radical space of possibilities, our interdisciplinary studies need to recognize the central contribution of feminist theories and analyses of emotion and power as a way to understand the subtleties of hegemony and resistances.

NOTES

1. *Feeling Power: Emotions and Education* (New York: Routledge, 1999a). For a philosophical discussion of the dominant discourses of emotion in educational theory, see Boler (1997a); readers will find here ample bibliographic references to the literatures that inform a study of emotions, power and education.

2. I refer here specifically to the work of Michel Foucault and specifically his essay on "The Subject and Power" (1983).

3. See Cohen (1983). I also discuss this at length in Boler (1999).

4. See Boler (1999a).

5. See the *Oxford English Dictionary*, 2d. ed. (Oxford: Clarendon Press, 1998), 557.

6. I discuss pastoral power and education in Boler 1996, and in Chapter 2 of *Feeling Power* (Boler 1999a).

7. Underlying my chapter are such questions as: Why *should* students move from tenuous comfort in a world so deeply fraught with trauma and crisis? What educational goal justifies encouraging interrogation that creates emotional upheaval and possibly pain? What will be gained through the potentially painful experience of "seeing things differently," when already there is plenty on our students' plates as they juggle family, employment and social crises? Once I justify making the move to

disrupt familiarity, how do we seduce students to take intellectual and emotional risks that threaten what has come to be taken as common sense? The irony has long been recognized by thinkers from John Dewey to postmodernists that, on the one hand, individuals are resistant to change, while on the other, the ability to think flexibly and questions our values, assumptions and actions in an ethical light is what makes us human, creative, and is most likely to lead us to "freedom." On the most general level, education will always ironically encounter a fundamental resistance to change, along with change being a central potential of learning.

8. See "Cultural Studies: Two Paradigms," in Nicholas Dirks, Geoff Eley and Sherry Ortner (eds.), *Culture/Power/History: A Reader in Contemporary Social Theory.* (Princeton, NJ: Princeton University Press, 1994).

9. I explore the emotional dimensions of "powerlessness" in Boler (1996).

10. Kathleen Woodward writes a compelling call for "histories of emotion" in a special issue on the emotions in *Discourse: Theoretical Studies in Media and Culture* (1990–1991).

11. I examine this in Chapter Five, "A Feminist Politics of Emotion," in *Feeling Power* (Boler 1999a).

12. See Chapter Five of *Feeling Power* (1999a) where I explore this in greater depth; see also Boler (1999b), "Posing Feminist Questions to Freire."

13. On this see Woodward (1990–1991).

REFERENCES

Anzaldúa, Gloria. (1987) *Borderlands/La Frontera.* San Francisco: Spinsters/Aunt Lute.

Bartky, Sandra. (1990) *Femininity and Domination.* New York: Routledge.

Bee, Barbara. (1993) "Critical Literacy and the Politics of Gender." In C. Lankshear and P. McLaren (eds.), *Critical Literacy: Politics, Praxis, and the Postmodern.* Albany: State University of New York Press.

Benjamin, Jessica. (1988) *The Bonds of Love: Psychoanalysis, Feminism, and the Problem of Domination.* New York: Pantheon Books.

Boler, Megan. (1996) "License to Feel: Teaching in the Context of War." In D. Kellner and A. Cvetkovich, (eds.), *Articulating the Global and Local,* Politics and Culture Series. Boulder, CO: Westview Press.

———. (1997a) "The Risks of Empathy: Interrogating Multiculturalism's Gaze." *Cultural Studies,* 11(2): 253–273.

———. (1997b) "Disciplined Emotions: Philosophies of Educated Feelings." *Educational Theory,* 47(3) (Summer): 203–227.

———. (1999a) *Feeling Power: Emotions and Education.* New York: Routledge.

———. (1999b) "Posing Feminist Questions to Freire." In P. Roberts (ed.), *Paolo Freire and Education: Voices from New Zealand.* Palmerston North, NZ: Dunmore Press. Forthcoming.

Campbell, Sue. (1994) "Being Dismissed: The Politics of Emotional Expression." *Hypatia Journal of Women and Philosophy,* 9(3): 46–65.

Cohen, Sol. (1993) "The Mental Hygiene Movement, The Development of Personality and the School: The Medicalization of American Education." *History of Education Quarterly* (Summer): 123–149.

Dirks, Nicholas, Eley, Geoff and Ortner, Sherry (eds.). (1994) "Introduction." In *Culture/Power/History: A Reading in Contemporary Social Theory.* Princeton NJ: Princeton University Press.

Du Bois, W. E. B. [1903] (1989) *The Souls of Black Folk.* New York: Bantam Books.

Ellsworth, E. (1989) "Why Doesn't This Feel Empowering? Working Through the Repressive Myths of Critical Pedagogy." *Harvard Educational Review,* 59(3): 297–324.

Fanon, Frantz. (1967) *Black Skin, White Masks.* New York: Grove Press.

Ferguson, Ann. (1984) "The Subject and Power." In *Art After Modernism,* edited with an introduction by Brian Wallis. Boston: D. R. Godine.

———. (1991) *Sexual Democracy, Women, Oppression and Revolution.* Boulder, CO: Westview Press.

Foucault, Michel. (1976) *Mental Illness and Psychology.* New York: Harper and Row.

———. (1983). "Afterword: The Subject and Power." In Herbert Dreyfus and Paul Rabinow, *Michel Foucault: Beyond Structuralism and Hermeneutics.* Chicago: University of Chicago Press.

Frye, Marilyn. (1983) *The Politics of Reality.* New York: The Crossing Press.

Grossberg, Lawrence. (1992) *We Gotta Get Out of This Place.* New York: Routledge.

Hall, Stuart. (1994) "Cultural Studies: Two Paradigms." In Nicholas Dirks, Geoff Eley and Sherry Ortner (eds.), *Culture/Power/History: A Reader in Contemporary Social Theory.* Princeton: NJ: Princeton University Press.

Haraway, Donna. (1991) *Simians, Cyborgs, and Women: The Reinvention of Nature.* New York: Routledge.

Henriques, Julian et al. (eds.). (1984) *Changing the Subject.* New York: Methuen Press.

Hochschild, Arlie Russell. (1983) *The Managed Heart: Commercialization of Human Feeling.* Berkeley: University of California Press.

McFall, Lynne. (1991) "What's Wrong with Bitterness?" In C. Card (ed.), *Feminist Ethics.* Lawrence: University Press of Kansas.

Mead, Margaret. (1963) *Sex and Temperament.* New York: William Morrow.

Prescott, Daniel. (1938) *Emotions and the Educative Process: A Report of the Committee on the Relation of Emotion to the Educative Process.* Washington, DC: American Council on Education.

Rosaldo, Michelle Z. (1974) *Women, Culture and Society.* Stanford, CA: Stanford University Press.

———. (1984) "Toward an Anthropology of Self and Feeling." In Richard Shweder and Robert Levine (eds.), *Culture Theory: Essays on Mind, Self, and Emotion.* New York: Cambridge University Press.

Rubin, Gayle. (1975) "The Traffic in Women: Notes on the Political Economy of Sex." In R. Reiter (ed.), *Towards and Anthropology of Women.* New York: Monthly Review Press.

Walkerdine, Valerie. (1985) "On the Regulation of Speaking and Silence: Subjectivity, Class, and Gender in Contemporary Schooling." In C. Steedman et al. (eds.), *Language, Gender, and Childhood.* Boston: Routledge and Kegan Paul.

Williams, Raymond. (1977) *Marxism and Literature.* New York: Oxford University Press.

Woodward, Kathleen. (1990–1991) "Introduction" (special issue on "Discourses of the Emotions"). *Discourse Journal for Theoretical Studies in Media and Culture,* 13(1): 3–11.

Chapter 8

The Late Show: The Production of Film and Television Studies

ROGER HORROCKS

Every year in the university handbook new courses spring to life fully formed, seemingly the result of an orderly intellectual development. Behind the scenes, however, many of these courses have involved a lengthy history of proposals, challenges, objections, arguments about budgets, high claims and smouldering rivalries. Discussions of curricular change tend to focus on intellectual developments and underestimate other factors such as organizational politics and changes in the surrounding culture. In this chapter, which traces the development of film, television and media studies in some New Zealand schools and universities, I seek to examine the curriculum as a site of institutional as well as intellectual struggle. Though I admit to having a partisan point of view my aim is not simply to write another sentimental history of heroic new subjects struggling against a reactionary *ancien regime*, but rather to explore the complex of social forces that is always involved yet seldom documented.

Within any institution various individuals and groups compete for limited resources. Academics are particularly skilled in theorizing such conflicts in terms of large intellectual and cultural values, and this may be seen as evidence either of their seriousness or of their ability to rationalize self-interest. The curriculum in New Zealand universities tended, until the mid-1980s, to be discussed according to a rather solemn conception of "discipline," which discouraged the introduction of new subjects proposed by younger lecturers. This policy was theorized as a need to move slowly and carefully in order to maintain standards. It was increasingly challenged in intellectual terms by those involved with new forms of cultural theory, but in the end the forces that destabilized the curriculum were not intellectual but political and financial. After the 1984 election the government introduced a program of market liberalization (or New Right economics) that has had a huge impact on the universities and indeed on every area of our society. Successive New Zealand governments have shared the assumption that competition is a universal good and market forces need to be given the power to override social or cultural forces.[1] With budgets dependent upon student numbers in a more competitive marketplace, the universities have begun to move from one extreme to the other, scrambling in a sometimes unseemly way to develop a more attractive curriculum.

Film studies provides a clear example of this shift. Under the old system it struggled unsuccessfully for fourteen years to be admitted to the B.A. program at the University of Auckland. Each attempt was blocked because of fears that the introduction of undergraduate courses in film studies would lure students away from established disciplines. But by 1988 the university was worrried about student numbers. Its change of heart towards film studies involved other factors also—such as new people in management positions and praise from a review team for the existing M.A. paper—but it is clear that student demand carried a great deal of weight, along with the fact that other New Zealand universities and polytechnics were now rushing to develop their own programs. Over the past decade the field of film, television and media studies has continued to expand dramatically at Auckland and other tertiary institutions.

Such changes suggest that the new regime has had a positive effect, administering a healthy shakeup to the curriculum. But it is typical of recent political changes in New Zealand that they have been too rapid and too extreme. Throughout our university system the current situation is extremely volatile. It is difficult to give a new subject or department the careful nurturing required when it is likely to be expensively courted by the university for a year or two and then sidelined in favor of a newcomer. Peter Munz, Emeritus Professor of History at Victoria University, spoke for many academics when he made a recent public statement expressing concern over the state of the local university: "It is now being run as if it were a bank or a firm of stockbrokers. All this [has happened] under the pretext of saving money and of promoting financial efficiency."[2]

Curricular change still involves a complex field of forces with departments often in conflict with administrators and new subjects in conflict with old subjects (who suspect the newcomers of being opportunists with more glamour than brains). Although universities are forced to make higher claims for themselves than ever before, they struggle in the new environment to maintain adequate forms of quality control. These are worldwide problems. The changes of the last decade have highlighted the complex process of social construction involved in shaping the curriculum. Alongside theoretical analyses that seek to deconstruct the idea of disciplinarity we can now place historical accounts which document the rapid changes of thinking that have occurred in response to material and other changes (economic, technological, political and social) within the education system and the surrounding society. The example that follows does not seek to discredit the idea of discipline—indeed, "thick description" of the kind I have just described seems to me a basic method of film and television studies. Rather, it aims to document a sample local history, highlighting the political pressures, the complex chains of cause and effect, and the idiosyncracies of individuals and institutions that often seem more closely related to chaos theory than to the broad generalizations of philosophers of culture.

THE SCHOOL CURRICULUM

I will be discussing both schools and universities since I was witness to the turf battles in both areas of education and observed many common problems. Films have always occupied an important place in our society, as Gordon Mirams observed in 1945: "We New Zealanders are a nation of film fans. Only tea-drinking is a more popular form of diversion with us than picture-going [which] exerts an enormous influence upon our manners, customs, and fashions, our speech, our standards of taste, and our attitudes of mind. . . . Few persons would disagree with the assertion that the cinema's influence upon us is enormous and far-reaching." Educators, however, tended to see the film medium as a distraction. Education in those days was about books, particularly the classics, and not about films or any other form of contemporary popular culture. From my own schooldays I can remember only a couple of class trips to the cinema (we saw a film about the 1950 "Empire Games" and another about the Queen's 1953 visit to New Zealand). We kids were not sorry that our teachers ignored films since that left us with a culture of our own. We were the last New Zealand generation to grow up before television, and the Saturday matinee at the local cinema was our weekly escape from the boredom of home and school.

Television reached New Zealand in 1960. By then the medium of film had been in existence for 65 years and had been (as Mirams had noted) the most influential medium of popular culture. It had also developed its own forms of high culture—a half-century of great films and a sophisticated tradition of film theory and criticism. [3] The fact that New Zealand schools and universities had yet to pay any significant attention to film, apart from the efforts of a few isolated enthusiasts, seems from today's perspective a staggering example of how out of touch our education system has sometimes been. Yet one can see why educators committed to high culture and to the print medium regarded film as a rival, a competitor. Since then a similar time lag has occurred in the case of television. Despite the profound influence of television on our lives (for better or worse), the amount of serious attention that teachers have paid to this medium over the past thirty-seven years seems again a case of "too little, too late" (with the exception of a few enthusiasts). Television poses a greater challenge than film because it has less interest in high culture—but what if education were seen as having a responsibility to analyze culture as a whole, a task that would necessarily involve studying popular culture and the mass media?

The slowness of the education system in coming to terms with film and television points to a wider problem. Each decade has seen the introduction of at least one important new technology or medium—how to keep up with them all? Those who grew up in New Zealand in the 1960s and 1970s were the first television generation. The children of the 1980s might be described as the video generation since video was a revolutionary medium that not only introduced new kinds of games but also gave us video cameras with instant playback. It made it possible to "read" or study films as closely as books with the help of the still-frame button (without the previous risk of breaking or scratching the film). The children coming to school in the 1990s may be described as the computer generation, another profound change. Of course not all children have had the opportunity or desire to engage with these new media, but my summary serves to suggest how rapidly our society has changed in terms of its media environment. As for the education environment, it has lagged several generations behind film, television and video, yet it has perhaps been better prepared for the computer. The fact that the computer was so obviously a tool of commerce as well as of culture helped to attract support from politicians, parents and corporate sponsors.

For teachers the desire to extend the curriculum often has the character of a crusade. This was certainly the case with the wave of teachers in the 1960s and 1970s who championed film as a suitable subject for education. They were energized by the emergence of the "art house" cinema in New Zealand in the 1960s, which specialized in the new wave of European films. The university students who had argued about what really happened at Marienbad had no doubts that film was an important modern art—and if that was the case, why shouldn't it be studied alongside literature? An important precondition for the growth of film study in New Zealand schools and universities was the development of an intellectual film culture, through the film society movement (established in 1946), annual film schools, specialist cinemas and international film festivals (from 1969).

Another important context was the upsurge in New Zealand filmmaking from the late 1960s. That New Zealanders could and should make their own films may seem an obvious idea today but it was certainly not obvious then. During the first thirty-five years of my life only three feature films were made in New Zealand, compared with the tens of thousands of overseas feature films screened here during that period. Out of the counterculture of the 1960s emerged groups determined to overcome the technical and financial problems, and by 1978 there was enough local film activity to persuade the government to create a Film Commission, another important part of the jigsaw. There were teachers who saw a link between the two struggles (or crusades): the struggle of filmmaking to gain a foothold in New Zealand and the struggle of film teaching to find a place in the local curriculum.

There continues to be a supportive relationship between these two activities, similar to the way schools provide an audience for local literature. The existence of an industry was not essential to the teaching of film but it did allow for a more sophisticated dialogue between theory and practice in our vicinity, and it provided a vocational argument for the inclusion of the subject in the school curriculum.

That process was initiated by individual enthusiasts. By 1977 at least six high schools in Auckland had teachers promoting the study of films as part of English.[4] These teachers knew one another and shared what resources they could find. (Campaigns to extend the curriculum are not only a crusade but also something of a conspiracy.) At the beginning of the 1980s such enthusiasts gained official support from the new *Forms 3–5 Statement of Aims*. This controversial curriculum acknowledged the fact that a revolution in communication had occurred through media such as film and television in which words were constantly linked with images. Now English needed to teach "watching," "viewing" and "shaping" as well as "reading." Few schools responded fully to the challenge of this remarkable new framework, but it certainly provided film teachers with new opportunities.

The year 1983 was a key year with the publication of the *Statement of Aims* backed by a series of in-service training courses. And there was the establishment of the Association of Film and Television Teachers to build on a network of teachers that had developed in order to share the kinds of resources that were not provided by the education system.[5] This was arguably the best way for curricular change to come about, with official or "top down" initiatives lending support to grass-roots activities. Interestingly this was a period in which a number of other important changes were happening to English. The 1983 NZATE Conference, for example, focused on "culture" as a challenge to monoculturalism in the New Zealand education system. There were also accusations that the traditional canon had a white, male bias. These new ideas were met with vigorous opposition from some university professors, and there was a certain amount of passive resistance from principals and heads of departments.

Today film study has become a regular if limited part of English teaching. Initial resistance was based largely on the belief that films were competitors to books, but some of this resistance was overcome by showing that films could also be regarded as "high culture." It was eventually accepted that "reading" skills could be taught by studying complex film "texts" as an occasional change from literary texts. Today there is a tendency to see books and films (or at least some films) as allies in the battle against the vulgarities of television. English would be better placed to deal with television if it could move closer to cultural studies (as it is doing in some university courses). This would also enable it to explore film from other angles—as "popular culture," for example, or as industry. The development of "media studies" as a school subject has been driven by this sense of need, and it is now taught in quite a few schools as a sixth form option. Unfortunately despite a great deal of lobbying it is still not possible to take media studies as a "bursary" subject (that is, in the major examinations held in the last year of high school study). This missing rung in the academic ladder discourages many schools and students from becoming involved in the subject at earlier levels. Both schools and universities suffer from this gap. (During the 1980s schools appeared to be leading universities in their coverage of media topics, but over the past decade the field has developed more rapidly at tertiary level.)

Working on the latest version of the English curriculum gave me an insight into the current debates. The new curriculum uses the category "visual language" to encourage the study of a wide range of media "texts." This term covers forms of communication other than isolated oral or written language—combinations of word and image, for example, or any of the types of sign studied by semiotics. Basically this is a continuation of the approach introduced by the 1983 *Statement of Aims*. Like most curricula it is the end result of a push and pull between various political and intellectual forces. At one stage the visual language strand was in danger of being dropped altogether because of powerful lobbying by an influential group of business people who sought to return to an old-fashioned "reading and writing" curriculum. In the end, visual language was retained but this was a qualified victory since teachers were left to decide how much importance to give it in relation to other modes of language.

In general the attempts to introduce some form of television studies into New Zealand schools have been an almost total failure. To offer an occasional lesson as part of English hardly seems an adequate response by the education system to one of the most influential (most exciting, most dangerous) media of the century. Existing subjects have succeeded in blocking the development of television studies, media studies or film studies except as a minor part of English. Media teaching has attracted some dedicated teachers, but unfortunately they have not included a charismatic individual such as Gordon Tovey who successfully championed the subject of art.[6] Art had struggled to make any headway in New Zealand schools until 1946 when Tovey's appointment as National Supervisor Art and Craft coincided with a new government and a sympathetic assistant director of education (Clarence Beeby). This historical conjunction delivered significant resources to art and the subject took off. In comparison, media teachers have simply not been in the right political place at the right time (except for the curricular statement of 1983).

Although the education system has made few concessions in intellectual or political terms, it has at least paid some attention to social changes such as the development of the local film and television industries and the demand by students for more media examples (which now even the most conservative teacher cannot ignore). At the same time there have been counterpressures from parents and lobby groups seeking to strengthen traditional forms of education, with "media studies" being cited as a prime example of the degeneracy of education overseas. Currently some teachers hope it may be possible to link media studies with the government's plans for more "technology" teaching, although this remains a somewhat desperate strategy.

THE UNIVERSITY CURRICULUM

My parallel story line is the development of film and television studies at the University of Auckland. Things are going well for it today but—like so many new subjects—it bears the scars of a long institutional struggle. Before 1970 the only teaching of film and television in Auckland as subjects in their own right appears to have been through adult education courses, an important arena for the development of new subjects. Robert Chapman pioneered the study of television news and current affairs as an aspect of political studies. Tom Hutchins, a lecturer in photography at the Elam School of Fine Arts, had several talented students making 16mm films, and in 1970 he proposed the establishment of a film school. The university accepted the idea and Hutchins went on leave to look at overseas film schools. When he returned he found the university had changed its mind—a dramatic example of missed opportunities in light of the upsurge in local filmmaking that was to occur in the 1970s. There was also an unsuccessful attempt to introduce women's studies around 1970, and that too would have been superbly timed, but in those days the university was more interested in studying history than in making it. Nevertheless, Hutchins continued to teach filmmaking as best he could, and feminist lecturers and students played a significant part in the 1970s upsurge.

As an English lecturer I made my first attempt to launch a film paper in 1970. Departments in those days were ruled from the top and I failed to obtain permission. Later I tried to organize an interdisciplinary paper at masters level, enlisting the support of Robin Scholes (art history) and a lecturer from one of the language departments. But the latter was prohibited from taking part by his head of department. Soon after, the lecturer shifted to an Australian university where he had more scope for his interest in films. In 1975 our M.A. paper was successfully launched as a joint venture between English and art history. Scholes was a valuable contributor because she had recently returned from England with a knowledge of French film theory (via magazines such as *Screen*). She left after two years to join the film industry and subsequently became the producer of *Once Were Warriors, Broken English* and other important films. There is often a strong element of historical accident in the way subjects develop, for if I had left the university before Scholes, film would have developed as part of art history rather than part of English.

The paper averaged forty students and for the next twenty or so years it was one of the largest M.A. papers in the arts faculty. In general the university appeared to view the paper as an eccentricity, the kind of specialized enthusiasm that could be indulged at masters level. My main problems were not intellectual but administrative. I was required to run my course on a budget of $200 per year which was in line with other English papers but hopelessly inadequate when it came to renting films. In those prevideo days I had to beg, borrow and steal films to fill my schedule. My department was always fearful that a film course might attract large bills. Also, there was no possibility of a purpose-built classroom. For each film class I had personally to borrow the projector from the other side of the campus and tape up the curtains in the classroom in an attempt to provide adequate blackout. I received complaints about noise because the rooms were not soundproofed. Physically as well as culturally the arts faculty was the home of books, and in those precomputer days there were academics who seemed to regard most forms of technology as a threat to the humanities. They would complain (with some justification, perhaps) that the excited students running round making a film with a borrowed 16mm camera were neglecting their other studies.

Although I had a number of supportive colleagues,[7] some continued to look upon film study as the Trojan horse of popular culture infiltrating the university. In the 1970s any proposal to teach or study popular culture was likely to be viewed as a joke or as hippie hokum (by members of the university's research committee, for example). But new subjects gradually modify the environment and at some stage they cease to seem alien. Changes in the surrounding culture can also show them in a new light. Meanwhile I felt fortunate to be teaching my masters paper because the students were excited to be studying a subject that seemed directly relevant to their own culture. Also, in the early days, it was the only course of its kind in Auckland and therefore attracted many talented enthusiasts.

Let me briefly summarize the rest of its history. I made a number of attempts to expand downwards from the M.A. into the B.A. In those days departments had a chance once every five years to propose sizeable developments and I applied on two occasions, unsuccessfully. I now had steady support from the English Department which had found that films could coexist with literature, but elsewhere in the university there were still fears that film studies would seduce too many students away from established subjects. To mount undergraduate courses I needed faculty approval. It is always a dilemma for people promoting new subjects to decide how much time they are prepared to spend on the necessary lobbying. My 1986 attempt to introduce film studies at first-year level was driven by desperation because I now saw other universities and polytechnics preparing to introduce programs. This time I seemed to be making good progress, but I was headed off at the pass by two prominent professors who insisted that masters was still the only appropriate level for such a dubious subject.

This was the one occasion I felt like giving up my campaign. Other tertiary institutions now jumped ahead of Auckland, in one case creating an entire department with unseemly haste (or so it seemed to my jaundiced eyes). I was pleased, however, to see former students obtain jobs as lecturers. Tertiary education had suddenly entered a period of accelerated change. Heads of department ceased to be monarchs for life, and there was the sense of a new generation coming to power. The government cut funding and encouraged competition in the tertiary sector and suddenly, in all parts of the country, the old conservatism was replaced by a scramble for student fees. The curriculum began to face a whole new set of dangers such as the possibility of being led astray by its pursuit of research funding, sponsorship, overseas students and other sources of revenue.

In 1989 I was at last able to infiltrate the B.A. with a film and television studies paper. Then, with strong support from a new dean, I was able to set up a Center for Film, Television and Media Studies and a B.A. program with core papers at Stages One, Two and Three which the student could combine with relevant papers from other departments. Film papers emerged even from conservative language departments as their emphasis shifted from "language" to "culture," responding both to the growing academic interest in cultural approaches and to the declining enrolments in pure language courses. Film and television studies continues to be a complex subject area since each of the two media incorporates language, the visual arts, music, theatre and many other elements—but complex or not, the subject is now firmly established with its own office, logo, director, handbook, senior scholars, publications, conferences and a flood of students. It is almost time for the T-shirt and the alumni reunion.

From a business point of view a successful new brand name and range of products have been established. But what exactly is this brand? Can our subject claim to be a discipline? My colleagues and I are now cautiously expanding the scope of our teaching to include other media, and we sum up the rationale of our program in this way: "The social and cultural importance of the mass media of communication call for a centre of teaching and research where these media become a primary subject of enquiry. This enquiry needs to be informed by a knowledge of the media in their complex specificity—their particular histories and contexts and the traditions of theory and analysis that have developed around them." Eventually we will probably shorten the name of our program to "media studies," a snappier brand name; but the advantage of our present title is the specific history it carries with it—the fact that we first taught film studies, then television studies, and now are learning to teach media studies. Each move has involved a fruitful juxtaposition—comparing and contrasting the medium of film with the medium of television, for example, and at the same time comparing and contrasting them in terms of theory and criticism. Our intellectual (and pedagogical) journey has proceeded slowly and carefully enough to remain coherent.

It would not be difficult to argue that our subject is a "discipline," but is that necessary? Institutional politics does make it a matter of consequence. Even in my own university, which has made a very serious attempt to establish interdisciplinary "programs" (as distinct from "departments"), there are still subtle differences of status such as the fact that students cannot take programs for the major as well as the minor subject of their B.A. More generally, it is inevitable that interdisciplinary programs should feel insecure when they have watched their counterparts in the United States as well in New Zealand suffering from the ebb and flow of academic fashion. Again, interdisciplinary programs based on cooperation between departments are not easy to manage. With all the best will in the world there are sometimes disagreements about the sharing of student numbers, and lecturers who divide their time between two departments or programs may have less visibility when it comes to decisions about leave or promotion. Nevertheless, interdisciplinary teaching can be very successful, and apart from the advantage to the university in moving its staff around efficiently, many lecturers find that the intellectual stimulation far outweighs the problems. Media studies in New Zealand has provided a meeting place of this kind for people interested in cultural studies, gender studies, semiotics, postmodernism and other currents of thought. But there are strong (and often unconscious) differences in the discourses that lecturers bring from the disciplines in which they were trained, and someone must be able to act as translator or mediator to manage the inevitable collisions. Ideally all the lecturers in a program develop this kind of interdisciplinary competence. But meanwhile there is always the fear that institutional pressures will bring the process of exploration to a premature end. As the result of some cost-cutting exercise, for example, centers or departments below a certain size (even those showing steady growth) may no longer be considered viable. This happened recently at two New Zealand universities where media studies departments were required to merge with a larger department (English, in both cases).

In conclusion, media teaching provides a particularly eventful case study in terms of the relationship between schools, universities and the surrounding society. What seems to emerge from our study is a disturbingly high level of historical accident, usually the effects of politics (both inside and outside the institution) distorting the logical development of the subject. How powerless and cynical should this make us feel? It can still be argued that the basic process proceeds in a rational fashion. A new subject can be a starter only if it has a solid basis. Persistence will eventually pay off in most cases. Issues of social relevance will usually get a hearing. A new subject is likely to benefit from the required process of gradual development. And universities have carefully designed procedures for evaluating new subjects (procedures that today in most cases achieve a sensible balance between maintaining standards and seizing opportunities). In general terms, this process deserves our continued support. At the same time we must recognize the extent to which this process is vulnerable to political pressures, such as governments determined to impose on education the wrong kinds of competition and the wrong management model.

Ironically at tertiary level film and television studies has benefited more than most subjects from the new political environment; and it is difficult for me to speak of the university and its values being under threat when for years I have heard academics using that same rhetoric to block the development of my own subject. Also, in curriculum terms, the university still clearly has some catching up to do. It remains a perennial problem that established subjects are suspicious of any development that may compete with them for resources. Nevertheless, my own conclusion is the need to be realistic rather than cynical. One of the lessons of recent New Zealand politics has been the danger of cynicism which has grown so widespread that the capacity for protest and outrage has been muted.

Studying the curriculum process serves to clarify (if mostly by negative example) how the ideal procedures might function. Within universities we can campaign not only for our individual subjects but for a better system, something that can operate between the two extremes of rigid conservatism (which blocked the development of film and television studies in the university for nearly thirty years and is still blocking it in our schools) and rootless opportunism (the scramble for short-term gains in line with the government's "more market" approach). But we need clearly to distinguish this institutional argument from the external crisis, which may in the near future require academics to develop political skills of a less familiar kind in order to defend the very existence of the university.

NOTES

1. For an example of how these ideas have operated in the field of public policy, see my essay "Conflicts and Surprises in New Zealand Television," *Continuum: The Australian Journal of Media and Culture*, 10(1) (1996): 50–63.

2. See "University Run 'As If It Were a Bank,' " *Evening Post*, March 28, 1998: 4.

3. See for example, Gerald Mast, Marshall Cohen and Leo Braudy (eds.), *Film Theory and Criticism: Introductory Readings*, 4th ed. (Oxford: Oxford University Press, 1992).

4. Some of this early history was documented in my essay "Experiments in Film Teaching" in *English in New Zealand*, July 1977: 4–9.

5. AFTT is still active today as NAME (the National Association of Media Educators) which continues to publish the magazine *Script*.

6. See Carol Henderson, *A Blaze of Colour: Gordon Tovey, Artist Educator* (Christchurch, NZ: Hazard Press, 1998).

7. Professors J. C. Reid and M. K. Joseph were two members of the English Department whose interest in films had long preceded mine. Reid had reviewed films for the *Auckland Star* for many years, and Joseph had published essays on film topics.

Chapter 9

The Development of Maori Studies in Tertiary Education in Aotearoa/New Zealand

RANGINUI WALKER

The development of Maori studies in New Zealand tertiary education is a microcosm of the emergence and incorporation of cultural studies in the academy. Some of its international counterparts I have visited are Sami studies in Norway, Aboriginal studies across the Tasman, Hawaiian studies at the University of Hawaii, the Native Indian Teacher Education Program at UBC, Inuit studies at the University of Anchorage, Chicano studies at University of California, Santa Cruz, and the Native Indian Law Program at the University of Arizona, Alberquerque. These programs have in common with Maori studies a history of colonization, subjection to cultural imperialism and a protracted struggle for cultural survival and emancipation against the powerful forces of the nation-state, the political economy and the ideology of assimilation. The existence of these programs in the academy is testimony to the resilience of indigenous people who were subjected to the dehumanizing project of European expansionism into the New World. This chapter attempts to answer some of the historical, epistemological and political questions, underlying the emergence of cultural studies with reference to the Maori case in tertiary education.

THE NATION STATE

The founding cultures of the nation-state in New Zealand are derived from the two disparate traditions of Maori and Pakeha. Maori belong to the tradition-oriented world of tribalism, with its emphasis on kinship, respect for ancestors, spirituality and millennial connectedness with the natural world. Pakeha, on the other hand, were the bearers of modernity, the Westminster system of government, scientific positivism, the capitalist mode of production and the monotheism of Christianity. The philosophic difference between the two cultures is encapsulated in the prophetic aphorism:

E kore te uku e piri ki te rino, ka whitikia e te ra ka ngahoro.

Clay will not unite with iron, when it is dried by the sun it crumbles away.

The colonization of New Zealand by the British in the nineteenth century transformed Maori society from the time-warp of tradition to modernity. The salient features of the transition include trading land and natural resources for material goods from Europe, adoption of the cash nexus, population collapse, conversion to Christianity, engagement with the metropolis by treaty and the dehumanising experience of colonization. Its most debilitating effects include loss of land, disempowerment of chiefs and cultural erosion.

Despite the culturally debilitating effects of colonization, tribal memory was not erased by state policies of domination, impoverishment and assimilation. The tribes engaged in a counterhegemonic struggle and continuous interrogation of power. This resistance, centered on the politics of culture and ethnicity, stands outside the Marxist interpretation of economic determinism, thus dooming the European project of assimilation to failure.

SCHOOLING AND CULTURAL SUBVERSION

Although the right of the Crown to govern was established by the Treaty of Waitangi in 1840, the Queen's writ did not extend into tribal areas. Sovereignty was not achieved over the whole of New Zealand until 1864 by what Brookfield characterized as a "revolutionary seizure of power" (Brookfield 1993: 43). While the sovereign authority of the nation-state was established by force, more subtle techniques were used to establish its moral leadership. One of the most potent of these was the use of schooling to "saturate" the consciousness of the colonized with the new order so that for them it becomes "the only world" (Apple 1990: 5).

Despite the packaging of education by the authorities as an objective, politically neutral enterprise underpinned by the ideology of equal opportunity, at its inception in New Zealand, schooling became one of the sites of domination, resistance and struggle. The contradiction is inherent in Gramsci's identification of the role of schooling in the production of intellectuals as functionaries and subalterns of the state (Gramsci 1971: 10–12).

Larrain concurs with Gramsci that the ideology underlying education legitimates the contradiction of schooling reproducing structural relations of inequality, thus enabling the ruling class to carry out their reproductive practices without interruption (Larrain 1979: 47). Consequently, Maori, as a subordinated class, beneath even the meanest strata of the dominant culture, were imbued with a feeling of *whakama*, a crippling sense of inferiority and shame in the face of the grand narrative of the colonizer. This hegemonic function of schooling was evident at the outset.

The missionaries, who were the first teachers and advance guard of modernity, had a low opinion of natives whom they characterized as "infidel New Zealanders," "governed by the prince of darkness" (Elsmore 1985: 15–16). Their cultural practices were regarded as "filthy and debasing." This un-Christian denial of Maori: humanity rationalized and validated the missionary project of cultural invasion. Their mission of conversion to Christianity was synonymous in their minds with converting the native from barbarism to civilization.

Education began in New Zealand in 1816 with the opening of the first mission school by Kendall at Rangihoua in the Bay of Islands. Although the curriculum consisted of reading, writing and arithmetic, the underlying purpose of the schools was religious indoctrination. Maori were eager consumers of schooling, hoping to access knowledge that enabled Pakeha to produce enormous ships, powerful weapons and an amazing array of material goods (Elsmore 1985: 14). But they were thwarted by the missionary policy of translating only scriptural knowledge into Maori, thereby denying them access to secular knowledge.

In 1847 Governor Grey's Education Ordinance subsidized the mission schools in the hope of assimilating Maori by isolating them from the "demoralising influence of the Maori villages," thereby "assimilating Maori to the habits and usages of the European" (Ewing and Shallcrass 1970: 28). To promote assimilation, one-twentieth of government revenue was devoted to mission schools, provided instruction was given in the English language. The system was reinforced by the Native Schools Act of 1858, which gave grants of £7,000 to boarding schools where English was the medium of instruction.

The Land Wars of the 1860s disrupted Grey's plan of assimilation. After the wars, the plan was revived through the Native Schools Act of 1867. The native schools, established in tribal areas, were the Trojan horse of cultural invasion. At first they were administered by the Department of Native Affairs, then handed over to the Department of Education in 1879. The following year the Inspector of Native Schools drew up a code for the schools. Teachers in the infant school were expected to have some knowledge of the Maori language as an aid to teaching English and inducting children into school routines. To this end, junior assistants were engaged from the local community. Thereafter English became the medium of instruction.

To speed up the replacement of Maori by the English language, the Inspector of Native Schools urged teachers in 1905 to speak English only in the playground. Overzealous teachers interpreted the instruction to be a general prohibition of the use of Maori in school precincts. Thereafter school for Maori became a cultural battleground as generations of pupils up to 1950 claimed they were given corporal punishment for speaking Maori at school. By the 1960s the suppression of Maori language had taken its toll. Only 26 percent of new entrants at primary school spoke Maori as their first language (Schwimmer 1968: 75).

At first, Maori leaders, including Sir Apirana Ngata, acquiesced to the hegemonic role of schooling, believing mastery of English would enable Maori to gain access to Pakeha culture and its professions. In 1939 Ngata changed his mind when he understood the corrosive effect that schooling had on Maori language and culture. In the foreword to *Nga Moteatea* (1928: xiii) he wrote:

There are Maoris, men and women, who have passed through the Pakeha *whare waananga* and felt shame at their ignorance of their native culture. They would learn it, if they could, if it were available for study as the culture of the Pakeha has been ordered for them to learn. . . . It is possible to be bicultural, just as bilingualism is a feature of Maori life today.

Ngata had already come to that political understanding long before he penned those words. In 1923 he initiated transforming action by arguing in Parliament that the government should support the publication of research into Maori culture. He clearly understood the relationship between power and knowledge—that is, the ability of the state to generate "truth" through research activity. The outcome of Ngata's efforts was the establishment of the Maori Ethnological Research Board to publish the work of Best, Buck and Skinner. Ngata adroitly used the imprimatur of the board to channel a request to the senate of the University of New Zealand to include Maori language as a subject of study for the Bachelor of Arts degree on the same footing as foreign languages. The senate stonewalled the request on the grounds there was no literature to support a teaching program (Walker 1990: 193). Ngata overcame the objection by citing the published works of Sir George Grey, *Nga Mahi a Nga Tupuna* and *Nga Moteatea*. To add to the literature, Ngata collected the poetic songs and chants of the Maori, which were published in 1924 as supplements to the Maori newspaper *Te Toa Takitin*. They were eventually published in three volumes of *Nga Moteatea* by the Polynesian Society, with the first volume appearing in 1959 (Walker 1990: 195).

The university senate's agreement to admit Maori language as a degree subject took a further twenty-five years to translate into action. Unfazed by the academy's reluctance, Ngata raised issues pertinent to the education curriculum at the Young Maori (Leaders) Conference he organized at Auckland University College in 1939. He asked the delegates to consider whether Maori language, history, traditions and literature should be taught in schools at the secondary and tertiary level (Young Maori Conference 1939: 9). The conference recommended the establishment of a Maori social and cultural center to promote Maori adult education through the Auckland University College, the WEA, Teachers College Technical College and the Museum (Young Maori Conference 1939: 46).

ADULT EDUCATION

The outbreak of World War II delayed Maori penetration of the academy until 1949 when Maharaia Winiata was appointed Maori tutor in adult education at Auckland. He was followed by Matiu Te Hau in 1952. The pedagogy of these tutors concentrated on what might be termed cultural reconstruction, validation and incorporation of Maori knowledge into the academy, albeit in the marginalized Department of University Extension. At least it was a baseline on which other incremental gains could be made. Their courses in Maori language, culture, history and the arts and crafts of weaving and carving were held off campus in Maori communities. The master carver Henare Toka of Ngaati Whaatua held his carving school in the Maori Community Centre in Fanshawe Street. This course provided support for the refurbishment of the meeting house at Judea Marae in Tauranga and carving for Te Puea Marae in Mangere. The latter was the first urban marae opened in 1965. Further south, at Omarumutu Marae in Opotiki, the decoration of the assembly hall was overseen by Pine Taiapa, another of the master carvers trained at the Rotorua school of carving.

Fundamental to the pedagogy of the Maori tutors in University Extension was the co-option of the traditional *hu* (Maori assembly) to address the problems facing Maori in education, health, land, housing and social welfare (Boshier 1980: 108–110). The model followed by the tutors was the Maori Leadership Conference initiated by Ngata in 1939. The conference was intended to be held annually but had been interrupted by the war. Both Winiata and Te Hau, who had attended the first conference, saw the benefit of taking up where Ngata had left off. In 1959 they organized the first postwar Maori Leaders Conference at Auckland University. The consciousness-raising effect of this conference was immediate, as requests for conferences came in from around the North Island. Regional Maori leadership conferences were held at Kaitaia, Ngaruawahia, Whakatane and Gisborne in 1960, and at Tauranga, Taupo, Rotorua and Wairoa in 1961. This outreach into the community raised the mana of the university among Maori people, because it was standard practice to take academics from education, Maori studies and anthropology as resource persons and rapporteurs for the conferences.

One of the spinoffs from these conferences was the establishment of Maori Education Advancement Committees to respond to the findings of the Hunn Report of 1960. There were others. The Ruatoria conference in 1962, for instance, launched the Play Centre movement into Maori communities. It also opened up a new area of discourse in family planning among Maori people at a time when rural Maori were ignorant of artificial methods of contraception. Unfortunately this problem-centered approach to community development sat uneasily within the traditional adult education courses derived from the liberal arts program of the academy. That disjunction was made explicit in the 1962–1963 reports of the Auckland Adult Education District:

In general the Maori people are still restricting their interest to discussion of topics that concern them today as community problems. . . . It would appear that the development of . . . study groups (on health, family planning, etc.) might lead to the development of a formal pattern of adult education. (Boshier 1980: 111)

After 1963, the university withdrew from involvement in Maori community affairs. The objective of the new Centre for Continuing Education was to provide courses of a sustained nature paralleling the academic courses of the university. By the time I joined the Centre for Continuing Education in 1970, the work of the Maori tutors had become more formal, with on-campus courses in their specialty subjects of language, culture, history and anthropology. The clientele changed from Maori to middle-class Pakeha. There was only 6 percent Maori enrollment in language, and none at all in the other courses (Boshier 1980: 112). Although the education of Pakeha about Maori culture and the effects of colonization was necessary, it was peripheral to the emancipatory project of the Maori. These obligations to the academy were met during the week. Maori needs, at more fundamental so-called "non academic" levels, were met by running courses on weekends and during vacations. The courses included training for Maori wardens, in-service courses for teachers of Maori language, seminars on committee procedure and urban gangs, and leadership conferences on land, fisheries, and three-tier farming.

The Maori leadership conferences were also revived to pursue the emancipatory agenda established in previous decades by Ngata, Winiata and Te Hau. Out of the 1970 conference on the theme of urbanization emerged the activist group Nga Tamatoa, which engaged in wide-ranging transforming action. Tamatoa mounted annual protests at Waitangi, founded Maori language day and pressed for the a one-year teacher training course for native speakers of Maori. Tamatoa played a critical role in the conscientization of modern Maori to their own oppression. They were the catalyst for subsequent events such as the Maori Land March of 1975, the occupation of Bastion Point in 1977, the Haka Party incident in 1979 and the Hikoi Ki Waitangi in 1984. These events culminated in the 1985 amendment to the Treaty of Waitangi Act granting retrospective power to the Waitangi Tribunal to 1840. That legislative change allowed the Tribunal to interrogate the past, rewrite history and promote the current treaty discourse on partnership and *tino rangatiratanga*.

The last of the Maori leadership conferences was the Maori Educational Development Conference of 1984. This conference marked a turning point in Maori understanding of the hegemonic role of schooling and set Maori education in the direction of kura kaupapa and waananga. These events indicate, that despite the academy's historical role of replicating structural relations of power and social stratification, the possibility exists, for those who dare, to engage in the politics of culture and the pedagogy of emancipation. Its protective mantle is academic freedom, and one of the university's legally defined roles to act as the critic and conscience of society.

TUURANGAWAEWAE (standing) IN THE ACADEMY

The appointment of Maori tutors in adult education coincided with the appointment of Bruce Biggs in 1951 as lecturer in Maori language. This post was established in the anthropology department by the foundation professor Ralph Piddington in the face of opposition from the professor of French. The latter argued at faculty that Maori was not a language of scholarship. It belonged to the Stone Age because it was an oral and not a written language. Dr. Bill Geddes, senior lecturer in anthropology, instructed Biggs to fetch Maori textbooks from the library. In due course he returned with *Nga Moteatea, Nga Mahi a Nga Tupuna*, the *Bible* and many others, including *Te Haerenga o te Manene*, the Maori translation of *The Pilgrim's Progress*. Geddes spread them on the table and invited members of faculty to inspect what would in effect be the student texts (Biggs 1977). Professor Piddington moved the motion for the inclusion of Maori, insisting that teaching the native language was integral to the discipline of anthropology. The successful passage of the motion unlocked the impasse following the university senate's listing of Maori as a subject for the Bachelor of Arts degree way back in 1929 (University of Auckland 1963: 4).

Although admitted into the academy, opposition in faculty to the teaching of level II Maori surfaced in 1952 on the old ground of insufficient literature. Sinclair observed that the opposition, as before, reflected the state of race relations in New Zealand rather than the paucity of literature. The liberals in faculty did a head count, and realizing they had the numbers, moved the motion for the acceptance of level II Maori (Sinclair 1983: 202).

At the outset, the core business of Maori studies was the teaching of *te reo Maori* (Maori language). The program was underpinned by structural analysis after Bruce Biggs returned to Auckland in 1957 with a Ph.D. in linguistics from the University of Indiana. His model for teaching the language, as set out in *Let's Learn Maori*, is well suited to nonnative speakers of the language. So was his introduction of the double vowel orthography to mark distinctions in the meanings of words with the same spelling. But "purists" and native speakers, who could distinguish the long and short vowels phonically or from the context of written material, resisted the change. Some, who conceded that vowel length is phonemic, preferred to mark vowel length with the macron. The advent of computer programs with macron capability is likely to settle the issue in favor of macron marking of the low vowel.

It is a truism that language is the vehicle of culture, and the admission of the Maori language into the academy paved the way for cultural studies which began as increments to the language program. These include *kawa* (marae protocol), *whaikorero* (oratory) and *waiata* (songs and chants). Neither *waiata* nor *whaikorero* could be taught in isolation from mythology and traditions, so the teaching of myths and tribal traditions became established parts of the program as well. Gradually, the material arts of *whakairo* (carving), *tukutuku* (decorative fiber work) and *raranga* (fiber weaving) were added to the program. The latest addition to the program is a stone workshop for the manufacture of adzes, chisels and other artifacts. The skills in stone technology have become so attenuated as a consequence of acculturation that this program teeters on the brink of cultural recovery, validation and incorporation into the academy.

Gradually, Maori studies at Auckland moved towards maturity when it occupied a purpose-built academic wing in 1986, and the university marae was opened in 1988. The marae became an adjunct to the teaching program and an interface between other departments, faculties and the community. Finally, after forty years under the mantle of anthropology, Maori studies became a department in its own right in 1991.

The path blazed for Maori studies at Auckland was later emulated by other universities, teachers colleges and polytechnics. The University of Victoria began teaching Maori studies as a part of anthropology in 1967. Leading this development was Koro Dewes, whose pedagogy of language immersion concentrated on training students to become competent speakers of Maori. The goal was to enable students to do *mihi* (formal speech of welcome) and *whaikorero* (speech in reply) on the marae. With oral fluency went knowledge of *tikanga* (customs and marae protocol). In 1975, Hirini Mead was appointed to the chair in Maori studies at Victoria. Thereafter, it became a separate department from anthropology. Mead's tenure of the chair saw the institution of a Maori graduation ceremony and the development of a marae on campus (Mead 1983). By 1979, Victoria, along with Auckland, was offering masters programs in Maori studies. Perhaps Mead's crowning achievement was the production of graduates who wrote their theses in Maori of such a high quality that they set a benchmark against which others would be measured.

Canterbury and Massey universities also come on stream with Maori studies in the 1970s under the wing of anthropology. At Canterbury the lecturer Bill Nepia modeled his language teaching on the program started by Dewes at Victoria. He also promoted scholarship in Maori literature with the recruitment of Margaret Orbell.

In 1970, Hugh Kawharu was appointed to the anthropology chair at Massey. He nurtured the development of Maori studies as a section of anthropology by recruiting native speakers of Maori to teach the language. Leading the program was Apirana Mahuika who followed Dewes' model of teaching. As staff and student numbers built up, Massey appointed Mason Durie as a professor of Maori studies in 1986. Thereupon Maori studies became a separate department from anthropology. Durie noted that the union of Maori studies with anthropology was at an end, allowing a more authentic Maori scholarship to emerge. For Durie, locating Maori studies within the confines of established disciplinary boundaries was academically unsound and ideologically and politically untenable (Durie 1995: 2). Clearly, Maori studies is at the cutting edge of culture and policy studies. But for the moment it is caught in the no-man's-land of being neither a traditional *waananga* (ancient school of tribal learning) nor an exclusively Western-oriented school of learning. For this reason, it is not the business of Maori studies to teach students how to be Maori. That is the prerogative of tribal *waananga* (Durie1995: 5).

In 1972, the University of Waikato established the first Maori studies and Research Centre headed by Robert Mahuta. The Maori studies section concentrated on teaching fluency in language and knowledge of *tikanga*, while the center concentrated solely on research. The center produced a series of reports establishing the social, economic, educational, health and demographic profile of the Waikato tribes that culminated in the *Tainui Report* of 1983. Thereafter the center focused on Treaty issues, the preparation of tribal claims, assisting tribal authorities to gather essential data and interpreting the information to facilitate negotiation with government (Centre for Maori Studies and Research 1989: 4). These efforts culminated in the Tainui Deed of Settlement of 1995 that brought to finality the Tainui Raupatu Claim for the confiscation of 1.2 million acres of land in 1864.

Otago began teaching Maori studies in 1983 with limited entry. In 1986 the enrolment limitation was lifted. Maori EFTS (full-time students) rose rapidly at the expense of anthropology. The number of students taking Maori soon outnumbered those taking foreign languages, so that Maori studies qualified for full department status. The departmental review of 1995 revealed glaring deficiencies in academic leadership, administration and curriculum development. The review findings highlight the essential fragility of Maori studies arising out of its own rapid growth on a shallow pool of fully qualified Maori academics. Otago moved rapidly to repair the situation by appointing Dr. Tania Ka'ai to a chair in Maori studies. This appointment, along with that of Ngahuia Te Awekotuku, brings to three the number of Maori studies departments out of seven headed by Maori with Ph.D.'s. This observation does not detract from Massey where the professor of Maori studies has a postgraduate degree in psychiatry. Without exception, all seven

Maori studies departments have over two-thirds of their staff studying for advanced degrees.

TEACHERS' COLLEGES

The establishment of Maori studies in University Extension and in the anthropology department at Auckland, provided Maori educators with a strong platform from which to lobby for admission of Maori studies into teachers colleges. Staff and students collaborated in mounting the Young Maori Leaders Conference of 1959 which recommended strengthening the case for Maori studies in the curriculum and expanding the teaching of Maori language in schools. To this end the conference recommended the appointment of full-time Maori studies lecturers at teachers colleges. Compared to universities, the lead-time between recommendation and action was considerably shortened. The first lectureship was established at Auckland Teachers' College that year, followed later by another appointment at Wellington. But these appointments were symptomatic of power relations of Pakeha dominance and Maori subjection.

The first appointee at Auckland was Harry Lambert, a nonspeaker of Maori. But to the Pakeha power-brokers Lambert was a "nice man," unlike Winiata. Winiata, who was a masters graduate, a native speaker and knowledgable on *tikanga*, was passed over. He was characterized by Pakeha as "having a chip on his shoulder." This metaphor was the condemnatory code for being pro-Maori and therefore a threat to Pakeha dominance. Further south the racism was less subtle. The appointee at Wellington was a Pakeha, the late Barry Mitcalfe. But in this case the power brokers erred. Mitcalfe was pro-Maori and engaged with his students in the counterhegemonic struggle against the establishment. The unequal struggle ended with Mitcalfe becoming an outcast and opting for the alternative lifestyle at Coromandel. He was replaced by Stephen O'Regan who in the fullness of time became an even more avenging angel than Mitcalfe as Sir Tipene O'Regan.

When Lambert left Auckland Teachers College in 1962 to take up the headmastership at Tikitiki, he was replaced by another safe appointment in a little-known conservative schoolteacher named Ranginui Walker. The incorporation of cultural studies such as flax weaving, *waiata, haka* and marae field trips to places like Ruatahuna and Te Kaha had immediate appeal for students. Enrollments in the Maori option increased considerably. Although student numbers justified additional staff, a whole decade passed before Maori studies became an independent department.

Well into the 1960s Palmerston North Teachers College resisted appointing Maori studies lecturers but eventually it capitulated. Young teachers trained at Palmerston complained they were ill-equipped to teach at schools in South Auckland. In 1970 the Auckland Secondary Teachers College appointed its first Maori studies lecturer. But in another country called the

South Island, the principal of Christchurch Teachers College, Dr. Colin Knight, opposed such an appointment well into the last decade. The ideology of one people was the rationale for his resistance.

Although the polytechnics were late in emulating universities and teachers colleges in establishing Maori studies, they did so rapidly over the last decade. Today Maori studies departments are established in seven universities, three teachers colleges, and 27 polytechnics.

CONCLUSION

In the forty-five years since introduction of Maori studies into tertiary education, pioneering tutors and professors have addressed the question of defining their subject and the content of its curriculum. For the tutors in University Extension it was *Te reo Maori* (Maori language) and *Tikanga Maori* (Maori culture and customs). For Bruce Biggs, the first professor of Maori studies, language comprised the basic and therefore major component of Maori studies. For him, the sociocultural component of Maori studies was secondary (Biggs 1977).

Hirini Mead, the second professor of Maori studies, embraced the term *Matauranga Maori* (Maori knowledge) coined by Salmond to encompass the whole field of Maori studies. For him, *Matauranga Maori* constitutes the knowledge base that Maori people must have if they are to be comfortable with their *Maoritanga* (identity) and competent in their dealings with other Maori (Mead 1983: 333). Mead adds a political component to Maori studies of an emancipatory pedagogy with the assertion:

There is no real option but for knowledge managers of our universities and departments of Maori Studies to become involved in the struggle of the Maori people to survive culturally. . . . Liberation is the opposite of cultural death. (Mead 1983: 340)

This means that the curriculum must also be dynamic and flexible enough to respond to the contemporary and the evolving needs of Maori people. Their *whakapapa*, their genealogy of knowledge, has to be expanded continuously to incorporate contemporary discourse of *tino rangatiratanga* (Maori sovereignty), the Treaty of Waitangi, tribal land claims and the post-settlement phase of Maori development.

This emancipatory project makes Maori studies an "uncomfortable science" because it creates tensions with the institution in which it is embedded by seeking to transform power relations of domination and subordination. The secession of Maori studies from anthropology was the first step in that transformation. With the advent of *Tomorrow's Schools*, the next step was secession from the academy and the establishment of tribal *waananga* as degree-granting institutions at Otaki and Whakatane. The advent of tribal *waananga* as competitors for student EFTS makes further transformations possible within the academy such as a *waananga Maori* under the rubric of a "school within a school." Provision for this development in Auckland is projected in the University's document *2001 Missions, Goals, and Strategies.*

REFERENCES

Apple, Michael W. (1990) *Ideology and Curriculum.* New York: Routledge, 5.

Biggs, Bruce. (1977) "Te Whakaako i Te Reo Maori i Te Whare Waananga o Akarana." Unpublished paper.

Boshier, Roger. (1980) *Towards a Learning Society: New Zealand Adult Education in Transition.* Vancouver: Learningpress, 108–112.

Brookfield, Frederic Morris. (1993) *Parliament, the Treaty and Freedom: Millennial Hopes and Speculations.* Auckland: F. Brookfield, 43.

Centre for Maori Studies and Research. (1989) *Annual Report,* 4.

Durie, M. H. (1995) "Maori Studies in New Zealand Universities: A Developmental Approach." Paper delivered at the University of Hawaii at Manoa, Honolulu, December 2.

Elsmore, Bronwyn. (1985) *Like Them that Dream: the Maori and the Old Testament.* Tauranga, NZ: Tauranga Moana Press, 14–16.

Ewing, John Lithgow and Shallcrass, Jack (eds.). (1970) *An Introduction to Maori Education: Selected Readings.* Wellington: New Zealand University Press, 28.

Gramsci, Antonio. (1971) *Selections from the Prison Notebooks of Antonio Gramsci;* ed. and trans. Quintin Hoare and Geoffrey Nowell Smith. London: Lawrence and Wishart, 10–12.

Larrain, Jorge. (1979) *The Concept of Ideology.* London: Hutchinson, 47.

Mead, S. M. (1983) "Te Toi Matauranga Maori Mo Nga Ra Kei Mua: Maori Studies Tomorrow." *Journal of the Polynesian Society* (September): 333, 340.

Ngata, Sir Apirana. (1928) Preface to *Nga moteatea, he maramara rere no nga waka maha/he mea kohikohi na A. T. Ngata.* Hastings, NZ: E. S. Cliff, xiii.

Schwimmer, Erik (ed.). (1968) *The Maori People in the Nineteen-Sixties: A Symposium.* New York: Humanities Press, 75.

Sinclair, Keith. (1983) *A History of the University of Auckland 1883–1983.* Auckland: Auckland University Press, 202.

University of Auckland. (1963) *Gazette,* 5(1): 4.

Walker, Ranginui J. (1990) *Ka whawhai tonu matou (Struggle Without End).* Auckland: Penguin, 193, 195.

Young Maori Conference. (1939) "Report on Young Maori Conference Held at Auckland University College May 22nd-May 26th, 1939," Auckland, New Zealand, 9, 46.

Chapter 10

Literacy Studies in Education: Disciplined Developments in a Postdisciplinary Age

COLIN LANKSHEAR

This chapter investigates literacy studies with particular reference to educational theory and practice. The argument is constructed in four parts. The first sketches some key elements and stages in the emergence of an explicit and well-subscribed focus on studies of literacy per se from the 1950s. It describes developments in and across established disciplinary areas like history, anthropology, linguistics, sociology and psychology—developments which, by the 1980s, saw a "sociocultural" conception of literacy and literacy studies emerge in opposition to the "traditional" conception.

The second part of the argument traces the related emergence of literacy as a focus of study within education specifically, revealing similar conceptual, theoretical and normative tensions operating here as occurred in developments outside educational theory and practice. The discussion grounds the claim that what we count as *literacy* and, hence, as literacy *studies*, is contestable and that choices and decisions must be made. Arguments are provided for the view that literacy and its study should be framed in terms of the sociocultural approach. What should count and be encouraged as literacy studies in educational and wider academic inquiry and practice is identified here as what has become known, variously, as "socioliteracy studies" (Gee 1996); "sociocultural literacy" (Gee, Hull and Lankshear 1996), and "the 'new' literacy studies" (Barton 1994; Gee 1996; Street 1995).

The third part presents a current picture of literacy studies (thus framed) in education. This includes accounts of key goal statements, constructs, programmatic values, methodological approaches and practical implications.

The final part looks briefly at critical literacy in relation to socioliteracy studies as a whole.

PART 1: GENERAL BACKGROUND

Historical Studies of Literacy

Since the 1950s, the notion of *literacy*—as distinct from "reading," "writing," "composition," "grammar," "rhetoric" and so on—has come increasingly to name a focus for theoretical, conceptual and research activities across a range of disciplinary areas.

Much of the early work was done by historians. Harvey Graff (1991) argues that by the 1990s historians were entering a third generation of literacy studies. He identifies the first generation of historical studies of literacy as comprising work from the late 1960s and into the 1970s by people like Stone (1969), Cipolla (1969) and Schofield (1968). This work was foreshadowed in the 1950s by that of Webb (1955) and Hoggart (1957) on British working class readers and by Fleury and Valmary in France. The "first generation" literacy historians made the case for the direct study of literacy as an important historical factor. It traced at a general level major chronological trends, transitions and passages in literacy over periods and identified factors tied closely to changes in the course of literacy across time, together with its dynamics, distributions and impacts.

Graff's second generation of historical literacy studies comprised subsequent work by Johansson (1977), Lockridge (1974), Cressy (1980), Houston (1983, 1985), Graff (1979), and others. These studies established and drew on the *quantitative* record of literacy—mainly using census data, signatory sources and the like—in a closer and more detailed way than previously. Second generation researchers sought close evidentially-based historical interpretations of changing patterns of literacy, particularly in terms of the distribution of literacy and different literacy levels within given populations. They also related trends in literacy to economic and social developments, including mass schooling, and to social class formation. Other work foregrounded literacy in relation to demographic behavior, cultural development, social class stratification, family formation and the like. It also considered literacy in relation to literary, cultural and publishing issues and themes as, for example, in the various histories of the press and newspapers produced during this period.

Graff saw evidence of an inchoate third generation of historical literacy studies beginning to emerge at the beginning of the 1990s. This would involve work that moved from the more quantitative evidential base employed in the previous generations to embrace also *critical* questions concerned particularly with developing a cultural politics and political economy of literacy in history—including literacy's relations with class, gender, age and culture. Issues of conceptualization and contextualization of literacy within history would become central, benefiting from the insights of landmark studies in sociocultural approaches to literacy, such as those by Scribner and Cole (1981) and Heath (1983)—and, indeed, from interdisciplinary perspectives and collaborations more generally. Potentially fruitful innovations like "historical ethnographies" were in the offing, along with possibilities for comparative historical work. Graff envisaged increased interest on the part of historians in developing new conceptualizations of context in the historical study of literacy. This would, among other things, temper the earlier focus on literacy as an *independent* variable with a stronger sense of literacy as a *dependent* variable. In Graff's view, the work of this third generation would be to make the shift from "historical studies of literacy" to "histories that would encompass literacy within their context and conceptualization"; that is, from "the history of literacy" to "literacy in history" (Graff 1991: xxii).

During the same period addressed by Graff, further important work, much of it with a broadly historical and cultural focus, was being done across other disciplinary areas and across a range of themes. Some focused on "the Gutenberg phenomenon"—the rise of the printing press as a decisive moment in human communication. Seminal works here included Davis' "Printing and the People" in *Society and Culture in Modern France* (1975), Eisenstein's *The Printing Press as an Agent of Change* (1979) and Joyce et al.'s *Printing and Society in Early America* (1983). These studies mainly worked across history, sociology and anthropology, typically from crossdisciplinary perspectives. Within the broad concern with the emergence of mass print in the context of social practice and change, a number of scholars focused more particularly on the significance of the printing press for the Reformation. Early studies like R. W. Scribner's (1981) *For the Sake of Simple Folk: Popular Propaganda for the German Reformation*, and Strauss' (1978) *Luther's House of Learning* paved the way for numerous subsequent studies—including some within education—of the nexus between the Gutenberg press and Protestantism (e.g., Luke 1989).

Crossdisciplinary Treks to "The Great Divide"

The period from the early 1960s to the early 1980s also brought landmark work by scholars working at various interfaces between philosophy, classical studies, anthropology, history and linguistics. This work profoundly influenced the development and direction of literacy studies from the mid-1980s. Eric Havelock, Jack Goody and Walter Ong are widely recognized as most influential here (see Gee 1996; Graff 1991; Street 1984).

Havelock's *Preface to Plato* (1963), Goody and Ian Watt's 1963 paper "The Consequences of Literacy," Goody's *The Domestication of the Savage Mind* (1977) and Ong's *Orality and Literacy* (1982) identified literacy— construed as the advent of the alphabetic system and writing—as a major factor in epistemic, cultural and historical change. Their arguments are variations around the theme that "literacy makes for a 'great divide' between

human cultures and their ways of thinking . . . and modes of cultural organization" (Gee 1996: 49–50). Literacy is seen as a key factor, if not *the
salient factor*, that enables the transition from "primitive" to "advanced"
culture.

Havelock, for example, argued that writing frees humans from dependence on memory and from "emotional trappings" necessary for purposes of
recall. That is, a written text permits emotional detachment from texts and,
with that, the possibility for objective reflection upon their content. New
ways and possibilities for thinking, judging, synthesizing, comparing and so
on are seen to accompany the emergence of "an abstract language of de-
scriptive science to replace a concrete language of oral memory" (Gee 1996:
50; Havelock 1963: 209).

Goody and Watt's variation on this theme was that important analytical
and logical procedures like syllogistic reasoning and identifying contradictions seem to be a function of writing, since writing permits expression of
ideas to be ordered, manipulated and compared as *visible* artifacts. In *The
Domestication of the Savage Mind*, Goody argued that the sorts of traits
typically seen as distinguishing "advanced" cultures from "primitive cultures" are linked to changes in means and methods of communication, particularly writing. Goody saw the development of writing as crucially linked
to "the growth of individualism, the growth of bureaucracy and of more
depersonalized and more abstract systems of government, as well as to the
development of the abstract thought and syllogistic reasoning that culminate
in modern science" (Gee 1996: 51).

Further elaboration of this theme came from the work of Ong (1977,
1982), who argued that committing language to space profoundly increases
its potential and restructures thought. Going still further than Goody and
Havelock before him, Ong (1982: 14) argued in *Orality and Literacy* that
literacy—writing—is "absolutely necessary for the development not only of
science but also history, philosophy, explicative understanding of literature
and of any art, and indeed for the explanation of language (including oral
speech) itself."

Across "The Great Divide": Crossdisciplinary Contributions to Sociocultural Study of Language and Literacy

The contributions of scholars like Havelock, Goody, Ong and others in
similar vein promoted literacy within humanities and social science domains
alike as a powerful independent variable which was instrumental in cultures
moving from "primitiveness" to "advanced" states of development. At the
very time this broad line of development was unfolding, however, very different work was under way across anthropology, linguistics, sociology and
socially oriented domains of psychology. This work was highly diverse, while

sharing a broad common interest in language and communication as *social practice*. The tradition it spawned soon came into direct conflict with the "great divide"/ "independent variable" thesis. This conflict provided a key focus for Brian Street (1984) and others (e.g., Cazden 1998; Cook-Gumperz 1986; de Castell, Luke and Luke 1989; Edelsky, C. 1990; Gee 1990; Hodge and Kress 1988; Lankshear and Lawler 1987; Levine 1986; Luke 1988; Michaels 1981; Scollon and Scollon 1981; Stubbs 1980) who were involved throughout the 1980s in crystallizing and making explicit a distinctively *sociocultural* paradigm of literacy studies.

This latter line of development was very complex, involving many strands of activity and influence, not all of which can be identified here, let alone described in the depth they warrant. The following selections are indicative, but by no means exhaustive.

In a recent paper James Gee (1998a) describes a broad trend in theory and research within social sciences and humanities dating from the 1970s, which he calls "the social turn." This was a turn "away from focusing on individuals and their 'private' minds and towards interaction and social practice" (1). Gee maps more than a dozen of the myriad discernible "movements" which collectively made up the "social turn." These movements included the emerging sociocultural approach to literacy and several which strongly influenced and were subsequently taken into the "new" literacy studies (Gee 1998a; Gee 1996: chap. 3).

Gee specifically identifies ethnomethodology, conversation analysis and interactional sociolinguistics; ethnography of communication; sociohistorical psychology based on the work of Vygotsky and his associates and Bakhtin; situated cognition; cultural models theory; cognitive linguistics; the new science and technology studies pioneered by the work of Latour; modern composition theory; connectionism (in cognitive science); narrative studies; evolutionary approaches to mind and behavior; modern developments in sociology associated particularly with the work of Giddens; work in poststructuralism and postmodern social theory centred on "discourse"; and the emerging "new" literacy studies (Gee 1998a).

Classic early work in sociocultural literacy studies with an explicit educational focus was, perhaps, especially influenced by developments in ethnography of communication and sociolinguistics spearheaded by people like Dell Hymes (1974, 1980) and by western adoptions of sociohistorical psychology and related work done earlier in the century in the Soviet Union by Vygotsky and Luria. Shirley Brice Heath's major ethnographic study of language patterns and effects within community, home and school settings across distinct social groups in a region of the United States owed much to—and, in turn, contributed greatly to—the ethnography of communication (Knobel 1997). Heath's 1983 book, *Ways with Words*, is widely acknowledged as a seminal foundation study in the sociocultural approach to literacy and literacy studies.

Likewise, Sylvia Scribner and Michael Cole's 1981 book, *The Psychology of Literacy*—itself very much an ethnographically based study—forced a major rethink of traditional approaches in psychology to the cognitive effects of literacy through its rigorous engagement with a problematic owing much to the earlier Soviet work in sociohistorical psychology (Gee 1996, 1998a; Street 1984; Wertsch 1985).

Besides these "social turn movement" influences, other notable early lines of influence on the emerging sociocultural paradigm included the work of Paulo Freire in Brazil and other third world settings from the 1960s and work done in the "new" sociology of education during the 1970s.

Freire's "pedagogy of the oppressed" (Freire 1972, 1973, 1974) explicitly denounced psychologistic-technicist reductions of literacy, insisting instead that "word" and "world" are dialectically linked, and that education for liberation involved relating word and world within transformative cultural praxis. Freire asserted the impossibility of literacy operating outside of social practice and, consequently, outside processes of creating and sustaining or re-creating social worlds. For Freire, the crucial issues concerned the *kinds* of social worlds humans create in and through their language-mediated practices, the interests promoted and subverted therein and the historical option facing education of serving as either an instrument of liberation or of oppression.

The "new" sociology of education addressed processes by which and ways in which schooling and school knowledge contributed to reproducing sociocultural stratification along class, race–ethnic and gender lines. Some of this work focused more or less specifically on the workings of language within the larger historical "logic" of reproduction. Work contributing to the "new" sociology corpus by Basil Bernstein (1971, 1975) and Pierre Bourdieu and Jean-Claude Passeron (Bourdieu 1977; Bourdieu and Passeron 1971) is widely recognized as having provided important formative support for the sociocultural approach to literacy.

In 1984 Brian Street presented a telling statement of these two traditions and what was at stake between them. His book, *Literacy in Theory and Practice* can be read as the first explicit programmatic account of literacy studies from the sociocultural point of view. The conceptual heart of his book comprised the juxtaposition of two "models" of literacy: the "autonomous" model (based on the "traditional" view of literacy) and the "ideological" model (based on the "sociocultural" view). Street's account and endorsement of the "ideological" model underpins his extended critique of theoretical and practical work in literacy based on the notion of literacy as autonomous.

Briefly, the autonomous model construes literacy as existing independently of specific contexts of social practice; having autonomy from material enactments of language in such practices; and producing effects independently of contextual social factors. Accordingly, literacy is seen as independent of and impartial toward trends and struggles in everyday life—a "neutral" variable.

The "ideological" model rejects the notion of an essential literacy lying behind actual social practices involving texts. What literacy *is* consists in the forms textual engagement takes within specific material contexts of human practice. These forms, which Street calls "conceptions and practices of reading and writing" (plus, we would add, imaging, keying, viewing, etc.), evolve and are enacted in contexts involving particular relations and structures of power, values, beliefs, goals and purposes, interests, economic and political conditions and so on. Hence, the consequences of literacy flow not from literacy "itself" but from the conjoint operation of the text-related components and all the other factors integral to the practices in question. The myriad literacies that play out in social life should be seen as integral components of larger practices, simultaneously reflecting and promoting particular values, beliefs, social relations, patterns of interests, concentrations of power and the like. In no way, then, can literacy be seen as "neutral" or as a producer of effects in "its own right."

PART 2: TOWARD LITERACY STUDIES IN EDUCATION

Some Developments and Complications within Education

Theoretical, pedagogical and research activity concerned with aspects of reading and writing have continued uninterrupted throughout this century within education. Much of it has been dominated by paradigms from psychology and has aimed to understand reading, writing, spelling and comprehension as cognitive and behavioral processes in order to improve teaching and learning approaches to mastering written texts. While this tradition is long and widely established, it tended not to be identified as "literacy" work until quite recently. Those working in the field did so mainly under the rubric of "reading," "writing" and related terms, as reflected in the names of long established journals and professional associations: e.g., The International Reading Association, which publishes *The Reading Teacher*, and the U.S.-based National Reading Conference, which publishes *The Journal of Reading Behavior*.

Nonetheless, enclaves of educational inquiry concerned explicitly with literacy per se did exist. For example, from at least the 1950s scholars concerned with the economics of education and educational development and planning, among others, were vitally concerned with social implications and efficacies of *literacy*. This concern was writ large, for instance, in the World Literacy Program of UNESCO from the 1950s. In addition, of course, within adult and continuing education and extensions studies departments in countries like the United States, Britain, Australia, New Zealand and

Canada, there has been an interest in adult literacy for several decades, often associated with migrant populations as well as educationally disadvantaged individuals from the native-speaking mainstream. Certainly, "functional literacy" has been a clearly and strongly defined area of research and pedagogical interest in the United States and elsewhere since the Second World War. Nonetheless, until the late 1970s, an educational interest couched explicitly in terms of *literacy* remained quite marginal.

During the past two decades, however, talk of literacy in relation to school-based learning and teacher education has become increasingly common. The term has increasingly displaced references to "reading" and "writing" in policy statements and school learning programs, as well as in the names of courses, subjects, departments, schools and divisions within teacher education institutions. "Literacy studies" has emerged as a generic name for diverse activities in research and scholarship broadly concerned with understanding and enhancing the production, reception and transmission of texts. At the same time, "literacy" has become a major focus for teacher professional development and policy formulation within education systems. In many cases, the change in terminology has not been accompanied by any substantial visible change in practice (Lankshear 1993). Familiar paradigms, questions and procedures for inquiry remain intact but now go under a different name.

At an institutional level, surface manifestations of the emergence of literacy studies include the growing numbers of schools, departments, divisions, research centers and other organizational units within teacher education faculties whose names profess a direct concern with literacy studies. Many of the larger teacher education faculties in Australian universities have schools or divisions of language and literacy education, for instance. Other indices include the names of academic and professional journals, professional associations, categories within publishers' lists and book series, etc. In some cases, these examples have involved name changes from earlier incarnations. For example, the former Australian Reading Association, which is affiliated with the International Reading Association, was renamed the Australian Literacy Educators' Association in 1993 and its journal, formerly the *Australian Journal of Reading* became the *Australian Journal of Language and Literacy*.

Within education, then, the situation with respect to something called "literacy studies" is complex, especially when we ask what counts as literacy studies and from what time can we talk about the serious emergence of literacy studies as a field of educational endeavor. At least four "tendencies" are readily apparent in the period from the 1950s.

Long-standing studies of reading and writing processes, characteristics of written language and the like, which were not thought of—and whose authors did not think of themselves—in terms of *literacy*.

1. Work in this same tradition which, from the (late)1980s onward, reidentified as *literacy* work, while remaining firmly within "nonsocial"—e.g., psychology of individuals, literature and literary theory, physiology, etc.—paradigms.

2. Studies grounded in larger study of social and cultural periods, milieus, processes, and changes, explicitly identified as studies of *literacy*, but where "literacy" was broadly and unproblematically defined as (alphabetic) writing, ability to sign or similar quantitative notions.

3. Literacy studies grounded firmly in an understanding of literacy as sociocultural practice. This tradition has made rapid and widespread advances since the mid 1980s and today boasts an impressive literature and research base.

How we understand the emergence of literacy studies in education and the scope of the field will depend crucially on where we stand in relation to these broad "tendencies" and on our approach to "literacy" as a socially contested concept. It will also depend, of course, on what kind of questions we take questions about the nature and emergence of literacy studies to be.

For example, if we take a purely "operational" approach, such that literacy studies is a matter of whatever is done within institutional settings or forums that self-define as departments, journals or research centers concerned with literacy education, we will arrive at a view that takes in everything from theories about and methodologies for teaching children's literature to ethnographic analyses of computer-mediated communication practices via approaches to teaching and learning the mechanics of encoding and decoding print and surveys of literacy "levels." By contrast, if we adopt some kind of prescriptive definition of literacy, the account we provide of the field will be much narrower and more focused.

If we focus on *explicit* reference to "literacy," the emergence of a literacy studies focus within education has, then, been rapid. Of course, to the extent that literacy is understood generally and by implication in terms of reading, writing, transmitting and receiving texts, we might say that there has been a concern with literacy studies for as long as there has been a theoretical and research concern with education—it was just a matter of nomenclature. This accords with Gee's (1990, 1996, 1998a, 1998b) notion of the *new* literacy studies, based on his distinction between the "traditional" conception of literacy as reading and writing (an "old" literacy studies) and the more recently informed conception of literacy as *sociocultural practice*. From the perspective of literacy as reading and writing we can identify the great mass of educational work on reading, writing and the like as literacy studies, even though it mainly did not fall under the rubric of what will be identified here as literacy studies. When we focus on literacy studies as the study of literacy as a profoundly *social* phenomenon, however, it is clear that literacy studies in education really only begins to emerge with anything like a critical mass from the 1980s.

There are, then, at least two related issues to be resolved that bear directly on further discussion of the nature and emergence of literacy studies from an educational point of view: namely, (a) what kind of questions are we asking in the first place (quantitative/qualitative; operational/normative; descriptive/prescriptive)? and (b) what stand are we to take with regard to radically competing constructions of literacy?

In education, as in other disciplines and areas of practice noted above, literacy has traditionally been thought of in terms of reading and writing—although with interesting variations. Educationists have mostly seen literacy as "a largely *psychological* ability—something true to do with our heads" (Gee, Hull and Lankshear 1996: 1) and, to that extent, a somewhat private possession. This reflects the heavy domination of educational research and theory by psychology throughout this century. Being literate has meant mastering decoding and encoding skills, entailing cognitive capacities involved in "cracking the alphabetic code," word formation, phonics, grammar, comprehension and so on (referred to by Gee 1998b as "design features" of language). Encoding and decoding skills serve as building blocks for doing other things and for accessing meanings. According to this view, once one is literate one can get on with learning—by studying subjects in a curriculum or by other print-mediated means. Once people are literate they can use "it" (the skill repertoire, the ability) in all sorts of ways as a means to pursuing diverse benefits (employment, knowledge, recreational pleasure, personal development, economic growth, innovation, etc.). Of course, this predominantly "psychological" view has been complemented in educational thinking by the more "external" notion of literacy as a tool or technology. This is strongly reflected at present in notions of technological literacy as involving mastery of computers.

If we go along with this traditionally dominant view of literacy within education we can say that "literacy studies" have been going on in educational inquiry as far back as we care to go, and that it matters little whether or not the activities have been *named* in terms of "literacy" or not. The contingent fact that interest in literacy *as such* has escalated dramatically during the past twenty to twenty-five years within countries like our own might be explained quite simply by reference to successive pronouncements of educational "crisis" and "falling standards." These have attended growing awareness of the extent and speed of contemporary social, economic, technological and demographic change, and fears of being "overtaken" by other countries. This has been a period in which literacy has been "rediscovered" locally as a key element of "human capital" (Luke 1992)—overlapping with numerous mass mobilizations around literacy (campaigns/crusades) in "third world" or "underdeveloped" countries—and where postindustrialism has been recognized as "upping the ante" for literacy in the "developed" world (Levett and Lankshear 1994: 28). In an intriguing parallel development, the notion of a critical mass of literate people being a crucial variable for economic take-off into industrialism (see, for example, Anderson and Bowman 1966), which was still playing out in the third world, received a second generation replay for *post*industrialism.

Within this context, "literacy" came to name the most urgent educational tasks of the day and, correspondingly, a good deal of work that had always been going on under other names suddenly became "literacy" work. As a leading educational theme and task, "literacy" was "everywhere"—in "functional," "cultural" and "critical" spaces and at all "levels" from "basic" to "higher order" literacies, by way of "technological literacy" "scientific literacy," and the like (Lankshear 1998). In Australia, the embrace was near to total. 1991 brought *The Australian Language and Literacy Policy* (DEET 1991). Schools, divisions and departments of language and literacy education mushroomed within amalgamated (teacher) educational faculties. Entire research project programs devoted to literacy—some of them falling within the prestigious Commonwealth Competitive Grants Scheme rubric—emerged, generating impetus for research centres specializing in literacy research. Adult and workplace literacy became big business, enjoying exponential increases in funding. A National Languages and Literacy Institute of Australia was formed with federal funding to play a strategic role in policy implementation.

The whole "shebang"—which serves neatly as a trope for literacy studies from the "literacy-as-being-about-reading-and-writing" perspective—accommodates pretty much anything and everything to do with the universe of written texts under the umbrella of literacy studies: from work on the most mechanistic approaches to diagnosing and "curing" disabilities with encoding and decoding to the most esoteric reaches of literary theory via approaches to children's literature, "big books" pedagogy, planning and programming for classroom language and literacy education, critical approaches to reading, writing and viewing and the theory and methodology of second/other/foreign language education. In this construction of literacy studies, it's all (equally) a part of the mix. Proponents of the most decontextualized skills-based approaches to teaching and researching reading and writing cohabit with literary theorists, proponents of cultural literacy, genre theorists and advocates of the "new" literacy studies, among others.

This, however, is not the line I will take here. I do not accept the "traditional" view of literacy but, rather, the sociocultural view. Neither do I accept an operational approach to the question of what constitutes literacy studies, whereby literacy studies includes what(ever) is undertaken in schools of departments of literacy education or centers for literacy studies and the like. Instead, I share Gee's (1996) view that "literacy" should be recognized as a socially contested concept. Hence, I take the question of what constitutes literacy studies as a domain of academic practice to be *normative*.

Framing "Literacy Studies" for Education: For a Sociocultural Paradigm

The kinds of questions we ask about literacy studies and the issue of how we frame literacy are not minor matters but, rather, amount to nothing less than taking up a stance for or against particular discursive practices.

Building educational theory and practice on the traditional, autonomous view of literacy has undesirable consequences. By contrast, educational endeavor is advanced in progressive ways by taking seriously the questions of how literacy should be framed and what we should count as falling under literacy studies, and answering these questions in terms of a sociocultural perspective.

Gee makes two important points here. First, he identifies literacy as an example of a "socially contested term," and argues that debate about literacy "ultimately comes down to moral choices about what theories one wants to hold based on the sorts of social worlds these theories underwrite in the present or make possible in the future" (Gee 1996: 123). Second, he claims that

> arguing about what words (ought to) mean is not a trivial business—it is not "mere words," "hair splitting," or "just semantics"—when these arguments are over . . . socially contested terms. Such arguments are what lead to the adoption of social beliefs and the theories behind them, and these theories and beliefs lead to social action and the maintenance and creation of social worlds. (15–16)

This is the approach I assume here. Taking "literacy" to be a social contested term clearly entails approaching the question of what constitutes literacy studies as a normative matter. Accordingly, we need to note the sorts of grounds and arguments advanced by proponents of *sociocultural* conceptions of "literacy" and literacy studies. My stance is that literacy studies is best understood in terms of academic/scholarly/research activities that seek to understand literacy as sociocultural practice, to build on these understandings ethically, politically and pedagogically, and to advance them conceptually and theoretically.

Toward a Sociocultural Approach to Literacy Studies

Understanding literacy as sociocultural practice means that reading and writing can only be understood in the context of the social, cultural, political, economic, historical practices to which they are integral; of which they are a part. This view lies at the heart of what Gee (1996) calls the "new" literacy studies, or socioliteracy studies—which is what will count as literacy studies (proper) for the rest of this discussion (see also Barton 1994; Street 1984, 1993, 1995). The relationship between human *practice* and the production, distribution, exchange, refinement, contestation, etc., of *meanings* is a key idea here. Human practices are meaningful ways of doing things or getting things done (Franklin 1990). There is no practice without meaning, just as there is no meaning outside of practice. Within contexts of human practice, language (words, literacy, texts) gives meaning to contexts and, dialectically, contexts give meaning to language. Hence, there is no reading or writing in any meaningful sense of the terms outside of social practices or discourses.

These elementary points are fundamental to the grounds advanced in support of a sociocultural perspective on literacy against the traditional view. Three main grounds can be distinguished in the literature. I will sketch these briefly by way of introducing a fuller account of (socio)literacy studies.

1. *We cannot make sense of our experience of literacy without reference to social practice.* If we see literacy as "simply reading and writing"—whether in the sense of encoding and decoding print, as a tool, skills or technology, or as some kind of psychological process—we cannot make sense of our literacy experience. In short (see Gee, Hull and Lankshear 1996: 1–4 for the detailed argument), reading (or writing) is always reading *something in particular* with *understanding*. Different kinds of text require "somewhat different backgrounds and somewhat different skills" if they are to be *read* (i.e., meaningfully). Moreover, particular texts can be read in different ways, contingent upon different people's experiences of practices in which these texts occur. A Christian Fundamentalist, for example, will read texts from the Bible in radically different ways from, say, a liberation theology priest.

Learning to read and write particular kinds of texts in particular ways presupposes immersion in social practices where participants "not only *read* texts of this type in this way but also *talk* about such texts in certain ways, *hold certain attitudes and values* about them, and *socially interact* over them in certain ways" (Gee, Hull and Lankshear 1996: 3). Different histories of "literate immersion" yield different forms of reading and writing as practice. The texts we read and write—*any and all* texts we read and write, even the most arid (and otherwise meaningless) drill and skill, remedial session "readings"—are integral elements of "lived, talked, enacted, value-and-belief-laden practices" engaged in under specific conditions, at specific times and in specific places (3). Consequently, it is impossible to abstract or decontextualize "literacy bits" from their larger embedded practices and have them still *mean* what they do in fact mean experientially. This, however, is what the traditional conception of literacy does, in effect, try to do—and to this extent it is incoherent.

2. *The sociocultural model has necessary theoretical scope and explanatory power.* The sociocultural model provides a proven basis for framing, understanding and addressing some of the most important literacy education issues we face: issues that cannot be framed effectively—let alone addressed—from the traditional perspective on account of its individualist, "inner," or

"abstracted skills and processes" orientation. These include issues of *patterned* differentials in literacy outcomes and learning achievements across social groups and apparently *anomalous* instances of learners who demonstrate competence in diverse social practices and their embedded literacies, yet fail to come to terms with school literacy.

Burgeoning work in socioliteracy studies (Barton and Hamilton 1998; Barton and Ivanic 1991; Heath 1983; Knobel 1997, 1998; Moll 1992) highlights important inherent differences between characteristically *school* literacies and those integral to wider social practices. It also documents some of the ways in which and extent to which there is a closer "fit" for some social groups between school literacies and their wider discursive experiences and acquisitions than there is for other social groups (Gee 1991, 1996). These differences "cut two ways" within the context of school learning.

First, as Heath's work (1982, 1983) shows, children from diverse social groups may learn to decode and encode print in the literal sense (i.e., be able to read words from a page and write words on a page) without being able to "cash in" this learning on equitable terms in respect of "valorized" school literacies. Heath (1982), for example, shows how working-class children performed comparably with middle-class children in entry level grades on literacy tasks, but fell progressively behind in subsequent grades. This, she argued, was a function of literacy in subsequent grades drawing on particular "ways" of talking, believing, valuing, acting and *living out* that transcend (merely) mechanical aspects of encoding and decoding texts *and that are differentially available within the social practices (discourses) of different social groups* (see, e.g., Gee 1991, 1996; Heath 1982; Lankshear 1997). The traditional conception of literacy is powerless to get at these kinds of analyses and explanations.

Second, many learners who are highly proficient at certain text-mediated practices in out-of-school contexts come to grief with school literacy even, at times, to the extent of performing badly on what appear to be routine encoding and decoding tasks. (For a classic recent example, see Michele Knobel's (1997, 1998) account of Jacques. For an equally graphic parallel from the adult world, see Kell's (1996) account of Winnie TsoTso. Pedagogical approaches that draw on the traditional conception of literacy and try to enhance—or "remediate"—learning by focusing more explicitly and intensely on the "design features" of literacy (Gee 1998b) often fail. A sociocultural approach offers fruitful ways of understanding and addressing what is going on here that are not available from the traditional approach to literacy. These include analyzing ineffective pedagogies from the standpoint that they confuse "learning" and "acquisition" (Gee 1991; Krashen 1982; Lankshear 1997: chap. 3) and/or that they do not differentiate between the "design" and "function" features of language and, hence, fail to build upon the distinction in pedagogically informed and effective ways (Gee 1998b). Many students may simply fail to grasp the point of school literacies on account of the gulf that often exists between school practices and the "real life" or "mature versions of social practices" learners experience in their larger lives. These "real world" practices are typically a long way removed from "essayism" and the "initiation-response-evaluation" routines so prevalent in school discourse (Cazden 1998; Gee, Hull and Lankshear 1996: chap. 1; Michaels 1981).

More generally, of course, sociocultural perspectives on literacy and learning provide powerful bases for pedagogical interventions aimed at "high quality" learning. These are becoming increasingly influential in shaping learning approaches beyond school classrooms, and are exemplified by models of learning derived from work in situated cognition (e.g., Lave and Wenger 1991), sociohistorical psychology (Wertsch 1991), ethnography of communication (Heath and Mangiola 1991; Moll 1992), and cognitive science (Bereiter and Scardamalia 1993; Brown et al. 1993); as well as from work based on cultural apprenticeship (Rogoff 1990) and various approaches to critical literacy, collaborative and cooperative education and distributed cognition (e.g., Bizzell 1992; Bloome and Green 1991; Edwards and Mercer 1987; cf., Gee, Hull and Lankshear 1996: chap. 3 for an overview).

3. *"Unwanted" theoretical trappings and implications for social worlds.* Proponents of socioliteracy studies identify a raft of theoretical tendencies and implications attaching to the traditional view of literacy which they argue are educationally, morally and politically regressive. For example, they see the traditional view going hand-in-glove with *quantitative* approaches and worldviews like psychometrics, measurable levels of academic (dis)ability and (il)literacy, quantifications of "functionality" and so on. These lend themselves to constructing learners who experience difficulties with school literacy as "deficit systems" (e.g., as having inadequate or inappropriate home support for school learning; not enough books—or the right kind of books—in the home, etc.) or, in many cases, as "learning disabled," "academically challenged," "slow learners," "ADD," etc. Such theories and constructs support the creation of particular kinds of "social worlds" (Gee 1996: 123). Policies and practices emphasizing diagnostic assessment, remedial assistance programs, regular reporting against "profiles," "standards" or "benchmarks," packages of special learning-teaching techniques and the like are "natural" concomitants of the traditional view. More subtle "affiliations" include the creation of social worlds grounded in possessive individualism, commodification, and generalized logics of instrumental and measurable value (think: exchange values, comparative advantage, added value, competency portfolios, etc.).

Such theoretical "baggage" and its implications for the kinds of social worlds we create (and don't create) are writ large within the current education reform regime which, of course, gives very high priority to literacy (and numeracy) defined in thoroughly "traditional" and "autonomous" terms. Current education reform proposals construct literacy as individual-ized, standardized and commodified in the extreme. They constitute stan-dard English literacy as the indisputable norm, advocate the "technologizing" of literacy to unprecedented levels and tie the significance and value of literacy in increasingly narrow and instrumental ways to eco-nomic viability and demands of citizenship (see Lankshear 1998 for detailed discussion).

Not surprisingly, advocates of socioliteracy studies argue that their ap-proach provides a more morally acceptable and humane basis on which to base educational practice and social reform than do theories, concepts, val-ues and practices coalescing around the traditional view of literacy (cf., Gee 1996: 123).

PART 3: LITERACY STUDIES IN EDUCATION: A CURRENT PICTURE

Those working within literacy studies, as framed here, aim to enhance our conceptual and theoretical understanding of literacy as sociocultural practice and encourage educational practices that build on these understandings ped-agogically, ethically and politically. This work involves multiple component tasks. These include:

- providing theoretically informed accounts of sociocultural practice in general;
- clarifying literacy as (an integral component of) sociocultural practice;
- articulating a moral position and a political ideal to inform theoretical and practical work in literacy education;
- researching and analyzing literacy in use and the outcomes and effects of instances of literacy in use under their particular conditions of social practice;
- assessing examples of literacy in use in relation to moral and political ideals for literacy;
- advancing ideas for promoting literacy practices that promote these ideals and for redressing literacy practices that impede them; and
- informing literacy pedagogy with insights gained from the above-mentioned work.

The corpus of work falling under these descriptions is already vast, and generalizing from it is beyond the scope of this chapter. Contributions vary in scope as well as in their more detailed theoretical investments. For an ostensive definition of representative current work in literacy studies, we might reasonably look to Taylor and Francis' series, "Critical Perspectives on Literacy and Education," edited by Allan Luke.

Rather than attempt the futile task of reducing current work in socioli-teracy studies to a list of accurate generalizations, I will simply identify briefly some "artifacts" and "emphases" that may be seen as typical progressive "moves" within the discourse of socioliteracy studies and note some of their implications for literacy education. There are, of course, many besides those noted here.

A Sociocultural Definition of Literacy

Any acceptable and illuminating sociocultural definition of literacy has to make sense of reading, writing and meaning-making as integral elements of social practices. Such a definition is provided by Gee (1996), who defines literacy in relation to Discourses. Discourses are socially recognized ways of using language (reading, writing, speaking, listening), gestures and other semiotics (images, sounds, graphics, signs, codes), as well as ways of thinking, believing, feeling, valuing, acting/doing and interacting in relation to people and things, such that we can be identified and recognized as being a member of a socially meaningful group or as playing a socially meaningful role (cf., Gee 1991, 1996, 1998a). To be in, or part of, a Discourse means that others can recognize us as being a "this" or a "that" (a pupil, mother, priest, footballer, mechanic), or a particular "version" of a this or that (a reluctant pupil, a doting mother, a radical priest, a "bush" mechanic), by virtue of how we are using language, believing, feeling, acting, dressing, doing and so on. Language is a dimension of Discourse, but only one dimension, and Gee uses discourse (with a small "d") to mark this relationship. As historical "productions," Discourses change over time, but at any given point are sufficiently "defined" for us to tell when people are in them.

Gee distinguishes our *primary* Discourse from our various *secondary* Discourses. Our primary Discourse is how we learn to do and be (including speaking and expressing) within our family (or face-to-face intimate) group during our early life. It (we each have only one primary Discourse, although there are many different primary Discourses) comprises our first notions of who "people like us" are and what "people like us" do, think, value and so on. Our secondary Discourses (and we each have many of these, although they differ from person to person) are those we are recruited to through participation in outside groups and institutions, such as schools, clubs, workplaces, churches, political organizations and so on. These all draw upon and extend our resources from our primary Discourse and may be "nearer to" or "further away from" our primary Discourse. The further away a secondary Discourse is from our primary Discourse and our other secondary Discourses—as in the case of children from marginal social groups who struggle to get a handle on the culture of school classrooms—the more we have to "stretch" our discursive resources to "perform" within that Discourse. Often in such cases we simply are unable to operate the Discourse at the level of fluent performance.

Gee holds that any socially useful definition of literacy must build on the notion of Discourse and the distinction between primary and secondary Discourses. In part this is because the context of all language use is some specific social practice or other, which is always part of some Discourse or other. Gee defines literacy "as mastery (or fluent performance) of a secondary Discourse" (Gee 1996). Hence, to be literate means being able to handle all aspects of competent performance of the Discourse, including the literacy bits: that is, to be able to handle the various human and nonhuman elements of "coordinations" (Gee 1996; Knorr-Cetina 1992; Latour 1987) effected by Discourses. To play a role, be a particular identity, etc., is a matter of both "getting coordinated" as an element in a Discourse and of coordinating other elements. Language/literacy is a crucial element of discursive "coordinating," but it is only one aspect, and the other elements need to be "in sync" for fluent performance—*literacy*—to be realized.

This idiosyncratic, but powerful sociocultural conception of literacy has much to offer education.

- It honors the reality of myriad literacies—since there are myriad secondary Discourses.

- It takes the emphasis off "print competence" (skills, inner processes), while retaining a contingent link with "print" by virtue of the fact that most secondary Discourses (being non-face-to-face/nonkinship) involve "print"—which must now be extended to include digitally encoded language. This reminds us that literacy is never an end in itself but always a part of larger purposes. To this extent, we may get various "language/literacy bits" right, but to little effect, because of failures to get other elements "coordinated." This is why so many pupils can learn to encode and decode print/digital texts and yet fail to "achieve" in school and wider world Discourses.

- It denounces the misguided notion of "literacy" being "foundational" or "linked in a linear way" to larger practices. It is not as if we "learn the print stuff" and can then go on and "use it" in straightforward "applications" to "forms of life."

- To this extent it puts the emphasis within education in the right places, insisting that literacies be acquired "whole." This generates important issues of pedagogy, long silenced within education, but being increasingly recognized beyond formal schooling (Gee, Hull and Lankshear 1996: chaps. 1–3; Heath and McLaughlin 1994).

- It provides a basis for questioning the narrow and peculiar privileging of characteristic "School Discourse(s)," and the assumed relationships between school learning and wider domains of social practice (Gee, Hall and Lankshear 1996: chaps. 1–3; Heath and McLanghlin 1994).

- Similarly, it provides a basis for understanding patterned differentials in school literacy-mediated achievement—in terms of the fact that many primary Discourses are far removed from school Discourse(s).

- At the same time it helps explain why bridging the gap between primary Discourse experiences and secondary discursive competence proves so difficult. As is evident in our primary Discourse, coming to acquire mastery of the various coordinations takes a long time, and much of the mastery comes by way of immersed *acquisition* rather than through instructed *learning.*

• It focuses our attention on the arbitrariness and injustice inherent in historically produced hierarchies of Discourses and, therefore, in the processes whereby school-ing privileges certain literacies over others; thereby advantaging those whose pri-mary and other secondary Discourses "fit" more closely with the cultural selections of school and the wider social order (Gee 1991, 1996). This helps us "unmask" simplistic and ingenuous models and rhetorics of empowerment (for elaborations see Delgado-Gaitan 1990; Freire 1972; Lankshear 1994).

A Three-Dimensional View of Effective Literacy

From a sociocultural perspective, literacy must be seen in "3-D," as having three interlocking dimensions—the operational, the cultural and the critical—that bring together language, meaning and context (Green 1988: 160–163; Green 1997a, 1997b). An integrated view of literacy in practice and in pedagogy addresses all three dimensions simultaneously; none has any necessary priority over the others.

The *operational* dimension refers to the "means" of literacy, in the sense that it is in and through the medium of language that the literacy event happens. It involves competency with regard to the language system. To refer to the operational dimension of literacy is to point to the manner in which individuals use language in literacy tasks in order to operate effectively in specific contexts. The emphasis is on the written language system and how adequately it is handled. From this perspective, it is a question of in-dividuals being able to read and write in a range of contexts, in an appro-priate and adequate manner. This is to focus on the language aspect of literacy (see Green 1988, 1997a, 1997b; Lankshear, Bigum et al. 1997: vol. 1).

The *cultural* dimension involves what may be called the meaning aspect of literacy. It involves competency with regard to the meaning system. This is to recognize that literacy acts and events are not only *context* specific but also entail a specific *content.* It is never simply a case of being literate in and of itself but of being literate with regard to something, some aspect of knowledge or experience. The cultural aspect of literacy is a matter of un-derstanding texts in relation to contexts—to appreciate their meaning; the meaning they need to make in order to be appropriate; and what it is about given contexts of practice that makes for appropriateness or inappropriate-ness of particular ways of reading and writing. Take, for example, the case of a worker producing a spreadsheet within a workplace setting or routine. This is not a simple matter of "going into some software program" and "filling in the data." Spreadsheets must be *compiled*—which means knowing their purpose and constructing their axes and categories accordingly. To know the purpose of a particular spreadsheet requires understanding relevant elements of the culture of the immediate work context; to know why one is doing what one is doing now, how to do it and why what one is doing is appropriate.

The *critical* dimension of literacy has to do with the socially constructed nature of all human practices and meaning systems. In order to be able to participate effectively and productively in any social practice, humans must be socialized into it. But social practices and their meaning systems are always selective and sectional; they represent particular interpretations and classifications. Unless individuals are also given access to the grounds for selection and the principles of interpretation, they are merely socialized into the meaning system and are unable to take an active part in its transformation. The critical dimension of literacy is the basis for ensuring that participants cannot merely participate in a practice and make meanings within it, but can in various ways transform and *actively* produce it.

This "3-D" model provides a very useful adjunct to the definition of literacy in terms of secondary Discourses. It gives due significance to the operational dimension, which includes the mechanical aspects of encoding and decoding, while insisting on recognition that much more is required of a pedagogy for "effective literacy." In the current education reform context, this provides a valuable basis for critiquing unduly narrow constructions of effective literacy (cf., DEET 1991; DEETYA 1998). It also speaks usefully and powerfully to specific components of "literacy strategies" within current reform plans: such as reporting profiles, literacy "standards" or "benchmarks" and the like. For example, benchmarks would need to be framed in ways that honor literacy as sociocultural practice. They could not be reduced to (merely) textual "lowest common denominators," since text stands to literacy as discourse stands to Discourse in Gee's conceptual scheme. In addition, assessment would need to be of literacy *in practice*: that is, as an embedded and integrated component of Discourse events or "moves."

Applications of Cultural Apprenticeship Models of Learning to Literacy Pedagogy

Adopting a sociocultural frame for literacy studies opens the way for exploring the potential for literacy pedagogy to be informed and enhanced by models of learning developed within other component "movements" of "the social turn." In an account of what more "authentic" school-based curriculum and pedagogy might look like, Heath and McLaughlin (1994: 472) critique classroom pedagogies that "create 'authenticity' artificially rather than study contextually authentic curricula—authentic to youth—in supportive organizational structures." They argue that classroom educators can learn much from examining effective grass-roots organizations like the Girl Guides, Girls Club and drama groups. These provide rich social contexts and opportunities for "learning to learn for anything" everyday by means of "[cognitive and social] apprenticeship, peer learning, authentic tasks, skill-focused practices and real outcome measures," such as completed public projects, performances, displays and exhibitions (472.). Heath and McLaughlin believe these characteristic features of effective *authentic* learning converge in Barbara Rogoff's (1990; also Rogoff 1995) account of learning through sociocultural activity.

Rogoff advances three planes of analysis for interpreting and evaluating learning. These are apprenticeship, guided participation and participatory appropriation. They correspond with community, interpersonal and personal processes. While these planes are mutually constituting, interdependent and inseparable, identifying them individually enables particular aspects of a learning process to be brought into sharp focus for analytic purposes.

According to Rogoff, "apprenticeship" operates within a plane of community and institutional activity and describes "active individuals participating with others in culturally organized ways" (1995:142). The primary purpose of apprenticeship is to facilitate "mature participation in the activity by less experienced people" (142). Experts—who continue to develop and refine their expertise—and peers in the learning process are integral to Rogoff's account of apprenticeship (Rogoff 1995: 143). Both categories of participant find themselves "engaging in activities with others of varying experience" and moving through cycles of learning, teaching and practice. Investigating and interpreting sociocultural apprenticeship focuses attention on the activity being learned (with its concomitant skills, processes and content knowledge) and on its relationship with community practices and institutions—eschewing traditional conceptions of apprenticeship as an expert–novice dyad.

"Guided participation" encompasses "processes and systems of involvement between people as they communicate and co-ordinate efforts while participating in culturally valued activity" (Rogoff 1995: 143). It involves a range of interpersonal interactions. These include face-to-face interactions, side-by-side interactions (which are more frequent face-to-face interactions within everyday life) and other interactional arrangements where activities do not require everyone involved to be present. Hence, for Rogoff, guidance is provided by "cultural and social values, as well as [by] social partners" who may be local or distant (142).

"Participatory appropriation" refers to personal processes of ongoing and dynamic engagement with learning through socially contextualized and purposeful activities that ultimately transform the learner. Rogoff uses this concept to describe processes by which people "transform their understanding of and responsibility for activities through their own participation" (Rogoff 1995: 150). Here, analysis focuses on changes that learners undergo in gaining facility with an activity, as well as acceptable changes learners make to activities in the process of becoming "experts," enabling them to engage with subsequent similar activities and their social meanings.

As a model of pedagogy for effective learning, cultural apprenticeship has important implications for literacy education. By grounding learning as far as possible within settings where genuine opportunities are available for apprenticeship to skills and procedures and where conditions exist for guided participation and participatory appropriation, it minimizes counterproductive forms of abstract(ed) and decontextualized activity. At the same time it allows for skill refinement through repetition, drilling and the like (cf., the practice and training dimensions of sports and games)—but within situations and settings that approximate to "the real thing." With the drilling, habituation and repetition, in other words, come also concrete and embodied experiences of participation that convey situated cultural understanding.

At the same time, the cultural apprenticeship model is basically one of *enculturation*: learners are recruited to Discourses "from the inside." While this may be very effective for mastering operational and cultural dimensions of literacy, it may work against the "critical." This recovers for classroom learning an important role that—almost by definition—cannot be undertaken in situ and in role (i.e., the tasks of identifying and judging the values, purposes, interests, perspectives and the like that are written into particular Discourses and those that are thereby written out).

PART 4: CRITICAL LITERACY AND SOCIOLITERACY STUDIES

The relationship between critical literacy and socioliteracy studies is interesting from an historical-developmental perspective. By the early 1990s it was common for literacy theorists to speak of critical literacy as one of several competing Discourses of literacy—along with functional literacy and cultural literacy, among others. This largely reflected the emergence of a critical literacy "school" out of the work of Paulo Freire and the critical theory of the Frankfurt School. Critical literacy emerged as an aspect of the larger phenomenon of a radical alternative educational perspective (including such things as the "new" sociology, critical theory applied to education, critical pedagogy, etc.) to the long-standing "liberal" view of education. It was framed in conscious distinction from and opposition to cultural and functional models (the latter equating roughly with the "operational" component of the "3-D model"). This separation often served to marginalize critical literacy from achieving the broad-based constituency it sought, which called for ways of taking functional and cultural considerations seriously within a larger pedagogy.

With the emergence of a defined field of socioliteracy studies it is now easier to frame and pursue critical literacy work within the ambit of a transcendent sociocultural ideal of literacy: that is, as an integral component of literacy in three dimensions. Building on ideas already canvassed in this chapter, we can expand the brief statement of the "critical dimension" of the 3-D model by way of concluding this discussion.

Work within socioliteracy studies identifies at least three related levels of activity involved in the critical dimension of literacy: namely,

- developing a critical perspective on literacy per se. This is precisely the kind of thing the sociocultural approach to literacy exemplifies. Gee's account of "literacy," for example, invokes metalevel understandings of language in use which enable a critical stance to be adopted toward other constructions of literacy and their implications (see, for example, Gee 1996; Kress 1996; Lankshear 1997; Muspratt, Freebody and Luke 1997; New London Group 1996; Wallace 1992);

- engaging in critique of particular *texts* or specific instances of *literacy in use*. This involves developing and using techniques that reveal how texts do work and produce effects as elements of larger social practices and discursive "coordinations." This presupposes drawing on some theory or ideal—ethical, political, educational— as a basis for choosing and employing particular kinds of techniques in the first place, as well as for making judgments about textual practices/literacy in use in the light of the analysis performed (e.g., Gee 1998a, 1998b, 1996: chap. 5; Fairclough 1989, 1992; Kress 1985; Luke 1992; Schiffrin 1987, 1994); and

- making "critical readings" of Discourses and enacting forms of resistance or transformative practice on the basis of preferred ethical, political and educational values/ ideals (e.g., Gee 1996; Fairclough 1989; Lankshear 1997, Muspratt, Freebody and Luke 1997). This would include the kind of work that seeks to explain and critique the operation of school literacies as interest-serving selections from a larger culture, which systematically advantage some groups and language communities over others.

In a recent statement, Gee integrates these levels of activity in making a case for making concern with a particular kind of "work" central to socioliteracy studies. This is what he calls "enactive" and "recognition" work: work done by human beings as they go about "getting coordinated" and "coordinating other elements" within everyday participation in Discourses— a conception that owes much to the work of Latour (1987, 1991) and Knorr-Cetina (1992).

Gee argues that social worlds are created and sustained by human beings organizing and coordinating "materials" in ways that others (come to) recognize, to see as *meaningful*. These "materials" are, of course, the "stuff" of Discourses: "people, things, artifacts, symbols, tools, technologies, actions, interactions, times, places, ways of speaking, listening, writing, reading, feeling, thinking, valuing, etc." (Gee 1998a: 15). Our discursive practice involves "attempting to get other people to recognize people and things as having certain meanings and values within certain configurations or relationships" (14). Enactive work refers to these "attempts" (which, of course, are often "unconscious"—they come with recruitment to Discourses—but can, equally, be conscious—as in witting acts of transformative practice). Recognition work refers to the efforts by others to accept or reject such attempts—"to see or fail [refuse] to see things our way" (15).

These attempts and recognitions are precisely what produce, sustain, challenge, transform, etc., particular discursive effects, including those of particular concern to critical literacy theorists and educators: namely, the creation and maintenance of relations, processes, arrangements, etc., within which individuals and groups have markedly unequal access to "representational systems and mediational means," "linguistic knowledge," "cultural artifacts," "actual financial capital," "institutional entry" and "status" (Muspratt, Freebody and Luke 1997: 2). Enactive and recognition work is, then, political and ethical. And the stakes of such work are "always "up for grabs." "Actors, events, activities, practices, and Discourses do not exist in the world *except through* active work, work that is very often unstable and contested" (Gee 1998a: 17).

From this standpoint, critical literacy becomes a political project involving informed "enactment" and "recognition." Employing appropriate techniques of discourse analysis we can investigate how language is recruited, in conjunction with other "elements," for enactive and recognition work. From this basis we can engage in our own informed enactments and recognitions on the basis of our moral and political commitments and our larger sociocultural understanding of literacy and Discourse. In the end, it is precisely these possibilities that underwrite the importance of framing literacy studies in sociocultural terms—and fighting for that framing as enactive work.

CONCLUSION

Socioliteracy studies provides a case of postdisciplinary development that has helped achieve some important academic advances. It has provided people working within established fields of linguistics and language studies with an important *material* focus for ongoing theory development and application: namely, discurively embedded social practices mediated by literacy—notably, within diverse educational contexts. Work in linguistics is the richer for this. So is work within the academic study of education, which has access to a considerably wider range of theoretical, conceptual and research perspectives than previously.

In particular, the development of socioliteracy studies has helped the process of getting educational studies—in principle *always* a crossdisciplinary domain—out from under the tyranny of the narrow paradigms of psychology that have dominated educational inquiry throughout this century. Unfortunately, at the point of most practical application—the "chalkface"—education remains powerfully in the grip of psychologistic-technicist policy predilections. Even so, literacy studies in education provides a key battleground from which to continue the struggle against the psychology-technocracy "alliance" and to have sociocultural practices better understood for what they are. This remains our best hope for contributing academically to the pursuit of more humane and just agendas for social policy and development.

REFERENCES

Anderson, C. and Bowman, M. (eds.). (1966) *Education and Economic Development.* London: Frank Cass.

Bakhtin, M. (1986) *Speech Genres and Other Late Essays.* Austin: University of Texas Press.

Barton, D. (1994) *Literacy: An Introduction to the Ecology of Written Language.* Oxford: Blackwell.

Barton, D. and Hamilton, M. (1998) *Local Literacies.* London: Routledge.

Barton, D. and Ivanic, R. (eds.). (1991) *Writing in the Community.* London: Sage.

Bereiter, C. and Scardamalia, M. (1993) *Surpassing Ourselves: An Inquiry into the Nature and Implications of Expertise.* Chicago: Open Court.

Bernstein, B. (1971) *Class, Codes and Control,* vol. 1. London: Routledge.

———. (1975) *Class, Codes and Control,* vol. 2. London: Routledge.

Bizzell, P. (1992) *Academic Discourse and Critical Consciousness.* Pittsburgh: University of Pittsburgh Press.

Bloome, D. and Green, J. (1991) "Educational Contexts of Literacy." In W. Grabe (ed.), *Annual Review of Applied Linguistics,* 12: 49–70.

Bourdieu, P. (1977) "Cultural Reproduction and Social Reproduction." In J. Karabel and J. Halsey (eds.), *Power and Ideology in Education.* Oxford: Oxford University Press.

Bourdieu, P. and Passeron, J.-C. (1971) *Reproduction in Education, Society and Culture.* London: Sage.

Brown, A. et al. (1993) "Distributed Expertise in the Classroom." In G. Salomon (ed.), *Distributed Cognitions: Psychological and Educational Considerations.* New York: Cambridge University Press, 188–228.

Cazden, C. (1998) *Classroom Discourse: The Language of Teaching and Learning.* Portsmouth, NH: Heinemann.

Cipolla, C. (1969) *Literacy and Development in the West.* Harmondsworth: Penguin.

Cook-Gumperz, J. (ed.). (1986) *The Social Construction of Literacy.* Cambridge: Cambridge University Press.

Cressy, D. (1980) *Literacy and the Social Order.* Cambridge: Cambridge University Press.

Davis, N. (1975) "Printing and the People." In N. Davis, *Society and Culture in Early Modern France.* Stanford, CA: Stanford University Press, 189–226.

de Castell, S., Luke, A. and Luke, C. (1989) *Language, Authority and Criticism.* London: Falmer Press.

DEET/Department of Employment, Education and Training, Australia. (1991) *Australia's Language: The Australian Language and Literacy Policy.* Canberra: Australian Government Publishing Service.

DEETYA/Department of Employment, Education and Training and Youth Affairs, Australia. (1998) *Literacy for All: The Challenge for Australian Schools.* Canberra: Australian Government Publishing Service.

Delgado-Gaitan, C. (1990) *Literacy for Empowerment*. London: Falmer Press.

Edelsky, C. (1990) *With Literacy and Justice for All*. London: Falmer Press.

Edwards, D. and Mercer, N. (1987) *Common Knowledge: The Development of Understanding in the Classroom*. London: Methuen.

Eisenstein, E. (1979) *The Printing Press as an Agent of Change*, 2 vols. Cambridge: Cambridge University Press.

Fairclough, N. (1989) *Language and Power*. London: Longman.

————. (ed.). (1992) *Critical Language Awareness*. London: Longman.

Franklin, U. (1990) *The Real World of Technology*. Montreal: CBC Enterprises.

Freire, P. (1972) *Pedagogy of the Oppressed*. Harmondsworth: Penguin.

————. (1973) *Cultural Action for Freedom*. Harmondsworth: Penguin.

————. (1974) *Education for Critical Consciousness*. London: Sheed and Ward.

Gee, J. P. (1990) *Social Linguistics and Literacies: Ideology in Discourses*. London: Falmer Press.

————. (1991) "What Is Literacy?" In C. Mitchell and K. Weiler (eds.), *Rewriting Literacy: Culture and the Discourse of the Other*. New York: Bergin & Garvey, 1–11.

————. (1996) *Social Linguistics and Literacies: Ideology in Discourses*, 2nd ed. London: Taylor and Francis.

————. (1998a) "The New Literacy Studies and the 'Social Turn.' " Madison: University of Wisconsin–Madison Department of Curriculum and Instruction (mimeo).

————. (1998b) "Preamble to a Literacy Program." Madison: University of Wisconsin–Madison Department of Curriculum and Instruction (mimeo).

Gee, J. P., Hull, G. and Lankshear, C. (1996) *The New Work Order: Behind the Language of the New Capitalism*. Boulder, CO: Westview Press.

Goody, J. (1977) *The Domestication of the Savage Mind*. Cambridge: Cambridge University Press.

Goody, J. and Watt, I. (1963) "The Consequences of Literacy." *Comparative Studies in History and Society*, 5: 304–345.

Graff, H. (1979) *The Literacy Myth: Literacy and Social Structure in the Nineteenth-Century City*. New York: Academic Press.

————. (1991) *The Literacy Myth: Literacy and Social Structure in the Nineteenth-Century City*, 2nd ed. London: Transaction Publishers.

Green, B. (1988) "Subject-Specific Literacy and School Learning: A Focus on Writing." *Australian Journal of Education*, 32(2): 156–179.

————. (1997) "Literacy, Information and the Learning Society." Keynote address at the Joint Conference of the Australian Association for the Teaching of English, the Australian Literacy Educators' Association and the Australian School Library Association. Darwin: Darwin High School, Northern Territory, Australia, July 8–11.

Havelock, E. (1963) *Preface to Plato*. Cambridge, MA: Harvard University Press.

Heath, S. B. (1982) "What No Bedtime Story Means: Narrative Skills at Home and School." *Language in Society*, 11(1): 49–76

————. (1983) *Ways with Words: Language, Life and Work in Communities and Classrooms*. Cambridge: Cambridge University Press.

Heath, S. B. and Mangiola, L. (1991) *Children of Promise: Literate Activity in Lin-*

guistically and Culturally Diverse Classrooms. Washington, DC: National Education Association of the United States.

Heath, S. B. and McLaughlin, M. (1994) "Learning for Anything Everyday." *Journal of Curriculum Studies,* 26(5): 471–489.

Hodge, R. and Kress, G. (1988) *Social Semiotics.* Ithaca, NY: Cornell University Press.

Hoggart, R. (1957) *The Uses of Literacy: Aspects of Working Class Life.* London: Chatto.

Houston, R. (1983) "Literacy and Society in the West, 1500–1800." *Social History,* 8: 269–293.

———. (1985) *Scottish Literacy and the Scottish Identity: Illiteracy and Society in Scotland and Northern England, 1600–1800.* Cambridge: Cambridge University Press.

Hymes, D. (1974) *Foundations of Sociolinguistics.* Philadelphia: University of Pennsylvania Press.

———. (1980) *Language in Education: Ethnolinguistic Essays.* Washington, DC: Center for Applied Linguistics.

Johansson, E. (1977) *The History of Literacy in Sweden.* Educational Reports, Umea, no. 12. Umea, Sweden: Umea University and School of Education.

Joyce, W. et al. (eds.). (1983) *Printing and Society in Early America.* Worcester, MA: American Antiquarian Society.

Kell, C. (1996) "Literacy Practices in an Informal Setting in the Cape Peninsula." In M. Prinsloo and M. Breier (eds.), *The Social Uses of Literacy: Theory and Practice in Contemporary South Africa.* Amsterdam: John Benjamins.

Knobel. M. (1997) "Language and Social Practices in Four Adolescents' Everyday Lives." Ph.D. thesis, Queensland University of Technology, Faculty of Education.

———. (1998) *Everyday Literacies: Language, Discourse and Social Practice.* New York: Peter Lang.

Knorr-Cetina, K. (1992) "The Couch, the Cathedral, and the Laboratory: On the Relationship between Experiment and Laboratory in Science." In A. Pickering (ed.), *Science as Practice and Culture.* Chicago: University of Chicago Press, 113–137.

Krashen, S. (1982) *Principles and Practice in Second Language Acquisition.* Hayward, CA: Alemany Press.

Kress, G. (1985) *Linguistic Processes in Sociocultural Practice.* Geelong, Australia: Deakin University Press.

———. (1996) *Before Writing: Rethinking Paths into Literacy.* London: Routledge.

Lankshear, C. (1993) Preface to C. Lankshear and P. McLaren (eds.), *Critical Literacy: Politics, Praxis and the Postmodern.* New York: SUNY Press.

———. (1994) "Literacy and Empowerment: Discourse, Power, Critique." *New Zealand Journal of Educational Studies,* 29(1): 59–72.

———. (1997) *Changing Literacies.* Philadelphia: Open University Press.

———. (1998) "Meanings of 'Literacy' in Education Reform Proposals." *Educational Theory,* 48(4): 351–372.

Lankshear, C., Bigum, C. et al. (1997) *Digital Rhetorics: Literacies and Technologies in Education—Current Practices and Future Directions,* 3 vols. Project Report, Children's Literacy National Projects. Brisbane: QUT/DEETYA.

Lankshear, C. and Lawler, M. (1987) *Literacy, Schooling and Revolution*. London: Falmer Press.

Latour, B. (1987) *Science in Action*. Cambridge, MA: Harvard University Press.

———. (1991) *We Have Never Been Modern*. Cambridge, MA: Harvard University Press.

Lave, J. and Wenger, E. (1991) *Situated Learning: Legitimate Peripheral Participation*. New York: Cambridge University Press.

Levett, A. and Lankshear, C. (1994) "Literacies, Workplaces and the Demands of New Times." In M. Brown (ed.), *Literacies and the Workplace: A Collection of Original Essays*. Geelong, Australia: Deakin University Press.

Levine, K. (1986) *The Social Context of Literacy*. London: Routledge.

Lockridge, K. (1974) *Literacy in Colonial New England*. New York: Norton.

Luke, A. (1988) *Literacy, Textbooks and Ideology*. London: Falmer Press.

———. (1992) "Literacy and Work in New Times." *Open Letter*, 3(1): 3–15.

Luke, C. (1989) *Pedagogy, Printing and Protestantism*. Albany, NY: SUNY Press.

Michaels, S. (1981) " 'Sharing Time': Children's Narrative Styles and Differential Access to Literacy." *Language in Society*, 10: 423–442.

Moll, L. (1992) "Literacy Research in Community and Classrooms: A Sociocultural Approach." In R. Beach et al. (eds.), *Multidisciplinary Perspectives on Literacy Research*. Urbana, IL: NCRE/NCTE, 211–244.

Muspratt, S., Freebody, P. and Luke, A. (eds.). (1997) *Constructing Critical Literacies*. Cresskill, NJ: Hampton Press.

New London Group (1996) "A Pedagogy of Multiliteracies: Designing Social Futures." *Harvard Educational Review*, 66(1): 60–92.

Ong, W. (1977) *Interfaces of the Word*. Ithaca, NY: Cornell University Press.

———. (1982) *Orality and Literacy: The Technologizing of the Word*. London: Methuen.

Rogoff, B. (1990) *Apprenticeship in Thinking: Cognitive Development in a Social Context*. Cambridge: Cambridge University Press.

———. (1995) "Observing Sociocultural Activity on Three Planes: Participatory Appropriation, Guided Participation, Apprenticeship." In J. Wertsch, P. del Rio and A. Alvarez (eds.), *Sociocultural Studies of Mind*. New York: Cambridge University Press.

Schiffrin, D. (1987) *Discourse Markers*. Cambridge: Cambridge University Press.

———. (1994) *Approaches to Discourse*. Oxford: Blackwell.

Schofield, R. (1968) "The Measurement of Literacy in Pre-Industrial England." In J. Goody (ed.), *Literacy in Traditional Societies*. Cambridge: Cambridge University Press, 311–325.

Scollon, R. and Scollon, S. (1981) *Narrative, Literacy and Face in Interethnic Communication*. Norwood, NJ: Ablex.

Scribner, R. (1981) *For the Sake of Simple Folk: Popular Propaganda for the German Reformation*. Cambridge: Cambridge University Press.

Scribner, S. and Cole, M. (1981) *The Psychology of Literacy*. Cambridge, MA: Harvard University Press.

Stone, L. (1969) "Literacy and Education in England, 1640–1900." *Past and Present*, 42: 69–139.

Strauss, G. (1978) *Luther's House of Learning*. Baltimore: John Hopkins University Press.

Street, B. (1984) *Literacy in Theory and Practice*. Cambridge: Cambridge University Press.

———. (ed.) (1993) *Cross-Cultural Approaches to Literacy*. Cambridge: Cambridge University Press.

———. (1995) *Social Literacies: Critical Approaches to Literacy in Development, Ethnography and Education*. London: Longman.

Stubbs, M. (1980) *Language and Literacy*. London: Routledge.

Vygotsky, L. (1978) *Mind in Society: The Development of Higher Psychological Processes*. M. Cole, V. John-Steiner, S. Scribner and E. Souberman (eds.). Cambridge, MA: Harvard University Press.

Wallace, C. (1992) "Critical Language Awareness in the EFL Classroom." In N. Fairclough (ed.), *Critical Language Awareness*. London: Longman, 59–92.

Webb, R. (1955) *The British Working Class Reader*. London: Allen and Unwin.

Wertsch, J. (1985) *Vygotsky and the Social Formation of Mind*. Cambridge, MA: Harvard University Press.

———. (1991) *Voices of the Mind: A Sociocultural Approach to Mediated Action*. Cambridge, MA: Harvard University Press.

Chapter 11

Doing Cultural Studies: Youth and the Challenge of Pedagogy

HENRY A. GIROUX

In our society, youth is present only when its presence is a problem, or is regarded as a problem. More precisely, the category "youth" gets mobilized in official documentary discourse, in concerned or outraged editorials and features or in the supposedly disinterested tracts emanating from the social sciences at those times when young people make their presence felt by going "out of bounds," by resisting through rituals, dressing strangely, striking bizarre attitudes, breaking rules, breaking bottles, windows, heads, issuing rhetorical challenges to the law (Hebdige 1988: 17–18).

A recent commentary in the *Chronicle of Higher Education* claimed that the field of cultural studies is "about the hottest thing in humanities and social-science research right now, but it's largely peopled by scholars in literature, film and media, communications, and philosophy" (*Chronicle of Higher Education* 1993: A8). Given the popularity of cultural studies for a growing number of scholars, I have often wondered why so few academics have incorporated cultural studies into the language of educational reform. If educators are to take seriously the challenge of cultural studies, particularly its insistence on generating new questions, models and contexts in order to address the central and most urgent dilemmas of our age, they must critically address the politics of their own location. This means understanding not only the ways in which institutions of higher education play their part in shaping the work we do with students, but also the ways in which our vocation as educators supports, challenges or subverts institutional practices that are at odds with democratic processes and the hopes and opportunities we provide for the nation's youth. In what follows, I want to explore not only why educators refuse to engage the possibilities of cultural studies, but also why scholars working within a cultural studies framework often refuse to take seriously pedagogy and the role of schools in the shaping of democratic public life.

Educational theorists demonstrate as little interest in cultural studies as cultural studies scholars do in the critical theories of schooling and pedagogy. For educators, this indifference may be explained in part by the narrow technocratic models that dominate mainstream reform efforts and structure education programs. Within such a tradition, management issues become more important than understanding and furthering schools as democratic public spheres.[1] Hence, the regulation, certification and standardization of teacher behavior is emphasized over creating the conditions for teachers to undertake the sensitive political and ethical roles they might assume as public intellectuals who selectively produce and legitimate particular forms of knowledge and authority. Similarly, licensing and assimilating differences among students is more significant than treating students as bearers of diverse social memories with a right to speak and represent themselves in the quest for learning and self-determination. While other disciplines have appropriated, engaged and produced new theoretical languages in keeping with changing historical conditions, colleges of education have maintained a deep suspicion of theory and intellectual dialogue and thus have not been receptive to the introduction of cultural studies.[2] Other explanations for this willful refusal to know would include a history of educational reform that has been overly indebted to practical considerations that often support a long tradition of anti-intellectualism. Moreover, educators frequently pride themselves on being professional, scientific and objective. Cultural studies challenges the ideological and political nature of such claims by arguing that teachers always work and speak within historically and socially determined relations of power.[3] Put another way, educators whose work is shaped by cultural studies do not simply view teachers and students either as chroniclers of history and social change or recipients of culture, but as active participants in its construction.

The resistance to cultural studies may also be due to the fact that it reasserts the importance of comprehending schooling as a mechanism of culture and politics, embedded in competing relations of power that attempt to regulate and order how students think, act and live.[4] Since cultural studies is largely concerned with the critical relationship among culture, knowledge and power, it is not surprising that mainstream educators often dismiss cultural studies as being too ideological or simply ignore its criticisms regarding how education generates a privileged narrative space for some social groups and a space of inequality and subordination for others.

Historically, schools and colleges of education have been organized around either traditional subject-based studies (math education) or into largely disciplinary/administrative categories (curriculum and instruction). Within this type of intellectual division of labor, students generally have had few opportunities to study larger social issues. This slavish adherence to structuring the curriculum around the core disciplinary subjects is at odds with the field of cultural studies, whose theoretical energies are largely focused on interdisciplinary issues, such as textuality and representation refracted through the dynamics of gender, sexuality, subordinated youth, national identity, colonialism, race, ethnicity and popular culture.[5] By offering educators a critical language through which to examine the ideological and political interests that structure reform efforts in education, such as nationalized testing, standardized curriculum and efficiency models, cultural studies incurs the wrath of mainstream and conservative educators, who often are silent about the political agendas that underlie their own language and reform agendas.[6]

Cultural studies also rejects the traditional notion of teaching as a technique or set of neutral skills and argues that teaching is a social practice that can only be understood through considerations of history, politics, power and culture. Given its concern with everyday life, its pluralization of cultural communities and its emphasis on multidisciplinary knowledge, cultural studies is less concerned with issues of certification and testing than it is with how knowledge, texts and cultural products are produced, circulated and used. In this perspective, culture is the ground "on which analysis proceeds, the object of study, and the site of political critique and intervention" (Grassberg et al. 1992: 5). This in part explains why some advocates of cultural studies are increasingly interested in "how and where knowledge needs to surface and emerge in order to be consequential" with respect to expanding the possibilities for a radical democracy (Bennett 1984: 32).

Within the next century, educators will not be able to ignore the hard questions that schools will have to face regarding issues of multiculturalism, race, identity, power, knowledge, ethics and work. These issues will play a major role in defining the meaning and purpose of schooling, the relationship between teachers and students and the critical content of their exchange in terms of how to live in a world that will be vastly more globalized, high tech and racially diverse than at any other time in history. Cultural studies offers enormous possibilities for educators to rethink the nature of educational theory and practice, as well as what it means to educate future teachers for the twenty-first century (see Giroux 1988, 1992).

At the same time, it is important to stress that the general indifference of many cultural studies theorists to the importance of critical pedagogy as a form of cultural practice does an injustice to the politically charged history of cultural studies, one which points to the necessity for combining self-criticism with a commitment to transforming existing social and political problems. It is not my intention here to replay the debate regarding what the real history of cultural studies is, though this is an important issue. Instead, I want to focus on the importance of critical pedagogy as a central aspect of cultural studies and on cultural work as a pedagogical practice. This suggests analyzing cultural studies for the insights it has accrued as it has moved historically from its previous concerns with class and language to its more recent analysis of the politics of race, gender, identity and ethnicity. This is not meant to suggest that the history of cultural studies needs to be laid out in great detail as some sort of foundational exegesis. On the contrary, cultural studies needs to be approached historically as a mix of founding moments, transformative challenges and self-critical interrogations (Nelson 1991: 32). And it is precisely the rupturing spirit that informs elements of its interdisciplinary practice, social activism and historical awareness that prompts my concern for the current lacunae in cultural studies regarding the theoretical and political importance of pedagogy as a founding moment in its legacy.

In what follows, I want to take up these concerns more concretely as they bear on what Dick Hebdige calls the "problem of youth" and the necessary importance of this issue for educators and other cultural workers (Hebdige 1988: 17–18). In constructing this line of thought, I begin by making the case that pedagogy must become a defining principle of any critical notion of cultural studies. This position is developed, in part, to expand the meaning and relevance of pedagogy for those engaged in cultural work both in and outside of the university. I then argue for the pedagogical practice of using films about youth not only as legitimate objects of social knowledge that offer representations in which youth can identify their desires and hopes, but also as pedagogical texts that play a formative role in shaping the social identities of youth. Through an analysis of four Hollywood films about youth, I hope to show how the more progressive elements of critical pedagogical work can inform and be informed by cultural studies' emphasis on popular culture as a terrain of significant political and pedagogical importance. I will conclude by developing the implications cultural studies might have for those of us who are concerned about reforming schools and colleges of education.

THE ABSENCE OF PEDAGOGY IN CULTURAL STUDIES

It is generally argued that cultural studies is largely defined through its analysis of culture and power, particularly with regard to its "shifting of the terrain of culture toward the popular" while simultaneously expanding its critical reading of the production, reception, use and effects of popular texts (Hall 1992: 22). Texts in this case constitute a wide range of aural, visual and printed signifiers; moreover, such texts are often taken up as part of a broader attempt to analyze how individual and social identities are mobilized, engaged and transformed within circuits of power informed by issues of race, gender, class, ethnicity and other social formations. All of these concerns point to the intellectual and institutional borders that produce, regulate and engage meaning as a site of social struggle. Challenging the ways in which the academic disciplines have been used to secure particular forms of authority, cultural studies has opened up the possibility for questioning how power operates in the construction of knowledge while simultaneously redefining the parameters of the form and content of what is being taught in institutions of higher education. In this instance, struggles over meaning, language and textuality have become symptomatic of a larger struggle over the meaning of cultural authority, the role of public intellectuals and the meaning of national identity. While cultural studies proponents have provided an enormous theoretical service in taking up the struggle over knowledge and authority, particularly as it affects the restructuring of the curriculum in many colleges and universities, such struggles often overlook some of the major concerns that have been debated by various theorists who work within the diverse tradition of critical pedagogy. This is especially surprising since cultural studies draws its theoretical and political inspiration from feminism, postmodernism, postcolonialism and a host of other areas that have at least made a passing reference to the importance of pedagogy.

I want to argue that cultural studies is still too rigidly tied to the modernist, academic disciplinary structures that it often criticizes. This is not to suggest that it does not adequately engage the issue of academic disciplines. In fact, this is one of its most salient characteristics.[7] What it fails to do is critically address a major prop of disciplinarity, which is the notion of pedagogy as an unproblematic vehicle for transmitting knowledge. Lost here is the attempt to understand pedagogy as a mode of cultural criticism for questioning the very conditions under which knowledge and identities are produced. Of course, theorists such as Gayatri Spivak, Stanley Aronowitz and others do engage the relationship between cultural studies and pedagogy, but they constitute a small minority.[8] The haunting question here is, What is it about pedagogy that allows cultural studies theorists to ignore it?

One answer may lie in the refusal of cultural studies theorists either to take schooling seriously as a site of struggle or to probe how traditional pedagogy produces particular social histories, how it constructs student identities through a range of subject positions. Of course, within radical educational theory, there is a long history of developing critical discourses of the subject around pedagogical issues.[9]

Another reason cultural studies theorists have devoted little attention to pedagogy may be due to the disciplinary policing that leaves the marks of its legacy on all areas of the humanities and liberal arts. Pedagogy is often deemed unworthy of being taken up as a serious project; in fact, even popular culture has more credibility than pedagogy. This can be seen not only in the general absence of any discussion of pedagogy in cultural studies texts, but also in those studies in the humanities that have begun to engage pedagogical issues. Even in these works there is a willful refusal to acknowledge some of the important theoretical gains in pedagogy that have gone on in the last twenty years.[10] Within this silence lurks the seductive rewards of disciplinary control, a refusal to cross academic borders and a shoring up of academic careerism, competitiveness and elitism. Of course, composition studies, one of the few fields in the humanities that does take pedagogy seriously, occupies a status as disparaging as the field of education.[11] Hence, it appears that the legacy of academic elitism and professionalism still exercises a strong influence on the field of cultural studies, in spite of its alleged democratization of social knowledge.

CULTURAL STUDIES AND PEDAGOGY

In what follows, I want to make a case for the importance of pedagogy as a central aspect of cultural studies. In doing so, I first want to analyze the role that pedagogy played in the early founding stages of the Birmingham Centre for Cultural Studies.[12] I then want to define more specifically the central dimensions of pedagogy as a cultural practice. But before I address these two important moments of critical pedagogy as a form of cultural politics, I think it is important to stress that the concept of pedagogy must be used with respectful caution. Not only are there different versions of what constitutes critical pedagogy, but there is also no generic definition that can be applied to the term. At the same time, there are important theoretical insights and practices that are woven through various approaches to critical pedagogy. It is precisely these insights, which often define a common set of problems, that serve to delineate critical pedagogy as a set of conditions articulated within the shifting context of a particular political project. These problems include, but are not limited to, the relationship between knowledge and power, language and experience, ethics and authority, student agency and transformative politics, and teacher location and student formations.

Richard Hoggart and Raymond Williams addressed the issue of pedagogy in a similar manner in their early attempts to promote cultural studies in Britain. As founding figures in the Birmingham Centre for Cultural Studies, Hoggart and Williams believed that pedagogy offered the opportunity to link cultural practice with the development of radical cultural theories. Not only did pedagogy connect questions of form and content, it also introduced a sense of how teaching, learning, textual studies and knowledge could be addressed as political issues that bring to the foreground considerations of power and social agency. According to Williams, the advent of cultural studies in the 1930s and 1940s emerged directly out of the pedagogical work that was going on in adult education. The specificity of the content and context of adult education provided cultural studies with a number of issues that were to direct its subsequent developments in Birmingham. These included the refusal to accept the limitations of established academic boundaries and power structures, the demand for linking literature to the life situations of adult learners and the call that schooling be empowering rather than merely humanizing.[13]

For Williams there is more at stake here than reclaiming the history of cultural studies; he is most adamant in making clear that the "deepest impulse [informing cultural studies] was the desire to make learning part of the process of social change itself" (Williams 1989a: 158). It is precisely this attempt to broaden the notion of the political by making it more pedagogical that reminds us of the importance of pedagogy as a cultural practice. In this context, pedagogy deepens and extends the study of culture and power by addressing not only how culture is produced, circulated and transformed, but also how it is actually negotiated by human beings within specific settings and circumstances. In this instance, pedagogy becomes an act of cultural production, a process through which power regulates bodies and behaviors as "they move through space and time." (Fiske 1994: 20) While pedagogy is deeply implicated in the production of power/knowledge relationships and the construction of values and desires, its theoretical center of gravity begins not with a particular claim to new knowledge, but with real people articulating and rewriting their lived experiences within rather than outside of history. In this sense, pedagogy, especially in its critical variants, is about understanding how power works within particular historical, social and cultural contexts in order to engage and, when necessary, to change such contexts.[14]

The importance of pedagogy to the content and context of cultural studies lies in the relevance it has for illuminating how knowledge and social identities are produced in a variety of sites in addition to schools. For Raymond Williams, one of the founding concepts of cultural studies was that cultural education was just as important as labor, political and trade union education. Moreover, Williams believed that limiting the study of culture to higher education was to run the risk of depoliticizing it. Williams believed that education in the broad, political sense was essential not only for engaging, challenging and transforming policy, but was also the necessary referent for stressing the pedagogical importance of work shared by all cultural workers who engage in the production of knowledge. This becomes clear in Williams' notion of permanent education. He writes:

This idea [permanent education] seems to me to repeat, in a new and important idiom, the concepts of learning and of popular democratic culture which underlie the present book. What it valuably stresses is the education force of our whole social and cultural experience. It is therefore concerned, not only with continuing education, of a formal or informal kind, but with what the whole environment, its institutions and relationships, actively and profoundly teaches. To consider the problems of families, or of town planning, is then an educational enterprise, for these, also, are where teaching occurs. And then the field of this book, of the cultural communications which, under an old shadow, are still called mass communications, can be integrated, as I have always intended, with a whole social policy. For who can doubt, looking at television or newspapers, or reading the women's magazines, that here, centrally, is teaching, and teaching financed and distributed in a much larger way than in formal education? (Williams 1967: 14–15)

Building upon Williams' notion of permanent education, pedagogy in this sense provides a theoretical discourse for understanding how power and knowledge mutually inform each other in the production, reception, and transformation of social identities, forms of ethical address and "desired versions of a future human community" (Simon 1992: 15). By refuting the objectivity of knowledge and asserting the partiality of all forms of pedagogical authority, critical pedagogy initiates an inquiry into the relationship between the form and content of various pedagogical sites and the authority they legitimate in securing particular cultural practices.

I want to be more specific about the importance of pedagogy for cultural studies and other emerging forms of interdisciplinary work by analyzing how youth are increasingly being addressed and positioned through the popular media, changing economic conditions, an escalating wave of violence and the emergence of discourse that Ruth Conniff has aptly called "the culture of cruelty" (Conniff 1992: 16–20). I will then address, both through theory and through examples of my own teaching, how the pedagogy implicit in a spate of Hollywood films about youth culture reinforces dominant racist and cultural stereotypes, but in so doing also creates the conditions for rewriting such films through diverse critical pedagogical strategies.

MASS CULTURE AND THE REPRESENTATION OF YOUTH(S)

Youth have once again become the object of public analysis. Headlines proliferate like dispatches from a combat zone, frequently coupling youth and violence in the interests of promoting a new kind of causal relationship. For example, "gangsta rap" artist Snoop Doggy Dogg was featured on the front cover of an issue of *Newsweek*.[15] This message is that young black men are selling violence to the mainstream public through their music. But according to Newsweek, the violence is not just in the music—it is also embodied in the lifestyles of the rappers who produce it. The potential victims in this case are a besieged white majority of male and female youth. Citing a wave of arrests among prominent rappers, the story reinforces the notion that crime is a racially coded word for associating black youth with violence.[16]

The statistics on youth violence point to social and economic causes that lie far beyond the reach of facile stereotypes. On a national level, U.S. society is witnessing the effects of a culture of violence in which close to twelve U.S. children aged nineteen and under die from gun fire each day. According to the National Center for Health Statistics, "Firearm homicide is the leading cause of death of African-American teenage boys and the second leading cause of death of high school age children in the United States" (Colatosti 1994: 59).

What is missing from these reports is any critical commentary on underlying causes that produce the representations of violence that saturate the mass media. In addition, there is little mention of the high numbers of infants and children killed every year through "poverty-related malnutrition and disease." Nor is the U.S. public informed in the popular press about "the gruesome toll of the drunk driver who is typically White" (Sklar 1993: 52). But the bad news doesn't end with violence.

The representations of white youth produced by dominant media within recent years have increasingly portrayed them as lazy, sinking into a self-indulgent haze and oblivious to the middle-class ethic of working hard and getting ahead. Of course, what the dominant media do not talk about are the social conditions that are producing a new generation of youth steeped in despair, violence, crime, poverty and apathy. For instance, to talk about black crime without mentioning that the unemployment rate for black youth exceeds forty percent in many urban cities serves primarily to conceal a major cause of youth unrest. Or to talk about apathy among white youth without analyzing the junk culture, poverty, social disenfranchisement, drugs, lack of educational opportunity and commodification that shape daily life removes responsibility from a social system that often sees youth as simply another market niche.

A failing economy that offers most youth the limited promise of service-sector jobs, dim prospects for the future and a world of infinite messages and images designed to sell a product or to peddle senseless violence as another TV spectacle, constitutes, in part, the new conditions of youth. In light of radically altered social and economic conditions, educators need to fashion alternative analyses in order to understand what is happening to our nation's youth. Such a project seems vital in light of the rapidity in which market values and a commercial public culture have replaced the ethical referents for developing democratic public spheres. For example, since the 1970s, millions of jobs have been lost to capital flight and technological change has wiped out millions more. In the last twenty years alone, the U.S. economy lost more than five million jobs in the manufacturing sector.[17] In the face of extremely limited prospects for economic growth over the next decade, schools will be faced with an identity crisis regarding the traditional assumption that school credentials provide the best route to economic security and class mobility for a large proportion of our nation's youth. As Stanley Aronowitz and I have pointed out elsewhere:

The labor market is becoming increasingly bifurcated: organizational and technical changes are producing a limited number of jobs for highly educated and trained people-managers, scientific and technological experts, and researchers. On the other hand, we are witnessing the disappearance of many middle-level white collar subprofessions. . . . And in the face of sharpening competition, employers typically hire a growing number of low paid, part-time workers. . . . Even some professionals have become free-lance workers with few, if any, fringe benefits. These developments call into question the efficacy of mass schooling for providing the "well-trained" labor force that employers still claim they require. (Aronowitz and Giroux 1993: 4–5)

In light of these shattering shifts in economic and cultural life, it makes more sense for educators to reexamine the mission of the school and the changing conditions of youth rather than blaming youth for the economic slump, the culture of racially coded violence or the hopelessness that seems endemic to dominant versions of the future.

But rethinking the conditions of youth is also imperative in order to reverse the mean-spirited discourse of the 1980s, a discourse that has turned its back on the victims of U.S. society and has resorted to both blaming and punishing them for their social and economic problems. This is evident in states such as Michigan and Wisconsin, which subscribe to "Learnfare" programs designed to penalize a single mother with a lower food allowance if her kids are absent from school. In other states, welfare payments are reduced if single mothers do not marry. Micky Kaus, an editor at the *New Republic*, argues that welfare mothers should be forced to work at menial jobs, and if they refuse, Kaus suggests that the state remove their children from them. Illiterate women, Kaus argues, could work raking leaves.[18] There is an indifference and callousness in this kind of language that now spills over to discussions of youth. Instead of focusing on economic and social conditions that provide the nation's youth, especially those who are poor and live on the margins of hope, with food, shelter, access to decent education and safe environments, conservatives such as former Secretary of Education William Bennett talk about imposing national standards on public schools, creating voucher systems that benefit middle-class parents and doing away with the concept of "the public" altogether. There is more at work here than simply ignorance and neglect.

It is in the dominant discourse on values that one gets a glimpse of the pedagogy at work in the culture of mean-spiritedness. Bennett (1996) for instance, in his book, *The Book of Virtues: A Treasury of Great Moral Stories*, finds hope in "Old Mr. Rabbit's Thanksgiving Dinner" in which the rabbit instructs us that there is more joy in being helpful than being helped. This discourse of moral uplift may provide soothing and inspirational help for children whose parents send them to private schools, establish trust-fund annuities for their future and connect them to the world of political patronage, but it says almost nothing about the culture of compressed and concentrated human suffering that many children have to deal with daily in this country. In part, this can be glimpsed in the fact that over seventy percent of all welfare recipients are children. In what follows, I want to draw from a number of insights provided by the field of cultural studies to chart out a different cartography that might be helpful for educators to address what might be called the changing conditions of youth.

FRAMING YOUTH

The instability and transitoriness characteristically widespread among a diverse generation of eighteen- to twenty-five-year-old youth is inextricably rooted in a larger set of postmodern cultural conditions informed by the following: a general loss of faith in the modernist narratives of work and emancipation; the recognition that the indeterminacy of the future warrants confronting and living in the immediacy of experience; an acknowledgment that homelessness as a condition of randomness has replaced the security, if not misrepresentation, of home as a source of comfort and security; an experience of time and space as compressed and fragmented within a world of images that increasingly undermine the dialectic of authenticity and universalism. For many youth, plurality and contingency—whether mediated through media culture or through the dislocations spurned by the economic system, the rise of new social movements or the crisis of representation and authority—have resulted in a world with few secure psychological, economic or intellectual markers. This is a world in which one is condemned to wander within and between multiple borders and spaces marked by excess, otherness and difference. This is a world in which old certainties are ruptured and meaning becomes more contingent, less indebted to the dictates of reverence and established truth. While the circumstances of youth vary across and within terrains marked by racial and class differences, the modernist world of certainty and order that has traditionally policed, contained and insulated such difference has given way to a shared postmodern culture in which representational borders collapse into new hybridized forms of cultural performance, identity and political agency. As the information highway and MTV condense time and space into what Paul Virilio calls "speed space," new desires, modes of association and forms of resistance inscribe themselves into diverse spheres of popular culture (Virilio 1991). Music, rap, fashion, style, talk, politics and cultural resistance are no longer confined to their original class and racial locations. Middle-class white kids take up the language of gangsta rap spawned in neighborhood turfs far removed from their own lives. Black youth in urban centers produce a bricolage of style fashioned from a combination of sneakers, baseball caps and oversized clothing that integrates forms of resistance and style later to be appropriated by suburban kids whose desires and identities resonate with the energy and vibrancy of the new urban funk. Music displaces older forms of textuality and references a terrain of cultural production that marks the body as a site of pleasure, resistance, domination and danger (Epstein 1994; Ross and Rose

1994). Within this postmodern culture of youth, identities merge and shift rather than become more uniform and static. No longer belonging to any one place or location, youth increasingly inhabit shifting cultural and social spheres marked by a plurality of languages and cultures.

Communities have been refigured as space and time mutate into multiple and overlapping cyberspace networks. Bohemian and middle-class youth talk to each other over electronic bulletin boards in coffee houses in North Beach, California. Cafes and other public salons, once the refuge of beatniks, hippies and other cultural radicals, have given way to members of the hacker culture. They reorder their imaginations through connections to virtual reality technologies and produce forms of exchange through texts and images that have the potential to wage a war on traditional meaning, but also run the risk of reducing critical understanding to the endless play of random access spectacles.

This is not meant to endorse a Frankfurt School dismissal of popular culture in the postmodern age.[19] On the contrary, I believe that the new electronic technologies with their proliferation of multiple stories and open-ended forms of interaction have altered not only the pedagogical context for the production of subjectivities, but also how people "take in information and entertainment" (Parkes 1994: 54). Produced from the centers of power, mass culture has spawned in the name of profit and entertainment a new level of instrumental and commodified culture. On the other hand, popular culture offers resistance to the notion that useful culture can only be produced within dominant regimes of power. This distinction between mass and popular culture is not meant to suggest that popular culture is strictly a terrain of resistance. Popular culture does not escape commodification, racism, sexism and other forms of oppression, but it is marked by fault lines that reject the high/low culture divide while simultaneously attempting to affirm a multitude of histories, experiences, cultural forms and pleasures. Within the conditions of postmodern culture, values no longer emerge unproblematically from the modernist pedagogy of foundationalism and universal truths, or from traditional narratives based on fixed identities with their requisite structure of closure. For many youths, meaning is in rout, media has become a substitute for experience and what constitutes understanding is grounded in a decentered and diasporic world of difference, displacement and exchanges.

The intersection among cultural studies and pedagogy can be made more clear through an analysis of how the pedagogy of Hollywood has attempted in some recent films to portray the plight of young people within the conditions of a postmodern culture. I will focus on four films: *River's Edge* (1986), *My Own Private Idaho* (1991), *Slacker* (1991) and *Juice* (1992). These films are important as arguments and framing devices that in diverse ways attempt to provide a pedagogical representation of youth. They point to some of the economic and social conditions at work in the formation of different racial and economic strata of youth, but they often do so within a narrative that combines a politics of despair with a fairly sophisticated depiction of the alleged sensibilities and moods of a generation of youth growing up amid the fracturing and menacing conditions of a postmodern culture. The challenge for progressive educators is to question how a critical pedagogy might be employed to appropriate the more radical and useful aspects of cultural studies in addressing the new and different social, political and economic contexts that are producing the twenty-something generation. At the same time, there is the issue of how a politics and project of pedagogy might be constructed to create the conditions for social agency and institutionalized change among diverse sectors of youth.

WHITE YOUTH AND THE POLITICS OF DESPAIR

For many youth, showing up for adulthood at the fin de siècle means pulling back on hope and trying to put off the future rather than taking up the modernist challenge of trying to shape it.[20] Popular cultural criticism has captured much of the ennui among youth and has made clear that "what used to be the pessimism of a radical fringe is now the shared assumption of a generation" (Anshaw 1992: 27). Cultural studies has helped to temper this broad generalization about youth in order to investigate the more complex representations at work in the construction of a new generation of youth that cannot be simply abstracted from the specificities of race, class or gender. And yet, cultural studies theorists have also pointed to the increasing resistance of a twenty-something generation of youth who seem neither motivated by nostalgia for some lost conservative vision of America nor at home in the new world order paved with the promises of the expanding electronic information highway.[21] While "youth" as a social construction has always been mediated, in part, as a social problem, many cultural critics believe that postmodern youth are uniquely "alien," "strange" and disconnected from the real world. For instance, in Gus Van Sant's film *My Own Private Idaho*, the main character, Mike, who hustles his sexual wares for money, is a dreamer lost in fractured memories of a mother who deserted him as a child. Caught between flashbacks of mom, shown in 8-mm color, and the video world of motley street hustlers and their clients, Mike moves through his existence by falling asleep in times of stress only to awaken in different geographic and spatial locations. What holds Mike's psychic and geographic travels together is the metaphor of sleep, the dream of escape, and the ultimate realization that even memories cannot fuel hope for the future. Mike becomes a metaphor for an entire generation of lower-middle-class youth forced to sell themselves in a world with no hope, a generation that aspires to nothing, works at degrading McJobs, and lives in a world in which chance and randomness rather than struggle, community and solidarity drive their fate.

A more disturbing picture of white, working-class youth can be found in *River's Edge*. Teenage anomie and drugged apathy are given painful expression in the depiction of a group of working-class youth who are casually told by John, one of their friends, that he has strangled his girlfriend, another member of the group, and left her nude body on the riverbank. The group at different times visits the site to view and probe the dead body of the girl. Seemingly unable to grasp the significance of the event, the youth initially hold off from informing anyone of the murder and with different degrees of concern initially try to protect John, the teenage sociopath, from being caught by the police. The youth in *River's Edge* drift through a world of broken families, blaring rock music, schooling marked by dead time and a general indifference. Decentered and fragmented, they view death, like life itself, as merely a spectacle, a matter of style rather than substance. In one sense, these youth share the quality of being "asleep" that is depicted in *My Own Private Idaho*. But what is more disturbing in *River's Edge* is that lost innocence gives way not merely to teenage myopia, but also to a culture in which human life is experienced as a voyeuristic seduction, a video game, good for passing time and diverting oneself from the pain of the moment. Despair and indifference cancel out the language of ethical discriminations and social responsibility while elevating the immediacy of pleasure to the defining moment of agency. In *River's Edge*, history as social memory is reassembled through vignettes of 1960s types portrayed as either burned-out bikers or as the ex-radical turned teacher whose moralizing relegates politics to simply cheap opportunism. Exchanges among the young people in *River's Edge* appear like projections of a generation waiting either to fall asleep or to commit suicide. After talking about how he murdered his girlfriend, John blurts out, "You do shit, it's done, and then you die." Another character responds, "It might be easier being dead." To which her boyfriend replies, "Bullshit, you couldn't get stoned anymore." In this scenario, life imitates art when committing murder and getting stoned are given equal moral weight in the formula of the Hollywood spectacle, a spectacle that in the end flattens the complex representations of youth while constructing their identities through ample servings of pleasure, death and violence.

River's Edge and *My Own Private Idaho* reveal the seamy and dark side of a youth culture while employing the Hollywood mixture of fascination and horror to titillate the audiences drawn to these films. Employing the postmodern aesthetic of revulsion, locality, randomness and senselessness, the youth in these films appear to be constructed outside of a broader cultural and economic landscape. Instead, they become visible only through visceral expressions of psychotic behavior or the brooding experience of a self-imposed comatose alienation.

One of the more celebrated white youth films of the 1990s is Richard Linklater's *Slacker*. A decidedly low-budget film, *Slacker* attempts in both form and content to capture the sentiments of a twenty-something generation of middle-class white youth who reject most of the values of the Reagan/Bush era but have a difficult time imagining what an alternative might look like. Distinctly nonlinear in format, *Slacker* takes place in a twenty-four-hour time frame in the college town of Austin, Texas. Building upon an antinarrative structure, *Slacker* is loosely organized around brief episodes in the lives of a variety of characters, none of whom are connected to each other except to provide the pretext to lead the audience to the next character in the film. Sweeping through bookstores, coffee shops, auto-parts yards, bedrooms and rock music clubs, *Slacker* focuses on a disparate group of young people who possess little hope in the future and drift from job to job speaking a hybrid argot of bohemian intensities and New Age pop-cult babble.

The film portrays a host of young people who randomly move from one place to the next, border crossers with little, if any, sense of where they have come from or where they are going. In this world of multiple realities, youth work in bands with the name "Ultimate Loser" and talk about being forcibly put in hospitals by their parents. One neopunker even attempts to sell a Madonna pap smear to two acquaintances she meets in the street: "Check it out, I know it's kind of disgusting, but it's like sort of getting down to the real Madonna." This is a world in which language is wedded to an odd mix of nostalgia, popcorn philosophy and MTV babble. Talk is organized around comments like: "I don't know . . . I've traveled . . . and when you get back you can't tell whether it really happened to you or if you just saw it on TV." Alienation is driven inward and emerges in comments like "I feel stuck." Irony slightly overshadows a refusal to imagine any kind of collective struggle. Reality seems too despairing to care about. This is humorously captured in one instance by a young man who suggests: "You know how the slogan goes, workers of the world, unite? We say workers of the world, relax." People talk, but appear disconnected from themselves and each other, lives traverse each other with no sense of community or connection. There is a pronounced sense in *Slacker* of youth caught in the throes of new information technologies that both contain their aspirations and at the same time hold out the promise of some sense of agency.

At rare moments in the film, the political paralysis of narcissistic forms of refusal is offset by instances in which some characters recognize the importance of the image as a vehicle for cultural production, as a representational apparatus that cannot only make certain experiences available but can also be used to produce alternative realities and social practices. The power of the image is present in the way the camera follows characters throughout the film, at once stalking them and confining them to a gaze that is both constraining and incidental. In one scene, a young man appears in a video apartment surrounded by televisions that he claims he has had on for years. He points out that he has invented a game called "Video Virus" in which, through the use of a special technology, he can push a button and insert himself onto any screen and perform any one of a number of actions. When asked by another character what this is about, he answers: "Well, we all know the psychic powers of the televised image. But we need to capitalize on it and make it work for us instead of working for it." This theme is taken up in two other scenes. In one short clip, a graduate history student shoots the video camera he is using to film himself, indicating a self-consciousness about the power of the image and the ability to control it at the same time. In the concluding scene, a carload of people, each equipped with their Super 8 cameras, drive up to a large hill and throw their cameras into a canyon. The film ends with the images being recorded by the cameras as they cascade to the bottom of the cliff in what suggests a moment of release and liberation.

In many respects, these movies largely focus on a culture of white male youth who are both terrified and fascinated by the media, who appear overwhelmed by "the danger and wonder of future technologies, the banality of consumption, the thrill of brand names, [and] the difficulty of sex in alienated relationships" (Kopkind 1992: 183). The significance of these films rests, in part, in their attempt to capture the sense of powerlessness that increasingly affects working-class and middle-class white youth. But what is missing from these films, along with the various books, articles and reportage concerning what is often called the "Nowhere Generation," "Generation X," "13thGen" or "Slackers" is any sense of the larger political, racial and social conditions in which youth are being framed, as well as the multiple forms of resistance and racial diversity that exist among many different youth formations. What in fact should be seen as a social commentary about "dead-end capitalism" emerges simply as a celebration of refusal dressed up in a rhetoric of aesthetics, style, fashion and solipsistic protests. Within this type of commentary, postmodern criticism is useful but limited because of its often theoretical inability to take up the relationship between identity and power, biography and the commodification of everyday life or the limits of agency in an increasingly globalized economy as part of a broader project of possibility linked to issues of history, struggle and transformation.[22]

In spite of the totalizing image of domination that structures *River's Edge* and *My Own Private Idaho*, and the lethal hopelessness that permeates *Slacker*, all of these films provide opportunities for examining the social and cultural context to which they refer in order to enlarge the range of strategies and understandings that students might bring to them to create a sense of resistance and transformation. For instance, many of my students who viewed *Slacker* did not despair over the film, but interpreted it to mean that "going slack" was viewed as a moment in the lives of young people that, with the proper resources, offered them a period in which to think, move around the country, and chill out in order to make some important decisions about their lives. Going slack became increasingly more oppressive as the slack time became drawn out far beyond their ability to end or control it. The students also pointed out that this film was made by Linklater and his friends with a great deal of energy and gusto, which in itself offers a pedagogical model for young people to take up in developing their own narratives.

BLACK YOUTH AND THE VIOLENCE OF RACE

With the explosion of rap music into the sphere of popular culture and the intense debates that have emerged around the crisis of black masculinity, the issue of black nationalism and the politics of black urban culture, it is not surprising that the black cinema has produced a series of films about the coming of age of black youth in urban America. What is unique about these films is that, unlike the black exploitation films of the 1970s, which were made by white producers for black audiences, the new wave of black cinema is being produced by black directors and aimed at black audiences.[23] With the advent of the 1990s, Hollywood has cashed in on a number of talented young black directors such as Spike Lee, Allen and Albert Hughes, Julie Dash, Ernest Dickerson and John Singleton. Films about black youth have become big business—in 1991 *New Jack City* and *Boyz N the Hood* pulled in over $100 million between them. Largely concerned with the inequalities, oppression, daily violence and diminishing hopes that plague black communities in the urban war zone, the new wave of black films has attempted to accentuate the economic and social conditions that have contributed to the construction of "Black masculinity and its relationship to the ghetto culture in which ideals of masculinity are nurtured and shaped" (Dyson 1994: 155).

Unlike many of the recent films about white youth whose coming-of-age narratives are developed within traditional sociological categories such as alienation, restlessness and anomie, black film productions such as Ernest Dickerson's *Juice* (1992) depict a culture of nihilism that is rooted directly in a violence whose defining principles are homicide, cultural suicide, internecine warfare and social decay. It is interesting to note that just as the popular press has racialized crime, drugs and violence as a black problem, some of the most interesting films to appear recently about black youth have been given the Hollywood imprimatur of excellence and have moved successfully as crossover films to a white audience. In what follows, I want briefly to probe the treatment of black youth and the representations of masculinity and resistance in the exemplary black film, *Juice*.

Juice (street slang for respect) is the story of four young Harlem African-American youth who are first portrayed as kids who engage in the usual antics of skipping school, fighting with other kids in the neighborhood, clashing with their parents about doing homework and arguing with their siblings over using the bathroom in the morning. If this portrayal of youthful innocence is used to get a general audience to comfortably identify with these four black youth, it is soon ruptured as the group, caught in a spiraling wave of poverty and depressed opportunities, turns to crime and violence as a way to both construct their manhood and solve their most immediate problems. Determined to give their lives some sense of agency, the group moves from ripping off a record store to burglarizing a grocery market to the ruthless murder of the store owner and eventually each other. Caught in a world in which the ethics of the street are mirrored in the spectacle of TV violence, Bishop, Quincy, Raheem and Steel (Tupac Shakur, Omar Epps, Kahalil Kain and Jermaine Hopkins) decide, after watching James Cagney go up in a blaze of glory in *White Heat*, to take control of their lives by buying a gun and sticking up a neighborhood merchant who once chased them out of his store. Quincy is hesitant about participating in the stickup because he is a talented disc jockey and is determined to enter a local deejay contest in order to take advantage of his love of rap music and find a place for himself in the world.

Quincy is the only black youth in the film who models a sense of agency that is not completely caught in the confusion and despair exhibited by his three friends. Trapped within the loyalty codes of the street and in the protection it provides, Quincy reluctantly agrees to participate in the heist. Bad choices have major consequences in this typical big-city ghetto, and Quincy's sense of hope and independence is shattered as Bishop, the most violent of the group, kills the store owner and then proceeds to murder Raheem and hunt down Quincy and Steele, since they no longer see him as a respected member of the group. Quincy eventually buys a weapon to protect himself, and in the film's final scene, confronts Bishop on the roof. A struggle ensues, and Bishop plunges to his death. As the film ends, one onlooker tells Quincy, "You got the juice," but Quincy rejects the accolade ascribing power and prestige to him and walks away.

Juice reasserts the importance of rap music as the cultural expression of imaginable possibilities in the daily lives of black youth. Not only does rap music provide the musical score that frames the film, it also plays a pivotal role by socially contextualizing the desires, rage and independent expression of black male artists. For Quincy, rap music offers him the opportunity to claim some "juice" among his peers while simultaneously providing him with a context to construct an affirmative identity along with the chance for real employment. Music in this context becomes a major referent for understanding how identities and bodies come together in a hip-hop culture that at its most oppositional moment is testing the limits of the American dream. But *Juice* also gestures, through the direction of Ernest Dickerson, that if violence is endemic to the black ghetto, its roots lie in a culture of violence that is daily transmitted through the medium of television. This is suggested in one powerful scene in which the group watches on television both the famed violent ending of James Cagney's *White Heat* and the news bulletin announcing the death of a neighborhood friend as he attempted to rip off a local bar. In this scene, Dickerson draws a powerful relationship between what the four youth see on television and their impatience over their own lack of agency and need to take control of their lives. As Michael Dyson (1994) points out:

Dickerson's aim is transparent: to highlight the link between violence and criminality fostered in the collective American imagination by television, the consumption of images through a medium that has replaced the Constitution and the Declaration of Independence as the unifying fiction of national citizenship and identity. It is also the daily and exclusive occupation of Bishop's listless father, a reminder that television's genealogy of influence unfolds from its dulling effects in one generation to its creation of lethal desires in the next, twin strategies of destruction when applied in the black male ghetto. (163)

While Dyson is right in pointing to Dickerson's critique of the media, he overestimates the importance given in *Juice* to the relationship between black-on-black violence and those larger social determinants that black ur-ban life both reflects and helps to produce. In fact, it could be argued that the violence portrayed in *Juice* and similar films, such as *Boyz N the Hood, New Jack City*, and especially *Menace II Society*, "feeds the racist national obsession that Black men and their community are the central locus of the American scene of violence" (Njeri 1993: 33).

Although the violence in these films is traumatizing as part of the effort to promote an antiviolence message, it is also a violence that is hermetic, sutured and sealed within the walls of the black urban ghetto. While the counterpart of this type of violence, in controversial white films such as *Reservoir Dogs* is taken up by most critics as part of an avant garde aesthetic, the violence in the recent wave of black youth films often reinforces for middle-class viewers the assumption that such violence is endemic to the black community. The only salvation gained in portraying such inner-city hopelessness is that it be noticed so that it can be stopped from spreading like a disease into the adjoining suburbs and business zones that form a colonizing ring around black ghettoes. Because films such as *Juice* do not self-consciously rupture dominant stereotypical assumptions that make race and crime synonymous, they often suggest a kind of nihilism that Cornel West (1992) describes as "the lived experience of coping with a life of hor-rifying meaninglessness, hopelessness and (most important) lovelessness" (40).

Unfortunately, West's notion of nihilism is too tightly drawn and while it may claim to pay sufficient attention to the loss of hope and meaning among black youth, it fails to connect the specificity of black nihilism to the nihilism of systemic inequality, calculated injustice and moral indifference that operates daily as a regime of brutalization and oppression for so many poor youth and youth of color in this country. Itabari Njeri forcefully captures the failure of such an analysis and the problems that films such as *Juice*, in spite of the best intentions of their directors, often reproduce. Commenting on another coming-of-age black youth film, *Menace II Society*, he writes:

> The nation cannot allow nearly 50% of black men to be unemployed, as is the case in many African-American communities. It cannot let schools systematically brand normal black children as uneducable for racist reasons, or permit the continued brutalization of blacks by police, or have black adults take out their socially engendered frustrations on each other and their children and not yield despair and dysfunction. This kind of despair is the source of the nihilism Cornel West described. Unfortunately, the black male-as-menace film genre often fails to artfully tie this nihilism to its poisonous roots in America's system of inequality. And because it fails to do so, the effects of these toxic forces are seen as causes. (Njeri 1933: 34)

In both pedagogical and political terms, the reigning films about black youth that have appeared since 1990 may have gone too far in producing narratives that employ the commercial strategy of reproducing graphic violence and then moralizing about its effects. Violence in these films is tied to a self-destructiveness and senselessness that shocks but often fails to inform the audience about either its wider determinations or the audience's possible complicity in such violence. The effects of such films tend to reinforce for white middle-class America the comforting belief that nihilism as both a state of mind and a site of social relations is always somewhere else— in that strangely homogenized social formation known as "black" youth.

Of course, it is important to note that *Juice* refrains from romanticizing violence, just as it suggests at the end of the film that Quincy does not want the juice if it means leading a life in which violence is the only capital that has any exchange value in African-American communities. But these sentiments come late and are too underdeveloped. One pedagogical challenge presented by this film is for educators and students to theorize about why Hollywood is investing in films about black youth that overlook the complex representations that structure African-American communities. Such an inquiry can be taken up by looking at the work of black feminist filmmakers such as Julie Dash and the powerful and complex representations she offers black women in *Daughters of the Dust* or the work of Leslie Harris, whose film *Just Another Girl on the IRT* challenges the misogyny that structures the films currently being made about black male youth. Another challenge involves trying to understand why large numbers of black, urban, male youth readily identify with the wider social representations of sexism, homophobia, misogyny and gaining respect at such a high cost to themselves and the communities in which they live. Films about black youth are important to engage in order to understand both the pedagogies that silently structure their representations and how such representations pedagogically work to educate crossover white audiences. Most importantly, these films should not be dismissed because they are reductionist, sexist or one dimensional in their portrayal of the rite of passage of black male youth; at most, they become a marker for understanding how complex representations of black youth get lost in racially coded films that point to serious problems in the urban centers, but do so in ways that erase any sense of viable hope, possibility, resistance and struggle.

Contemporary films about black youth offer a glimpse into the specificity of otherness; that is, they cross a cultural and racial border and in doing so perform a theoretical service in making visible what is often left out of the dominant politics of representations. And it is in the light of such an opening that the possibility exists for educators and other cultural workers to take up the relationship among culture, power and identity in ways that grapple with the complexity of youth and the intersection of race, class and gender formations.

Combining cultural studies with pedagogical theory would suggest that students take these films seriously as legitimate forms of social knowledge that reveal different sets of struggles among youth within diverse cultural sites. For white youth, these films mimic a coming-of-age narrative that indicts the aimlessness and senselessness produced within a larger culture of commercial stupification; on the other hand, black youth films posit a not-coming-of-age narrative that serves as a powerful indictment of the violence being waged against and among African-American youth. Clearly, educators can learn from these films and in doing so bring these different accounts of the cultural production of youth together within a common project that addresses the relationship between pedagogy and social justice, on the one hand, and democracy and the struggle for equality on the other. These films suggest that educators need to ask new questions and develop new models and new ways of producing an oppositional pedagogy that is capable of understanding the different social, economic and political contexts that produce youth differently within varied sets and relations of power.

Another pedagogical challenge offered by these films concerns how teachers can address the desires that different students bring to these popular cultural texts. In other words, what does it mean to mobilize the desires of students by using forms of social knowledge that constitute the contradictory field of popular culture? In part, it means recognizing that while students are familiar with such texts, they bring different beliefs, political understandings and affective investments to such a learning process. Hence, pedagogy must proceed by acknowledging that conflict will emerge regarding the form and content of such films and how students address such issues. For such a pedagogy to work, Fabienne Worth argues that "students must become visible to themselves and to each other and valued in their differences" (Worth 1993: 27). This suggests giving students the opportunity to decenter the curriculum by structuring, in part, how the class should be organized and how such films can be addressed without putting any one student's identity on trial. It means recognizing the complexity of attempting to mobilize students' desires as part of a pedagogical project that directly addresses representations that affect certain parts of their lives and acknowledging the emotional problems that will emerge in such teaching.

At the same time, such a pedagogy must reverse the cycle of despair that often informs these accounts and address how the different postmodern conditions and contexts of youth can be changed in order to expand and deepen the promise of a substantive democracy. In part, this may mean using films about youth that capture the complexity, sense of struggle and diversity that marks different segments of the current generation of young people. In this case, cultural studies and pedagogical practice can mutually inform each other by using popular cultural texts as serious objects of study. Such texts can be used to address the limits and possibilities that youth face in different social, cultural and economic contexts. Equally important is the need to read popular cultural texts as part of a broader pedagogical effort to develop a sense of agency in students based on a commitment to changing oppressive contexts by understanding the relations of power that inform them.

The pedagogical challenge represented by the emergence of a postmodern generation of youth has not been lost on advertisers and market research analysts. According to a 1992 study by the Roper Organization, the current generation of eighteen to twenty-nine-year-olds have an annual buying power of $125 billion. Addressing the interests and tastes of this generation, "McDonald's, for instance, has introduced hip-hop music and images to promote burgers and fries, ditto Coca-Cola, with its frenetic commercials touting Coca-Cola Classic" (Hollingsworth 1993: 27). Benetton, Esprit, The Gap and other companies have followed suit in their attempts to identify and mobilize the desires, identities and buying patterns of a new generation of youth.[24] What appears as a despairing expression of the postmodern condition to some theorists becomes for others a challenge to invent new market strategies for corporate interests. In this scenario, youth may be experiencing the indeterminacy, senselessness and multiple conditions of postmodernism, but corporate advertisers are attempting to theorize a pedagogy of consumption as part of a new way of appropriating postmodern differences among youth in different sites and locations. The lesson here is that differences among youth matter politically and pedagogically, but not as a way of generating new markets or registering difference simply as a fashion niche.

What educators need to do is to make the pedagogical more political by addressing both the conditions through which they teach and what it means to learn from a generation that is experiencing life in a way that is vastly different from the representations offered in modernist versions of schooling. This is not to suggest that modernist schools do not attend to popular culture, but they do so on very problematic terms, which often confine it to the margins of the curriculum. Moreover, modernist schools cannot be rejected outright. As I have shown elsewhere, the political culture of modernism, with its emphasis on social equality, justice, freedom and human agency, needs to be refigured within rather than outside of an emerging postmodern discourse.[25]

The emergence of the electronic media coupled with a diminishing faith in the power of human agency has undermined the traditional visions of schooling and the meaning of pedagogy. The language of lesson plans and upward mobility and the forms of teacher authority on which it was based have been radically delegitimated by the recognition that culture and power are central to the authority/knowledge relationship. Modernism's faith in the past has given way to a future for which traditional markers no longer make sense.

CULTURAL STUDIES AND YOUTH: THE PEDAGOGICAL ISSUE

Educators and cultural critics need to address the effects of emerging postmodern conditions on a current generation of young people who appear hostage to the vicissitudes of a changing economic order, with its legacy of diminished hopes on the one hand, and a world of schizoid images, proliferating public spaces and an increasing fragmentation, uncertainty and randomness that structures postmodern daily life on the other. Central to this issue is whether educators are dealing with a new kind of student forged within organizing principles shaped by the intersection of the electronic image, popular culture and a dire sense of indeterminacy.

What cultural studies offers educators is a theoretical framework for addressing the shifting attitudes, representations and desires of this new generation of youth being produced within the current historical, economic and cultural juncture. But it does more than simply provide a lens for resituating the construction of youth within a shifting and radically altered social, technological and economic landscape: it also provides elements for rethinking the relationship between culture and power, knowledge and authority, learning and experience and the role of teachers as public intellectuals. In what follows, I want to point to some of the theoretical elements that link cultural studies and critical pedagogy and speak briefly to their implications for cultural work.

First, cultural studies is premised on the belief that we have entered a period in which the traditional distinctions that separate and frame established academic disciplines cannot account for the great diversity of cultural and social phenomena that have come to characterize an increasingly hybridized, postindustrial world. The university has long been linked to a notion of national identity that is largely defined by and committed to transmitting traditional Western culture.[26] Traditionally, this has been a culture of exclusion, one that has ignored the multiple narratives, histories and voices of culturally and politically subordinated groups. The emerging proliferation of diverse social movements arguing for a genuinely multicultural and multiracial society have challenged schools that use academic knowledge to license cultural differences in order to regulate and define who they are and how they might narrate themselves. Moreover, the spread of electronically mediated culture to all spheres of everyday intellectual and artistic life has shifted the ground of scholarship away from the traditional disciplines designed to preserve a "common culture" to the more hybridized fields of comparative and world literature, media studies, ecology, society and technology and popular culture.

Second, advocates of cultural studies have argued strongly that the role of culture, including the power of the mass media with its massive apparatuses of representation and its regulation of meaning, is central to understanding how the dynamics of power, privilege and social desire structure the daily life of a society.[27] This concern with culture and its connection to power has necessitated a critical interrogation of the relationship between knowledge and authority, the meaning of canonicity and the historical and social contexts that deliberately shape students' understanding of accounts of the past, present and future. But if a sea change in the development and reception of what counts as knowledge has taken place, it has been accompanied by an understanding of how we define and apprehend the range of texts that are open to critical interrogation and analysis. For instance, instead of connecting culture exclusively to the technology of print and the book as the only legitimate academic artifact, there is a great deal of academic work going on that analyzes how textual, aural and visual representations are produced, organized and distributed through a variety of cultural forms such as the media, popular culture, film, advertising, mass communications and other modes of cultural production.[28]

At stake here is the attempt to produce new theoretical models and methodologies for addressing the production, structure and exchange of knowledge. This approach to interdisciplinary and postdisciplinary studies is valuable because it addresses the pedagogical issue of organizing dialogue across and outside of the disciplines in order to promote alternative approaches to research and teaching about culture and the newly emerging technologies and forms of knowledge. For instance, rather than organize courses around strictly disciplinary concerns arising out of English and social studies courses, it might be more useful and relevant for colleges of education to organize courses that broaden student's understanding of themselves and others by examining events that evoke a sense of social responsibility and moral accountability. A course on "Immigration and Politics in Fin de Siècle America" could provide a historical perspective on the demographic changes confronting the United States and how such changes are being felt within the shifting dynamics of education, economics, cultural identity and urban development. A course on the Los Angeles uprisings could incorporate the related issues of race, politics, economics and education to address the multiple conditions underlying the violence and despair that produced such a tragic event.

Third, in addition to broadening the terms and parameters of learning, cultural studies rejects the professionalization of educators and the alienating and often elitist discourse of professionalism and sanitized expertise. Instead, it argues for educators as public intellectuals. Stuart Hall is instructive on this issue when he argues that cultural studies provides two points of tension that intellectuals need to address:

First, cultural studies constitutes one of the points of tension and change at the frontiers of intellectual and academic life, pushing for new questions, new models, and new ways of study, testing the fine lines between intellectual rigor and social relevance. . . . But secondly . . . cultural studies insist on what I want to call the vocation of the intellectual life. That is to say, cultural studies insists on the necessity to address the central, urgent, and disturbing questions of a society and a culture in the most rigorous intellectual way we have available. (Hall 1992: 11)

In this view, intellectuals must be accountable in their teaching for the ways in which they address and respond to the problems of history, human agency and the renewal of democratic civic life. Cultural studies strongly rejects the assumption that teachers are simply transmitters of existing configurations of knowledge. As public intellectuals, academics are always implicated in the dynamics of social power through the experiences they organize and provoke in their classrooms. In this perspective, intellectual work is incomplete unless it self-consciously assumes responsibility for its effects in the larger public culture while simultaneously addressing the most profoundly and deeply inhumane problems of the societies in which we live. Hence, cultural studies raises questions about what knowledge is produced in the university and how it is consequential in extending and deepening the possibilities for democratic public life. Equally important is the issue of how to democratize the schools to enable those groups that in large measure are divorced from or simply not represented in the curriculum to be able to produce their own representations, narrate their own stories and engage in respectful dialogue with others. In this instance, cultural studies must address how dialogue is constructed in the classroom about other cultures and voices by critically addressing both the position of the theorists and the institutions in which such dialogues are produced. Peter Hitchcock argues forcefully that the governing principles of any such dialogic exchange should include some of the following elements:

(1) attention to the specific institutional setting in which this activity takes place; (2) self-reflexivity regarding the particular identities of the teacher and students who collectively undertake this activity; (3) an awareness that the cultural identities at stake in "other" cultures are in the process-of-becoming in dialogic interaction and are not static as subjects; but (4) the knowledge produced through this activity is always already contestable and by definition is not the knowledge of the other as the other would know herself or himself. (Hitchcock 1993: 12)

Fourth, another important contribution of cultural studies is its emphasis on studying the production, reception and use of varied texts and how they are used to define social relations, values, particular notions of community, the future and diverse definitions of the self. Texts in this sense do not merely refer to the culture of print or the technology of the book, but to all those audio, visual and electronically mediated forms of knowledge that have prompted a radical shift in the construction of knowledge and the ways in which knowledge is read, received and consumed. It is worth repeating that contemporary youth increasingly rely less on the technology and culture of the book to construct and affirm their identities; instead, they are faced with the task of finding their way through a decentered cultural landscape no longer caught in the grip of a technology of print, closed narrative structures or the certitude of a secure economic future. The new emerging technologies that construct and position youth represent interactive terrains that cut across "language and culture, without narrative requirements, without character complexities. . . . Narrative complexity [has given] way to design complexity; story [has given] way to a sensory environment" (Parkes 1994: 50). Cultural studies is profoundly important for educators in that it focuses on media not merely in terms of how it distorts and misrepresents reality, but also on how media plays "a part in the formation, in the constitution, of the things they reflect. It is not that there is a world outside, 'out there,' which exists free of the discourse of representation. What is 'out there' is, in part, constituted by how it is represented" (Hall 1992a: 14).

I don't believe that educators and schools of education can address the shifting attitudes, representations and desires of this new generation of youth within the dominant disciplinary configurations of knowledge and practice. On the contrary, as youth are constituted within languages and new cultural forms that intersect differently across and within issues of race, class, gender and sexual differences, the conditions through which youth attempt to narrate themselves must be understood in terms of both the context of their struggles and a shared language of agency that points to a project of hope and possibility. It is precisely this language of difference, specificity and possibility that is lacking from most attempts at educational reform.

Fifth, it is important to stress that when critical pedagogy is established as one of the defining principles of cultural studies, it is possible to generate a new discourse for moving beyond a limited emphasis on the mastery of techniques and methodologies. Critical pedagogy represents a form of cultural production implicated in and critically attentive to how power and meaning are employed in the construction and organization of knowledge, desires, values and identities. Critical pedagogy in this sense is not reduced to the mastering of skills or techniques, but is defined as a cultural practice that must be accountable ethically and politically for the stories it produces, the claims it makes on social memories and the images of the future it deems legitimate. As both an object of critique and a method of cultural production, it refuses to hide behind claims of objectivity and works effortlessly to link theory and practice to enabling the possibilities for human agency in a world of diminishing returns. It is important to make a distinction here that challenges the liberal and conservative criticism that, since critical pedagogy attempts both to politicize teaching and teach politics, it represents a species of indoctrination. By asserting that all teaching is profoundly political and that critical educators and cultural workers should operate out of a project of social transformation, I am arguing that as educators we need to make a distinction between what Peter Euben calls political and politicizing education.

Political education, which is central to critical pedagogy, refers to teaching

students how to think in ways that cultivate the capacity for judgment essential for the exercise of power and responsibility by a democratic citizenry. . . . A political, as distinct from a politicizing education would encourage students to become better citizens to challenge those with political and cultural power as well as to honor the critical traditions within the dominant culture that make such a critique possible and intelligible. (Euben 1994: 14–15)

A political education means decentering power in the classroom and other pedagogical sites so the dynamics of those institutional and cultural inequalities that marginalize some groups, repress particular types of knowledge and suppress critical dialogue can be addressed. On the other hand, politicizing education is a form of pedagogical terrorism in which the issue of what is taught, by whom and under what conditions is determined by a doctrinaire political agenda that refuses to examine its own values, beliefs and ideological construction. While refusing to recognize the social and historical character of its own claims to history, knowledge and values, a politicizing education silences in the name of a specious universalism and denounces all transformative practices through an appeal to a timeless notion of truth and beauty. For those who practice a politicizing education, democracy and citizenship become dangerous in that the precondition for their realization demands critical inquiry, the taking of risks and the responsibility to resist and say no in the face of dominant forms of power.

CONCLUSION

Given its challenge to the traditional notion of teachers as mere transmitters of information and its insistence that teachers are cultural producers
deeply implicated in public issues, cultural studies provides a new and transformative language for educating teachers and administrators around the
issue of civic leadership and public service. In this perspective, teacher education is fashioned not around a particular dogma, but through pedagogical practices that address changing contexts, creating the necessary
conditions for students to be critically attentive to the historical and socially
constructed nature of the locations they occupy within a shifting world of
representations and values. Cultural studies requires that teachers be educated to be cultural producers, to treat culture as an activity, unfinished and
incomplete. This suggests that teachers should be critically attentive to the
operations of power as it is implicated in the production of knowledge and
authority in particular and shifting contexts. This means learning how to be
sensitive to considerations of power as it is inscribed on every facet of the
schooling process.

The conditions and problems of contemporary youth will have to be engaged through a willingness to interrogate the world of public politics, while
at the same time appropriating modernity's call for a better world but abandoning its linear narratives of Western history, unified culture, disciplinary
order and technological progress. In this case, the pedagogical importance
of uncertainty and indeterminacy can be rethought through a modernist
notion of the dream world in which youth and others can shape, without
the benefit of master narratives, the conditions for producing new ways of
learning, engaging and positing the possibilities for social struggle and solidarity. Critical educators cannot subscribe either to an apocalyptic empti-
ness or to a politics of refusal that celebrates the abandonment of authority
or the immediacy of experience over the more profound dynamic of social
memory and moral outrage forged within and against conditions of exploitation, oppression and the abuse of power.

The intersection of cultural studies and critical pedagogy offers possibilities for educators to confront history as more than simulacrum and ethics
as something other than the casualty of incommensurable language games.
Educators need to assert a politics that makes the relationship among authority, ethics and power central to a pedagogy that expands rather than
closes down the possibilities of a radical democratic society. Within this discourse, images do not dissolve reality into simply another text: on the contrary, representations become central to revealing the structures of power
relations at work in the public, in schools, in society and in the larger global
order. Pedagogy does not succumb to the whims of the marketplace in this
logic, nor to the latest form of educational chic; instead, critical pedagogy
engages cultural studies as part of an ongoing movement towards a shared

conception of justice and a radicalization of the social order. This is a task that not only recognizes the multiple relationships between culture and power, but also makes critical pedagogy one of its defining principles.

NOTES

Acknowledgement: I would like to thank Susan Searls, Doug Kellner and Stanley Aronowitz for their critical reading of this manuscript.

This chapter first appeared as "Doing Cultural Studies," *Harvard Educational Review*, 64(3) (Fall 1994): 278–308.

1. I provide a detailed critique of this issue in Henry A. Giroux, *Schooling and the Struggle for Public Life* (Minneapolis: University of Minnesota Press, 1988). See also Stanley Aronowitz and Henry A. Giroux, *Education Still Under Siege* (Westport, CT: Bergin & Garvey, 1993).

2. I take this issue up in detail in Henry A. Giroux, *Disturbing Pleasures: Learning Popular Culture* (New York: Routledge, 1994).

3. Feminist theorists have been making this point for years. For an example of some of this work as it is expressed at the intersection of cultural studies and pedagogy, see the various articles in *Between Borders: Pedagogy and the Politics of Cultural Studies*, eds. Henry A. Giroux and Peter McLaren (New York: Routledge, 1993).

4. The relationship between cultural studies and relations of government are taken up in Tony Bennett, "Putting Policy into Cultural Studies," in *Cultural Studies*, eds. Lawrence Grossberg, Cary Nelson and Paula Treichler (New York: Routledge, 1992), pp. 23–24.

5. For representative examples of the diverse issues taken up in the field of cultural studies, see Grossberg et al., "Cultural Studies," in *The Cultural Studies Reader*, ed. Simon During (New York: Routledge, 1993).

6. This is especially true of some of the most ardent critics of higher education. A representative list includes: William J. Bennett, *To Reclaim a Legacy: A Report on the Humanities in Higher Education* (Washington, DC: National Endowment for the Humanities, 1984); Stephen H. Balch and Herbert London, "The Tenured Left," *Commentary*, 82(4) (1986): 41–51; Lynne V. Cheney, *Tyrannical Machines: A Report on Education Practices Gone Wrong and Our Best Hopes for Setting Them Right* (Washington, DC: National Endowment for the Humanities, 1990); Roger Kimball, *Tenured Radicals: How Politics Has Corrupted Our Higher Education* (New York: Harper & Row, 1990); Dinesh D'Souza, *Illiberal Education: The Politics of Race and Sex on Campus* (New York: Free Press, 1991). For a highly detailed analysis of the web of conservative money, foundations and ideologies that connect the above intellectuals, see Ellen Messer-Davidow, "Manufacturing the Attack on Liberalized Higher Education," *Social Text*, 11(3) (1993): 40–80.

7. As a representative example of this type of critique, see any of the major theoretical sources of cultural studies, especially the Centre for Contemporary Cultural Studies at the University of Birmingham (England). For example, Stuart Hall, "Cultural Studies: Two Paradigms," in *Media, Culture, and Society*, eds. Richard Collins et al. (London: Sage Publications, 1986), pp. 34–48; and Stuart Hall, "Cultural Studies and the Center: Some Problematics and Problems," in *Culture, Media, Language: Working Paper in Cultural Studies*, eds. Stuart Hall et al. (London:

Hutchinson, 1980); Richard Johnson, "What Is Cultural Studies Anyway?" *Social Text*, 6(1) (1987): 38–40; Meaghan Morris, "Banality in Cultural Studies," *Discourse*, 10(2) (1988): 3–29.

8. See Stanley Aronowitz, *Roll Over Beethoven: Return of Cultural Strife* (Hanover, NH: University Press of New England, 1993); Gayatri C. Spivak, *Outside in the Teaching Machine* (New York: Routledge, 1993). See also a few articles in Grossberg et al., *Cultural Studies*. Also, see various issues of *College Literature* under the editorship of Kostas Mrysiades. It is quite revealing to look into some of the latest books on cultural studies and see no serious engagement of pedagogy as a site of theoretical and practical struggle. In David Punter, ed., *Introduction to Contemporary Cultural Studies* (New York: Longman, 1986), there is one chapter on identifying racism in textbooks. For more recent examples, see: Patrick Brantlinger, *Crusoe's Footprints: Cultural Studies in Britain and America* (New York: Routledge, 1990); Graeme Turner, *British Cultural Studies* (London: Unwin Hyman, 1990); John Clarke, *New Times and Old Enemies* (London: Harper Collins, 1991); Sarah Franklin, Celia Lury and Jackie Stacey, eds., *Off-Centre: Feminism and Cultural Studies* (London: Harper Collins, 1991). In neither of the following books published in 1993 is there even one mention of pedagogy: During, *The Cultural Studies Reader*; Valda Blundell, John Shepherd and Ian Taylor, eds., *Relocating Cultural Studies: Developments in Theory and Research* (New York: Routledge, 1993).

9. While there are too many sources to cite here, see R. W. Connell, D. J. Ashenden, S. Kessler and G. W. Dowsett, *Making the Difference* (Boston: Allen and Unwin, 1982); Julian Henriques, Wendy Hollway, Cathy Urwin, Couze Venn and Valerie Walkerdine, eds., *Changing the Subject* (London: Methuen, 1984); James T. Sears, *Growing Up Gay in the South: Race, Gender, and Journeys of the Spirit* (New York: Harrington Park Press, 1991); Michelle Fine, *Framing Dropouts* (Albany: State University of New York Press, 1991); Roger I. Simon, *Teaching against the Grain* (New York: Bergin & Garvey, 1992); James Donald, *Sentimental Education* (London: Verso Press, 1992).

10. For instance, while theorists such as Jane Tompkins, Gerald Graff, Gregory Ulmer and others address pedagogical issues, they do it solely within the referenced terrain of literary studies. Moreover, even those theorists in literary studies who insist on the political nature of pedagogy generally ignore, with few exceptions, the work that has gone on in the field for twenty years. See, for example, Shoshana Felman and Dori Lamb, *Testimony: Crisis of Witnessing in Literature, Psychoanalysis, and History* (New York: Routledge, 1992); Bruce Henricksen and Thais E. Morgan, *Reorientations: Critical Theories & Pedagogies* (Urbana: University of Illinois Press, 1990); Patricia Donahue and Ellen Quahndahl, eds., *Reclaiming Pedagogy: The Rhetoric of the Classroom* (Carbondale: Southern Illinois University Press, 1989); Gregory Ulmer, *Applied Grammatology* (Baltimore: Johns Hopkins University Press, 1985); Barbara Johnson, ed., *The Pedagogical Imperative: Teaching as a Literary Genre* (New Haven, CT: Yale University Press, 1983).

11. One interesting example of this occurred when Gary Olson, the editor of the *Journal of Advanced Composition*, interviewed Jacques Derrida. He asked Derrida, in the context of a discussion about pedagogy and teaching, if he knew of the work of Paulo Freire. Derrida responded, "This is the first time I've heard his name" (Gary Olson, "Jacques Derrida on Rhetoric and Composition: A Conversation," in *[Inter]views]: Cross-Disciplinary Perspectives on Rhetoric and Literacy*, eds. Gary Olson

and Irene Gale [Carbondale: Southern Illinois University Press, 1991], p. 133). It is hard to imagine that a figure of Freire's international stature would not be known to someone in literary studies who is one of the major proponents of deconstruction. So much for crossing boundaries. Clearly, Derrida does not read the radical literature in composition studies, because if he did he could not miss the numerous references to the work of Paulo Freire and other critical educators. See, for instance, C. Douglas Atkins and Michael L. Johnson, *Writing and Reading Differently: Deconstruction and the Teaching of Composition and Literature* (Lawrence: University of Kansas Press, 1985); Linda Brodkey, *Academic Writing as a Social Practice* (Philadelphia: Temple University Press, 1987); C. Mark Hurlbert and Michael Blitz, eds., *Composition & Resistance* (Portsmouth, NH: Heinemann, 1991).

12. It is worth noting that the term "cultural studies" derives from the Centre for Contemporary Cultural Studies at the University of Birmingham. Initially influenced by the work of Richard Hoggart, Raymond Williams and E. P. Thompson, the Centre's ongoing work in cultural studies achieved international recognition under the direction of Stuart Hall in the 1970s and later under Richard Johnson in the 1980s. For a useful history of the Centre written from the theoretical vantage point of one of its U.S. supporters, see Lawrence Grossberg, "The Formations of Cultural Studies: An American in Birmingham," in Blundell et al., *Relocating Cultural Studies*, pp. 21–66.

13. Williams is quite adamant in refuting "encyclopedia articles dating the birth of Cultural Studies from this or that book in the late 'fifties.'" He goes on to say that "the shift of perspective about the teaching of art and literature and their relation to history and to contemporary society began in Adult Education, it didn't happen anywhere else. It was when it was taken across by people with that experience to the Universities that it was suddenly recognized as a subject. It is in these and other similar ways that the contribution of the process itself to social change itself, and specifically to learning, has happened" (cited in Raymond Williams, "Adult Education and Social Change," *What I Came to Say* [London: Hutchinson-Radus, 1989], pp. 157–166). See also, Raymond Williams, "The Future of Cultural Studies," in *The Politics of Modernism*, ed. Tony Pickney (London: Verso, 1989), pp. 151–162.

14. Larry Grossberg goes so far as to argue that cultural studies "sees both history and its own practice as the struggle to produce one context out of another, one set of relations out of another." Lawrence Grossberg, "Cultural Studies and/in New Worlds," *Critical Studies in Mass Communications* (Annandale, VA: Speech Communication Association, forthcoming), p. 4.

15. See the November 29, 1993, issue of *Newsweek*. Of course, the issue that is often overlooked in associating "gangsta rap" with violence is that "gangsta rap does not appear in a cultural vacuum, but, rather, is expressive of the cultural crossing, mixing, and engagement of black youth culture with the values, attitudes, and concerns of the white majority." bell hooks, "Sexism and Misogyny: Who Takes the Rap?" *Z Magazine*, February 1994, p. 26. See also Greg Tate's spirited defense of rap in "Above and Beyond Rap's Decibels," *New York Times*, March 6, 1994, pp. 1, 36.

16. This is most evident in the popular media culture where analysis of crime in the United States is almost exclusively represented through images of black youth. For example, in the May 1994 issue of *Atlantic Monthly*, the cover of the magazine shows a black urban youth, without a shirt, with a gun in his hand, staring out at

the reader. The story the image is highlighting is about inner-city violence. The flurry of articles, magazines, films and news stories about crime produced in 1994 focuses almost exclusively on black youth, both discursively and representationally.

17. Stanley Aronowitz, "A Different Perspective on Educational Inequality," *The Review of Education/Pedagogy/Cultural Studies* (University Park, PA: Gordon and Breach, forthcoming), p. 15.

18. These quotes and comments are taken from a stinging analysis of Kaus in Jonathan Kozol, "Speaking the Unspeakable," unpublished manuscript (1993). The context for Kaus' remarks are developed in Mickey Kaus, *The End of Equality* (New York: Basic Books, 1992).

19. Theodor Adorno and Max Horkheimer, writing in the 1940s, argued that popular culture had no redeeming political or aesthetic possibilities. See Max Horkheimer and Theodor Adorno, *Dialectic of Enlightenment* (New York: Herder & Herder, 1944/1972), especially "The Culture Industry: Enlightenment as Mass Deception," pp. 120–167.

20. This section of the chapter draws from Henry A. Giroux, "Slacking Off: Border Youth and Postmodern Education," *Journal of Advanced Composition*.

21. For a critique of the so-called "twenty-something generation" as defined by *Time, U.S. News, Money, Newsweek* and the *Utne Reader*, see Chris de Bellis, "From Slackers to Baby Busters," *Z Magazine*, December 1993, pp. 8–10.

22. The contours of this type of criticism are captured in a comment by Andrew Kopkind, a keen observer of slacker culture, in "Slacking Toward Bethlehem," p. 187:

The domestic and economic relationships that have created the new consciousness are not likely to improve in the few years left in this century, or in the years of the next, when the young slackers will be middle-agers. The choices for young people will be increasingly constricted. In a few years, a steady job at a mall outlet or a food chain may be all that's left for the majority of college graduates. Life is more and more like a lottery—is a lottery—with nothing but the luck of the draw determining whether you get a recording contract, get your screenplay produced, or get a job with your M.B.A. Slacking is thus a rational response to casino capitalism, the randomization of success, and the utter arbitrariness of power. If no talent is still enough, why bother to hone your skills? If it is impossible to find a good job, why not slack out and enjoy life?

23. For an analysis of black American cinema in the 1990s, see Ed Guerrero, "Framing Blackness: The African-American Image in the Cinema of the Nineties," *Cineaste*, 20(2) (1993): 24–31.

24. I have called this elsewhere the pedagogy of commercialism. See Giroux, *Disturbing Pleasures*.

25. For an analysis of the relationship among modernist schooling, pedagogy and popular culture, see Henry A. Giroux and Roger I. Simon, "Popular Culture as a Pedagogy of Pleasure and Meaning," in *Popular Culture, Schooling, and Everyday Life*, eds. Henry A. Giroux and Roger Simon (Granby, MA: Bergin & Garvey, 1989), pp. 1–30; Henry A. Giroux and Roger I. Simon, "Schooling, *Popular Culture*, and a Pedagogy of Possibility," in Giroux and Simon, *Popular Culture*, pp. 219–236.

26. Anyone who has been following the culture wars of the past eight years is well aware of the conservative agenda for reordering public and higher education around

the commercial goal of promoting economic growth for the nation while simultaneously supporting the values of Western civilization as a common culture designed to undermine the ravages of calls for equity and multiculturalism. For a brilliant analysis of the conservative attack on higher education, see Ellen Messer-Davidow, "Manufacturing the Attack on Liberalized Higher Education," *Social Text*, 11(3) (1993): 40–80.

27. This argument is especially powerful in the work of Edward Said, who frames the reach of culture as a determining pedagogical force against the backdrop of the imperatives of colonialism. See Edward Said, *Culture and Imperialism* (New York: Alfred A. Knopf, 1993); see also Donaldo Macedo, *Literacies of Power* (Boulder, CO: Westview Press, 1994).

28. Selective examples of this work include: Carol Becker, ed., *The Subversive Imagination* (New York: Routledge, 1994); Giroux and McLaren, *Between Borders*; Roger Simon, *Teaching against the Grain*; David Trend, *Cultural Pedagogy: Art/Education/Politics* (Westport, CT: Bergin and Garvey, 1992); James Schwoch, Mimi White and Susan Reilly, *Media Knowledge: Readings in Popular Culture, Pedagogy, and Critical Citizenship* (Albany: State University of New York Press, 1992); Lawrence Grossberg, *We Gotta Get Out of This Place: Popular Conservatism and Postmodern Culture* (New York: Routledge, 1992). See also, Douglas Kellner, *Media Culture* (New York: Routledge, forthcoming); Jeanne Brady, *Schooling Young Children* (Albany: State University of New York Press, forthcoming).

REFERENCES

Anshaw, Carol. (1992) "Days of Whine and Poses." *Village Voice*, November 10: 27.

Aronowitz, Stanley. (1993) *Roll Over Beethoven: Return of Cultural Strife*. Hanover, NH: University Press of New England.

———. (1995) "A Different Perspective on Educational Inequality." *The Review of Education/Pedagogy/Cultural Studies*. University Park, PA: Gordon and Breach, 15.

Aronowitz, Stanley and Giroux, Henry A. (1993) *Education Still Under Siege*. Westport, CT: Bergin & Garvey, 4–5.

Atkins, C. Douglas and Johnson, Michael L. (1985) *Writing and Reading Differently: Deconstruction and the Teaching of Composition and Literature*. Lawrence: University of Kansas Press.

Balch, Stephen H. and London, Herbert. (1986) "The Tenured Left." *Commentary*, 82(4): 41–51.

Becker, Carol (ed.). (1994) *The Subversive Imagination*. New York: Routledge.

Bennett, Tony. (1992) "Putting Policy into Cultural Studies." In Lawrence Grossberg, Cary Nelson, and Paula Treichler (eds.), *Cultural Studies*. New York: Routledge, 23–24, 32.

Bennett, William. (1996) *The Book of Virtues: A Treasury of Moral Stories*. New York: Touchstone Books.

Bennett, William J. (1984) *To Reclaim a Legacy: A Report on the Humanities in Higher Education*. Washington, DC: National Endowment for the Humanities.

Blundell, Valda, Shepherd, John and Taylor, Ian (eds.). (1993) *Relocating Cultural Studies: Developments in Theory and Research*. New York: Routledge.

Brady, Jeanne. (1995) *Schooling Young Children: A Feminist Pedagogy for Libertory Learning*. Albany: State University of New York Press.

Brantlinger, Patrick. (1990) *Crusoe's Footprints: Cultural Studies in Britain and America*. New York: Routledge, 1990.

Brodkey, Linda. (1987) *Academic Writing as a Social Practice*. Philadelphia: Temple University Press.

Cheney, Lynne V. (1990) *Tyrannical Machines: A Report on Education Practices Gone Wrong and Our Best Hopes for Setting Them Right*. Washington, DC: National Endowment for the Humanities.

Clarke, John. (1991) *New Times and Old Enemies*. London: Harper Collins.

Colatosti, Camille. (1994) "Dealing Guns." *Z Magazine*, January: 59.

Connell, R. W., Ashenden, D. J., Kessler, S. and Dowsett, G. W. (1982) *Making the Difference*. Boston: Allen and Unwin.

Conniff, Ruth. (1992) "The Culture of Cruelty." *The Progressive*, September 16: 16–20.

D'Souza, Dinesh. (1991) *Illiberal Education: The Politics of Race and Sex on Campus*. New York: Free Press.

de Bellis, Chris. (1993) "From Slackers to Baby Busters." *Z Magazine*, December: 8–10.

Donahue, Patricia and Quahndahl, Ellen (eds.). (1989) *Reclaiming Pedagogy: The Rhetoric of the Classroom*. Carbondale: Southern Illinois University Press.

Donald, James. (1992) *Sentimental Education*. London: Verso Press.

During, Simon (ed.). (1993) *The Cultural Studies Reader*. New York: Routledge.

Dyson, Michael. (1994) "The Politics of Black Masculinity and the Ghetto in Black Film." In Carol Becker (ed.), *The Subversive Imagination: Artists, Society, and Social Responsibility*. New York: Routledge, 155, 163.

Epstein, Jonathon (ed.). (1994) *Adolescents and Their Music: If It's Too Loud, You're Too Old*. New York: Garland.

Euben, Peter. (1994) "The Debate Over the Canon." *Civic Arts Review*, 7(1): 14–15.

Felman, Shoshana and Lamb, Dori. (1992) *Testimony: Crisis of Witnessing in Literature, Psychoanalysis, and History*. New York: Routledge.

Fine, Michelle. (1991) *Framing Dropouts*. Albany: State University of New York Press.

Fiske, John. (1994) *Power Plays, Power Works*. London: Verso Press, 20.

"Footnotes." (1993) *Chronicle of Higher Education*, December 1: A8.

Franklin, Sarah, Lury, Celia and Stacey, Jackie (eds.). (1991) *Off-Centre: Feminism and Cultural Studies*. London: Harper Collins.

Giroux, Henry A. (1988) *Schooling and the Struggle for Public Life*. Minneapolis: University of Minnesota Press.

———. (1992) *Border Crossings: Cultural Workers and the Politics of Education*. New York: Routledge.

———. (1994a) *Disturbing Pleasures: Learning Popular Culture*. New York: Routledge, 1994.

———. (1994b) "Slacking Off: Border Youth and Postmodern Education." *Journal of Advanced Composition*, 14(2): 347–366.

Giroux, Henry A. and McLaren, Peter (eds.). (1993) *Between Borders: Pedagogy and the Politics of Cultural Studies.* New York: Routledge.

Giroux, Henry A. and Simon, Roger I. (1989a) "Popular Culture as a Pedagogy of Pleasure and Meaning." In Henry A. Giroux and Roger Simon (eds.), *Popular Culture, Schooling, and Everyday Life.* Granby, MA: Bergin & Garvey, 1–30.

Giroux, Henry A. and Simon, Roger I. (1989b) "Schooling, Popular Culture, and a Pedagogy of Possibility." In Henry A. Giroux and Roger I. Simon, *Popular Culture, Schooling, and Everyday Life.* Granby, MA: Bergin & Garvey, 219–236.

Grossberg, Lawrence. (1992) *We Gotta Get Out of This Place: Popular Conservatism and Postmodern Culture.* New York: Routledge.

———. (1993) "The Formations of Cultural Studies: An American in Birmingham." In V. Blundell et al., *Relocating Cultural Studies: Developments in Theory and Research.* New York: Routledge, 21–66.

———. "Cultural Studies and/in New Worlds." Critical Studies in *Mass Communications.* Annandale, VA: Speech Communication Association, 4: 1–22.

Grossberg, Lawrence et al. (1993) "Cultural Studies." In Simon During (ed.), *The Cultural Studies Reader.* New York: Routledge.

Grossberg, Lawrence, Nelson, Cary and Treichler, Paula (eds.). (1992) "Cultural Studies: An Introduction. In L. Grossberg, C. Nelson and P. Treichler, *Cultural Studies.* New York: Routledge, 5.

Guerrero, Ed. (1993) "Framing Blackness: The African-American Image in the Cinema of the Nineties." *Cineaste,* 20(2): 24–31.

Hall, Stuart. (1980) "Cultural Studies and the Center: Some Problematics and Problems." In Stuart Hall et al. (eds.), *Culture, Media, Language: Working Paper in Cultural Studies.* London: Hutchinson.

———. (1986) "Cultural Studies: Two Paradigms." In Richard Collins et al. (eds.), *Media, Culture, and Society.* London: Sage Publications, 34–48.

———. (1992a) "Race, Culture, and Communications: Looking Backward and Forward at Cultural Studies." *Rethinking Marxism,* 5(1): 11, 14

———. (1992b) "What Is This 'Black' in Popular Culture?" In Gina Dent (ed.), *Black Popular Culture.* Seattle: Bay Press, 22.

Hebdige, Dick. (1988) *Hiding in the Light.* New York: Routledge, 17–18.

Henricksen, Bruce and Morgan, Thais E. (1990) *Reorientations: Critical Theories & Pedagogies.* Urbana: University of Illinois Press.

Henriques, Julian, et al. (eds.). (1984) *Changing the Subject.* London: Methuen.

Hitchcock, Peter. (1993) "The Othering of Cultural Studies." *Third Text,* 25 (Winter 1993–1994): 12.

Hollingsworth, Pierce. (1993) "The New Generation Gaps: Graying Boomers, Golden Agers, and Generation X." *Food Technology,* 47(10): 30.

hooks, bell. (1994) "Sexism and Misogyny: Who Takes the Rap?" *Z Magazine,* February: 26.

Horkheimer, Max and Adorno, Theodor. (1944/1972) "The Culture Industry: Enlightenment as Mass Deception." In *Dialectic of Enlightenment.* New York: Herder and Herder, 120–167.

Hurlbert, C. Mark and Blitz, Michael (eds.). (1991) *Composition & Resistance.* Portsmouth, NH: Heinemann.

Johnson, Barbara (ed.). (1983) *The Pedagogical Imperative: Teaching as a Literary Genre*. New Haven, CT: Yale University Press.

Johnson, Richard. (1987) "What Is Cultural Studies Anyway?" *Social Text*, 6(1): 38–40.

Kaus, Mickey. (1992) *The End of Equality*. New York: Basic Books.

Kellner, Douglas. (1995) *Media Culture*. New York: Routledge.

Kimball, Roger. (1990) *Tenured Radicals: How Politics Has Corrupted Our Higher Education*. New York: Harper & Row.

Kopkind, Andrew. (1992) "Slacking Toward Bethlehem." *Grand Street*, 11(4): 183.

Kozol, Jonathan. (1993) "Speaking the Unspeakable." Unpublished manuscript.

Macedo, Donaldo. (1994) *Literacies of Power*. Boulder, CO: Westview Press.

Messer-Davidow, Ellen. (1993) "Manufacturing the Attack on Liberalized Higher Education." *Social Text*, 11(3): 40–80.

Morris, Meaghan. (1988) "Banality in Cultural Studies." *Discourse*, 10(2): 3–29.

Nelson, Cary. (1991) "Always Already Cultural Studies." *Journal of the Midwest Language Association*, 24(1): 32.

Njeri, Itabari. (1993) "Untangling the Roots of the Violence Around Us—On Screen and Off." *Los Angeles Times Magazine*, August 29: 33–34

Olson, Gary. (1991) "Jacques Derrida on Rhetoric and Composition: A Conversation." In Gary Olson and Irene Gale (eds.), *[Inter]views]: Cross-Disciplinary Perspectives on Rhetoric and Literacy*. Carbondale: Southern Illinois University Press, 133.

Parkes, Walter. (1994) "Random Access, Remote Control: The Evolution of Story Telling." *Omni*, January: 50, 54.

Punter, David (ed.). (1986) *Introduction to Contemporary Cultural Studies*. New York: Longman.

Ross, Andrew and Rose, Tricia (eds.). (1994) *Microphone Fiends: Youth Music and Youth Culture*. New York: Routledge.

Said, Edward. (1993) *Culture and Imperialism*. New York: Alfred A. Knopf.

Schwoch, James, White, Mimi and Reilly, Susan. (1992) *Media Knowledge: Readings in Popular Culture, Pedagogy, and Critical Citizenship*. Albany: State University of New York Press.

Sears, James T. (1991) *Growing Up Gay in the South: Race, Gender, and Journeys of the Spirit*. New York: Harrington Park Press.

Simon, Roger I. (1992) *Teaching against the Grain*. New York: Bergin & Garvey, 15.

Sklar, Holly (1993) "Young and Guilty by Stereotype." *Z Magazine*, July–August: 52.

Spivak, Gayatri C. (1993) *Outside in the Teaching Machine*. New York: Routledge.

Tate, Greg. (1994) "Above and Beyond Rap's Decibels." *New York Times*, March 6: 1, 36.

Trend, David. (1992) *Cultural Pedagogy: Art/Education/Politics*. Westport, CT: Bergin & Garvey.

Turner, Graeme. (1990) *British Cultural Studies*. London: Unwin Hyman.

Ulmer, Gregory. (1985) *Applied Grammatology*. Baltimore: Johns Hopkins University Press.

Virilio, Paul. (1991) *Lost Dimension*, trans. Daniel Moshenberg. New York: Semiotext[e].

West, Cornel. (1992) "Nihilism in Black America." In G. Dent (ed.), *Black Popular Culture*. Seattle: Bay Press, 40.

———. (1967) *Communications*, rev. ed. New York: Barnes and Noble, 14–15.

Williams, Raymond. (1989a) "The Future of Cultural Studies." In Tony Pickney (ed.) *The Politics of Modernism*. London: Verso, 151–162.

———. (1989b) "Adult Education and Social Change." In *What I Came to Say*. London: Hutchinson-Radus, 157–166.

Worth, Fabienne. (1993) "Postmodern Pedagogy in the Multicultural Classroom: For Inappropriate Teachers and Imperfect Spectators." *Cultural Critique*, 25 (Fall): 27.

Chapter 12

Humanities in the Postmodern

BRIAN OPIE

The challenge to (or the loss of) the grand (Enlightenment) narrative of the search for truth through reason as the defining purpose of the Western university is recognized in discussions ranging across the now traditional disciplines of the arts, humanities and the social sciences during the 1980s and 1990s. One account among many is that of Geoff Eley, writing from a position "in history":

Social history has become one site of a general epistemological uncertainty that characterizes large areas of academic-intellectual life in the humanities and the social sciences in the late twentieth century. This flux is perhaps more extensive in some places than others (in the sense that it pervades more disciplines more completely) and more central to disciplinary discussion in, say, literature and anthropology than in, say, sociology and the "harder" social sciences. Not by accident, the most radical and influential discussions have been occurring in areas that lack the constraining power of disciplinary traditions—especially women's studies and the emerging field of cultural studies. (Eley 1996: 194)

Eley encapsulates, from the perspective of the academic (rather than the manager), the key factors that necessarily involve the university as an institution in the destabilization and disruption of identity and function that characterize many of its disciplines, especially in the "nonsciences." The Sokal controversy is a recent and particularly striking instance of the intense politics in the domain of knowledge creation and critique that now actually or implicitly circulate through all Western universities, in which the boundaries separating the sciences and the humanities have been breached.[1] At each apparent disruption of the integrity of a discipline, the whole fabric of the university is supposed to be undermined. On the other hand, as Sosnowski notes about the situation of English literature, the breakdown of disciplines is also the release of a particular field of knowledge to modes of knowledge creation more appropriate to its objects of study and contexts of transmission and exchange:

I favor abandoning the notion of disciplinarity in the way we speak about ourselves. It invokes comparisons with the sciences. We should stop gauging our own efforts by comparison with the successes of the sciences, as has been our history. . . . I contend that the study of cultures is institutionally misbegotten and still suffers from an inbred residue of scientism. (Sosnoski 1995: 57)

Between them, Eley and Sosnoski identify a crucial aspect of disciplinarity as that which both blocks the formation of new kinds of knowledge and distorts the relation of the knower to certain objects of knowledge. In the postmodern, which is where they position their analyses, the "structural coherence" offered by the discipline is the primary means by which the modes and ends of enquiry constitutive of the "modern" university are perpetuated anachronistically into an era in which "intellectual flux" (Sosnoski 1995: 213) is a decisive characteristic. The historic and linguistic "turns" which most clearly mark the means by which humanities disciplines have been destabilized if not dissolved were located by Michel Foucault, most pertinently in his collocating discipline with regulation, exclusion and control, in contrast to language, which he collocated with heterogeneity and plentitude (Foucault 1981). As Eley suggests, cultural studies as a product of the postmodern is both transformative of and also marginal to the "modern" university because it lacks secure boundaries of its own while engaging with the objects and contents of many disciplines in the humanities and social sciences. The university, then, becomes a site in which more general forces of change can be observed, an instance of processes creating a new social formation of which Mark C. Taylor and Esa Saarinen write: "Postmodern society is radically decentred and thoroughly disseminated. As a result of this dispersion, the machine of socio-cultural reproduction is no longer controlled by centralised agencies" (Taylor and Saarinen: 1994a). Applied to the university, the breaking down of disciplines (rather than devolution as a managerial exercise) can be seen as exemplifying key features of postmodernity.

For Sosnoski in this situation, "Reminding ourselves that we live in a postmodern information age while we work in modern institutions seems an appropriate instance of self-reflexivity" (Sosnoski 1995: 50). Timothy Luke, in a paper to the 1995 HUMANZ Conference, went further by proposing, "albeit ironically and provisionally," that the humanities need to be rethought as "dehumanities," detaching from their parallel evolution to modern industrial culture as "informational economies and societies displace industrialism." The effect of making such a move is the writing of a "narrative of "dehumanization" to embrace a "dehuman" being that might be disclosed by a "dehumanities," or a critical applied humanities that could approach such man/machine, humanity/technology, woman/machine, subject/object, fragments and fusions with a new analytical attitude" (Luke 1996:1). The implication in both these statements that the model subject of the traditional humanities, teacher and critic, is also undergoing change is made explicit by Mark Taylor and Esa Saarinen when they affirm that "What our age needs is communicative intellect. For intellect to be communicative, it must be active, practical, engaged. In a culture of the simulacrum, the site of communicative engagement is electronic media" (Taylor and Saarinen 1994b), one site of which is the virtual university.

In each of these instances, the moment of an epistemic transition is clearly marked, and the unavoidable reframing of the discourses that constitute Western knowledge as well as the institutions that conserve, transmit and create that knowledge, has already taken place. I wish to focus my paper on one of the questions contributors to the series were asked to consider, and modify it to bring in the object and instance of my remarks, not an emergent discipline but an emergent organization, The Humanities Society of New Zealand/Te Whainga Aronui—HUMANZ.[2] By substituting HUMANZ for "cultural studies," the question reads: "To what extent does the emergence of HUMANZ reflect a changing mission of the university and changing relations between the university and the wider society?" My intention is to propose that the conditions affecting the articulation of cultural studies in the Western university are precisely those affecting the formation in the period of the postmodern of a public organization for the humanities in the context of both the universities and the academies or learned societies which complement them.

The title I gave to my chapter, "Humanities in the Postmodern," aims to advertise the "extent" as vividly as possible. I am taking as self-evident the proposition that New Zealand publicly and irrevocably entered postmodernity in 1984 with the end of the Muldoon era and the installation of a Labour government, a government which attempted to govern by separating the economy from society as domains of knowledge and policy formation just as it separated itself, in that process, from large sections of its past and the party membership. From that moment on, processes of globalization driven by transnational capital, which were already well advanced in the northern hemisphere, began to reengineer New Zealand society and culture with astonishing speed and effectiveness. An unfamiliar terminology rapidly pervaded the media and government, centered on the concept of "the market" as the reductive substitute in the discourse of economics for more elaborate and enriched concepts of society and culture that have traditionally characterized humanities discourses.[3]

Resistance to this change from within now traditional disciplinary conceptions of the humanities, except by rejection and withdrawal, has been very difficult. Three reasons for this situation are particularly relevant to the founding of HUMANZ:

1. The sciences successfully established the criteria in what I will call the modern or industrial university for achievement in knowledge work. One result was that the traditional emphasis in the humanities on the acquisition and teaching of sophisticated skills in reading and writing through the study of canonical texts from literature, history and moral philosophy came into conflict with the emphasis on the production of new knowledge through research associated with science. The evolution of the social sciences, taking the humanities' territory of society and culture and reframing it within the canons of scientific research, further disempowered or feminized the traditional humanities by calling attention to their apparent lack of discipline or methodology on which to found a claim to rank as equals in the production of knowledge. These relations of status were already deeply entrenched before 1984; what remained was for the necessary link between science, technology and the market to be articulated, both in government in the reform of the government's patronage of scientific and technological research, and in the university in the rapid expansion of commerce and management programs, the prioritization of research able to compete for external funding and the largely forced adoption of corporate models of governance and administration.

2. Within the new order, in which knowledge is a market commodity like anything else, the traditional humanities' valorization of the personal over the technological, the moral and imaginative over the scientific and economic, the minority over the mass audience and the nonvocational over the vocational has made reframing of the humanities in terms of their presence in the market almost impossible. Furthermore, from the perspective of public policy, the humanities do not exist; as a field of public knowledge, the humanities vanish into Vote: Education allocated state spending on the education sector or are partly subsumed under the statistical category of "the cultural sector."

3. The humanities are a product of the city (which includes but is not subsumed by the market) and of two associated technologies, writing and printing. I intend to take up this point again later, but it is important in this context because the humanities' uneasy relation to the materiality of their transmission and preservation has been magnified by the invention of new technologies of representation based, firstly, on the moving image rather than spoken or written language and, now, on digital multimedia. Although these new technologies have entered the classroom in various ways, and they and their distinctive products are studied in departments of film or media or communications studies, they remain on the margins of print-based humanities—which is to say that, in the media-dominated image world of the postmodern, the humanities (unlike the arts) are largely absent from the mass media.

The originating moment for HUMANZ was confirmation by the minister for research, science and technology after a meeting of deans of arts and humanities in 1990 that the humanities would not be permitted to compete for research funding from the Public Good Science Fund (PGSF). Given the title of the fund and its origin in the abolition of the Department of Scientific and Industrial Research, this exclusion should not have been surprising, although the situation exposed other boundary problems. How scientific are the social sciences, and how social scientific are (some of) the humanities? What kinds of knowledge are needed to meet government priorities, and why is it that the humanities were not regarded as able to contribute to advancing the nation's "social, environmental and economic goals."[4] It is a notable consequence of the priority model that the output framework for the PGSF is determined by large research areas shaped by prioritized applications of knowledge, not by academic disciplinary definitions.

At that originating moment, the complex situation of the humanities showed itself very clearly to those of us who took on the task of establishing a national organization. Because the term "humanities" was common internationally but not in New Zealand[5] and, in contrast to the United States, a professional exponent of the humanities could not be called a humanist (especially when the Humanist Society was one of the founding organizations), there was initial doubt about using that term in the name of the organization. As for the *kind* of organization—although a substantial majority of those participating in the development meetings did not want to set up an elite learned society based on the election of fellows, a small majority favored calling the organization an academy, the very name which creates an expectation, in New Zealand and overseas, that it is a learned society of that kind. If that part of the name looks back to an era in Europe when authority in an intellectual field or discipline was directly connected to seniority, the Maori name, Te Whainga Aronui, looks to the future.[6] As a bicultural organization, respecting two distinct traditions of knowledge within the partnership context of the Treaty of Waitangi, HUMANZ has to attempt to create forms of discourse about its purposes and aims that do not privilege Western academic conventions and assumptions. What, in other words, does constitute a postmodern New Zealand humanities?[7]

Also, by coming into existence in a space between the universities, the government, the national cultural institutions and interested societies and individuals, HUMANZ could not simply adopt a university representation of its field of interests. Many of the current difficulties experienced by overseas academies in meeting pressures for change, because their structures are too closely linked to traditional disciplinary divisions of the field of the humanities, were avoided in our case. On the other hand, the New Zealand government's refusal of the role of patron in the context of restructuring meant that, uniquely among such organizations internationally, HUMANZ could expect no government support. There was no alternative but to look to a broadly based personal membership, which meant asking why anyone would want to become a member—a fundamental and not simply answered question in the light of the apparent lack of interest since the 1920s among those in the humanities for a national organization complementary to the Royal Society of New Zealand to represent nationally the interests of that body of knowledge and its practitioners.

A crucial change in the conception of the purposes of government must be underlined here. As patron, the function of British-style governments was to ensure, by providing financial support, that public organizations contributing to the well-being and quality of society were able to perform these functions. In the new order of strategic planning and policy formation, government funding purchases outputs in these areas from such public organizations. Instead of making representations to government with the aim of advancing their interests, such organizations are now having to develop new competencies in order to meet these expectations of the state. In New Zealand, the Business Roundtable is the only organization yet fully developed on this model; not a learned society the members of which speak privately as equals to those in government, but a member-funded organization aimed at shaping the state's agendas by publishing research-based proposals for policy formation or revision.

An important larger framework for this situation is given in two papers in a recent issue of *Social Text*. Tom Moylan writes of the "now pervasive imbrication of economics and culture on the entire social fabric" and provides a brief history of this development as follows:

The long march of the New Right into governments around the world marked a crucial moment in the recent instrumentalization and privatization of culture; for, as Larry Grossberg argues in the case of the U.S., it was the New Right's understanding and appropriation of the counterculture that endowed the Right with the cultural force it needed to win. However, as Radhika Desai has demonstrated, the relationship between free market ideology, cultural practices, and the economic order had been persistently explored long before the Reagan-Thatcher victories by think tanks. . . . The body of theoretical analysis generated by these intellectual centers valorizes the market as the historically triumphant ideology and technology. Yet, unlike other versions of market-based economics, these projects have developed a more sophisticated and effective approach by paying acute attention to cultural dynamics and to the theories that address those dynamics, from hermeneutics to cultural studies. In what I would call "corporate cultural studies," the influence of the "interpretive turn" is quite evident. In the pages of the *Harvard Business Review*; in the restructuring projects at places like the Banff Center, M.I.T's Media Lab, and many universities; and in the outreach courses and consultancies offered by programs such as the Banff Center for Management, culture is constantly reutilized as an economic force. (Moylan 1995: 50–51)

For my purposes, what is of most importance in this description is the implication that the agents of corporate culture take theory work in the new humanities and social sciences much more seriously than do many of those who represent modern humanities and social sciences from positions of teaching and research in the universities. From a corporate perspective, from within the sectors and institutions where economic and political power is concentrated, postmodern intellectual and critical work in new formations like cultural studies is seen to be engaged competitively in the same endeavor, which is to constitute the dominant account of the terms and conditions of global cultural development. It would seem that the Right more than the Left realized the efficacy of Foucault's analysis of power and governmentality as discursive practices; the postmodern democratic state is an abstract engine endlessly reproducing itself in the discourses of public policy and market economics which together claim to be capable of totally representing the domains of culture and society.

It has to be an extreme irony that the university (the one institution in modern society that has thought of itself as uniquely the producer of new symbolic or discursive products), by lacking a Foucaultian theorization of itself, has failed to establish a new position for itself in the changed landscape of institutional power relations. In the university, the politically riven state of postmodern knowledge is underlined by Moylan when he notes how "academia plays a leading role in generating the cultural theory enlisted in restructuring, and it would be useful for those of us who are involved in cultural studies programs to have a clearer understanding of the role of these newly funded programs" (Moylan 1995: 53). We in New Zealand have considerable experience of how those sections of the university able to compete in the new funding structures do so (with whatever reluctance) without any consideration being given to the implications for the university as a distinctive kind of institution.

As for those sections of the university that are apparently irrelevant to this new order—principally the humanities, although "pure science" has provided unusual company in this marginal zone—it is very difficult to articulate and negotiate the terms of a new relationship to the postmodern state when disciplinary divisions of the field fail to map over the uses to which this knowledge is being (or should be) put in contemporary society. In particular, when the state thinks in terms of "the cultural sector" and not of the humanities, when it seeks to formulate "cultural policy" as a dimension of its rational management of the nation's stock of various kinds of capital, the kinds of knowledge and modes of discourse that have efficacy in the public sphere simply do not engage with those currently practiced in modern humanities.

There are clearly many humanities professionals—probably a substantial majority—in New Zealand who would explain this noncommunication as deafness on the part of those currently defining and producing the discourses of government. But the new humanities, those intellectual and cultural formations that do not respect the typical administrative categorization of knowledge (cultural studies is the obvious example), are both shaped by and are shaping the conditions of and for knowledge in the postmodern.[8] These theorized discourses deny that disciplinary content or the historical evolution of the university as an organization can now provide a pertinent or powerful basis for defining knowledge fields. Just as the state has become an abstraction, to be represented conceptually and not personally, so has knowledge in the humanities, re-presented as the theorization of culture. As Avery Gordon describes the situation:

The explosion of cultural studies has given us a nuanced understanding of culture's subtle and diffuse ways of weaving together a complicated web of human relations. The culturalist perspective reveals flexibility, social constructedness, variability, difference, diversity, and plentiful interpretive possibility. And it reveals that these are what make even the heavy power centers of our society operate delicately and with a deftness often hard to capture. The only problem is that these are precisely the modes that the corporation has discovered to better produce a new social order in its own image. We are in a historical moment in which culturalism is increasingly the form corporatism takes. (Gordon 1995: 23)

I hope that my opening parallel between the emergence of HUMANZ and of cultural studies as instances of the condition of postmodernity is beginning to seem justified. Neither is consonant with the modern university's representation of knowledge through its administration and curriculum, but each proposes a new map of cultural knowledge which is powerfully informed by the processes of globalization and conditioned by the challenge of the new economic order. McKenzie Wark defines this situation exactly when he gives a minihistory of the evolution of cultural studies in the preface to his recent book, *Virtual Geography:*

Cultural studies started [at Birmingham] with the event—the event of Thatcherism. It worked back through the vectors which form the contours of its powers, and very pragmatically picked the eyes out of a whole range of specialized knowledges which might help create a practical knowledge organized around the horizon of the event. That approach is still valid today, only the events requiring a critical cultural intervention are increasingly global in scope, and exceed the bounds of any particular national culture and hegemonic class order. If one starts from everyday life, as cultural studies did, from the experience of an ever-shifting combination of dominant, residual and emergent forces, then it is still possible to practice a kind of cultural studies, even when the vectors of power one must trace vastly exceed the bounds of the national popular. (Wark 1994: ix)

The Humanities Society of New Zealand is being put together as Wark proposes cultural studies was in Birmingham, not by appropriating or conforming to some existing institutional account of the humanities but through the creation of "a practical knowledge organized around the horizon of the event"; in the case of HUMANZ, the strange conjunction of the installation of a free market economy, the effects socially and culturally of digital information and communications technologies, the ratification of the Treaty of Waitangi and a vacant space where a national organization for the humanities should have already been located.

"The postmodern is our interregnum." That succinct formulation introduces the notion that I want to place in the foreground of the second part of my chapter, in which I intend to identify some of the principal factors requiring the abandonment of the typical representation of the humanities given in New Zealand universities. My argument is based on two propositions:

1. The departmentalization of the humanities in the university is an aberration, a consequence of the industrial mode of the Western university; the interregnum of the postmodern is a transitional period in which profoundly different institutional formations for the conservation and production of knowledge will take shape. If the humanities seemed irrelevant to the first phase—the capture of the state by free market economics—they are integral to the second, what Gordon described as culturalism. The elaboration of the new humanities in journals like *Social Text*, at applied research centers like the Center for Electronic Texts in the Humanities and the Centre for Cultural Policy Studies, with publishers like Eastgate Systems and through societies like the Society for Literature and Science is providing the conceptual coordinates for mapping this new terrain and the institutional forms which, like the think tanks of the Right, are able to mobilize intellectual resources in a relation of critique to the postmodern corporate state.

2. We are in a period of epistemic change, of no more and no less signficance than the Reformation and Romanticism. All are periods characterized by a heightened sense of catastrophe and the presence of the sublime; all feature a major social irruption through the invention of a new technology of communication; all are marked by a crisis in knowledge and subjectivity; all include an opening onto a "new world"; in each the city as the material embodiment of society and culture undergoes a radical shift in form and function.

The constituent elements in the sketch I want to give of humanities in the postmodern are: text, technology, the city and the state. These four comprise the conditions that originally produced the humanities as a body of qualitative or value-laden knowledge in the West, and they remain the key factors when the accretions of periodic institutional formation are stripped away.

TEXT/TECHNOLOGY

In *The Road Ahead*, Bill Gates offers an account of the genealogy of the computer which would be agreed with by those studying the history of printing or the history of communications:

The only other single shift that has had as great an effect on the history of communication (as the invention of the railway) took place in about 1450 [the invention of printing]. . . . The printing press did more than give the West a faster way to reproduce a book. . . . [The printed word] was the first mass medium—the first time knowledge, opinions, and experiences could be passed on in a portable, durable, and available form. As the written word extended the population's reach far beyond a village, people began to care about what was happening elsewhere. Printing shops quickly sprang up in commercial cities and became centers of intellectual exchange. Literacy became an important skill that revolutionized education and altered social structures. . . . The information highway will transform our culture as dramatically as Gutenberg's press did the Middle Ages. (Gates 1995: 89)

For those of us brought up on predigital humanities, printing was like the air one breathed, an invisible and unconsidered (except by those engaged in bibliographical study) dimension of daily life. The fact that humanities as we knew them—the subjects offered in the arts faculty—depended for their existence on the print book was entirely overlooked. Even the study of a text like Milton's *Areopagitica*, his pamphlet arguing for the freedom of the press, focused on its emphasis upon truth and reason and liberty of conscience, not on the technology and its material product, the book as the materialization of thought.

It is only very recently—about 400 years after the invention of the printing press—that systematic enquiry into the social and cultural significance of the technology rather than the contents of its products has been undertaken. Those near the beginning of its development could see it differently. Francis Bacon, for example, linked printing with gunpowder and the compass as the critical technologies in the turn of Europe away from its medieval past and towards its future imperial power and scientific achievement. But the intimate link of the humanities with print technology could, logocentrically, be misrecognized. The principal disturbing fact about printing to humanists was its inherent promiscuity, its openness to the market, in contrast to the rational and civilizing imperatives of humanism. Bill Gates' recognition of the epochal significance of print technology as a power for social and cultural change is itself a product of his belief in the equivalent or greater power of digital technology as the shaper of a new epoch that is already inclusively global in scope and corporate rather than imperial in character. It is a recognition that takes the connection between technology and the market for granted; the significant institutions are home, school and business, in contrast to the traditional focus of the humanities on the relation between the individual and the (city) state.

Since education has become the distinctive location of the humanities as other knowledges (and specifically the social sciences) displace the humanities expert from his earlier role of advisor to the state, it is worth noting how Bill Gates sees "the road ahead" for education and therefore its implications for the humanities. He gives a whole chapter to education ("Education: The Best Investment"), emphasizing the fundamental role of good teachers and strongly affirming that "technology can humanize the educational environment." The key terms in his thinking which explain his use of "humanize" are those of the individual and the corporation, which together produce the following analogy:

Just as information technology now allows Levi Strauss & Co. to offer jeans that are both mass-produced and custom fitted, information technology will bring mass customization to learning. Multimedia documents and easy-to-use authoring tools will enable teachers to "mass-customize" a curriculum. As with blue jeans, the mass customization of learning will be possible because computers will fine-tune the product . . . to allow students to follow somewhat divergent paths and learn at their own rates. (Gates 1995: 185)

Gates is tackling head on core issues in education here that derive from the perceived need to educate to ever higher levels an increasing proportion of the population, to allow for individual differences and to find the necessary financial and content resources. As he noted just prior to giving this example, "Corporations are reinventing themselves around the flexible opportunities afforded by information technology; classrooms *will have* to change as well" (185, my emphasis). If Levi Strauss & Co. does not immediately strike those of us "in the humanities" as an obvious model for reinventing education, we need to ask ourselves what alternative models we would offer. Are there examples of organizations that have reinvented themselves around new information technologies but on other than business principles? The question has to be asked this way because it will not be possible for organizations to remain functional if unconnected to the global communications system that digital information technologies have made possible. If the analogy to Levi Strauss can be positively extended as a model for a university, it would ironically reverse the current trend towards ever larger classes—the literal consequence of mass education. It might produce an organization in which arts and social sciences organized as disciplines are replaced by a library of texts with multiple, interconnected routes into the collection (a hypertextual institution). In its inclusion of a diversity of theory, method and objects of investigation (in other words, its capacity to provide for "mass-customization"), cultural studies could be the form of the humanities in such a hypertextual university.[9]

The key word for Gates is "information." He is less certain about the book, partly because "Most parents are delighted when a child curls up with an engrossing book, but [are] less enthusiastic when he spends hours at the computer." Part of the problem lies in children's experience of TV entertainment and the current lack of "entertainment quality interactive learning materials" (Gates 1995: 135). But I think that the actual problem with the book for Gates is that it is a technology which dissociates the reader from other readers, thought of as users of information. As he observes at the opening of his chapter, "Implications for Business":

As documents become more flexible, richer in multimedia content, and less tethered to paper, the ways in which people collaborate and communicate will become richer and less tied to location. . . . The information highway will revolutionize communications even more than it will revolutionize computing. (Gates 1995: 194, 197)

Even if the underlying model of the education process is questionable—and it should be noted that an unstated reason for not being "tethered to paper" is that the book as a communication device lacks the interactivity needed for an effective point-of-sale device—I think that the general point being made here is undeniable, and it has critical implications for our conception of "humanities in the postmodern." Digital information and communication technologies remove the physical separateness of different modes of textuality and therefore the disciplines that reify those technological differences as distinct areas of expertise. Traditional literacy, which it has been primarily the task of the humanities to teach, has been almost exclusively alphabetic. Print texts have used pictures as "illustrations" requiring no special training to read; literacy in other kinds of graphic and numeric representation has been left to other, nonhumanities disciplines to teach. "Information literacy," as the kind of literacy needed to "communicate and collaborate" with others on the information highway, requires as radical a revision of current humanities practices as would be required of current humanities disciplines if cultural studies were to be recognized as the exemplary case of or model for the new humanities.

A fine attempt to imagine this new humanities, in which the book as educational technology is individually focused, customized, multimedia and interactive, is to be found in Neal Stephenson's (1995) recent novel, *The Diamond Age*. The story is set in the middle of the next century, in a north Pacific world of ethnic enclaves transformed by the inventions of nanotechnology. The Anglo-American enclave is characterized by a return to Victorian values and customs, with the result that, while it is a high-achievement society, one of its leaders has concluded that it will inevitably decline unless some of its members are educated in ways that do not produce the stereotyped behaviors required by neo-Victorianism. The outcome is a book, called *A Young Lady's Illustrated Primer*: its inventor, Hackworth, gives it to Lord Finkle-McGraw, who commissioned it for his granddaughter:

He kept flipping through the book, waiting for something to happen. "It is unlikely to do anything interesting just now," Hackworth said. "It won't really activate itself until it bonds. . . . As we discussed, it sees and hears everything in its vicinity. . . . As soon as a little girl picks it up and opens the front cover for the first time, it will imprint that child's face and voice into its memory. . . . Whenever the child uses the book, then, it will perform a sort of dynamic mapping from the database onto her particular terrain." (95–96)

Hackworth secretly makes an extra copy of the book for his own daughter, but it is stolen from him and ends up in the hands of another girl from an impoverished family. This girl has no experience of books:

On the first page of the book was a picture of a little girl sitting on a bench. . . . The girl had her back to Nell; she was looking down a grassy slope sprinkled with little flowers towards a blue pond. . . . "once upon a time," said a woman's voice, "there was a little girl named Elizabeth who liked to sit in the bower in her grandfather's garden and read story-books." The voice was soft, meant just for her, with an expensive Victorian accent. (82–83)

Later, after the primer has adopted itself to its actual possessor:

Nell sat in the corner, opened the book, and started to read. She did not know all the words, but she knew a lot of them, and when she got tired, the book would help her sound out the words or even read the whole story to her, or tell it to her with moving pictures just like a cine. (135)

While such a book may be a dream of fiction—Neal Stephenson's novel creates this imagined book in the conventional narrative medium of the print novel—it also models a possibility of and in digital information technology that fulfill's the ideal relation to representation and to learning of the print book as a device able to evade institutional authority while mediating between the stock of knowledge necessary to be known and the individual and developmental needs of the learner. In this respect, Stephenson's view of the digital book is nostalgic rather than transformative in the sense assumed by Anthony Smith when he argues that "new information machines and their attendant institutions intrude deeply into the self, reshaping emotional and cultural outlook, redefining perceptual functions" (Smith 1993: 42–43). But Stephenson does share Smith's view of a world in which digital technologies become dominant, one in which "Our compatriots have become those who most deeply share our convictions" (Smith 1993: 57). In the world of *The Diamond Age*, the nation has been replaced by networks of cultural enclaves distributed through vast urban conglomerates.

THE CITY

Sir Thomas More's *Utopia*, written at the beginning of modern humanities, addresses directly the problem of speaking to power through the humanities. Formulating utopias—fictional alternatives to actual cities—is a proper action of the humanities, a narrative rather than an analytical mode of instituting a critique of society and culture. To redirect the attention of the humanities away from their preoccupation with their position in the university is to recover the city as their most proper object and content of enquiry, critique and knowledge production. Some of the most powerful conceptual work in this reorientation of postmodern humanities is the writing of future history by novelists like Neal Stephenson. Architecture as a mode of the humanities also figures significantly as field and metaphor, and I want to instance this domain through two citations.

The first is from the opening chapter of William J. Mitchell's *City of Bits: Space, Place and the Infobahn* in which he defines the new context that creates the need to "reimagine architecture and urbanism" and shows how completely this act of reimagining draws into itself the full scope of the humanities as someone like More understood their value in the formation of the new cities and nations of the sixteenth century. Mitchell writes that this new context is constituted by

the digital telecommunications revolution, the ongoing miniaturization of electronics, the commodification of bits, and the growing domination of software over materialized form. They adumbrate the emergent but still invisible cities of the twenty-first century. And they argue that the most crucial task before us is not one of putting in place the digital plumbing of broadband communications links and associated appliances (which we will certainly get anyway), nor even of producing electronically deliverable "content," but rather one of imagining and creating digitally mediated environments for the kinds of lives that we will want to lead and the sorts of communities that we will want to have.

What does it matter? Why should we care about this new kind of architectural and urban design issue? It matters because the emerging civic structures and spatial arrangements of the digital era will profoundly affect our access to economic opportunities and public services, the character and content of public discourse, the forms of cultural activity, the enaction of power, and the experiences that give shape and texture to our daily routines. Massive and unstoppable changes are under way, but we are not passive subjects powerless to shape our fates. If we understand what is happening, and if we can conceive and explore alternative futures, we can find opportunities to intervene, sometimes to resist, to organize, to plan, and to design. (Mitchell 1995: 5)[10]

Mitchell's answer to the effects of technocratic power is, like More's, the answer of the humanities when freed from the constraints of modern disciplinarity. Grounded in a conception of the city as the space in which humanity's most complex acts of social invention occur, in which whatever is meant by "the human" is made most available for knowledge, Mitchell's assertion of citizen power assumes that such assertions are always political, enacted and require "design"—that is, the materialization of virtual/fictional/imagined value and possibility.

Timothy Luke's name for applied critical humanities in the period of the postmodern, "dehumanities," takes up the same core issues in forming a powerful conception of the position and work of the humanities as a body of knowledge accumulated over time and apparently marginalized now by the technocratic knowledges. For him, too, the city provides the exemplary locus for thinking how cyberspace as a new space of sociability and citizenship can be properly developed. He notes that

Already the architectures of the info-city are being drawn by only a few major players—telecom, computer, banking, and financial service corporations—with very little public input. In turn, the designers working for these players are mainly technical-engineering experts, or the same minds and sensibilities that have already not done too well designing (wo)man/machine and society/system interfaces. Applied humanities analysis might flag these tendencies to bring another voice, a different eye, and an unusual touch to the construction of the info-city before it simply reproduces in virtual reality what already exists in material reality. (Luke 1996: 16)

Here the engagement is directly to the desire of technocratic knowledge to stand for all knowledge in the process of global reconstruction; the question is, how can applied humanities analysis find its voice outside the university, and what is the curriculum needed to train it?

THE STATE: CULTURAL POLICY

Evaluating and criticizing the activities of public and private sector organizations in cultural matters has been a part of the practice of the humanities since their modern inception. What has recently changed is the conception of the role of the state in relation to culture, as to any aspect of the activity of the society that comes within the range of government.

This change has been most clearly signaled in Australia in two ways that have not yet occurred in New Zealand: the production of a national policy for culture and the invention out of cultural studies of the field of cultural policy studies. Recently, in New Zealand, some steps have been taken in the former direction: firstly, in the production of the first collection of cultural statistics, through cooperation between Statistics NZ and the Ministry of Cultural Affairs; and secondly, through a proposal from the department of internal affairs that a new strategic result area for government should be established in the area of national identity.

In the context of globalization, in which it is usual to conclude (as Stephenson does in *The Diamond Age*) that the entity most likely to survive in the space between the global and the local is the city, not the nation, it is of considerable interest to ask why a government department is taking a particular interest in promoting the concept. It is clearly consonant with the development of nation studies, but in both modern humanities and cultural studies such fields arise in a curriculum to support a process of redefinition, as in New Zealand studies signaling locally a separation from the imperial curriculum of history, English literature and so on, or British studies signaling the loss of an imperial domain.

The context for the promotion of "national identity" in this instance seems to be provided by the consequences of government restructuring. A very clear indication of way restructuring generates very specific requirements for those who would seek to shape government decision making and policy formation is given in a recent speech by Christopher Blake, the CEO of the Ministry of Cultural Affairs, entitled, "What is the Government Doing in Culture?" In the latter half of the speech, it is noted that "The government-supported cultural sector has developed in a rather haphazard fashion" and that "a set of "first principles"—a vision of the desired outcomes of policy" is needed that will "allow gaps and anomalies to be more easily recognised, and that could provide some rationale for the division of labour between public and private endeavour" (Blake 1996: 7). I do not believe that it is possible to address the issues raised in this account from within the current disciplinary arrangements and professionalisms of the humanities, partly because those disciplines do not in any way match the representation of the cultural field in the present agencies of government, and partly because the discourses in which they represent themselves are no longer shared with those who manage the state.

In one respect, the account is a clear example of the discourse of bureaucratic rationality, aiming to bring more of the unmanaged terrain of the cultural within the purview of the government—not necessarily for the purposes of control, but for the purposes of being able to decide in what parts of the cultural the government does have an interest and a responsibility. Part of the mandate of the ministry, while it does not represent the whole of the government interest in the cultural, is "the development of coordinated Government policy in the 'cultural sector' " (Blake: 6.6). The development of a draft cultural framework is aimed at fulfilling this mandate, and it is important to note the purpose of such a document. It will "explain the benefits of government involvement in the cultural sector, and . . . make explicit the basis on which government makes policy for the sector"(6). The framework is based on four principles: nationhood, citizenship, quality of life and excellence. These principles are intended to translate the mission of the ministry—"to increase New Zealand's creative and intellectual potential and sustain and develop the nation's cultural heritage"—into four equal and interdependent outcomes (p. 8). In order to focus understanding, key terms have been defined as follows:

- *Cultural heritage*: Those parts of its material and intellectual inheritance that a nation or community seeks to maintain or develop, in practice or in record; the activities involved in the presentation and reinterpretation of this inheritance.
- *The arts*: The art forms of dance, film, literature, music, theatre and visual arts; the activities involved in their presentation, execution and interpretation; and the study and technical development of these art forms and activities.
- *The cultural sector*: The institutions, practitioners and consumers that serve and support the arts and cultural heritage.

I have listed these points in some detail because I think that it is important to realize how far removed from the representation of the humanities in the universities the terms of this account are.[11] And yet, to participate in the discussion of this draft document requires an ability to employ the concepts and forms of policy discourse and to understand as well as be able to critique a categorization of the cultural that has almost no resonance with the categorizations offered in the disciplinary arrangements of the university. Yet again, as I have already observed, the much broader perspectives and terminology of cultural studies provide a powerful means of engaging with this different mode of rationality, but such an engagement has to be able to employ the conventions of policy discourse that seek a high level of generality in contrast to the much more specialized focus of disciplinary discourses. The establishment of cultural policy studies in Australia, vigorously contested by those who saw the development as compromising cultural studies proper, is in my view a necessary response to the problem of bringing informed and theorized critique to bear in effective ways upon the processes of public policy formation. These processes and their distinctive mode of discourse are the most powerful forces shaping the direction of the postmodern state. At this juncture, to work in this space between the academic and the governmental seems to be a particular responsibility of an organization like HUMANZ.

There is one other development in this area of the governmental to which I wish to draw attention. The humanities have just gained entry into the Marsden Fund (New Zealand's science funding system). That ought to be filled with ambiguities—and I believe it is. However, what the situation vividly foregrounds is the clearest evidence one could want of a consequence of what Christopher Blake described as the haphazard development of the "government-supported cultural sector." In contrast to the arts and the humanities, science and technology policy is formulated by one ministry, the Ministry of Research, Science and Technology, which symbolizes the perceived centrality of those knowledges to national development and economic growth. The divisions of that sector are not disciplinary, but are defined in terms of government priorities for knowledge and the perceived importance of specific sectors of the economy. While all this is familiar enough now, such a framework for conceptualizing work in the humanities does not yet exist. And yet, if the humanities are to succeed in "the science funding system," adaptation to and of such a framework will be necessary. What this will involve is a rethinking of what is "applied" about the humanities, something of an irony when one considers that the originating purpose of the humanities was *only* applied—that is, civilizing society through literacy.

Within the materials produced by those writing science policy a most interesting issue has become apparent both in Australia and New Zealand. In Australia, the Australian Science and Technology Council (ASTEC) has recently argued strongly for the "Embedding [of] Science and Technology in Australian culture" because

Australian industry requires a community with a better understanding of S&T to provide a labour force with more adaptable skills and the flexibility to deal with on-going rapid technological change. An S&T literate community was identified as essential for investment in new and technologically high value-added industries. . . . S&T research can be hindered by community concerns often based on a poor understanding of S&T. . . . We need an S&T literacy (or "technacy") that will allow us *inter alia* to:

1. use S&T effectively in decision-making processes;

2. discuss and adapt new S&T developments;

3. appreciate science as part of our culture;

4. maximise benefits of S&T in our daily lives; and

5. build strong S&T systems and expertise, including an educated workforce. (ASTEC 1996: 61–62)

The strongest emphasis in these points is the need of the S&T system to be more completely integrated into Australian culture. The same position is adopted in the recently published *RS&T: 2010. The Government's Strategy for RS&T in New Zealand to the Year 2010.* The first goal of the strategy is "Fostering societal values and attitudes that recognise science and technology as critical to future prosperity"; and the second is "Ensuring an adequate level of investment in science as a component in national life which has cultural value in its own right" (RS&T: 2010, 1996: 3). These statements and their expansion in the document are more fully explicit than the ASTEC document about the cultural ground for science policy in New Zealand and the entry of the science system into overt cultural politics. Given the apparent security in government funding for science and technology, one may wonder why the need to change cultural thinking is so strongly felt. Given also a continuing confidence among practitioners of the humanities about their fundamental role in cultural formation through literacy, one may well conclude that such confidence is no longer well grounded if powerful organizations of the state can claim a cultural mission in such a proactive manner. Furthermore, the emphasis on intervention in the science documents is remarkably different from the approach taken by Christopher Blake in his speech. On the question of the government's role in culture, he says that it is "to provide the means, not to shape the ends. National identity, as I have suggested, shapes itself—cultural policy should not aim to construct it. . . . A democratic state is tested by its cultural policy: will it encourage the full creative and intellectual development of its people, without attempting to prescribe the results of that development?" (Blake 1997: 9).

CONCLUSION

These different views on the role of the state as an instrument of cultural formation provide an opening for an intervention from the new or postmodern humanities, an intervention that needs a discourse or discourses able to address the proactivity in culture of the science and technology sector. It has been the burden of this chapter that neither traditional humanities discourses and curricula, nor traditional humanities institutions, are able to provide the concepts, models and critical strategies needed to articulate a "dehumanities" or applied humanities capable of working beyond modern binaries such as science/humanities, machine/human and nature/culture. Cultural studies does now offer a means to these ends, and we in New Zealand have much to learn and adapt from the exciting and exemplary work being done by skillful exponents of cultural critique in Australia like Meaghan Morris and Ross Gibson. To borrow my conclusion from another whose cultural analysis I have already used in this paper, McKenzie Wark's aspiration for his own work can also describe the goal of both cultural studies and HUMANZ in New Zealand:

I want to create my understanding of the global, seen from the antipodes. It's a step towards recognizing that while one cannot escape the necessity of conceptualizing the global, it cannot be thought exclusively from the metropolitan centers. . . . If we are to take so terrifying a word [as the postmodern] with anything like the respect that its uncompromising self-negation deserves, then we must face up to the fact that it challenges all of the procedures, assumptions, and categories of the modern, including all those of scholarship, writing, and publishing. We no longer have roots, we have aerials. . . . One has to write differently not only because the form of what one writes about changes, but also because the community one writes for changes. We no longer have origins, we have terminals. (Wark 1994: xiv)

NOTES

1. See *Social Text*, Nos. 46–47 (Spring–Summer 1996) and No. 50 (Spring 1997).

2. Prior to 26 June 1997, HUMANZ was known as "The New Zealand Academy for the Humanities." The organization was inaugurated in 1993.

3. The recent arrival of the concept of "social capital" in public discourse signals the discovery of this deficiency by those who are concerned that the "economic growth" side of the policy binary has dominated government attention to the near exclusion of its other, "social cohesion." While "social capital" may appear to offer an opening for the humanities into the policy arena, the proponents of this move are not likely to be receptive to postmodern humanities.

4. RS&T: 2010, Strategic Overview, p. 16. In 1997, after this paper was first given, it was decided by the minister of research science and technology that the humanities should be able to apply for research funding in principle from the PGSF; in fact, applications had been allowed to the Marsden Fund which was created as a small fund within the PGSF to provide for nonprioritized research. This decision can be seen as another example of Sosnoski's "modern skeletons."

5. This situation is changing, as "arts" faculties become "humanities" or "humanities and social science" faculties; further "modern skeletons."

6. This name, a gift of Professor Wharehuia Milroy of Waikato University and Te Matawhanui, can be translated as "the goal or way ahead for the humanities."

7. An important contribution to thinking about this fundamental matter was made by Tania Ka'ai, professor of Maori studies at Otago University, in a paper on "The Concept of Aronui" presented to the 1996 HUMANZ conference.

8. Anthony Smith in *Books to Bytes. Knowledge and Information in the Postmodern Era* (London: British Film Institute, 1993), pp. 90–91, writes that

In academic practice, research is an interdisciplinary, collaborative process that passes across continents and across generations. . . . Knowledge is social and global in character, though it has been pressed into the moulds of individualism and nationalism. . . . The old knowledge culture was built around the notion of the text as a singular and eternal phenomenon. The new conception is based upon an infinity of versions, subject to permanent interpretation.

9. See Ikujiro Nonaka and Hiro Tekeuchi, *The Knowledge-Creating Company* (New York: Oxford University Press, 1995) for the use of literary hypertext as a model for postmodern business management.

10. Taylor and Saarinen make a similar observation:

In the netropolis, architecture becomes electrotecture. Electrotecture surpasses the techniques of computer-aided design by actually taking responsibility for fashioning cyberspace. If we increasingly dwell in cyberspace, the architect must find ways to design the electronic environment. There is no clear line separating the electrotect from either the imagologist or the computer programmer. In the netropolis, images and programs are no longer preliminary models that are the prelude to "real" building but constitute the living space for global villagers. (*Imagologies.* New York: Routledge, 1994: 4)

The invention of new terms also reflects back on older conventions and acceptances and suggests alternative ways of constructing the past as well as the future. What if, for example, the work of fiction in print culture was to be called "typotecture"?

11. They are also based on modern rather than postmodern categorizations—eg., heritage, creativity, industry.

REFERENCES

Australian Science and Technology Council (ASTEC). (1996) "Developing Long-Term Strategies for Science and Technology in Australia. Outcomes of the Study: Matching Science and Technology to Future Needs 2010." Canberra, Australia: Commonwealth of Australia.

Blake, Christopher. (1997) "What Is the Government Doing in Culture?" Unpublished paper, Wellington, Ministry of Cultural Affairs.

Eley, Geoff. (1996) "Is All the World a Text? From Social History to the History of Society Two Decades Later." In Terrence J. McDonald (ed.), *The Historic Turn in the Human Sciences*. Ann Arbor: University of Michigan Press, 194.

Foucault, Michel. (1981) "The Order of Discourse." In Robert Young (ed.), *Untying the Text: A Post-Structuralist Reader*. London: Routledge.

Gates, Bill with Myhrvold, Nathan and Rinearson, Peter. (1995) *The Road Ahead*. New York: Viking.

Gordon, Avery. (1995) "The Work of Corporate Culture: Diversity Management." *Social Text*, 44: 23.

Luke, Timothy W. (1996) "Humanities, Multimedia, and the Informational Society." *Sites*, 32 (Autumn): 1, 16, 40.

Mitchell, William J. (1995) *City of Bits: Space, Place and the Infobahn*. Cambridge, MA: The MIT Press.

Moylan, Tom. (1995) "People and Markets: Some Thoughts on Culture and Corporations in the University of the Twenty-First Century." *Social Text*, 44: 50–51.

Nonaka, Ikujiro and Tekeuchi, Hiro. (1995) *The Knowledge-Creating Company*. New York: Oxford University Press.

RS&T: 2010. (1996) *The Government's Strategy for Research, Science and Technology in New Zealand to the Year 2010*. Strategic Overview (August): 16.

Sosnoski, James J. (1995) *Modern Skeletons in Postmodern Closets. A Cultural Studies Alternative*. Charlottesville: University Press of Virginia, 57.

Smith, Anthony. (1993) *Books to Bytes. Knowledge and Information in the Postmodern Era*. London: British Film Institute, 42–43, 57, 90–91.

Stephenson, Neal. (1995) *The Diamond Age*. New York: Bantam Books, 82–83, 95–96, 135.

Taylor, Mark C. and Saarinen, Esa. (1994a) "Simcult." 1. *Imagologies: Media Philosophy*. New York: Routledge.

———. (1994b) "Communicative Practices." 2. *Imagologies: Media Philosophy*. New York: Routledge.

Wark, McKenzie. (1994) *Virtual Geography. Living with Global Media Events*. Bloomington: Indiana University Press, ix, xiv.

Index

About the Contributors

MEGAN BOLER is Assistant Professor in Education at Virginia Polytechnic and State University.

RUTH BUTTERWORTH is formerly Associate Professor of Political Studies at the University of Auckland, New Zealand.

HENRY A. GIROUX is Professor of Secondary Education and holds the Waterbury Chair at Penn State University.

ROGER HORROCKS is Associate Professor of Film and Television Studies at the University of Auckland, New Zealand.

COLIN LANKSHEAR is Adjunct Professor, Faculty of Education and Creative Arts, Central Queensland University, Australia.

TIMOTHY LUKE is Professor of Political Science at Virginia Polytechnic and State University.

ROBERT MARKLEY is Professor of English and holds the Jackson Distinguished Chair of British Literature at the University of West Virginia.

MAUREEN MOLLOY is Professor of Women's Studies at the University of Auckland, New Zealand.

WARREN MORAN is Professor of Geography at the University of Auckland, New Zealand.

BRIAN OPIE is Senior Lecturer in English, Film and Theatre at Victoria University of Wellington, New Zealand.

RAVI ARVIND PALAT is Senior Lecturer in Sociology at the University of Auckland, New Zealand.

MICHAEL PETERS is Associate Professor in Education at the University of Auckland, New Zealand.

RANGINUI WALKER was formerly Professor of Maori Studies and Pro-Vice Chancellor (Maori) at the University of Auckland, New Zealand.

ISBN 0-89789-626-2

9 780897 896269

HARDCOVER BAR CODE

Resources Centre

Centre for Teaching, Learning & Assessment

The University of Edinburgh

www.tla.ed.ac.uk